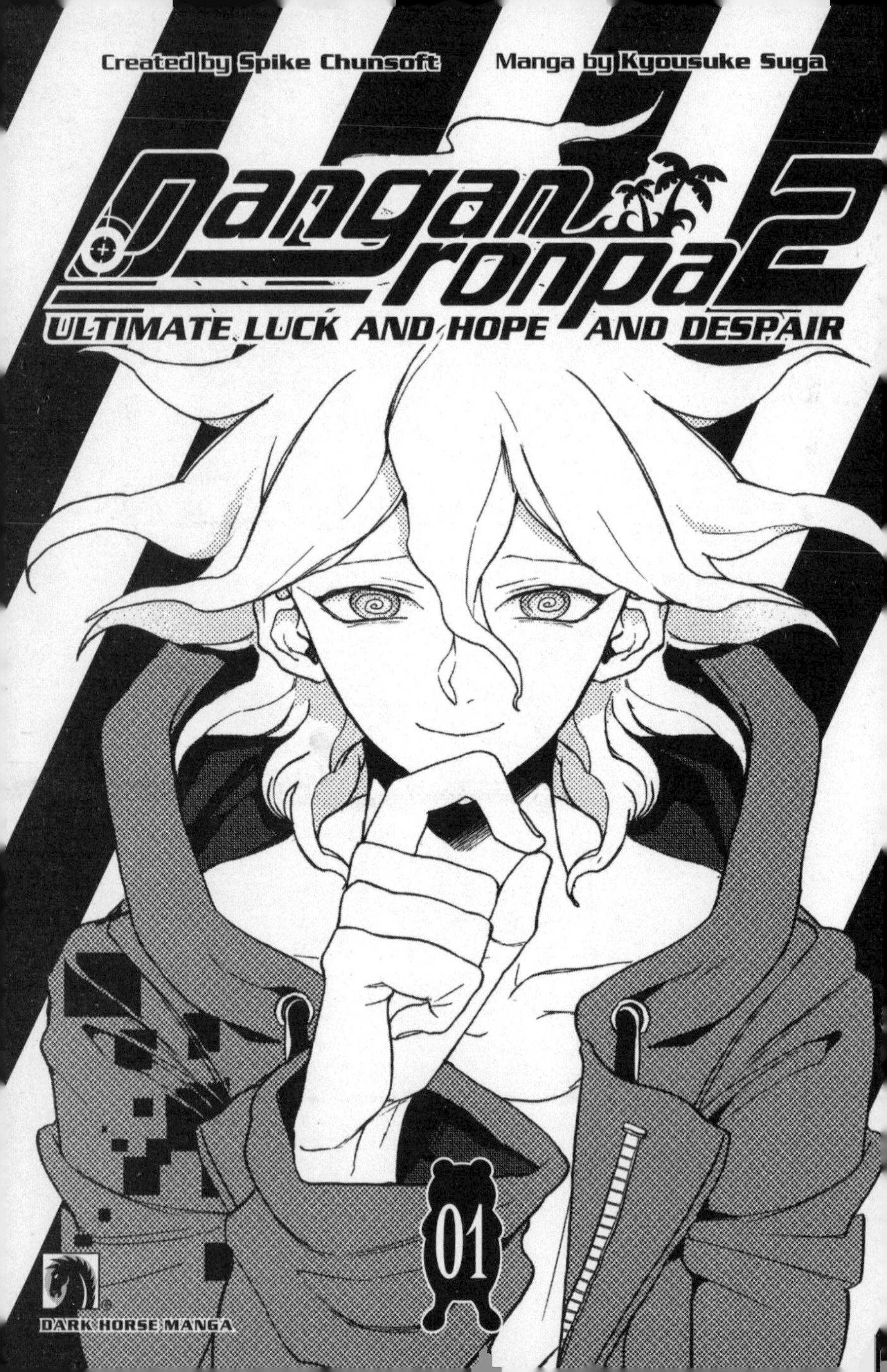
Created by Spike Chunsoft
Manga by Kyousuke Suga
Danganronpa 2
ULTIMATE LUCK AND HOPE AND DESPAIR
01
DARK HORSE MANGA

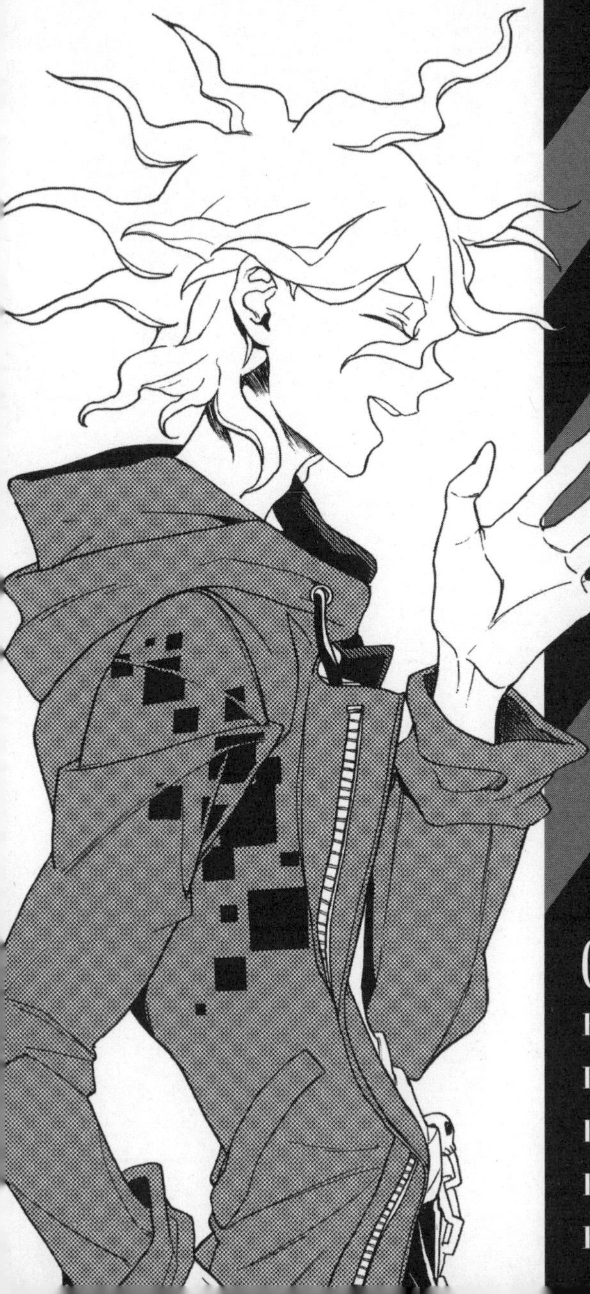

Translation by **Jackie McClure**
Lettering and touchup by **John Clark**
Edited by **Carl Gustav Horn**

CONTENTS

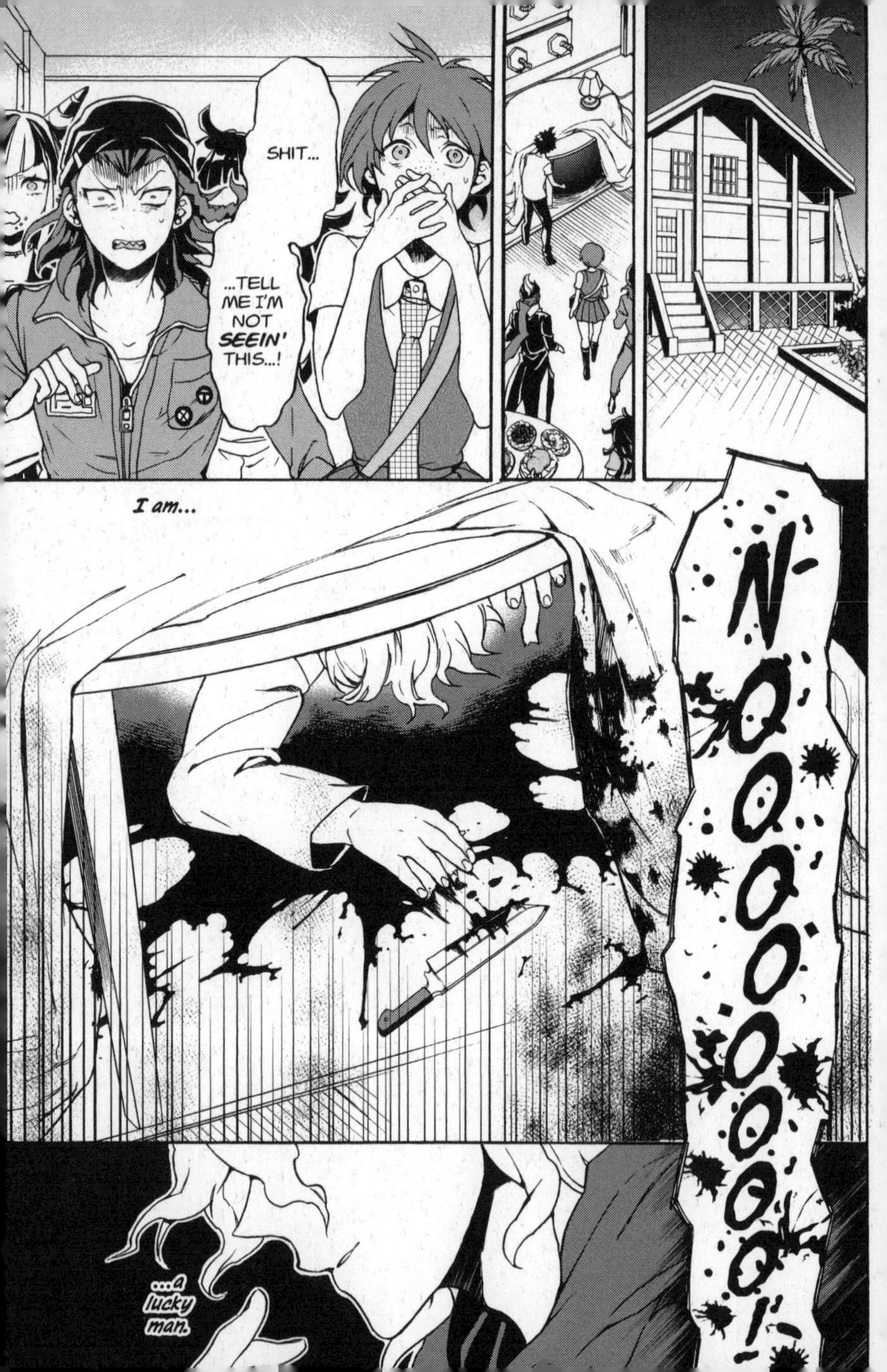
SHIT...
...TELL ME I'M NOT SEEIN' THIS...!
NOOOOOOOOOO!
I am...
...a lucky man.

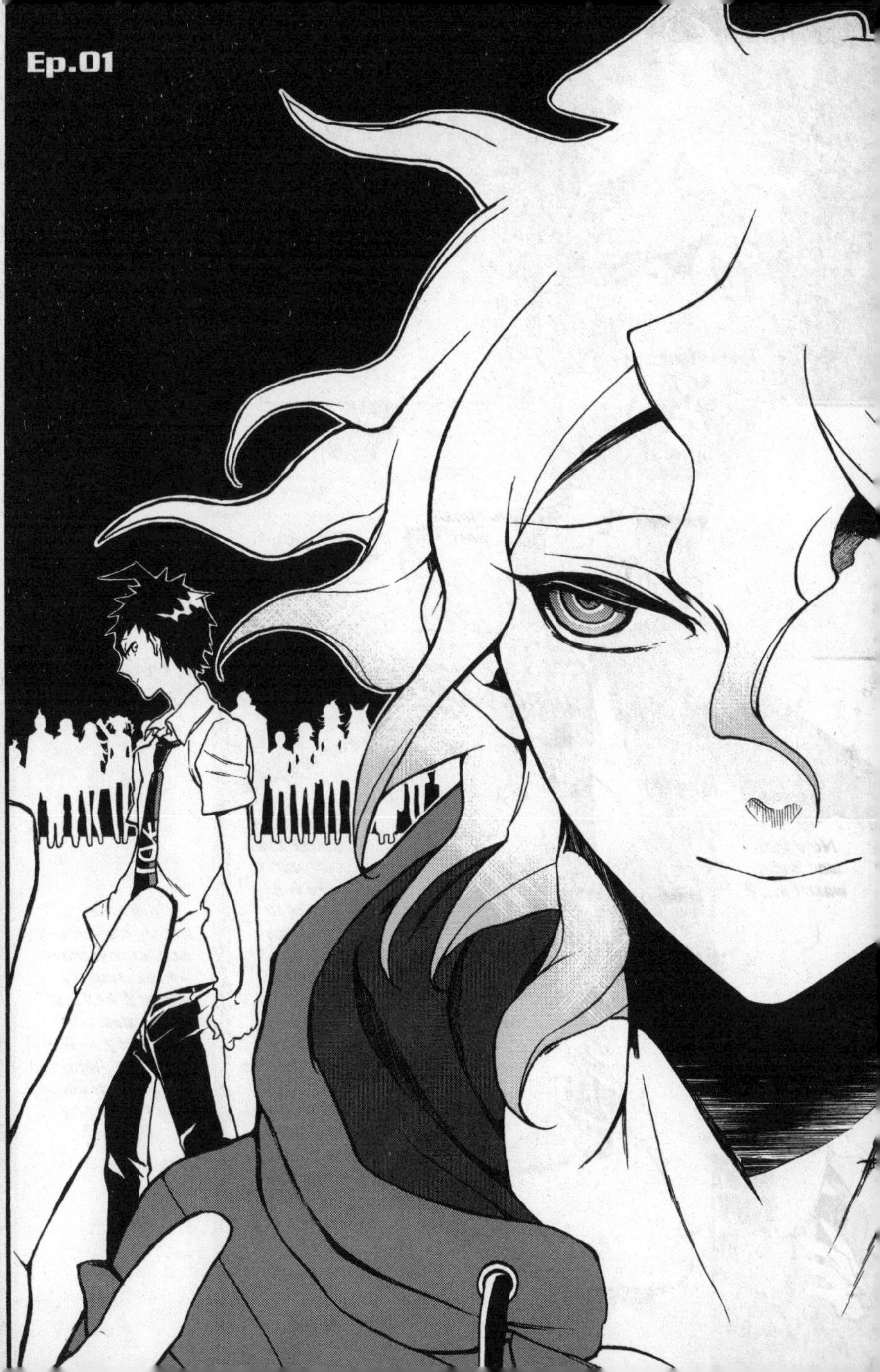
Ep.01

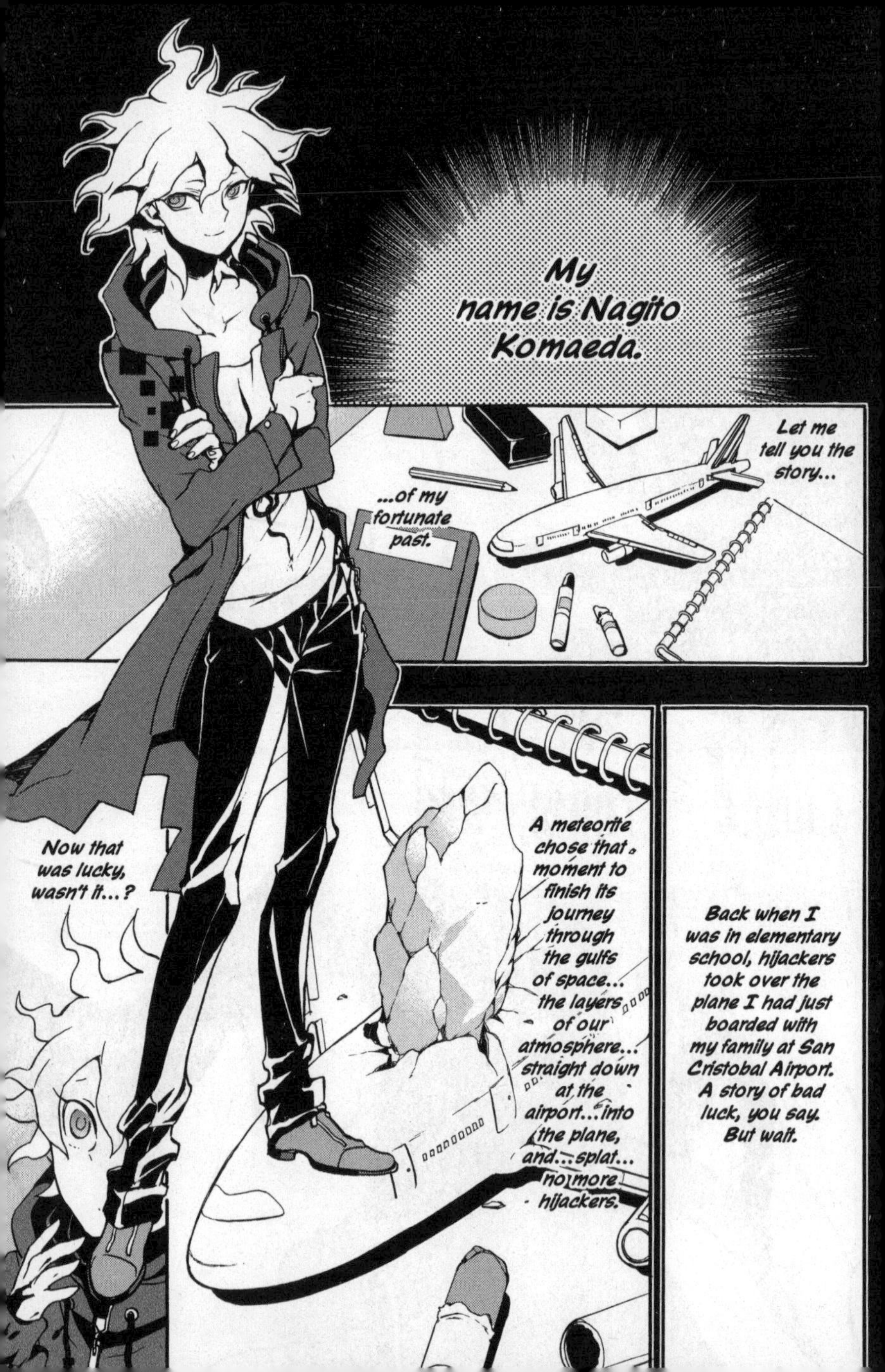
My name is Nagito Komaeda.
Let me tell you the story...
...of my fortunate past.
Back when I was in elementary school, hijackers took over the plane I had just boarded with my family at San Cristobal Airport. A story of bad luck, you say. But wait.
A meteorite chose that moment to finish its journey through the gulfs of space... the layers of our atmosphere... straight down at the airport... into the plane, and... splat... no more hijackers.
Now that was lucky, wasn't it...?

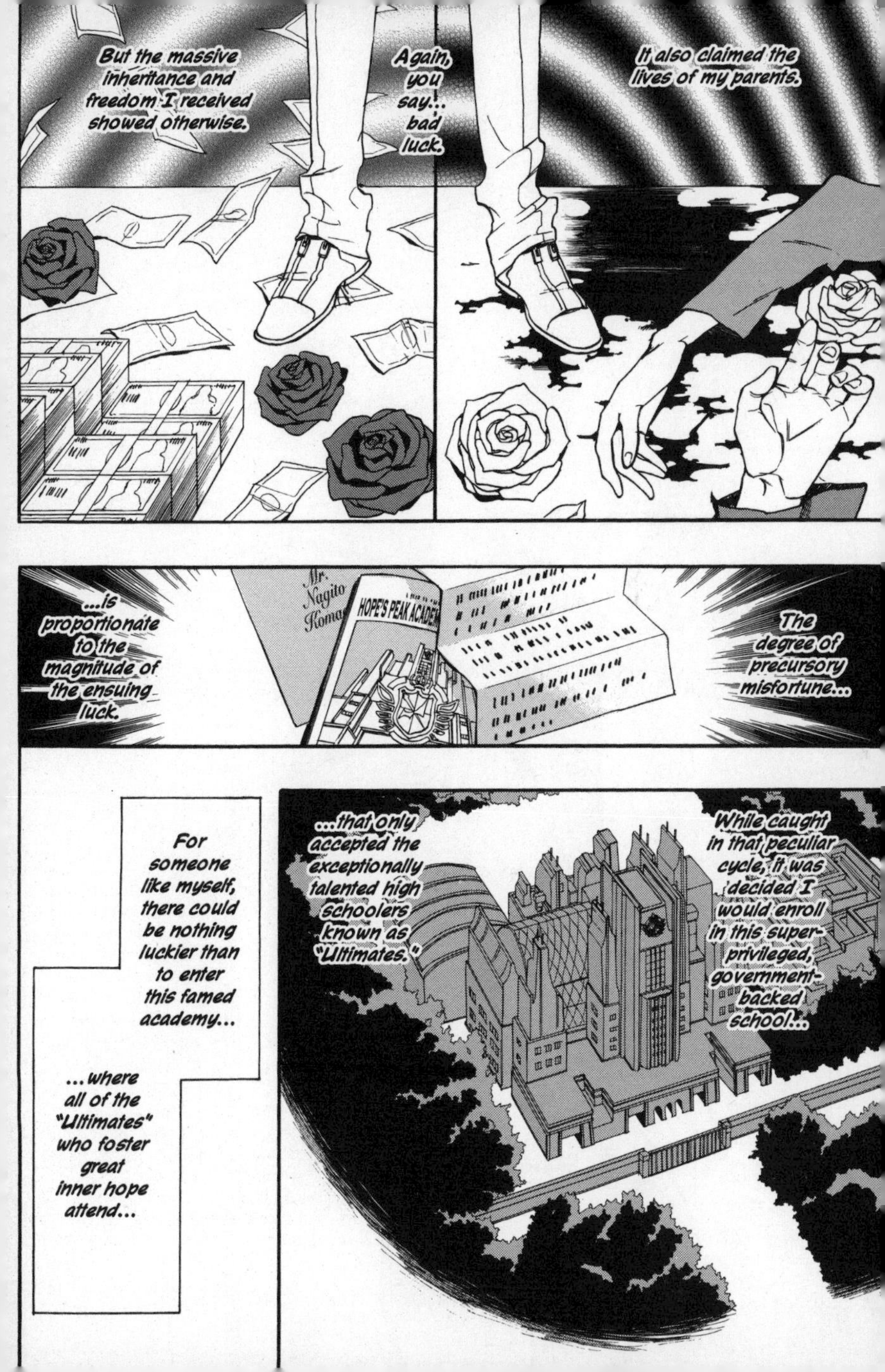
It also claimed the lives of my parents.
Again, you say... bad luck.
But the massive inheritance and freedom I received showed otherwise.
The degree of precursory misfortune...
Mr. Nagito Koma
HOPE'S PEAK ACADEM
...is proportionate to the magnitude of the ensuing luck.
While caught in that peculiar cycle, it was decided I would enroll in this super-privileged, government-backed school...
...that only accepted the exceptionally talented high schoolers known as "Ultimates."
For someone like myself, there could be nothing luckier than to enter this famed academy...
...where all of the "Ultimates" who foster great inner hope attend...

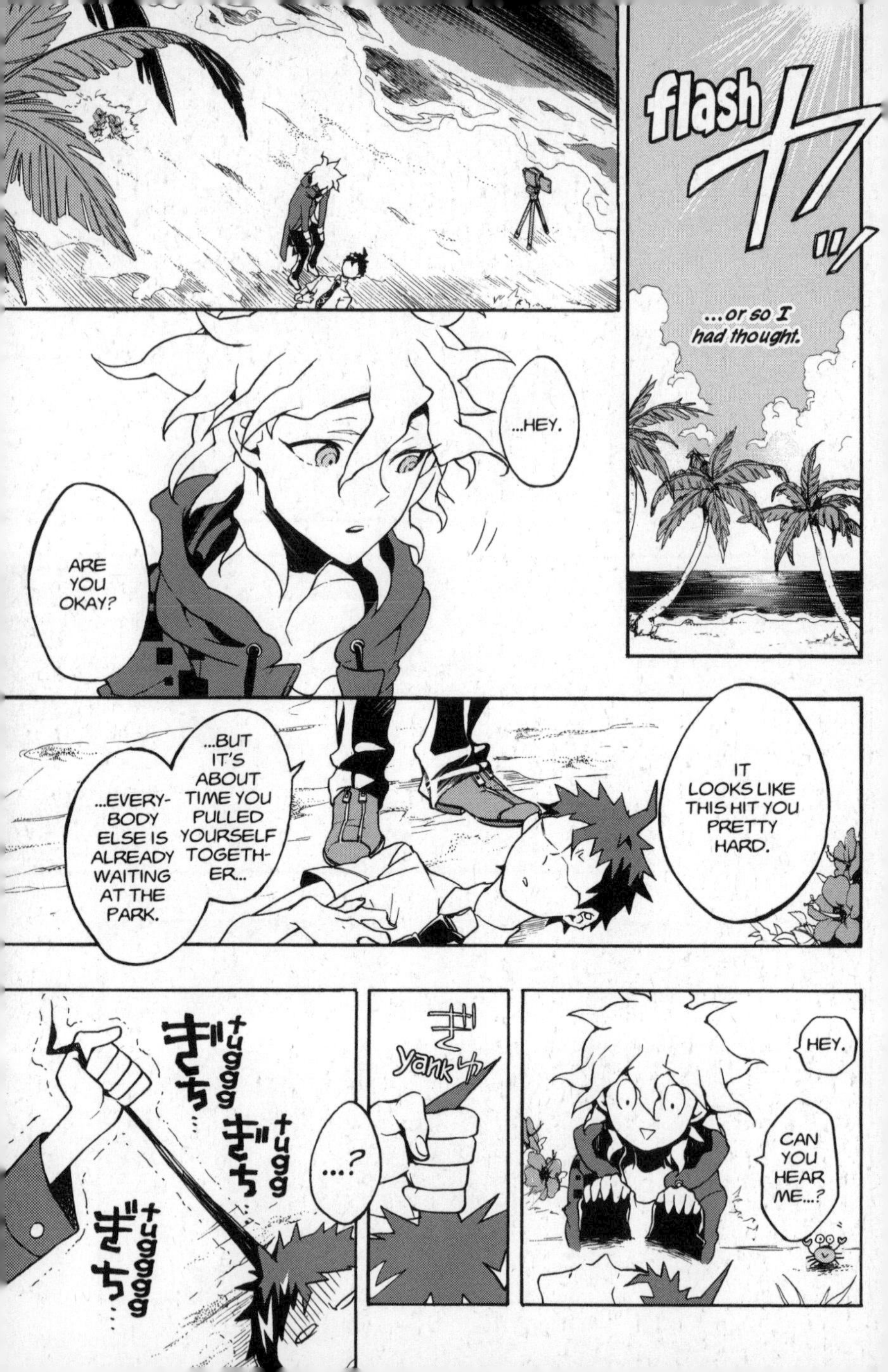
flash
...or so I had thought.
...HEY.
ARE YOU OKAY?
IT LOOKS LIKE THIS HIT YOU PRETTY HARD.
...BUT IT'S ABOUT TIME YOU PULLED YOURSELF TOGETH-ER...
...EVERY-BODY ELSE IS ALREADY WAITING AT THE PARK.
HEY.
CAN YOU HEAR ME...?
ぎゅ
yank
...?
ぎち tugg
ぎち tugg
ぎち tugg

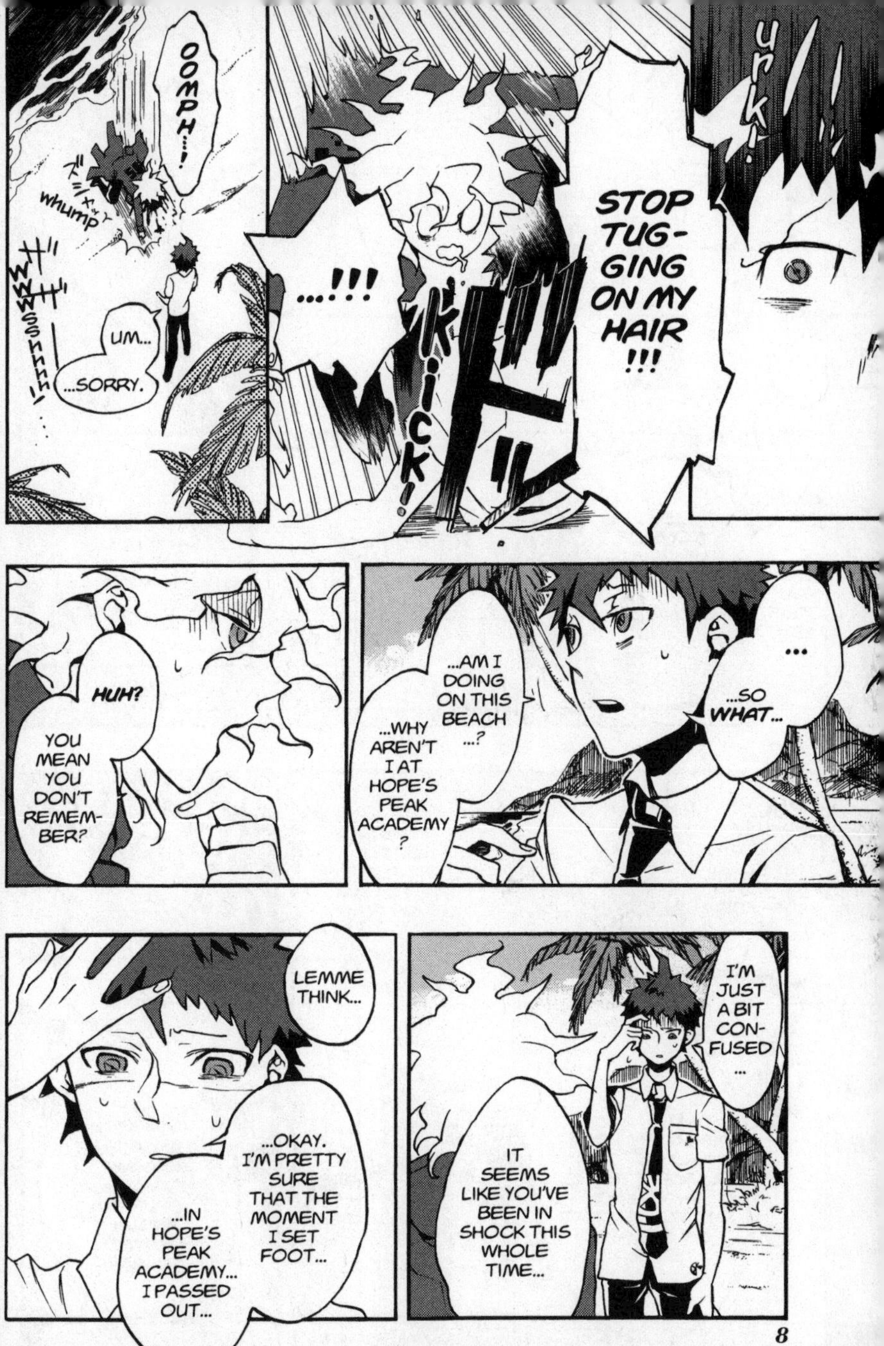

URK!
STOP TUGGING ON MY HAIR!!!
...!!!
KICK!
OOMPH...!
WHUMP
WWWSHHHH!!
UM...
...SORRY.
...
...SO WHAT...
...AM I DOING ON THIS BEACH...?
...WHY AREN'T I AT HOPE'S PEAK ACADEMY?
HUH?
YOU MEAN YOU DON'T REMEMBER?
I'M JUST A BIT CONFUSED...
IT SEEMS LIKE YOU'VE BEEN IN SHOCK THIS WHOLE TIME...
LEMME THINK...
...OKAY. I'M PRETTY SURE THAT THE MOMENT I SET FOOT...
...IN HOPE'S PEAK ACADEMY... I PASSED OUT...

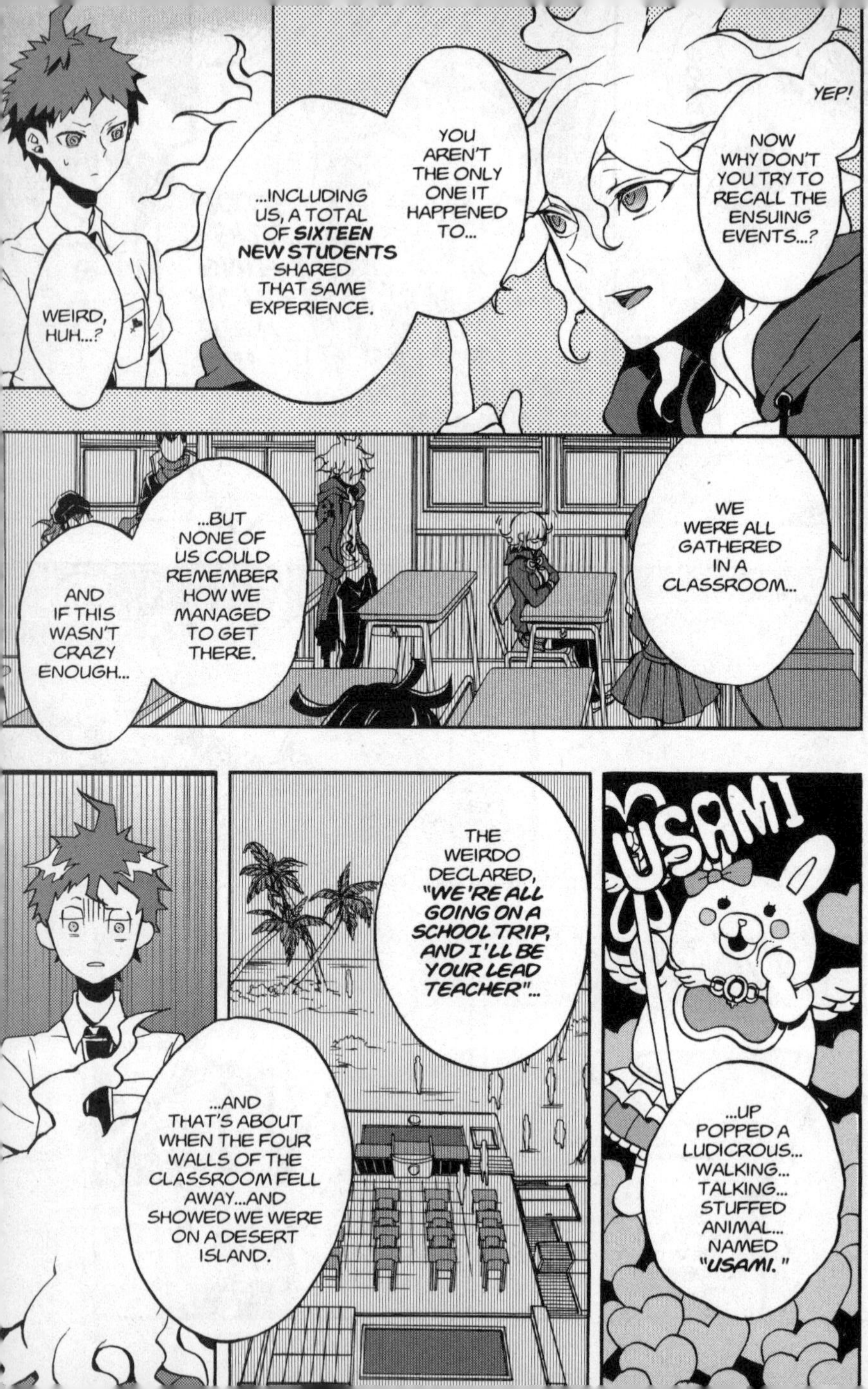
YEP!
NOW WHY DON'T YOU TRY TO RECALL THE ENSUING EVENTS...?
YOU AREN'T THE ONLY ONE IT HAPPENED TO...
...INCLUDING US, A TOTAL OF **SIXTEEN NEW STUDENTS** SHARED THAT SAME EXPERIENCE.
WEIRD, HUH...?
WE WERE ALL GATHERED IN A CLASSROOM...
...BUT NONE OF US COULD REMEMBER HOW WE MANAGED TO GET THERE.
AND IF THIS WASN'T CRAZY ENOUGH...
USAMI
...UP POPPED A LUDICROUS... WALKING... TALKING... STUFFED ANIMAL... NAMED "***USAMI.***"
THE WEIRDO DECLARED, ***"WE'RE ALL GOING ON A SCHOOL TRIP, AND I'LL BE YOUR LEAD TEACHER"***...
...AND THAT'S ABOUT WHEN THE FOUR WALLS OF THE CLASSROOM FELL AWAY...AND SHOWED WE WERE ON A DESERT ISLAND.

NO...
...THAT'S WRONG !!
ALLOW ME TO CUT THROUGH THOSE WORDS!
DON'T GET SO UPSET...
...I SINCERELY DOUBT THERE IS ANY TRUE CAUSE FOR ALARM.
...
...YOU THINK?
WELL, USAMI CLAIMED THAT ONCE WE BECOME GOOD BUDS...
...SHE'LL END THIS "SCHOOL TRIP" AND LET US OFF THE ISLAND. REMEMBER THAT...?
BUT SHOULD WE TAKE THAT AT FACE VALUE...?
I MEAN, IT'S OUTRIGHT FISHY WHERE SHE'S GOT THAT MONITOR AND CAMERA...
...IS SHE WATCHING OUR EVERY MOVE?
HMMM... WOULD SHE REALLY MONITOR US?
TRY A DIFFER-ENT ANGLE.
EVER THINK SHE MIGHT BE KEEPING TABS TO ENSURE NO HARM COMES TO US?
I'D BE COOL WITH THAT...

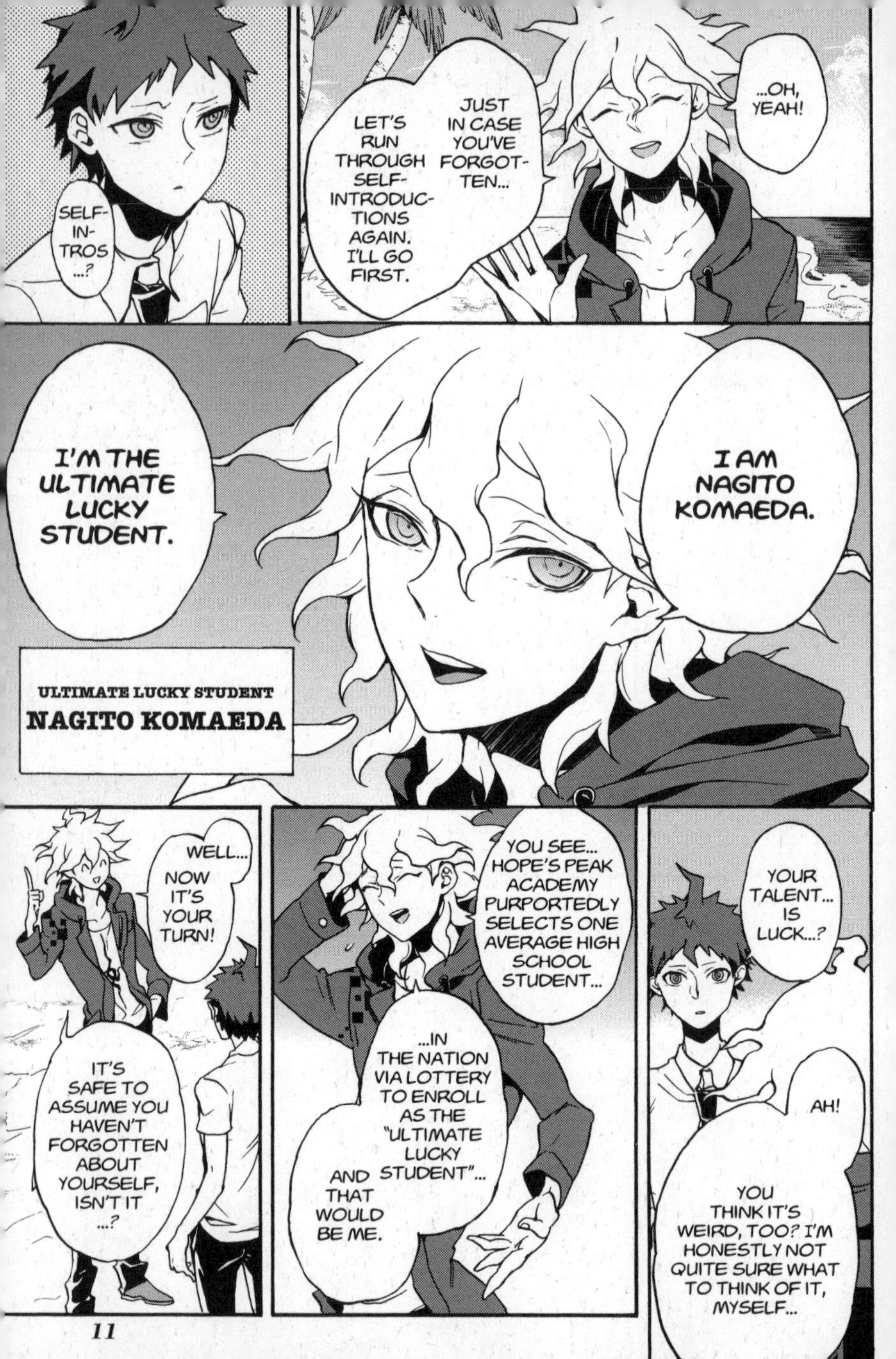
...OH, YEAH!
JUST IN CASE YOU'VE FORGOTTEN...
LET'S RUN THROUGH SELF-INTRODUCTIONS AGAIN. I'LL GO FIRST.
SELF-INTROS...?
I AM NAGITO KOMAEDA.
I'M THE ULTIMATE LUCKY STUDENT.
ULTIMATE LUCKY STUDENT
NAGITO KOMAEDA
YOUR TALENT... IS LUCK...?
AH!
YOU THINK IT'S WEIRD, TOO? I'M HONESTLY NOT QUITE SURE WHAT TO THINK OF IT, MYSELF...
YOU SEE... HOPE'S PEAK ACADEMY PURPORTEDLY SELECTS ONE AVERAGE HIGH SCHOOL STUDENT...
...IN THE NATION VIA LOTTERY TO ENROLL AS THE "ULTIMATE LUCKY STUDENT"...
AND THAT WOULD BE ME.
WELL... NOW IT'S YOUR TURN!
IT'S SAFE TO ASSUME YOU HAVEN'T FORGOTTEN ABOUT YOURSELF, ISN'T IT...?

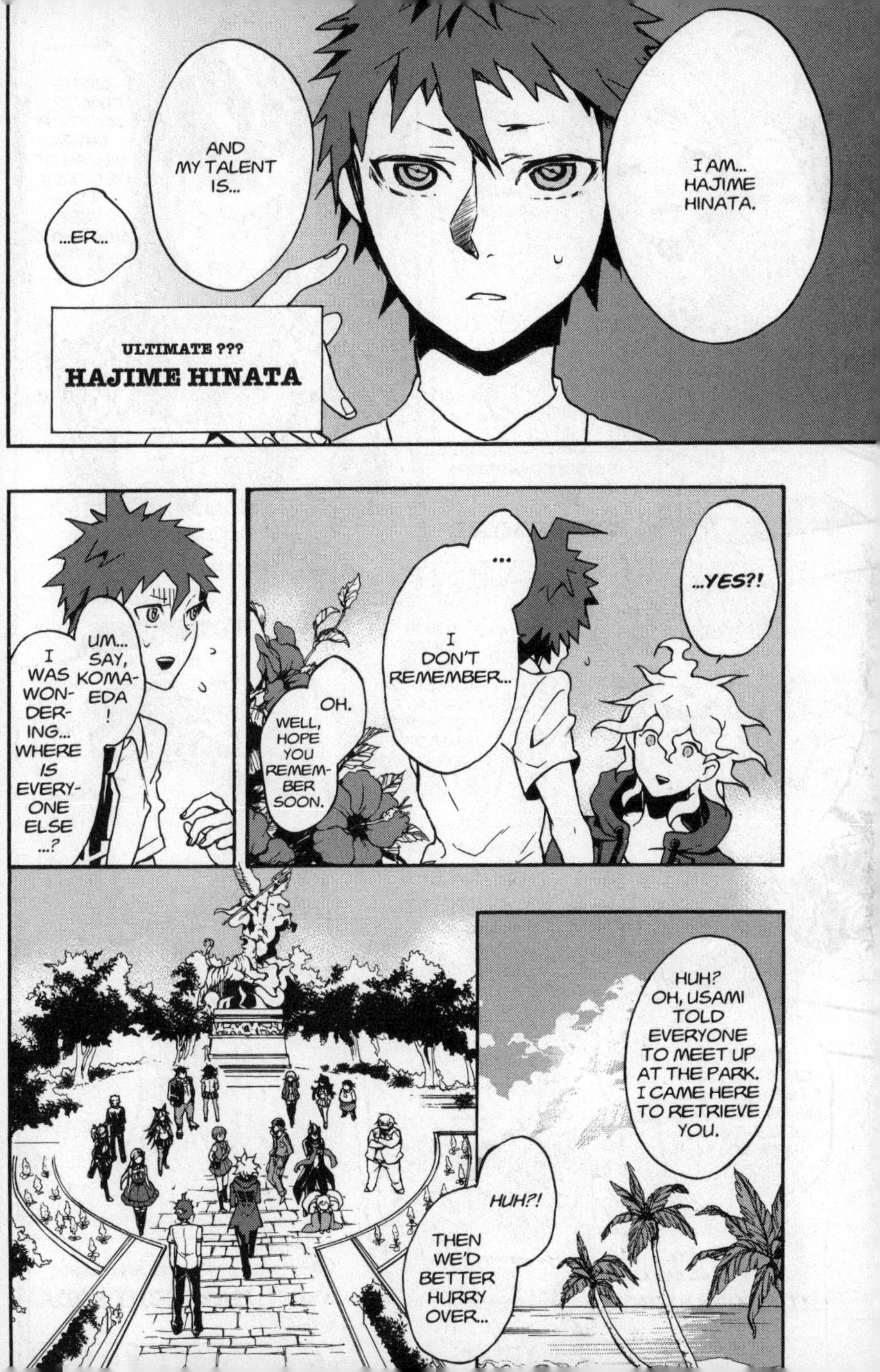
I AM... HAJIME HINATA.
AND MY TALENT IS...
...ER...
ULTIMATE ???
HAJIME HINATA
...YES?!
...
I DON'T REMEMBER...
OH.
WELL, HOPE YOU REMEMBER SOON.
UM... SAY, KOMAEDA!
I WAS WONDERING... WHERE IS EVERYONE ELSE...?
HUH? OH, USAMI TOLD EVERYONE TO MEET UP AT THE PARK. I CAME HERE TO RETRIEVE YOU.
HUH?!
THEN WE'D BETTER HURRY OVER...

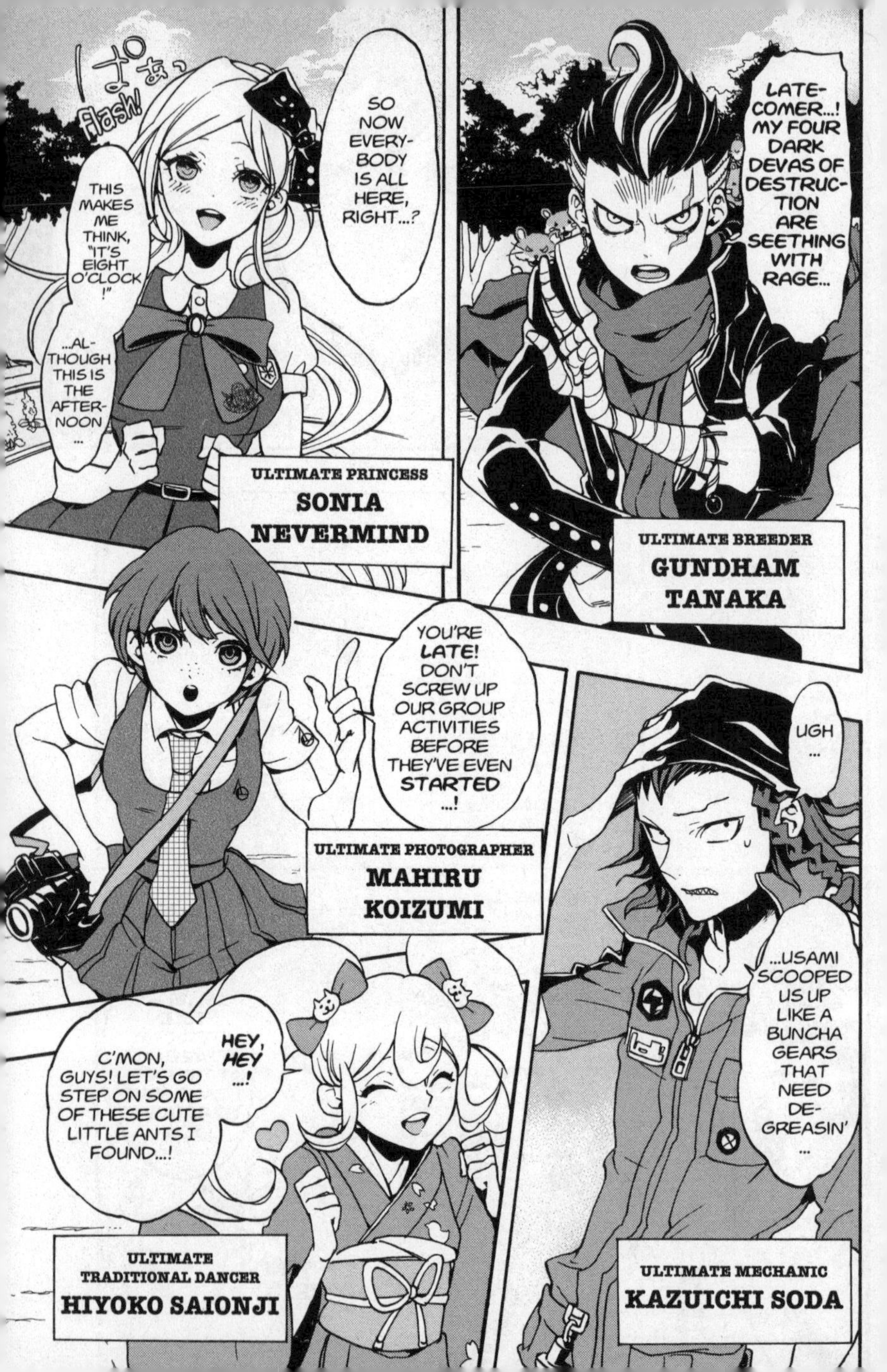
LATE-COMER...! MY FOUR DARK DEVAS OF DESTRUCTION ARE SEETHING WITH RAGE...
ULTIMATE BREEDER
GUNDHAM TANAKA
SO NOW EVERYBODY IS ALL HERE, RIGHT...?
ぱぁっ
FLASH!
THIS MAKES ME THINK, "IT'S EIGHT O'CLOCK!"
...ALTHOUGH THIS IS THE AFTERNOON...
ULTIMATE PRINCESS
SONIA NEVERMIND
UGH...
...USAMI SCOOPED US UP LIKE A BUNCHA GEARS THAT NEED DE-GREASIN'...
ULTIMATE MECHANIC
KAZUICHI SODA
YOU'RE LATE! DON'T SCREW UP OUR GROUP ACTIVITIES BEFORE THEY'VE EVEN STARTED...!
ULTIMATE PHOTOGRAPHER
MAHIRU KOIZUMI
HEY, HEY...!
C'MON, GUYS! LET'S GO STEP ON SOME OF THESE CUTE LITTLE ANTS I FOUND...!
ULTIMATE TRADITIONAL DANCER
HIYOKO SAIONJI

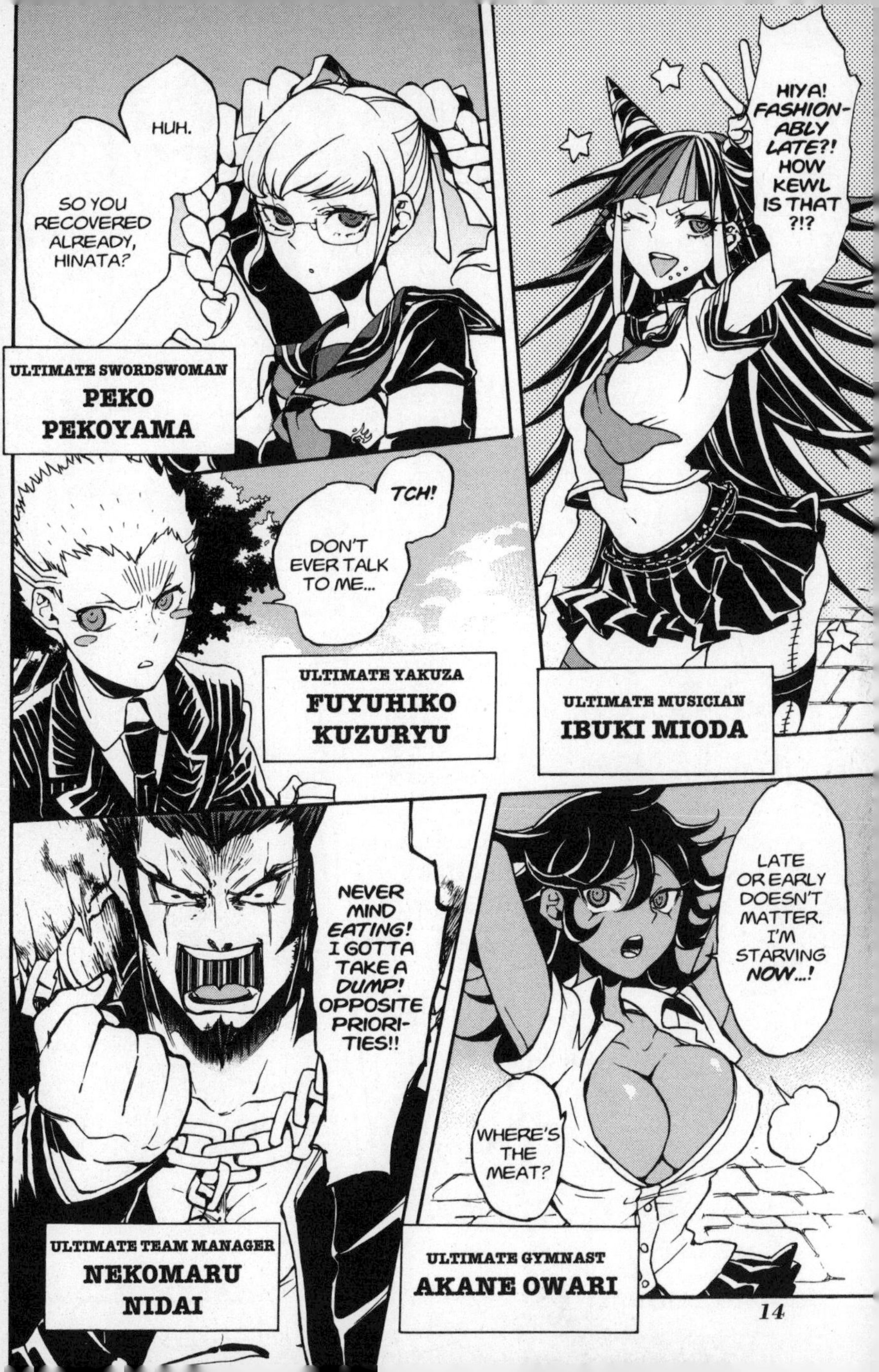
HIYA! FASHION-ABLY LATE?! HOW KEWL IS THAT ?!?
ULTIMATE MUSICIAN
IBUKI MIODA
HUH.
SO YOU RECOVERED ALREADY, HINATA?
ULTIMATE SWORDSWOMAN
PEKO PEKOYAMA
TCH!
DON'T EVER TALK TO ME...
ULTIMATE YAKUZA
FUYUHIKO KUZURYU
LATE OR EARLY DOESN'T MATTER. I'M STARVING NOW...!
WHERE'S THE MEAT?
ULTIMATE GYMNAST
AKANE OWARI
NEVER MIND EATING! I GOTTA TAKE A DUMP! OPPOSITE PRIORI-TIES!!
ULTIMATE TEAM MANAGER
NEKOMARU NIDAI

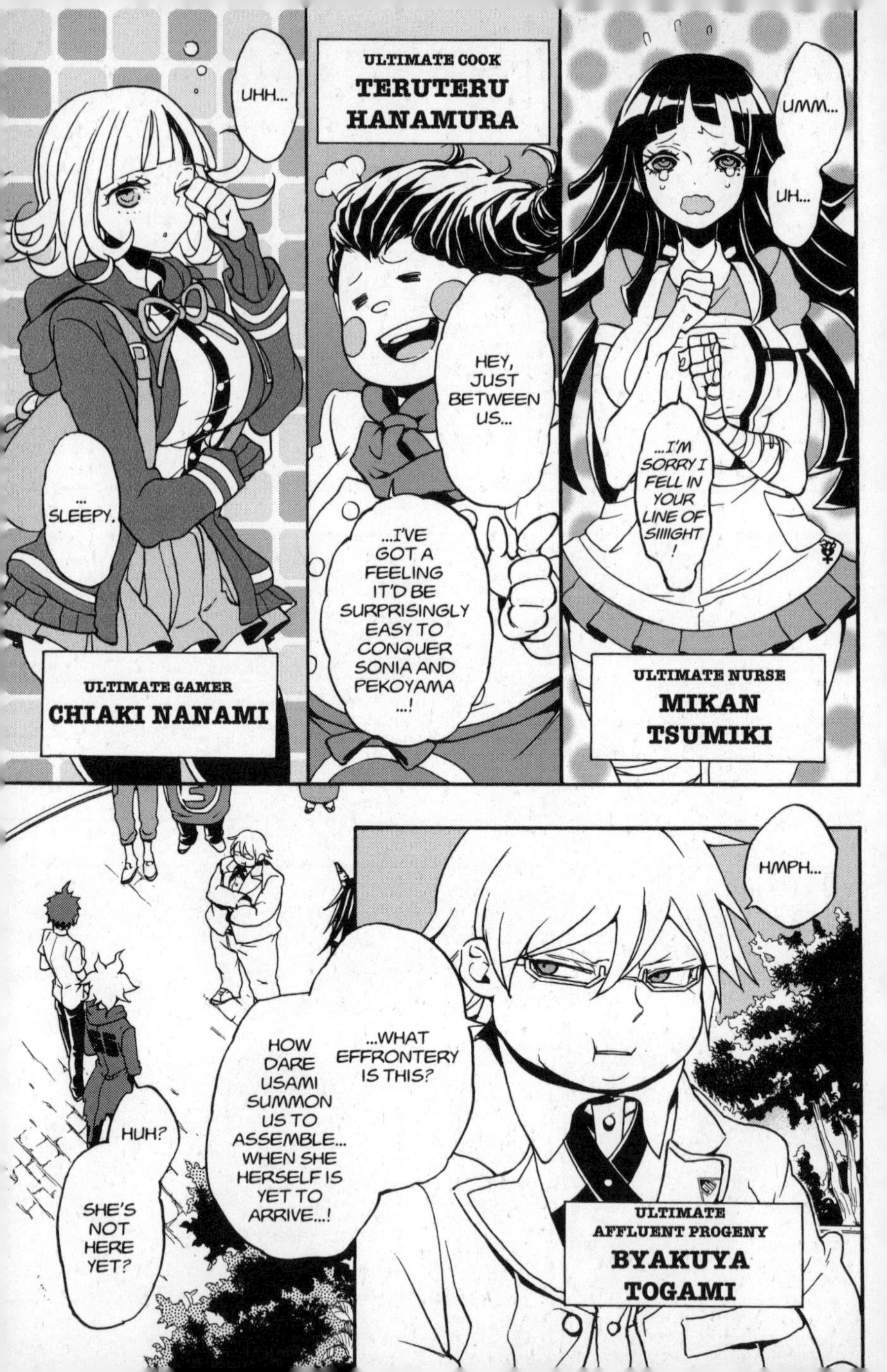
UMM...
UH...
...I'M SORRY I FELL IN YOUR LINE OF SIIIGHT!
ULTIMATE NURSE MIKAN TSUMIKI
ULTIMATE COOK TERUTERU HANAMURA
HEY, JUST BETWEEN US...
...I'VE GOT A FEELING IT'D BE SURPRISINGLY EASY TO CONQUER SONIA AND PEKOYAMA ...!
UHH...
... SLEEPY.
ULTIMATE GAMER CHIAKI NANAMI
HMPH...
...WHAT EFFRONTERY IS THIS?
HOW DARE USAMI SUMMON US TO ASSEMBLE... WHEN SHE HERSELF IS YET TO ARRIVE...!
ULTIMATE AFFLUENT PROGENY BYAKUYA TOGAMI
HUH?
SHE'S NOT HERE YET?

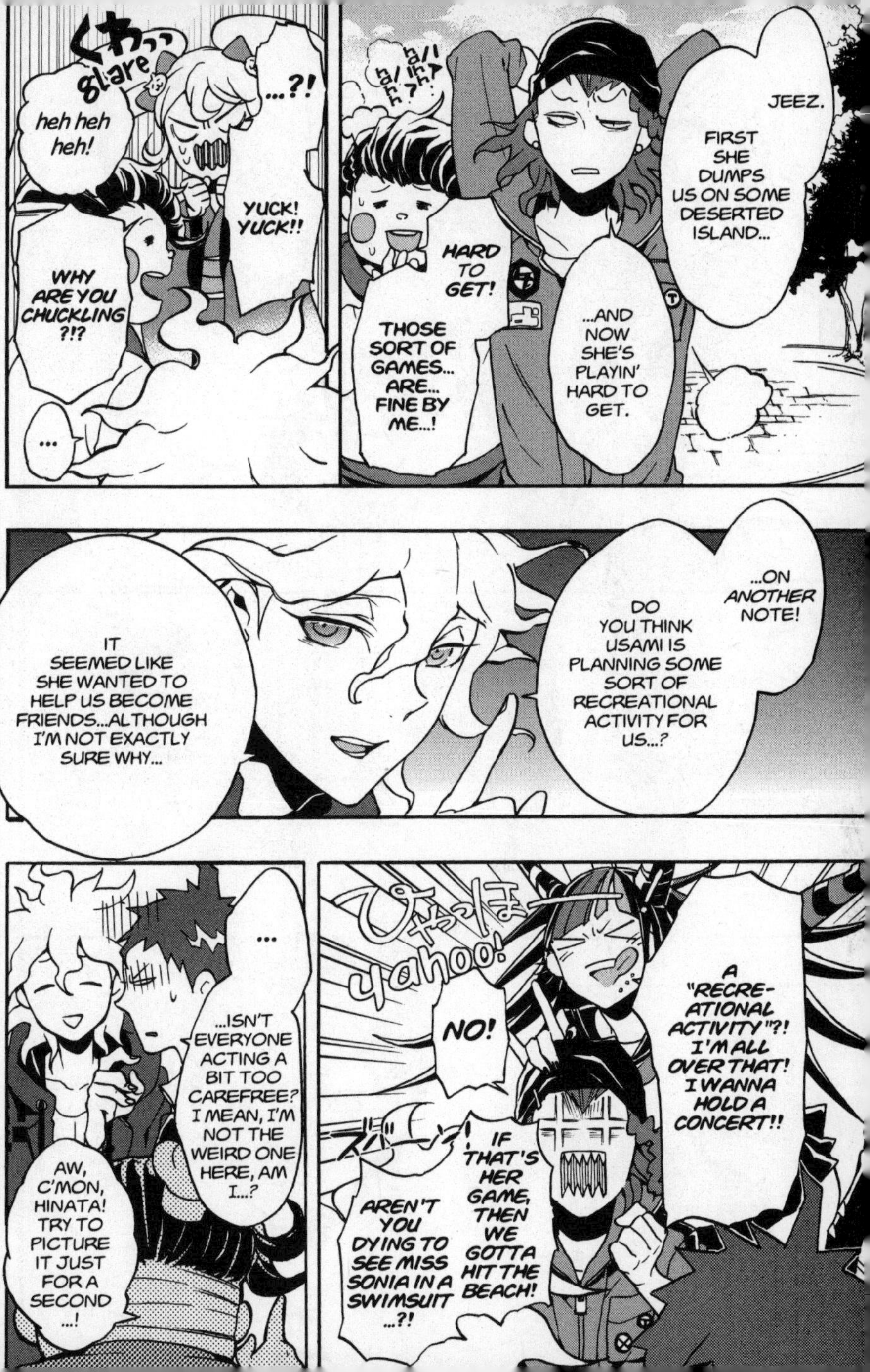
JEEZ.
FIRST SHE DUMPS US ON SOME DESERTED ISLAND...
...AND NOW SHE'S PLAYIN' HARD TO GET.
HARD TO GET!
THOSE SORT OF GAMES... ARE... FINE BY ME...!
...?!
glare
heh heh heh!
YUCK! YUCK!!
WHY ARE YOU CHUCKLING?!?
...
...ON ANOTHER NOTE!
DO YOU THINK USAMI IS PLANNING SOME SORT OF RECREATIONAL ACTIVITY FOR US...?
IT SEEMED LIKE SHE WANTED TO HELP US BECOME FRIENDS...ALTHOUGH I'M NOT EXACTLY SURE WHY...
yahoo!
A "RECRE-ATIONAL ACTIVITY"?! I'M ALL OVER THAT! I WANNA HOLD A CONCERT!!
NO!
IF THAT'S HER GAME, THEN WE GOTTA HIT THE BEACH!
AREN'T YOU DYING TO SEE MISS SONIA IN A SWIMSUIT ...?!
...
...ISN'T EVERYONE ACTING A BIT TOO CAREFREE? I MEAN, I'M NOT THE WEIRD ONE HERE, AM I...?
AW, C'MON, HINATA! TRY TO PICTURE IT JUST FOR A SECOND ...!

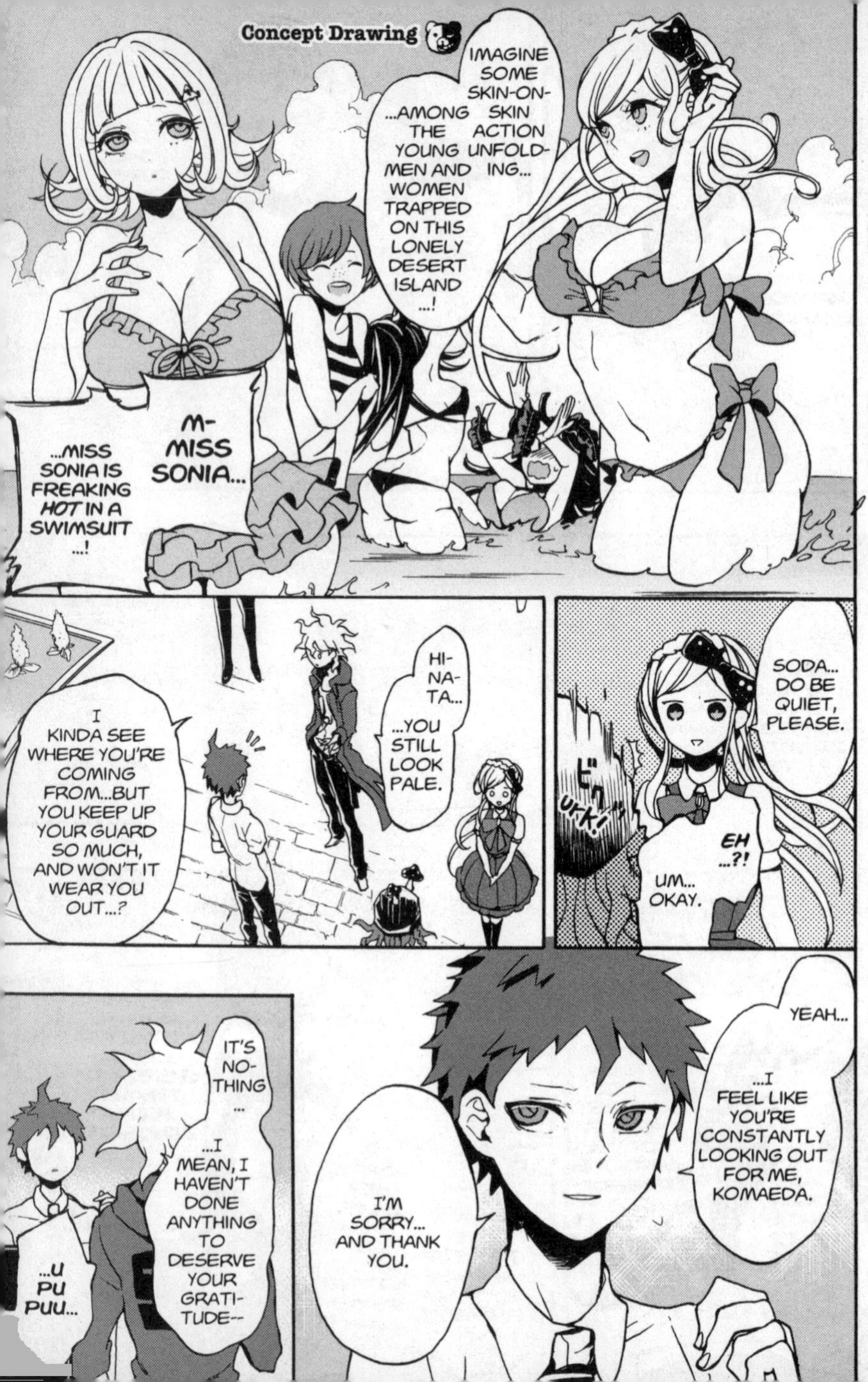
Concept Drawing
IMAGINE SOME SKIN-ON-SKIN ACTION UNFOLDING...
...AMONG THE YOUNG MEN AND WOMEN TRAPPED ON THIS LONELY DESERT ISLAND...!
M-MISS SONIA...
...MISS SONIA IS FREAKING *HOT* IN A SWIMSUIT...!
SODA... DO BE QUIET, PLEASE.
ビク URK!
EH...?!
UM... OKAY.
HI-NA-TA... ...YOU STILL LOOK PALE.
I KINDA SEE WHERE YOU'RE COMING FROM...BUT YOU KEEP UP YOUR GUARD SO MUCH, AND WON'T IT WEAR YOU OUT...?
YEAH...
...I FEEL LIKE YOU'RE CONSTANTLY LOOKING OUT FOR ME, KOMAEDA.
I'M SORRY... AND THANK YOU.
IT'S NOTHING...
...I MEAN, I HAVEN'T DONE ANYTHING TO DESERVE YOUR GRATITUDE--
...U PU PUU...

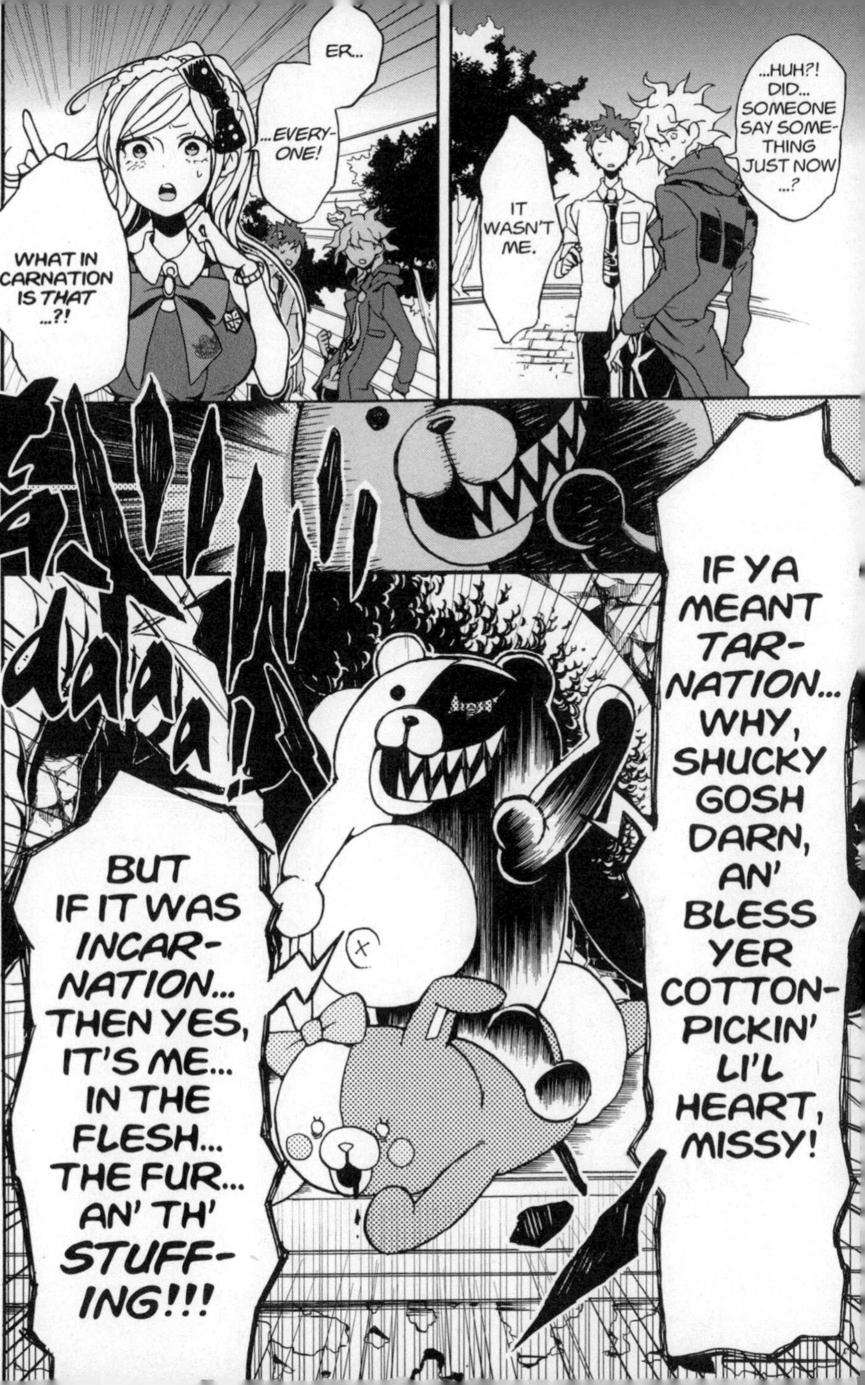
...HUH?! DID... SOMEONE SAY SOMETHING JUST NOW ...?
IT WASN'T ME.
ER...
...EVERYONE!
WHAT IN CARNATION IS THAT ...?!
IF YA MEANT TARNATION... WHY, SHUCKY GOSH DARN, AN' BLESS YER COTTON-PICKIN' LI'L HEART, MISSY!
BUT IF IT WAS INCARNATION... THEN YES, IT'S ME... IN THE FLESH... THE FUR... AN' TH' STUFFING!!!

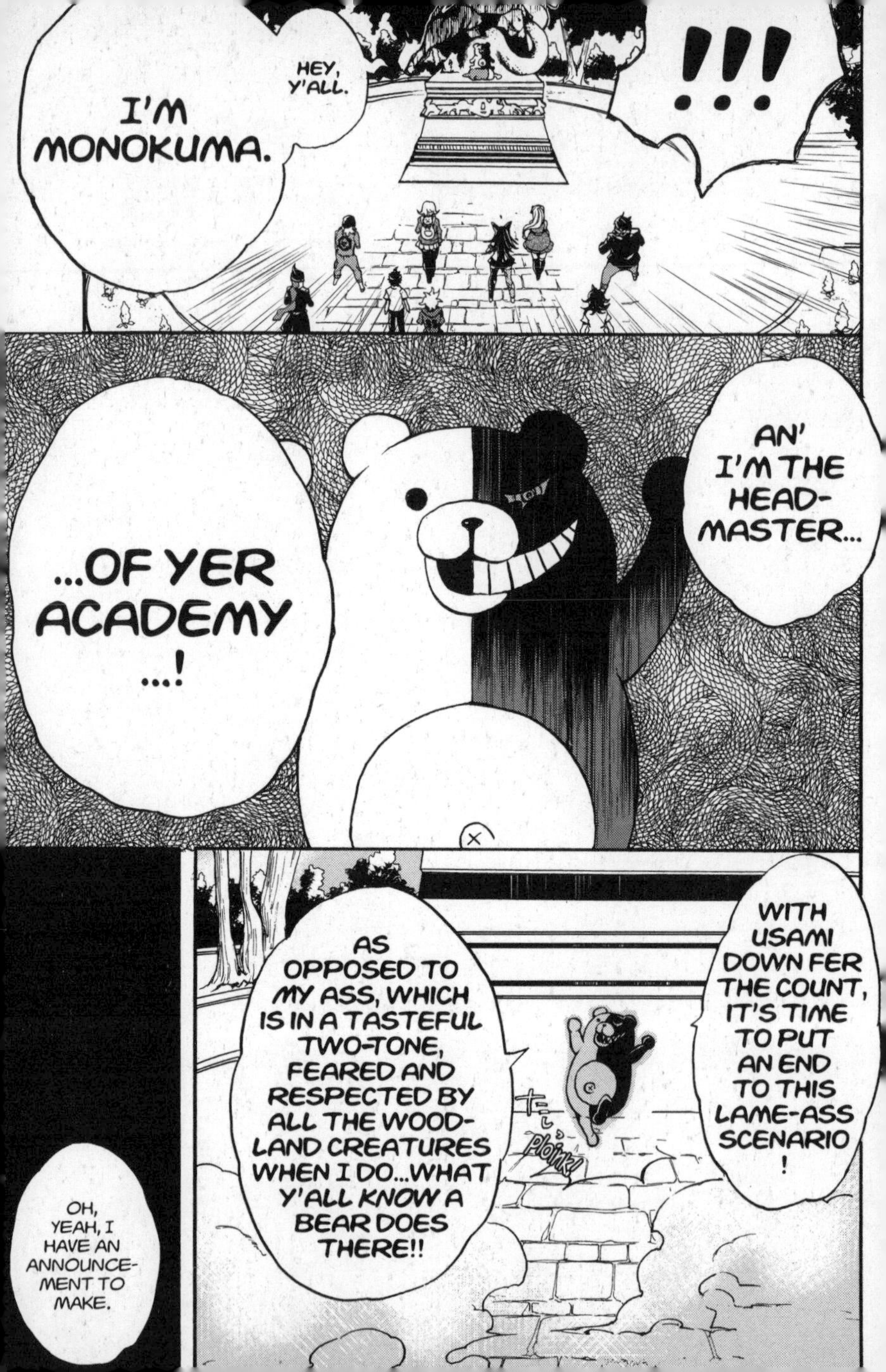
!!!
HEY, Y'ALL.
I'M MONOKUMA.
AN' I'M THE HEAD-MASTER...
...OF YER ACADEMY ...!
WITH USAMI DOWN FER THE COUNT, IT'S TIME TO PUT AN END TO THIS LAME-ASS SCENARIO !
AS OPPOSED TO MY ASS, WHICH IS IN A TASTEFUL TWO-TONE, FEARED AND RESPECTED BY ALL THE WOOD-LAND CREATURES WHEN I DO...WHAT Y'ALL KNOW A BEAR DOES THERE!!
Ploink!
OH, YEAH, I HAVE AN ANNOUNCE-MENT TO MAKE.

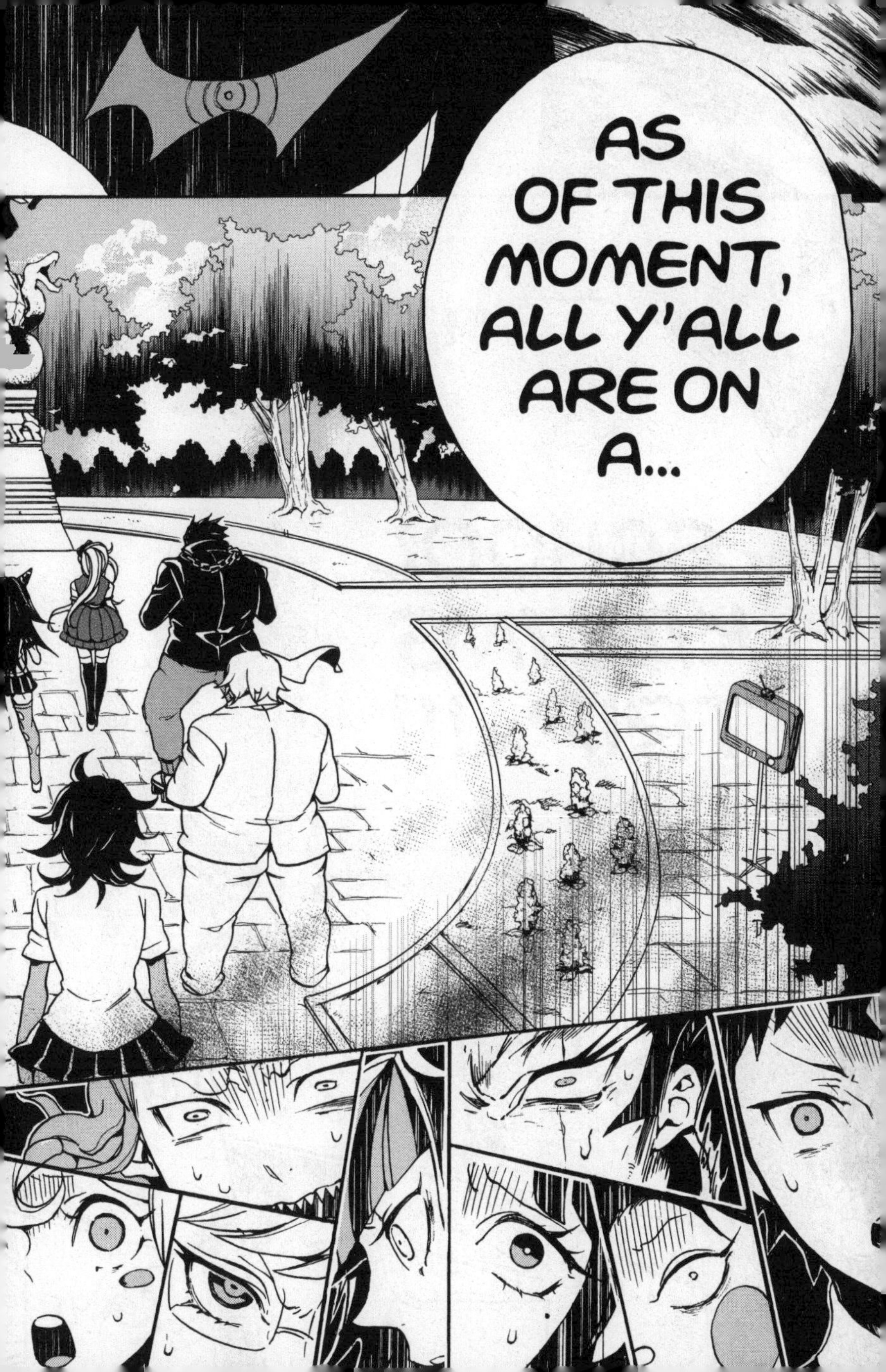
AS OF THIS MOMENT, ALL Y'ALL ARE ON A...

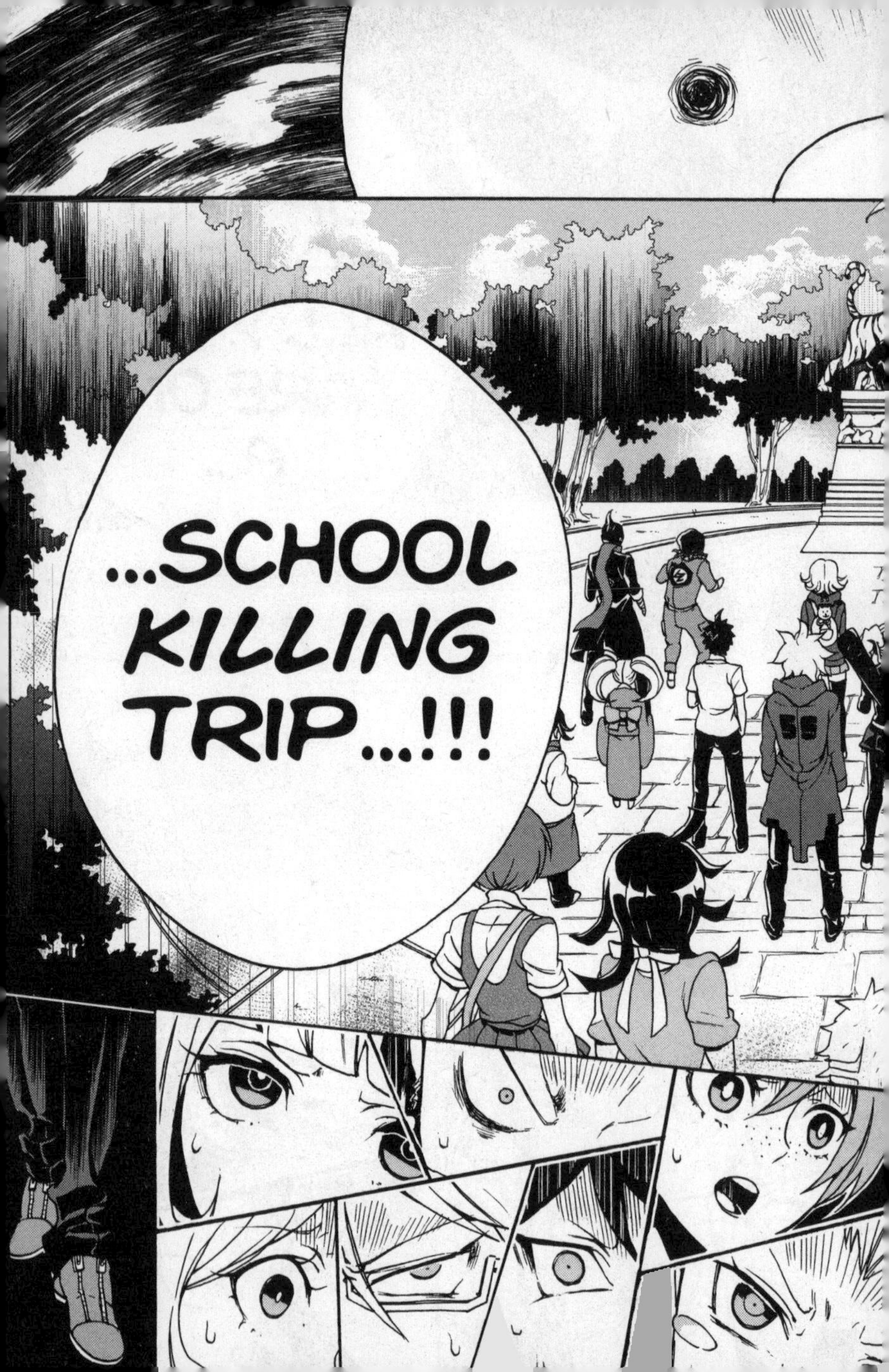
...SCHOOL KILLING TRIP...!!!

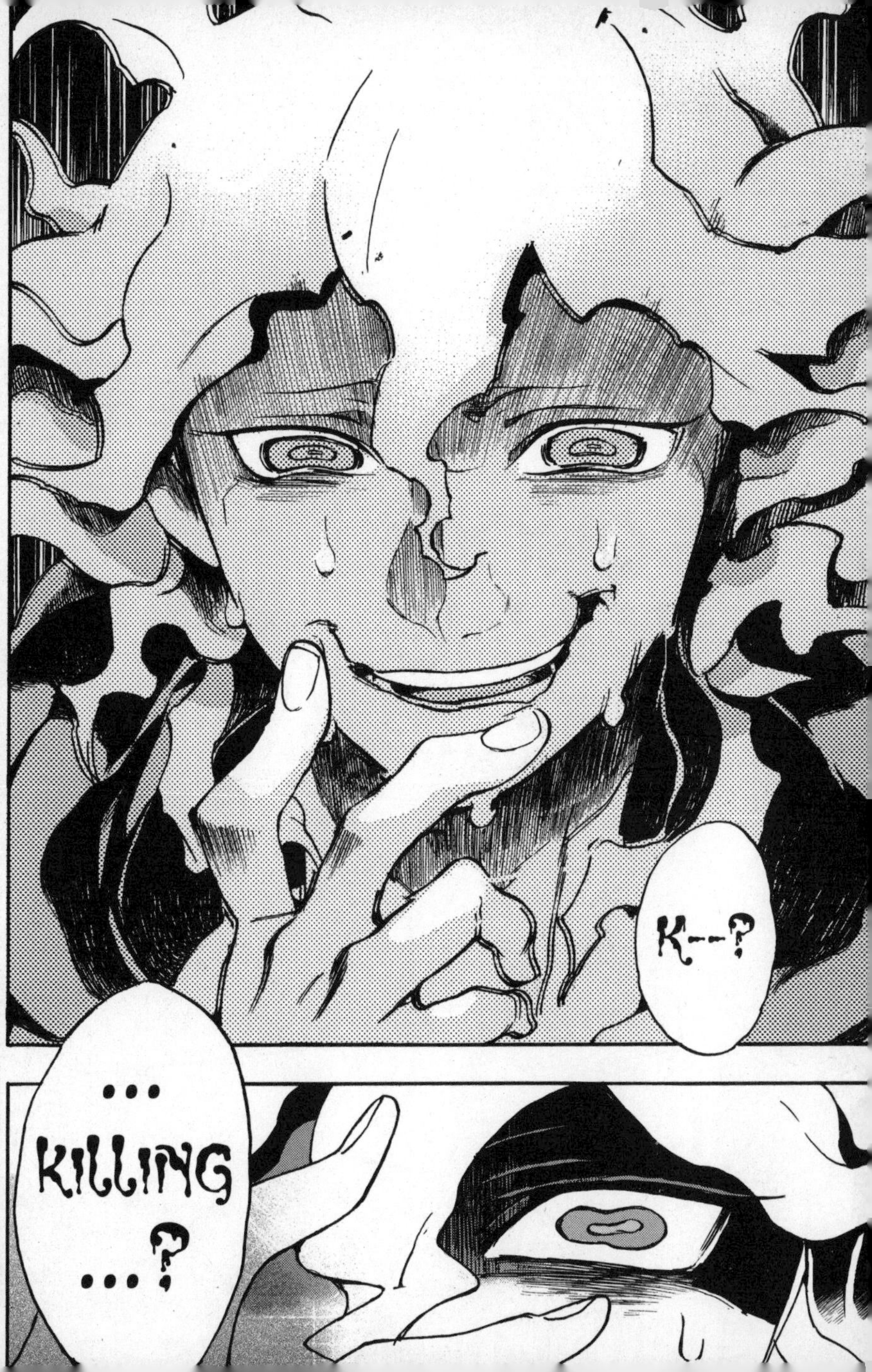
K---?
... KILLING ...?

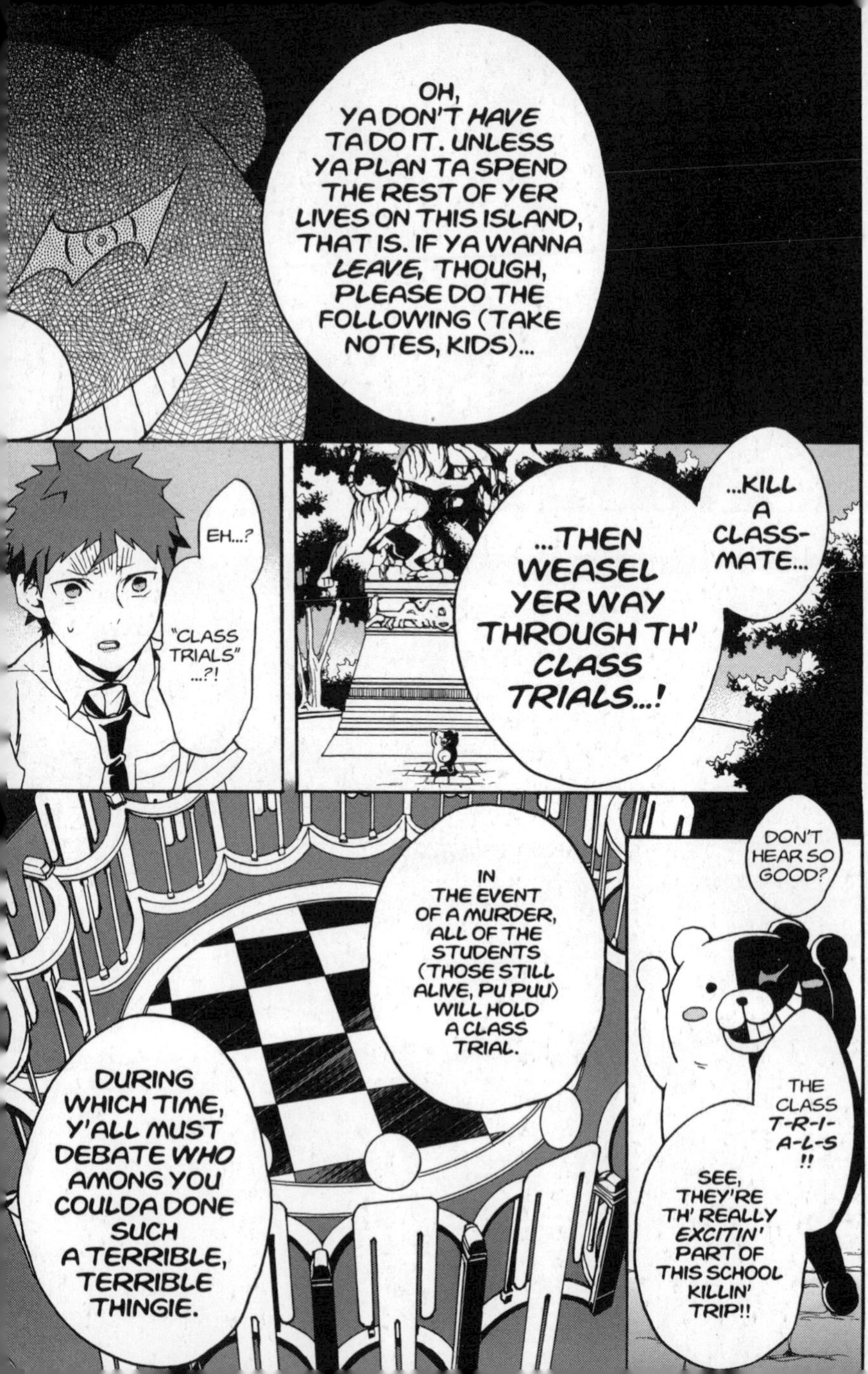
OH, YA DON'T *HAVE* TA DO IT. UNLESS YA PLAN TA SPEND THE REST OF YER LIVES ON THIS ISLAND, THAT IS. IF YA WANNA *LEAVE,* THOUGH, PLEASE DO THE FOLLOWING (TAKE NOTES, KIDS)...
...KILL A CLASS-MATE...
...THEN WEASEL YER WAY THROUGH TH' *CLASS TRIALS*...!
EH...?
"CLASS TRIALS" ...?!
DON'T HEAR SO GOOD?
THE CLASS *T-R-I-A-L-S*!!
SEE, THEY'RE TH' REALLY *EXCITIN'* PART OF THIS SCHOOL KILLIN' TRIP!!
IN THE EVENT OF A MURDER, ALL OF THE STUDENTS (THOSE STILL ALIVE, PU PUU) WILL HOLD A CLASS TRIAL.
DURING WHICH TIME, Y'ALL MUST DEBATE WHO AMONG YOU COULDA DONE SUCH A TERRIBLE, TERRIBLE THINGIE.

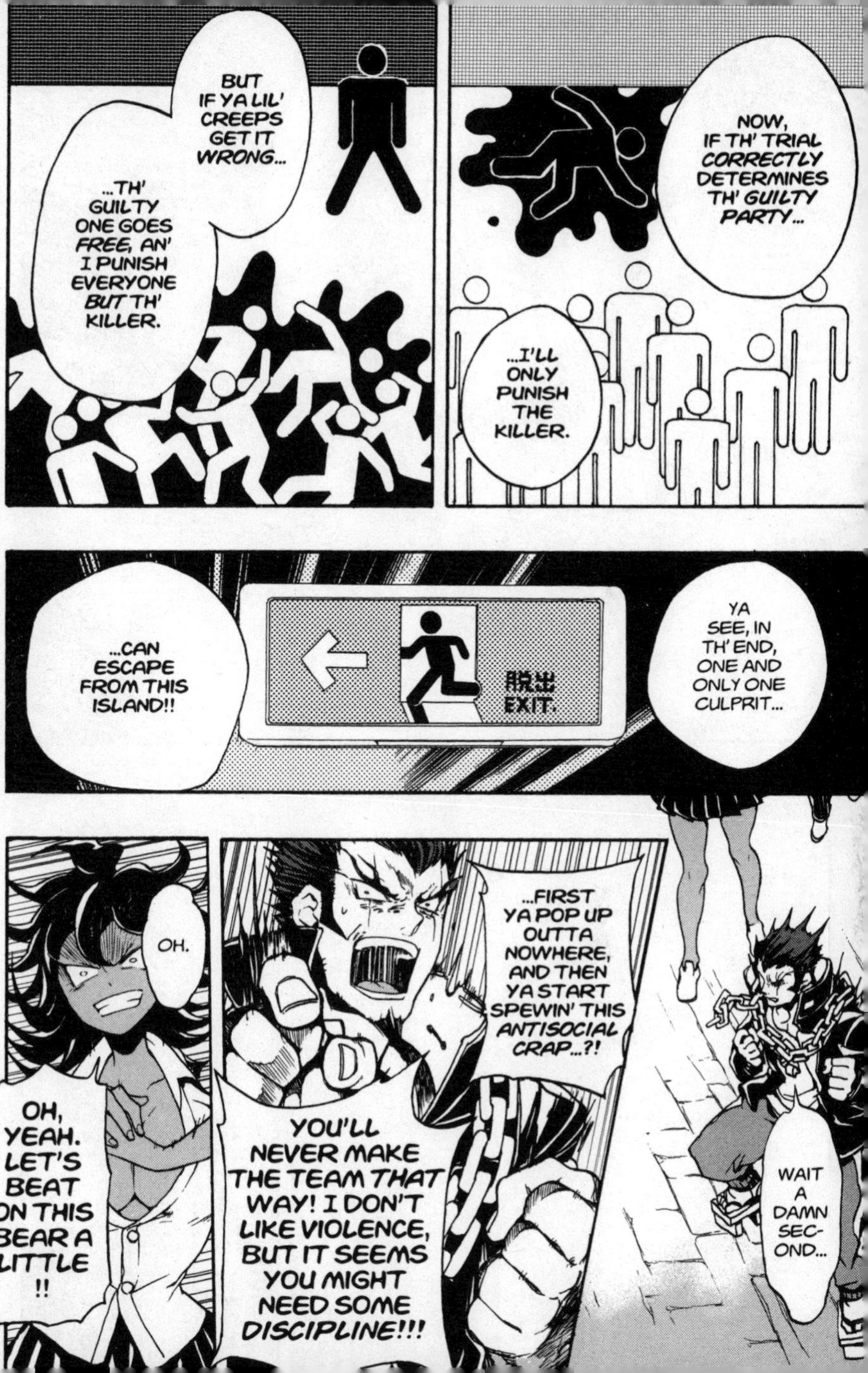
NOW, IF TH' TRIAL CORRECTLY DETERMINES TH' GUILTY PARTY...
...I'LL ONLY PUNISH THE KILLER.
BUT IF YA LIL' CREEPS GET IT WRONG...
...TH' GUILTY ONE GOES FREE, AN' I PUNISH EVERYONE BUT TH' KILLER.
YA SEE, IN TH' END, ONE AND ONLY ONE CULPRIT...
脱出
EXIT.
...CAN ESCAPE FROM THIS ISLAND!!
WAIT A DAMN SEC-OND...
...FIRST YA POP UP OUTTA NOWHERE, AND THEN YA START SPEWIN' THIS ANTISOCIAL CRAP...?!
YOU'LL NEVER MAKE THE TEAM THAT WAY! I DON'T LIKE VIOLENCE, BUT IT SEEMS YOU MIGHT NEED SOME DISCIPLINE!!!
OH.
OH, YEAH. LET'S BEAT ON THIS BEAR A LITTLE!!

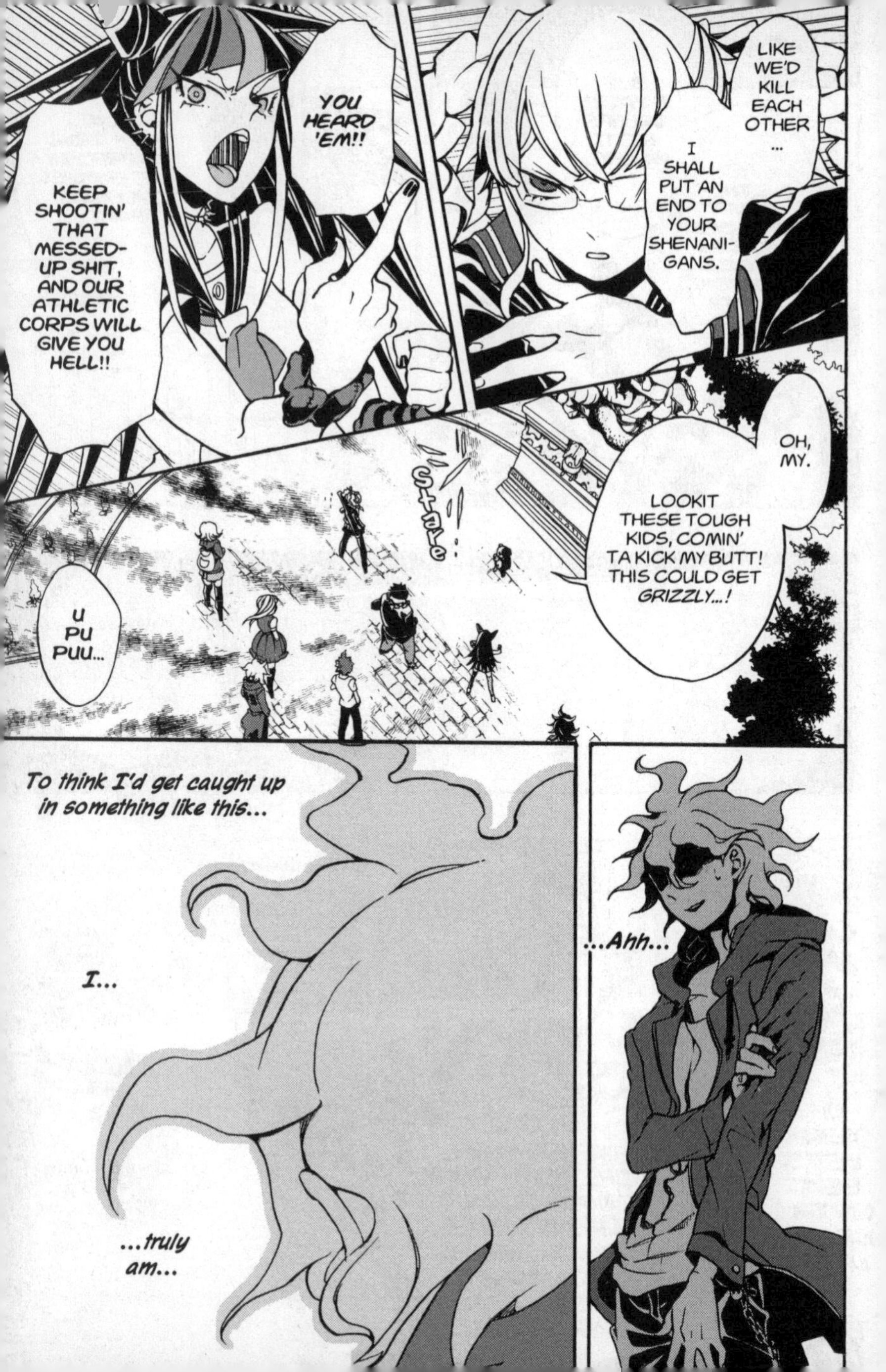
LIKE WE'D KILL EACH OTHER ...
I SHALL PUT AN END TO YOUR SHENANIGANS.
YOU HEARD 'EM!!
KEEP SHOOTIN' THAT MESSED-UP SHIT, AND OUR ATHLETIC CORPS WILL GIVE YOU HELL!!
OH, MY.
LOOKIT THESE TOUGH KIDS, COMIN' TA KICK MY BUTT! THIS COULD GET GRIZZLY...!
Stare
U PU PUU...
...Ahh...
To think I'd get caught up in something like this...
I...
...truly am...

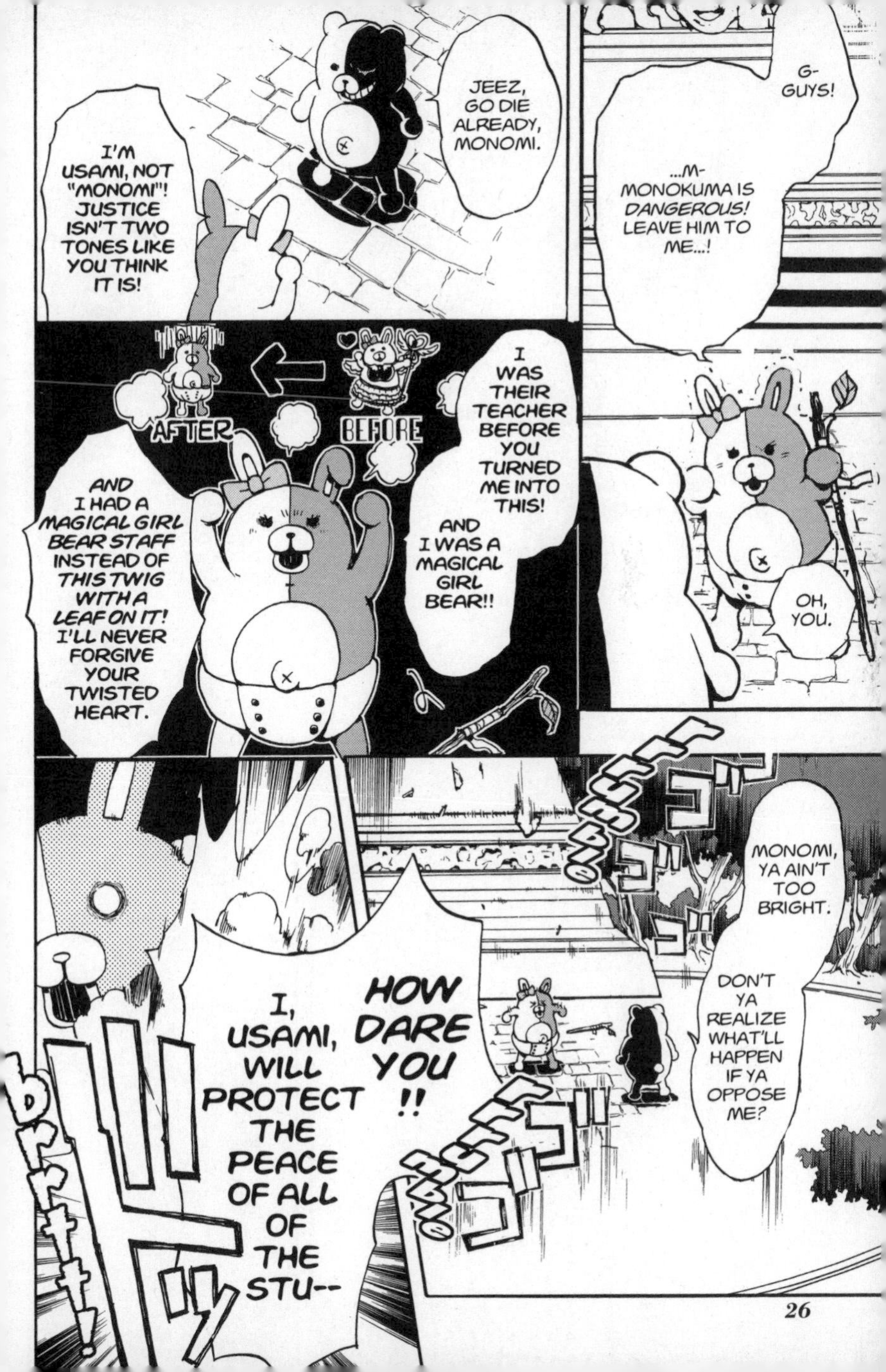
G-GUYS!
...M-MONOKUMA IS DANGEROUS! LEAVE HIM TO ME...!
JEEZ, GO DIE ALREADY, MONOMI.
I'M USAMI, NOT "MONOMI"! JUSTICE ISN'T TWO TONES LIKE YOU THINK IT IS!
OH, YOU.
I WAS THEIR TEACHER BEFORE YOU TURNED ME INTO THIS!
AND I WAS A MAGICAL GIRL BEAR!!
BEFORE
AFTER
AND I HAD A MAGICAL GIRL BEAR STAFF INSTEAD OF THIS TWIG WITH A LEAF ON IT! I'LL NEVER FORGIVE YOUR TWISTED HEART.
rumble
MONOMI, YA AIN'T TOO BRIGHT.
DON'T YA REALIZE WHAT'LL HAPPEN IF YA OPPOSE ME?
rumble
HOW DARE YOU!!
I, USAMI, WILL PROTECT THE PEACE OF ALL OF THE STU--
brrttt!

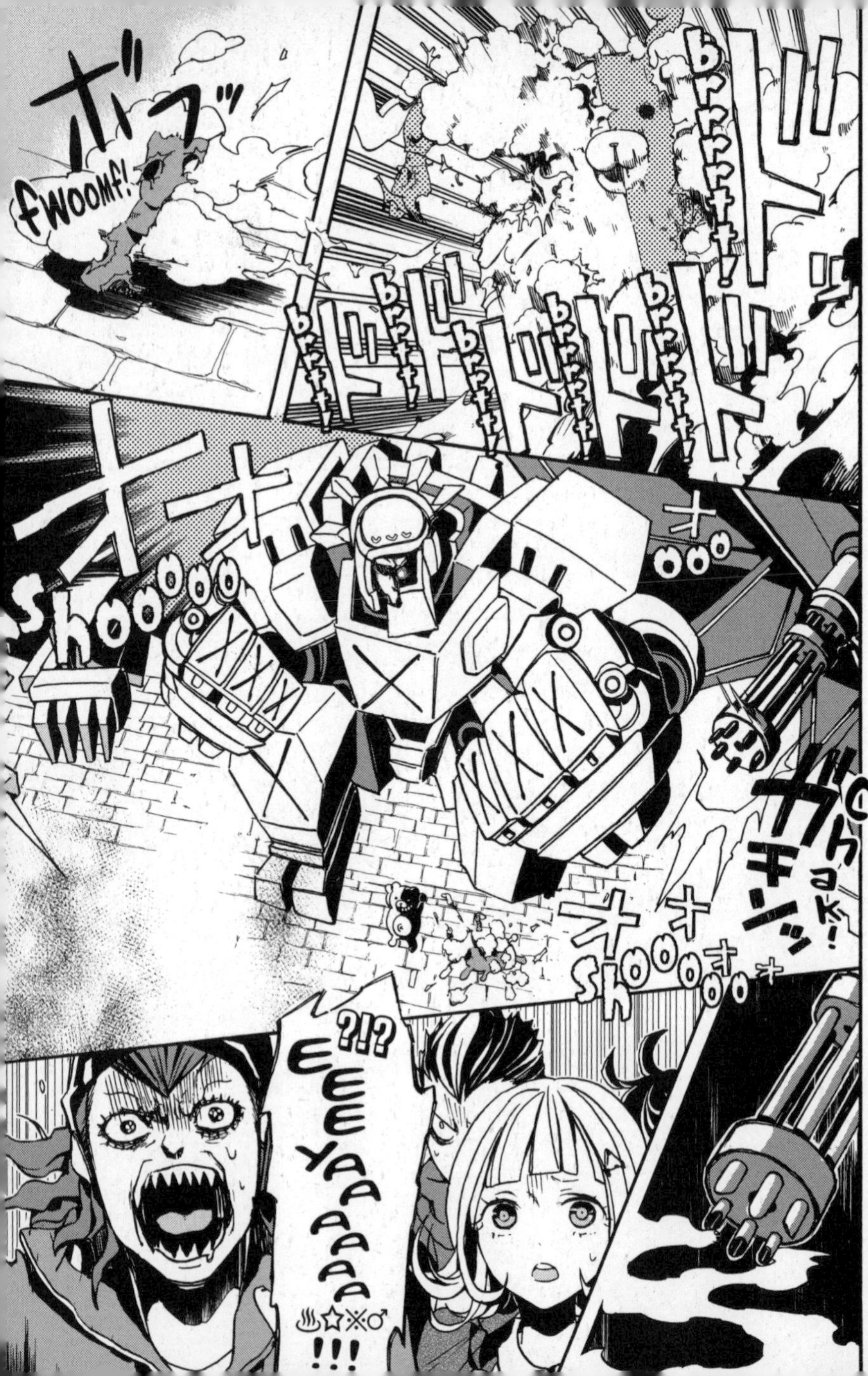

brrrrtt!
brrrrrtt!
brrrtt!
brrrtt!
brrrt!
ボブッ
fwoomf!
chak!
shooooo
shoooooo
?!?
EEEYAAAAAAA ♨☆※♂!!!

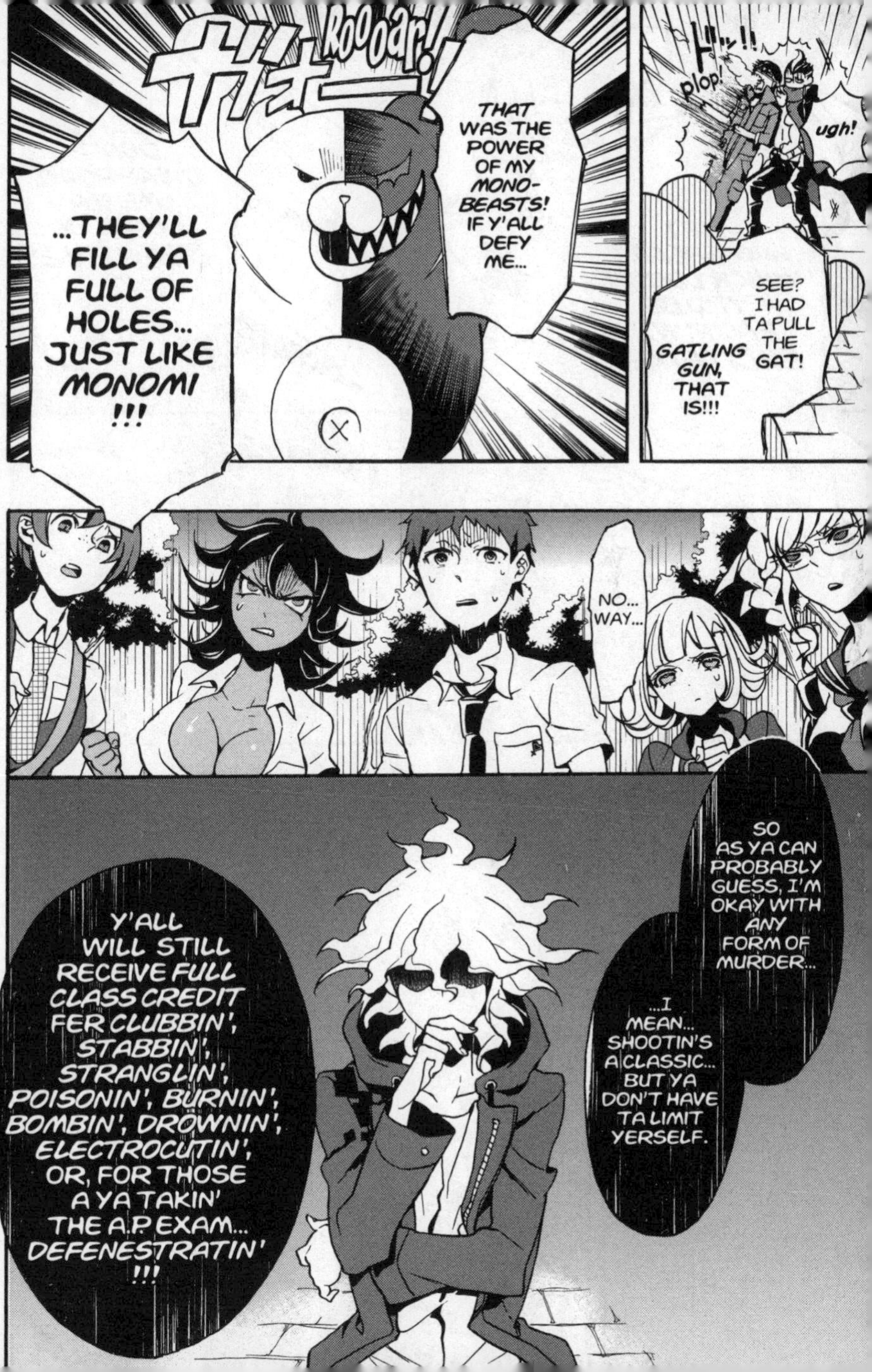
ドッ!!
plop!
ugh!
SEE? I HAD TA PULL THE GAT!
GATLING GUN, THAT IS!!!
ガオー!
ROOOAR!!
THAT WAS THE POWER OF MY MONO-BEASTS! IF Y'ALL DEFY ME...
...THEY'LL FILL YA FULL OF HOLES... JUST LIKE MONOMI !!!
NO... WAY...
SO AS YA CAN PROBABLY GUESS, I'M OKAY WITH ANY FORM OF MURDER...
...I MEAN... SHOOTIN'S A CLASSIC... BUT YA DON'T HAVE TA LIMIT YERSELF.
Y'ALL WILL STILL RECEIVE FULL CLASS CREDIT FER CLUBBIN', STABBIN', STRANGLIN', POISONIN', BURNIN', BOMBIN', DROWNIN', ELECTROCUTIN', OR, FOR THOSE A YA TAKIN' THE A.P. EXAM... DEFENESTRATIN' !!!

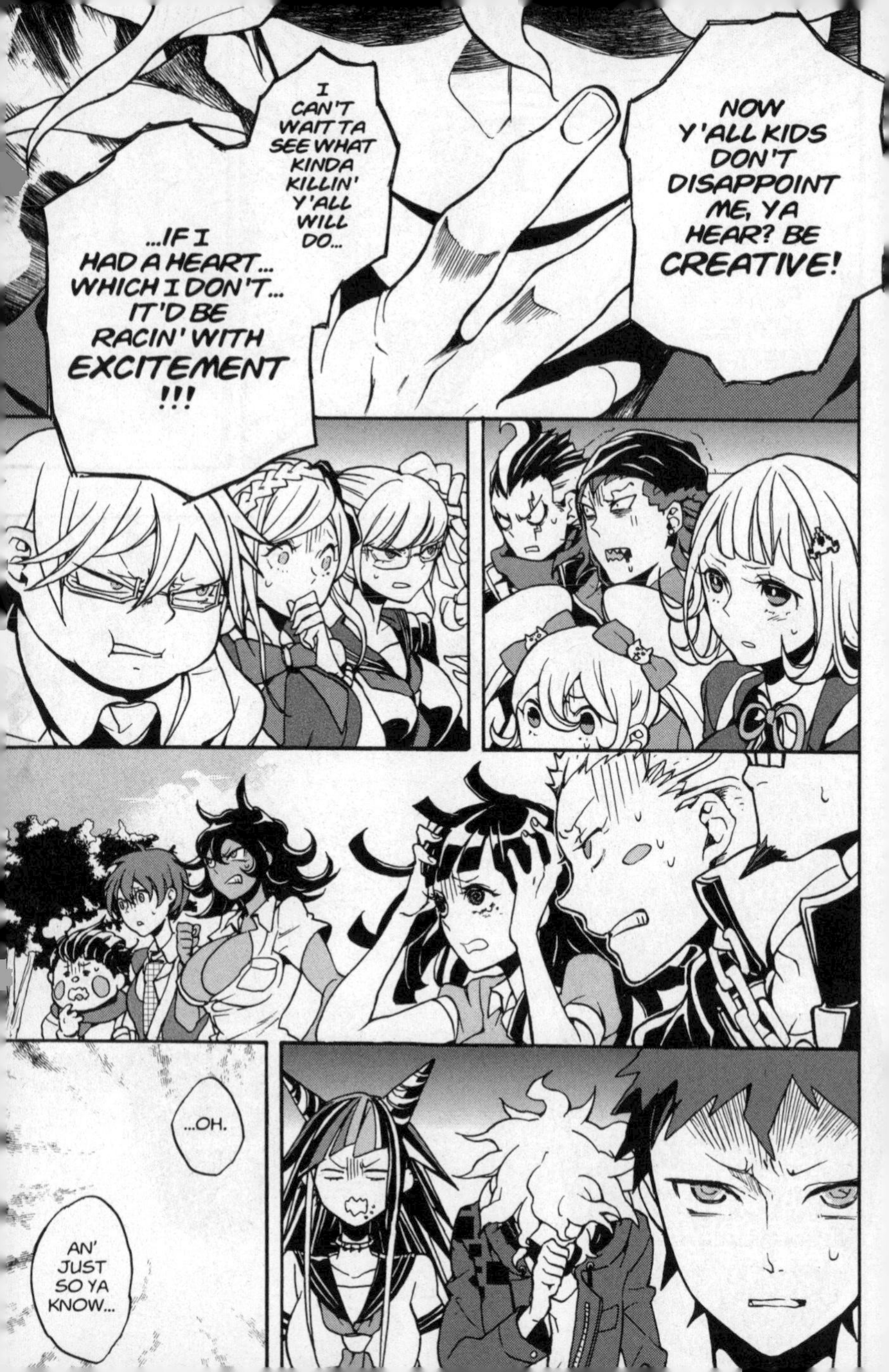
NOW Y'ALL KIDS DON'T DISAPPOINT ME, YA HEAR? BE CREATIVE!
I CAN'T WAIT TA SEE WHAT KINDA KILLIN' Y'ALL WILL DO...
...IF I HAD A HEART... WHICH I DON'T... IT'D BE RACIN' WITH EXCITEMENT !!!
...OH.
AN' JUST SO YA KNOW...

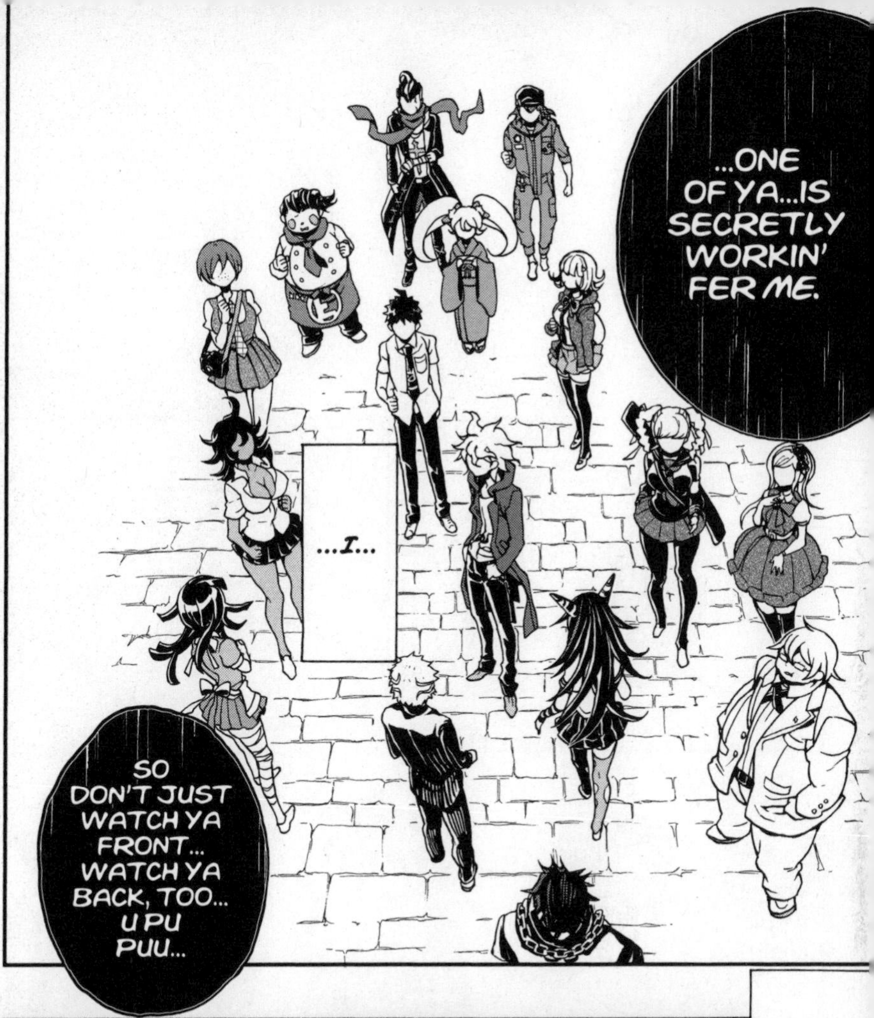
...ONE OF YA...IS SECRETLY WORKIN' FER ME.
...I...
SO DON'T JUST WATCH YA FRONT... WATCH YA BACK, TOO... UPU PUU...

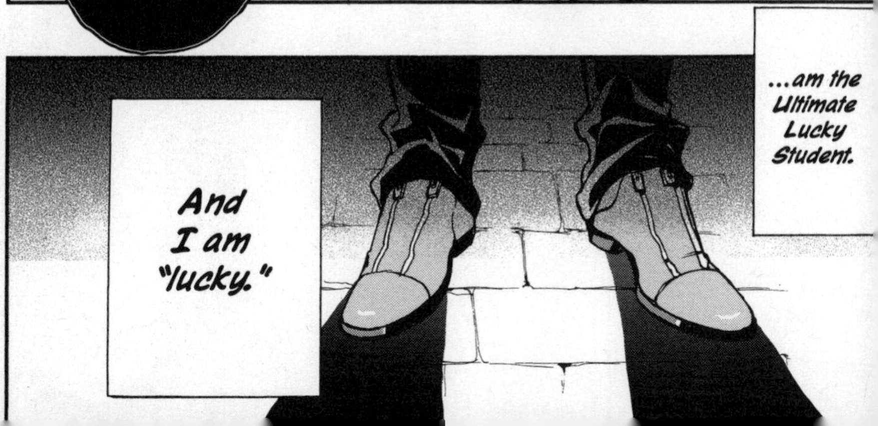
...am the Ultimate Lucky Student.
And I am "lucky."

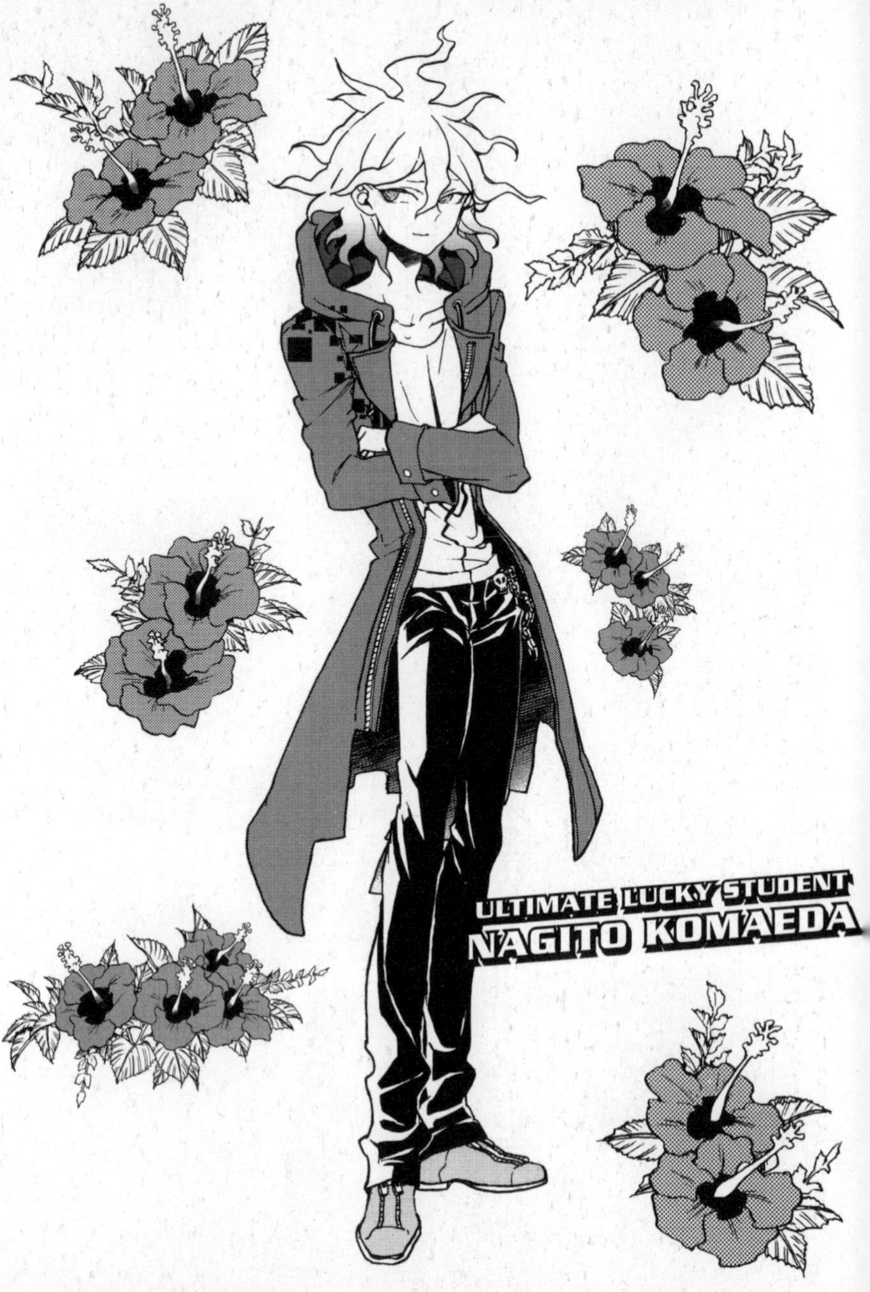
ULTIMATE LUCKY STUDENT
NAGITO KOMAEDA

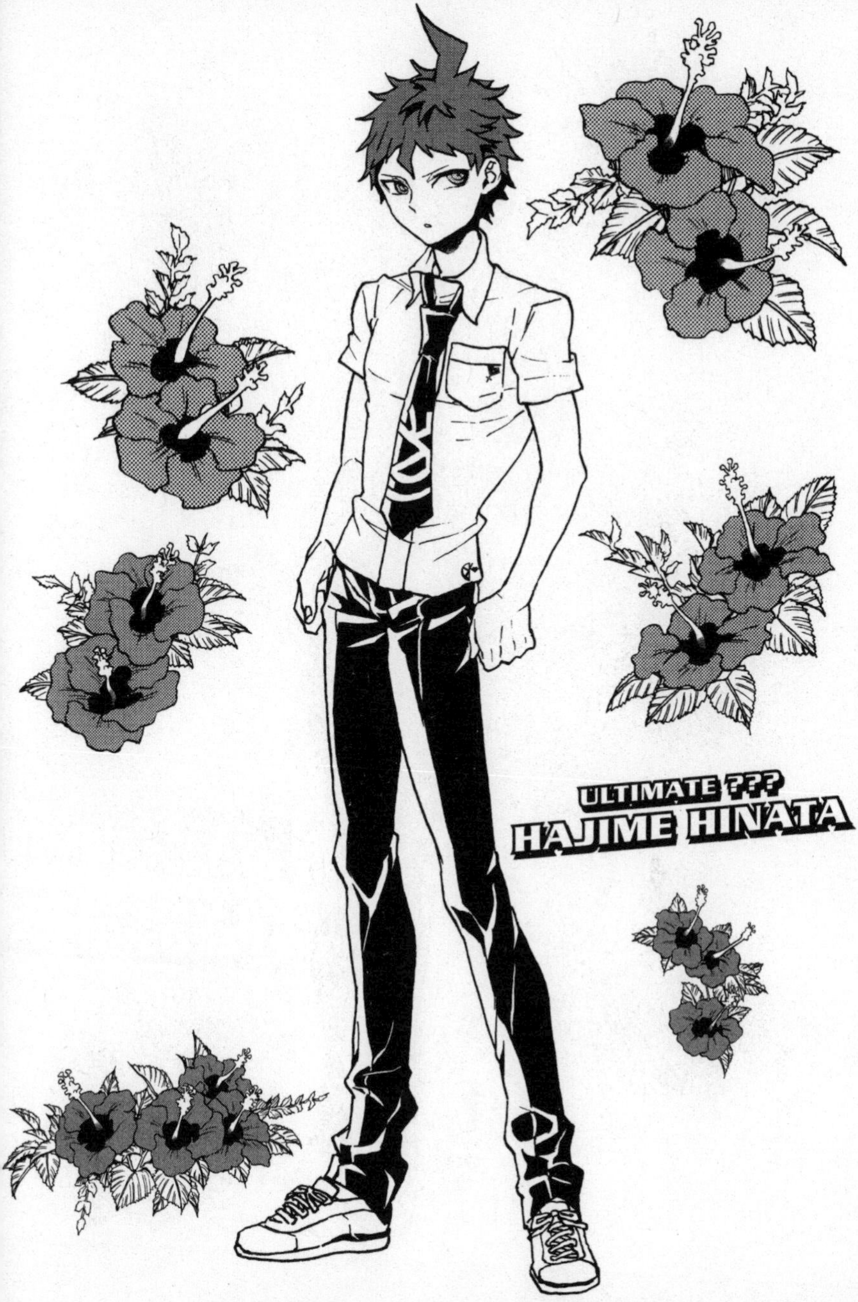
ULTIMATE ???
HAJIME HINATA

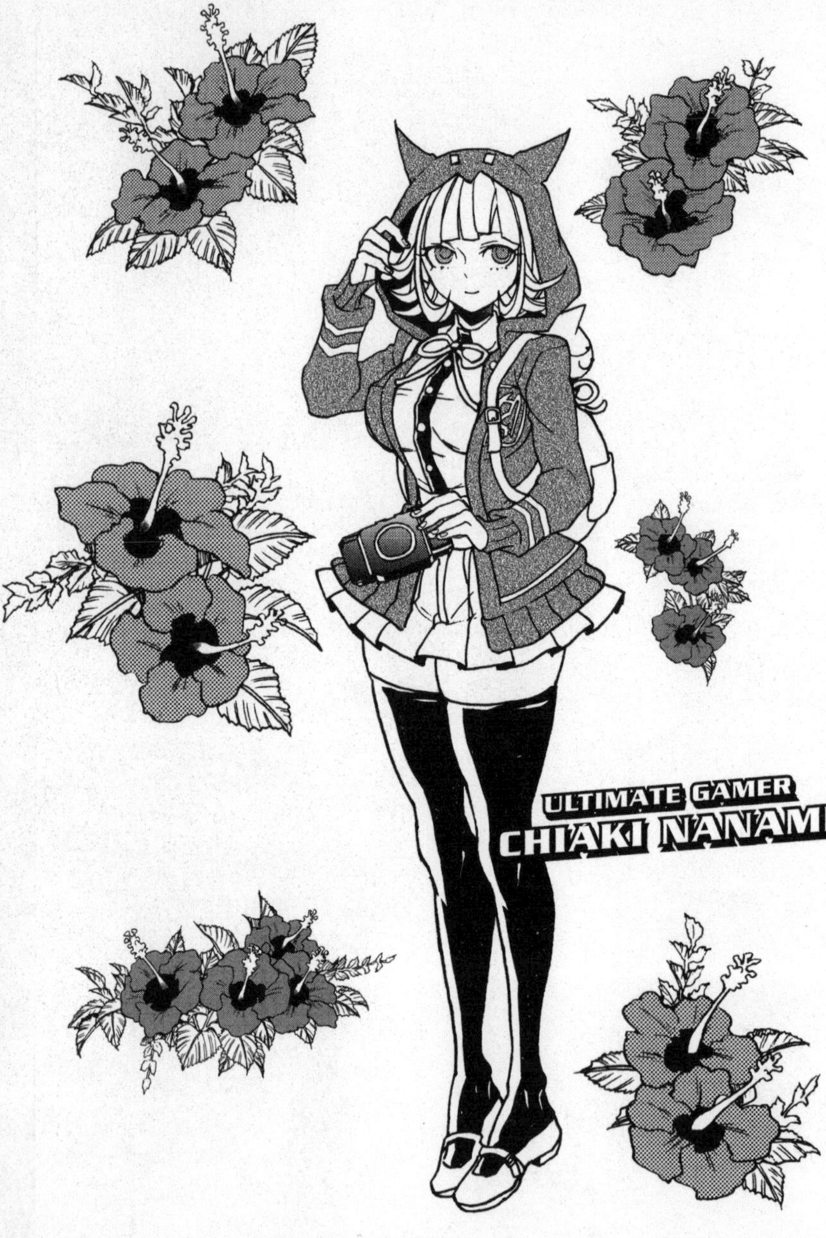
ULTIMATE GAMER
CHIAKI NANAMI

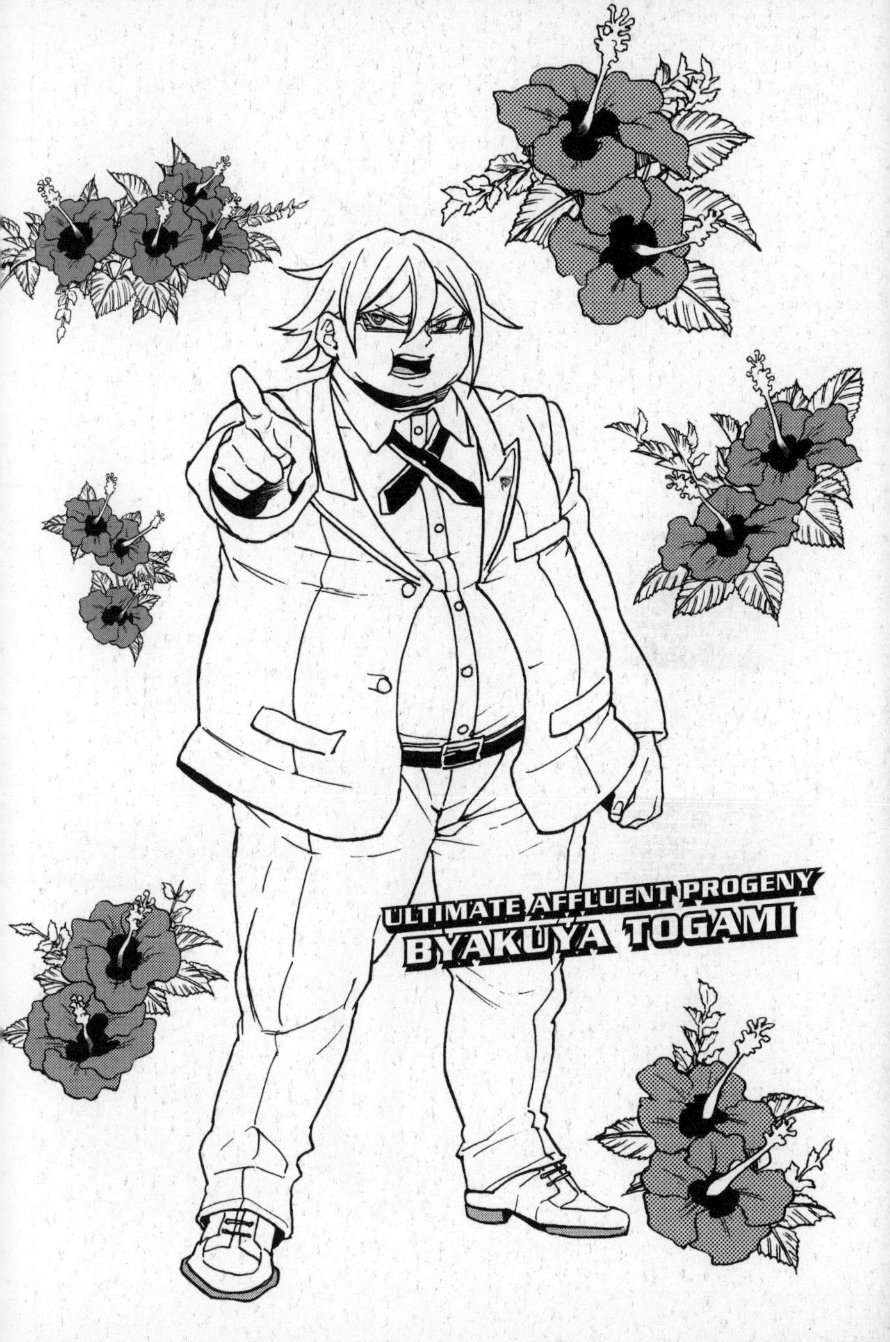
ULTIMATE AFFLUENT PROGENY
BYAKUYA TOGAMI

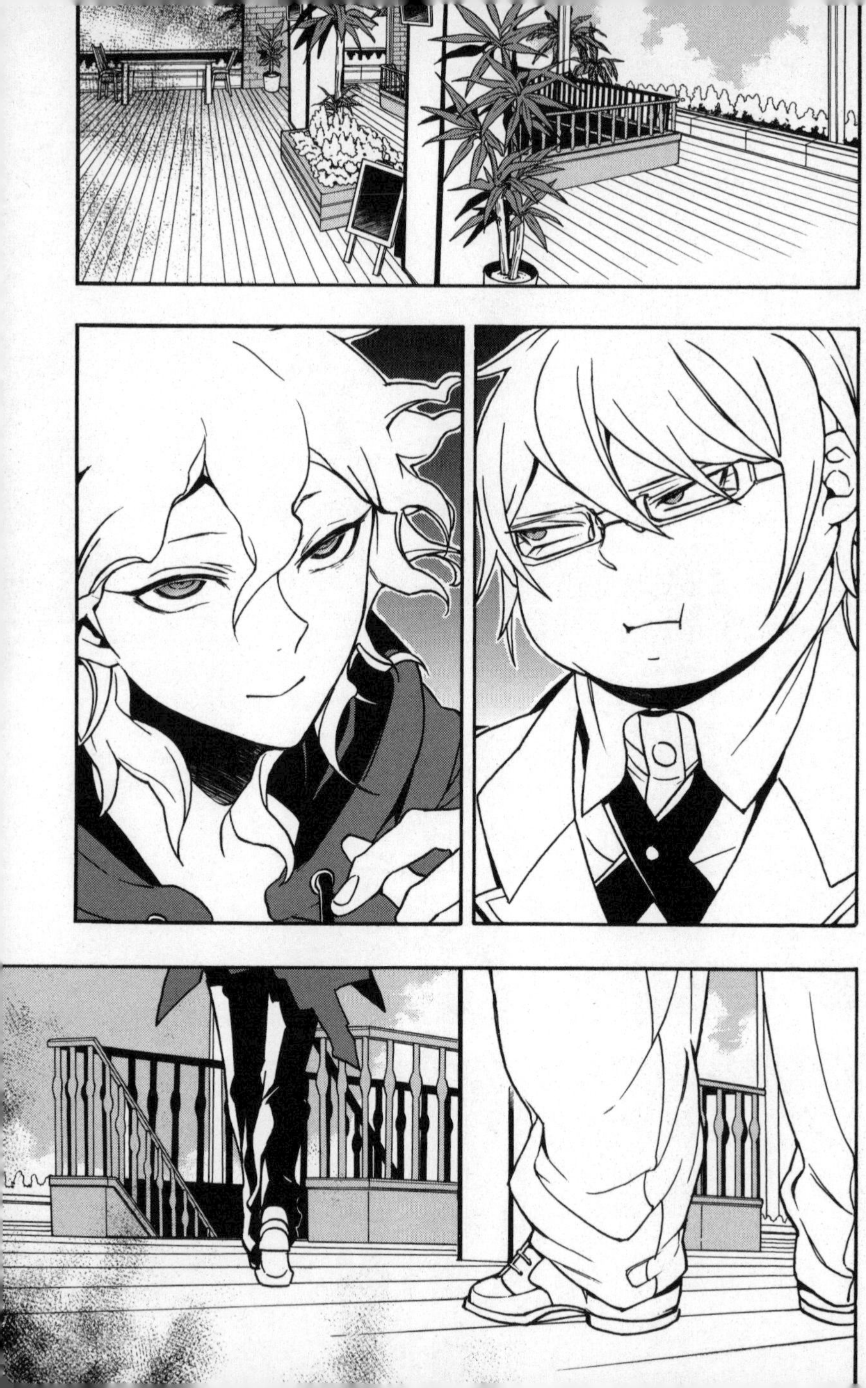

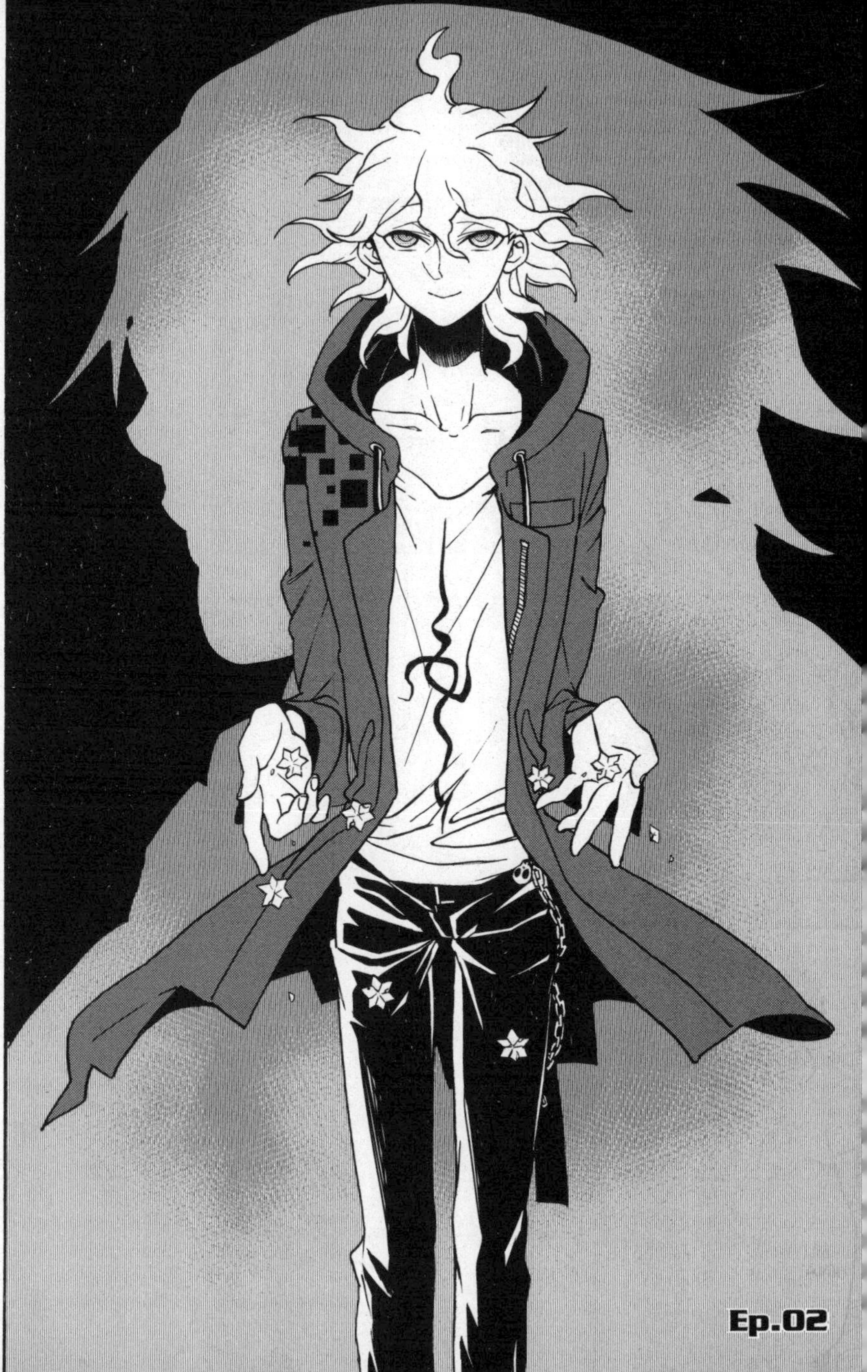
Ep.02

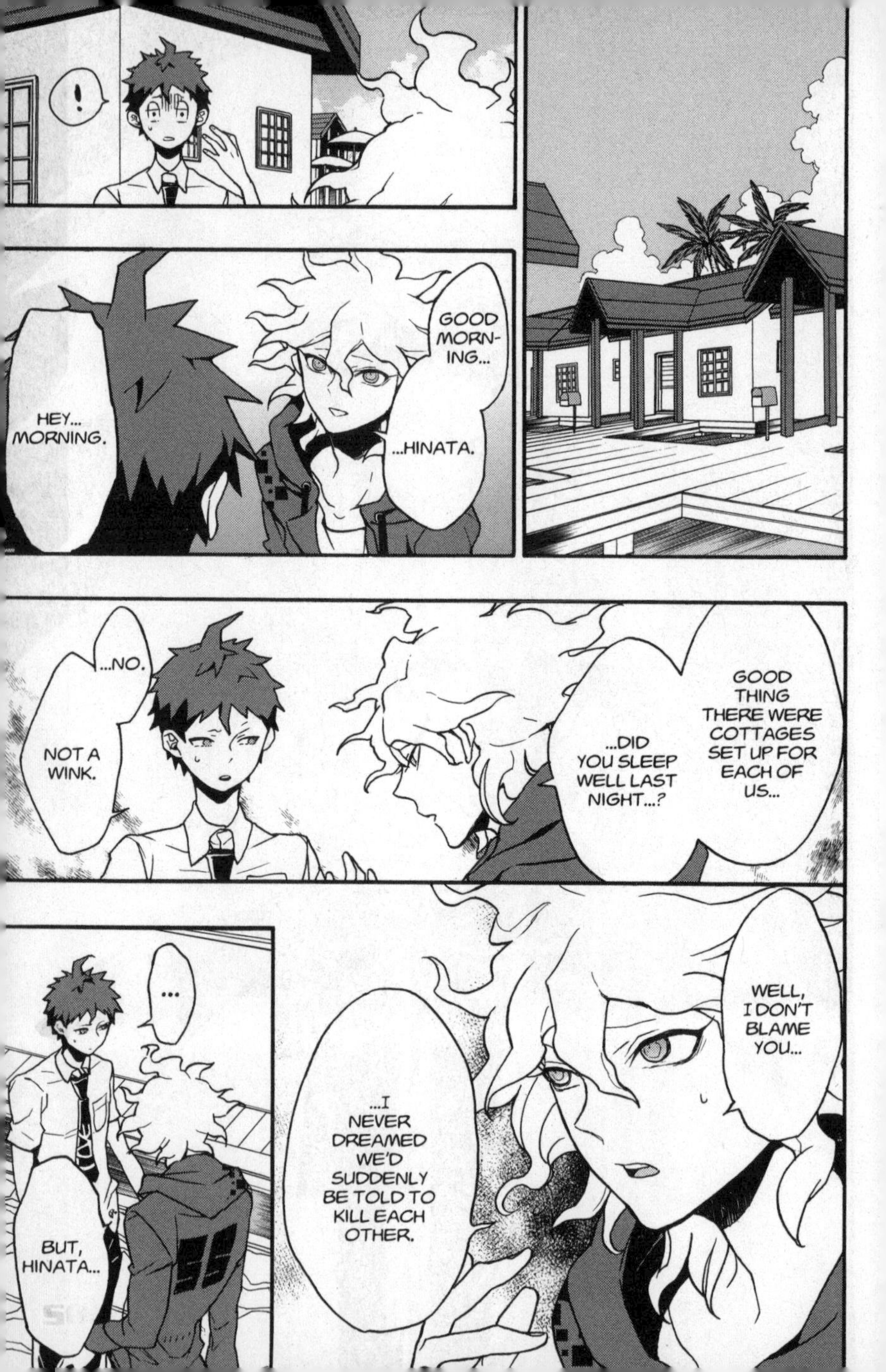
!
GOOD MORNING-ING...
...HINATA.
HEY... MORNING.
GOOD THING THERE WERE COTTAGES SET UP FOR EACH OF US...
...DID YOU SLEEP WELL LAST NIGHT...?
...NO.
NOT A WINK.
WELL, I DON'T BLAME YOU...
...I NEVER DREAMED WE'D SUDDENLY BE TOLD TO KILL EACH OTHER.
...
BUT, HINATA...

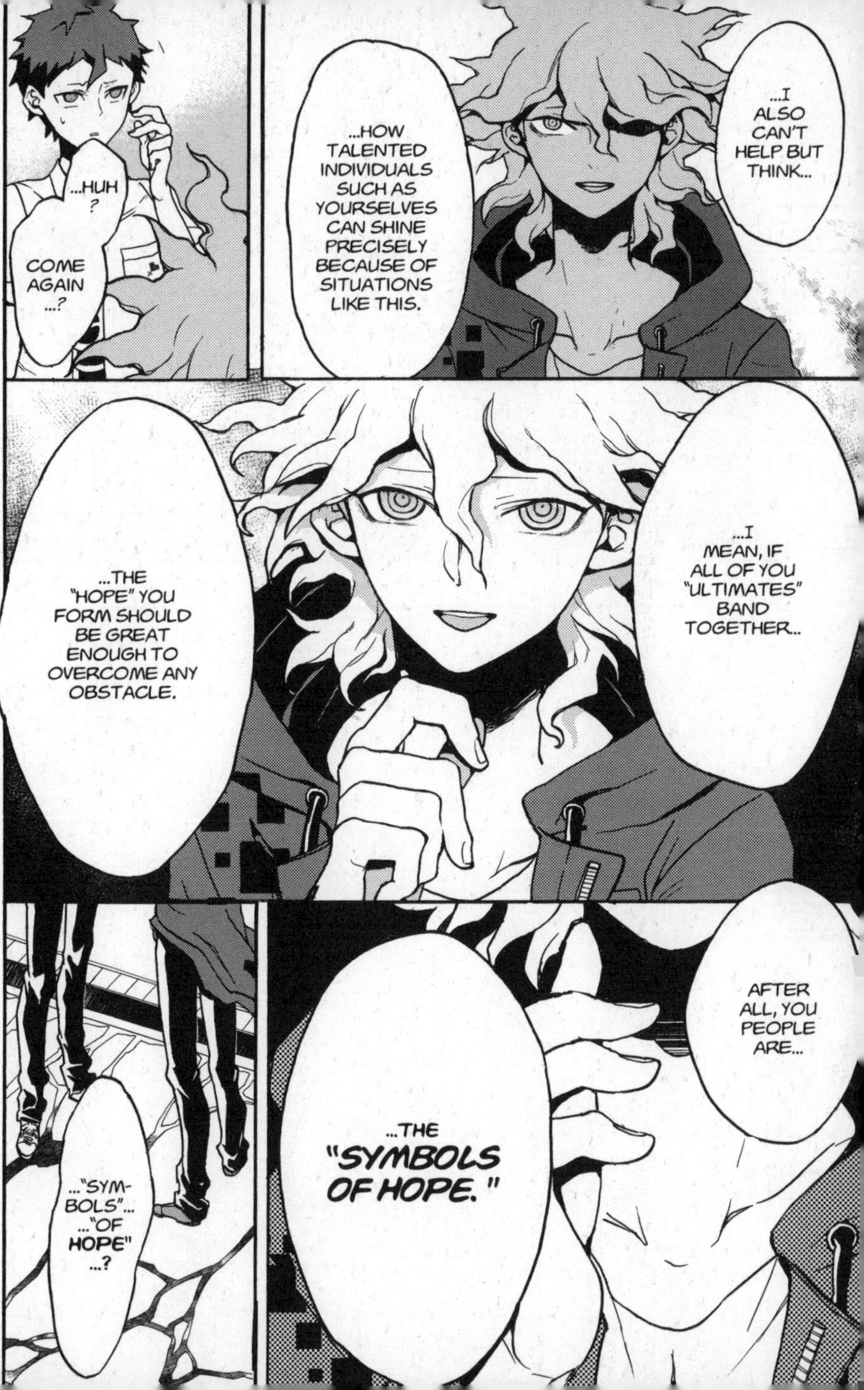
...I ALSO CAN'T HELP BUT THINK...
...HOW TALENTED INDIVIDUALS SUCH AS YOURSELVES CAN SHINE PRECISELY BECAUSE OF SITUATIONS LIKE THIS.
...HUH?
COME AGAIN...?
...I MEAN, IF ALL OF YOU "ULTIMATES" BAND TOGETHER...
...THE "HOPE" YOU FORM SHOULD BE GREAT ENOUGH TO OVERCOME ANY OBSTACLE.
AFTER ALL, YOU PEOPLE ARE...
...THE "SYMBOLS OF HOPE."
..."SYM-BOLS"... ..."OF HOPE"...?

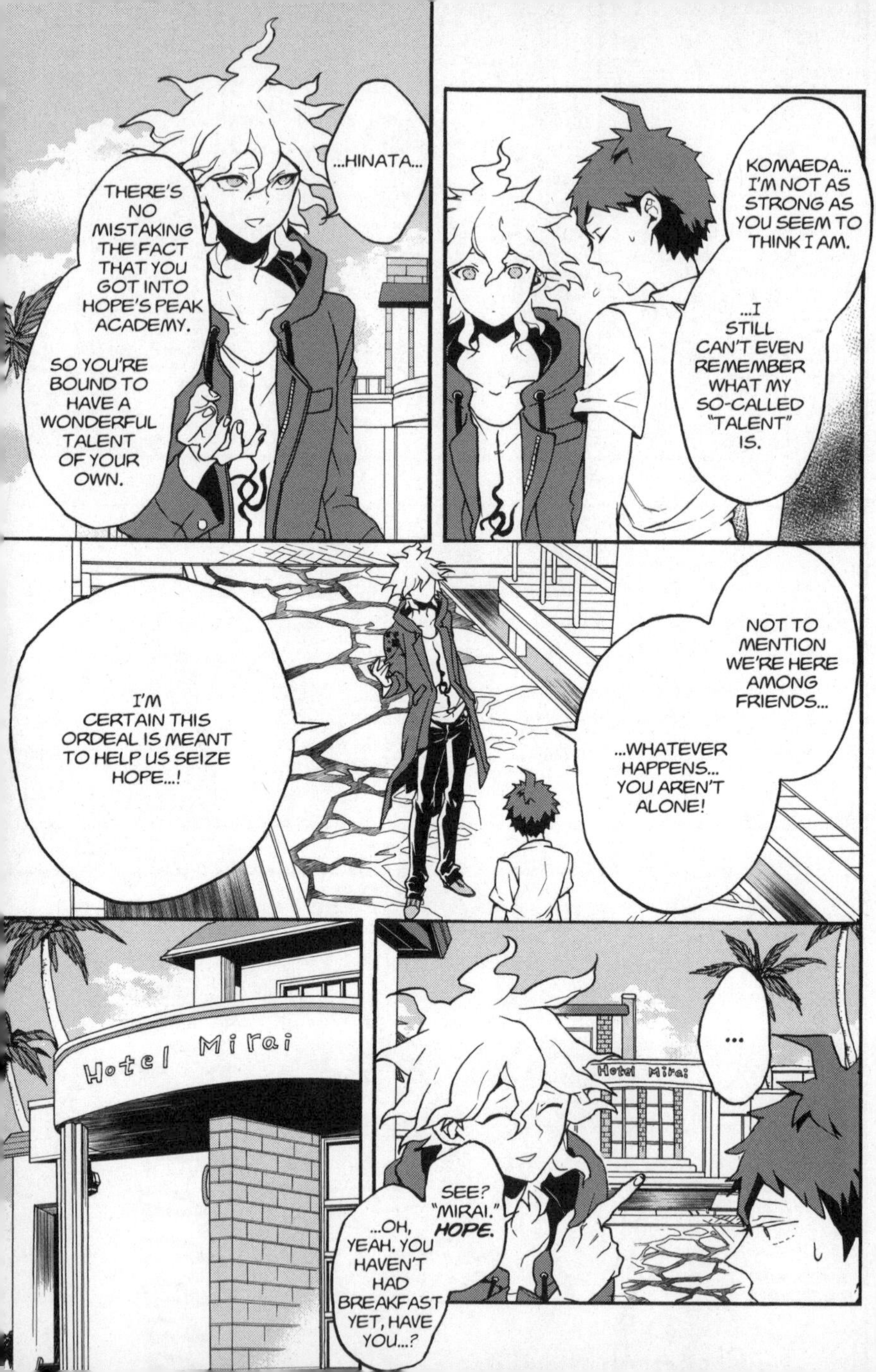
KOMAEDA... I'M NOT AS STRONG AS YOU SEEM TO THINK I AM.
...I STILL CAN'T EVEN REMEMBER WHAT MY SO-CALLED "TALENT" IS.
...HINATA...
THERE'S NO MISTAKING THE FACT THAT YOU GOT INTO HOPE'S PEAK ACADEMY.
SO YOU'RE BOUND TO HAVE A WONDERFUL TALENT OF YOUR OWN.
NOT TO MENTION WE'RE HERE AMONG FRIENDS...
...WHATEVER HAPPENS... YOU AREN'T ALONE!
I'M CERTAIN THIS ORDEAL IS MEANT TO HELP US SEIZE HOPE...!
...
Hotel Mirai
SEE? "MIRAI." **HOPE.**
...OH, YEAH. YOU HAVEN'T HAD BREAKFAST YET, HAVE YOU...?
Hotel Mirai

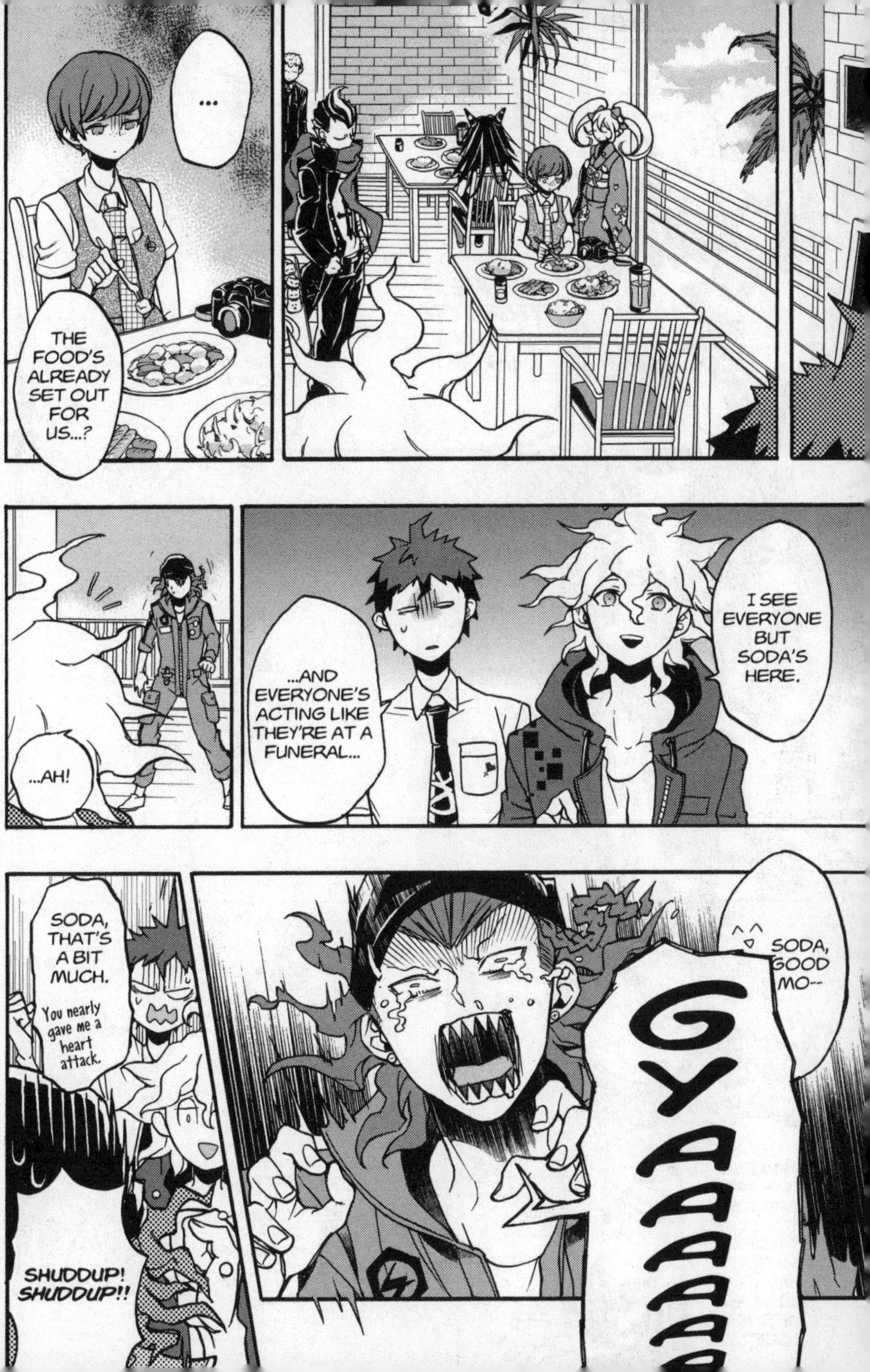
...
THE FOOD'S ALREADY SET OUT FOR US...?
I SEE EVERYONE BUT SODA'S HERE.
...AND EVERYONE'S ACTING LIKE THEY'RE AT A FUNERAL...
...AH!
^^ SODA, GOOD MO--
GYAAAAAA
SODA, THAT'S A BIT MUCH.
You nearly gave me a heart attack.
SHUDDUP! SHUDDUP!!

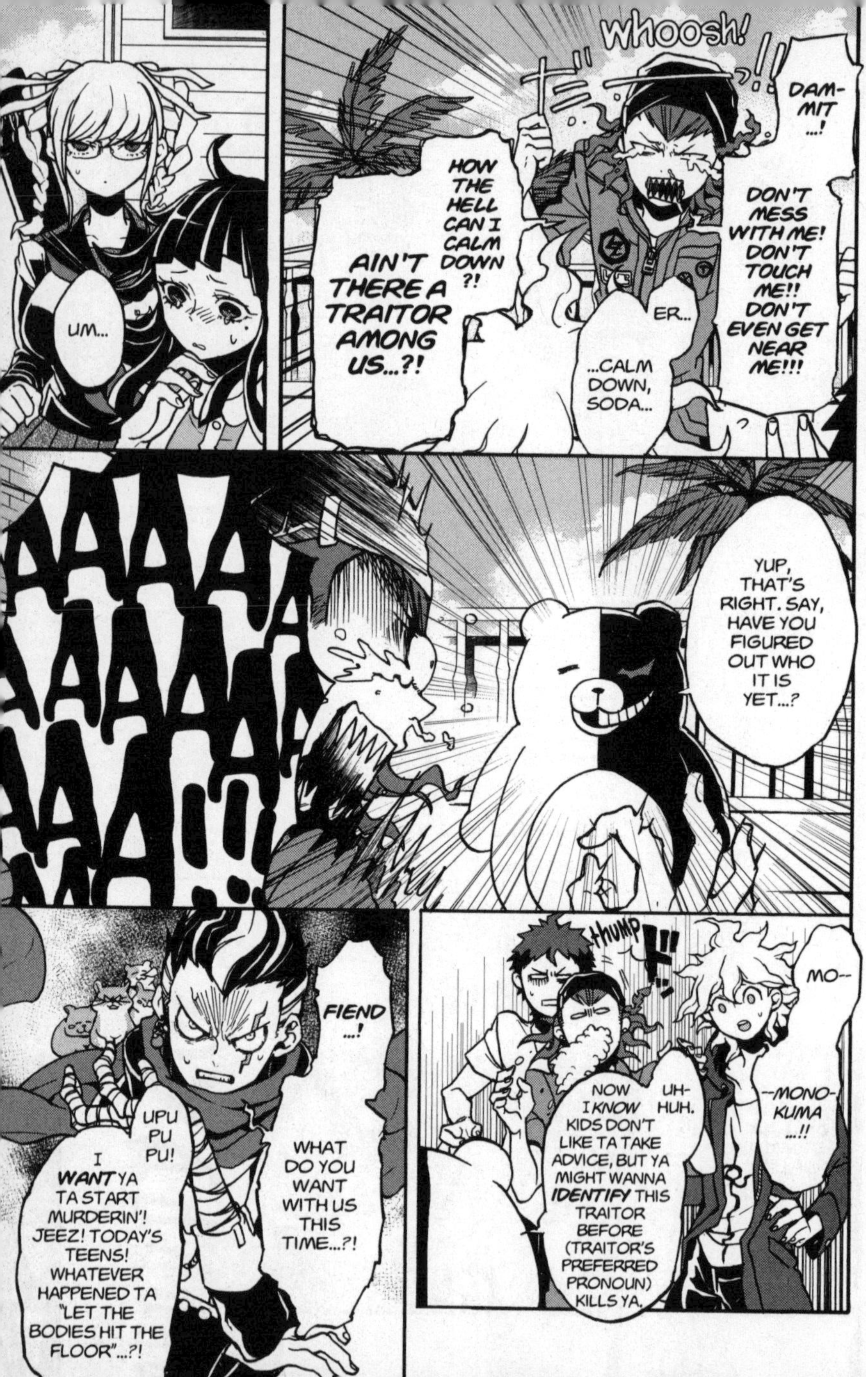
Whoosh!
DAM-MIT ...!
DON'T MESS WITH ME! DON'T TOUCH ME!! DON'T EVEN GET NEAR ME!!!
ER...
...CALM DOWN, SODA...
HOW THE HELL CAN I CALM DOWN ?!
AIN'T THERE A TRAITOR AMONG US...?!
UM...
YUP, THAT'S RIGHT. SAY, HAVE YOU FIGURED OUT WHO IT IS YET...?
AAAAAAAAAAAAAAAAAAAAAA!!
thump
MO--
--MONO-KUMA ...!!
UH-HUH.
NOW I KNOW KIDS DON'T LIKE TA TAKE ADVICE, BUT YA MIGHT WANNA IDENTIFY THIS TRAITOR BEFORE (TRAITOR'S PREFERRED PRONOUN) KILLS YA.
FIEND ...!
WHAT DO YOU WANT WITH US THIS TIME...?!
UPU PU PU!
I WANT YA TA START MURDERIN'! JEEZ! TODAY'S TEENS! WHATEVER HAPPENED TA "LET THE BODIES HIT THE FLOOR"...?!

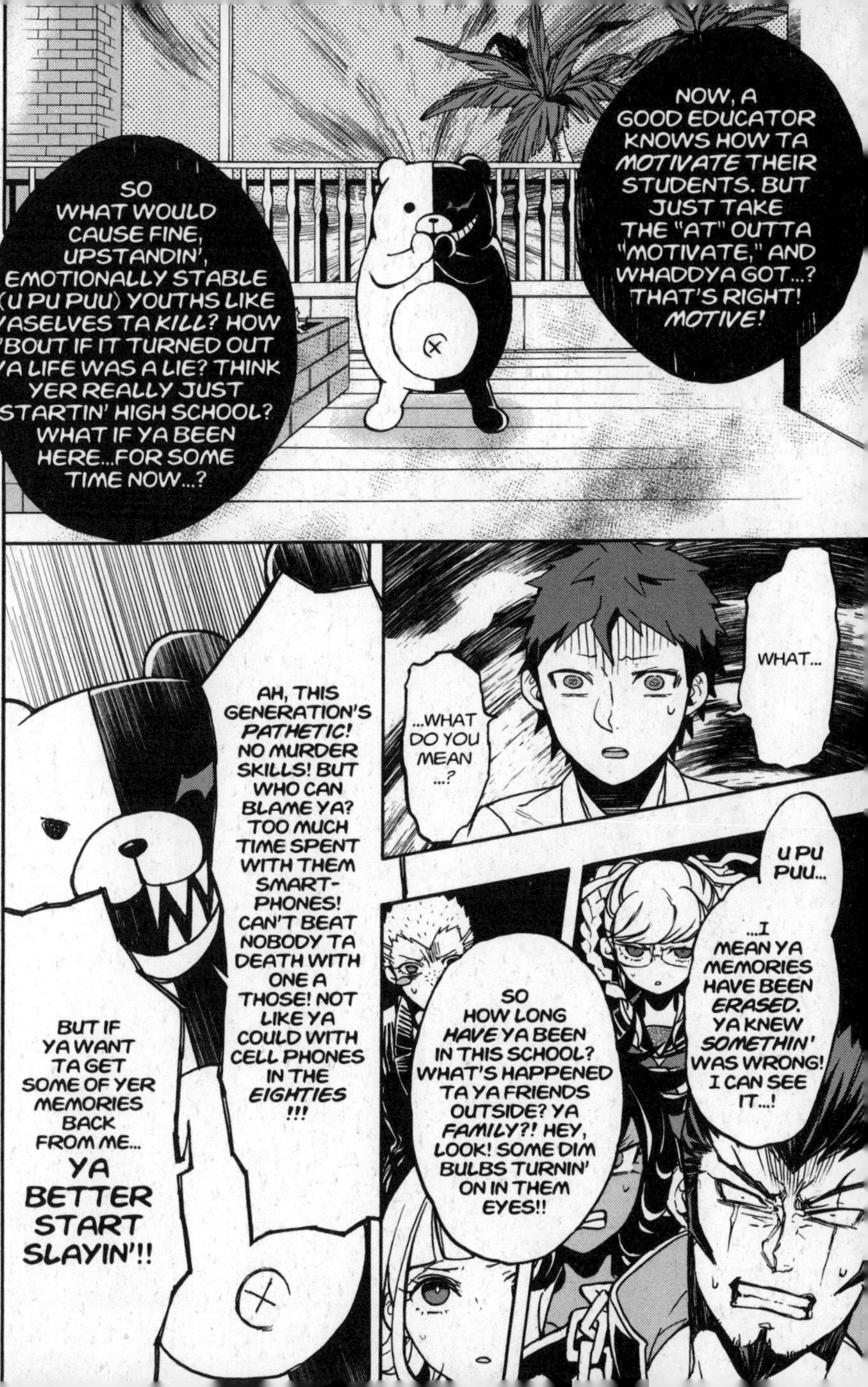
NOW, A GOOD EDUCATOR KNOWS HOW TA *MOTIVATE* THEIR STUDENTS. BUT JUST TAKE THE "AT" OUTTA "MOTIVATE," AND WHADDYA GOT...? THAT'S RIGHT! *MOTIVE!*
SO WHAT WOULD CAUSE FINE, UPSTANDIN', EMOTIONALLY STABLE (U PU PUU) YOUTHS LIKE YASELVES TA *KILL*? HOW 'BOUT IF IT TURNED OUT YA LIFE WAS A LIE? THINK YER REALLY JUST STARTIN' HIGH SCHOOL? WHAT IF YA BEEN HERE...FOR SOME TIME NOW...?
WHAT...
...WHAT DO YOU MEAN ...?
U PU PUU...
...I MEAN YA MEMORIES HAVE BEEN *ERASED*. YA KNEW *SOMETHIN'* WAS WRONG! I CAN SEE IT...!
SO HOW LONG *HAVE* YA BEEN IN THIS SCHOOL? WHAT'S HAPPENED TA YA FRIENDS OUTSIDE? YA *FAMILY*?! HEY, LOOK! SOME DIM BULBS TURNIN' ON IN THEM EYES!!
AH, THIS GENERATION'S *PATHETIC*! NO MURDER SKILLS! BUT WHO CAN BLAME YA? TOO MUCH TIME SPENT WITH THEM SMART-PHONES! CAN'T BEAT NOBODY TA DEATH WITH ONE A THOSE! NOT LIKE YA COULD WITH CELL PHONES IN THE *EIGHTIES* !!!
BUT IF YA WANT TA GET SOME OF YER MEMORIES BACK FROM ME... **YA BETTER START SLAYIN'!!**

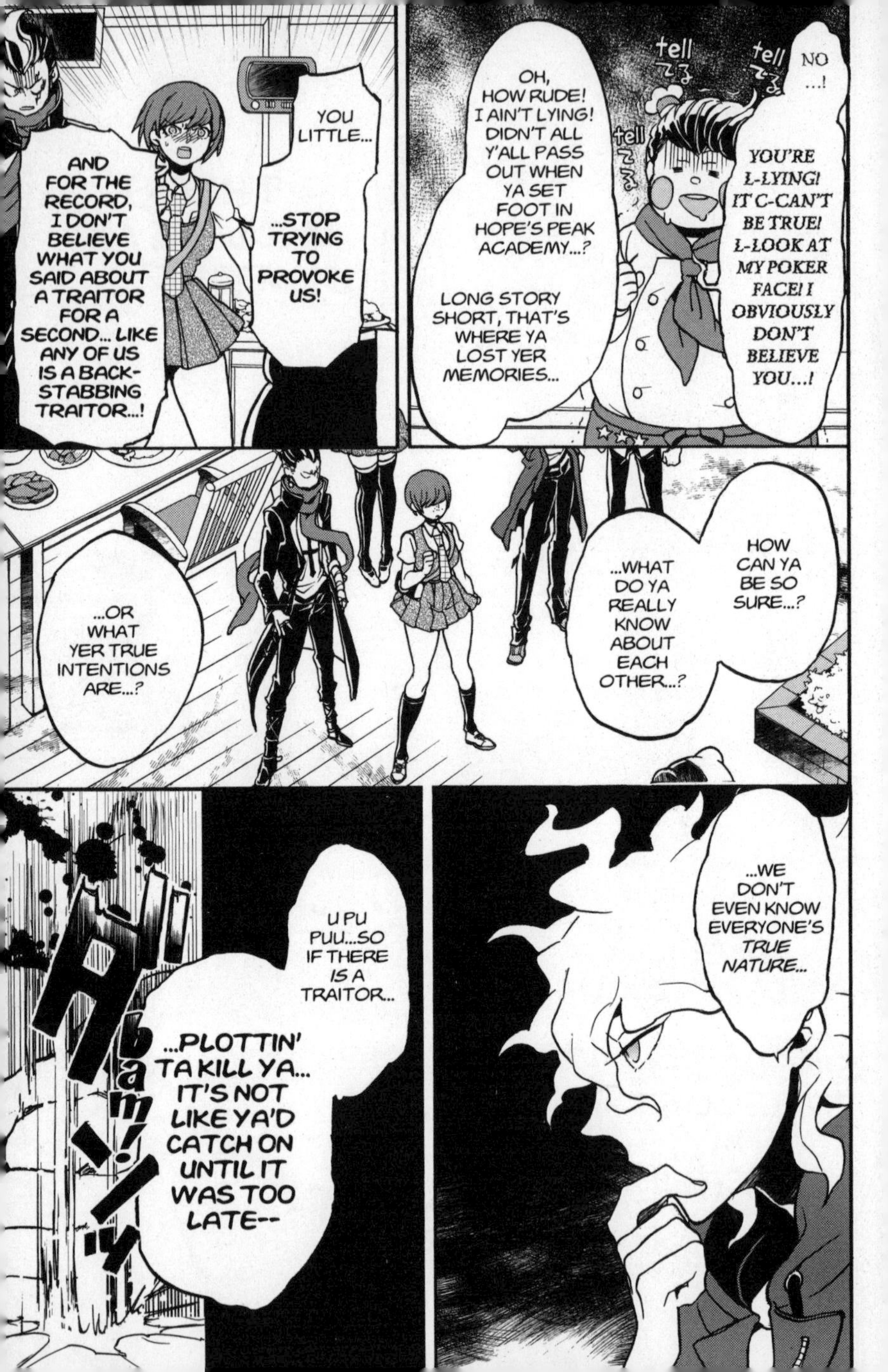
tell てる
tell てる
NO ...!
YOU'RE L-LYING! IT C-CAN'T BE TRUE! L-LOOK AT MY POKER FACE! I OBVIOUSLY DON'T BELIEVE YOU...!
tell てる
OH, HOW RUDE! I AIN'T LYING! DIDN'T ALL Y'ALL PASS OUT WHEN YA SET FOOT IN HOPE'S PEAK ACADEMY...?
LONG STORY SHORT, THAT'S WHERE YA LOST YER MEMORIES...
YOU LITTLE...
...STOP TRYING TO PROVOKE US!
AND FOR THE RECORD, I DON'T BELIEVE WHAT YOU SAID ABOUT A TRAITOR FOR A SECOND... LIKE ANY OF US IS A BACK-STABBING TRAITOR...!
HOW CAN YA BE SO SURE...?
...WHAT DO YA REALLY KNOW ABOUT EACH OTHER...?
...OR WHAT YER TRUE INTENTIONS ARE...?
...WE DON'T EVEN KNOW EVERYONE'S TRUE NATURE...
U PU PUU...SO IF THERE IS A TRAITOR...
...PLOTTIN' TA KILL YA... IT'S NOT LIKE YA'D CATCH ON UNTIL IT WAS TOO LATE--
bam!

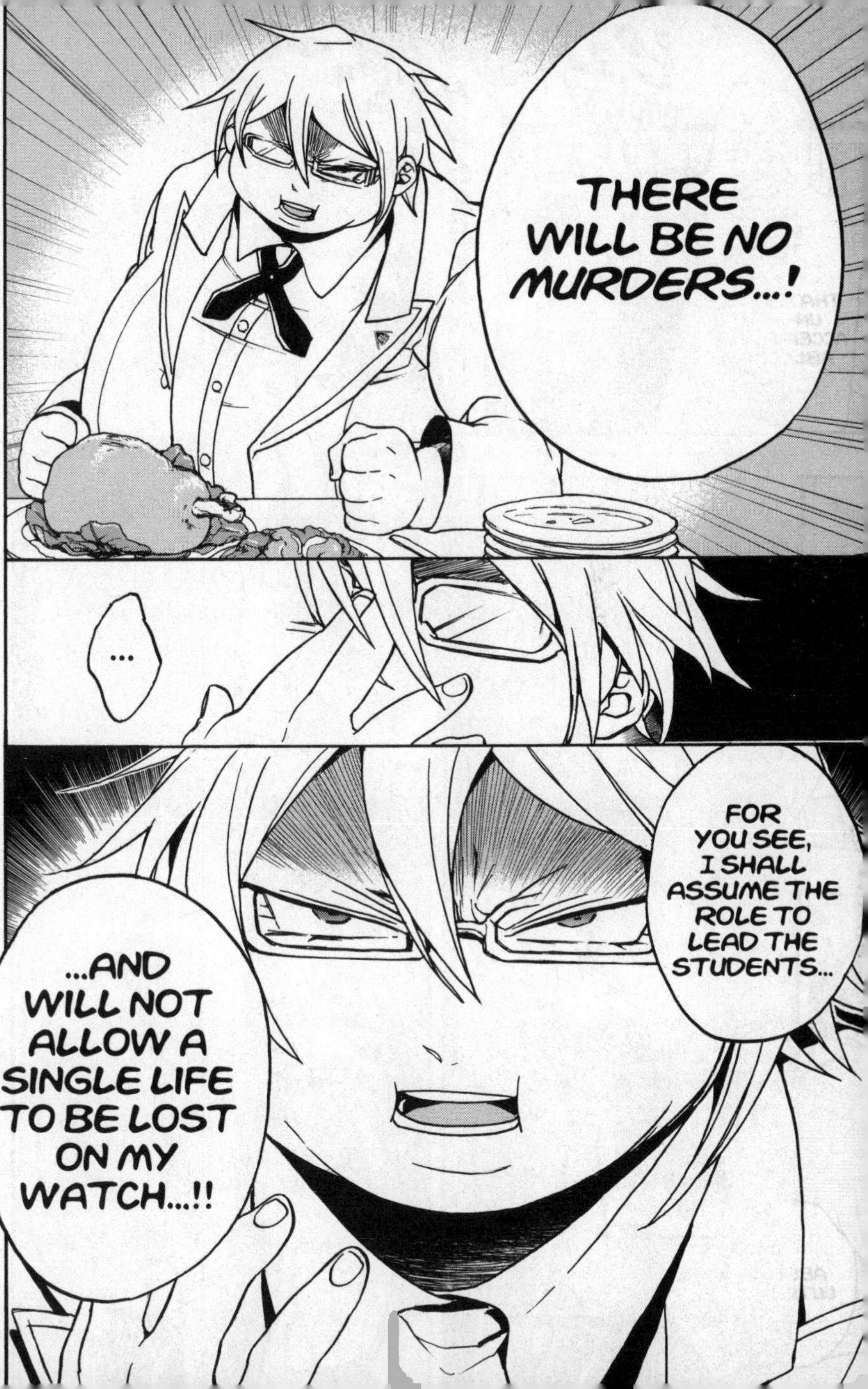
THERE WILL BE NO MURDERS...!
...
FOR YOU SEE, I SHALL ASSUME THE ROLE TO LEAD THE STUDENTS...
...AND WILL NOT ALLOW A SINGLE LIFE TO BE LOST ON MY WATCH...!!

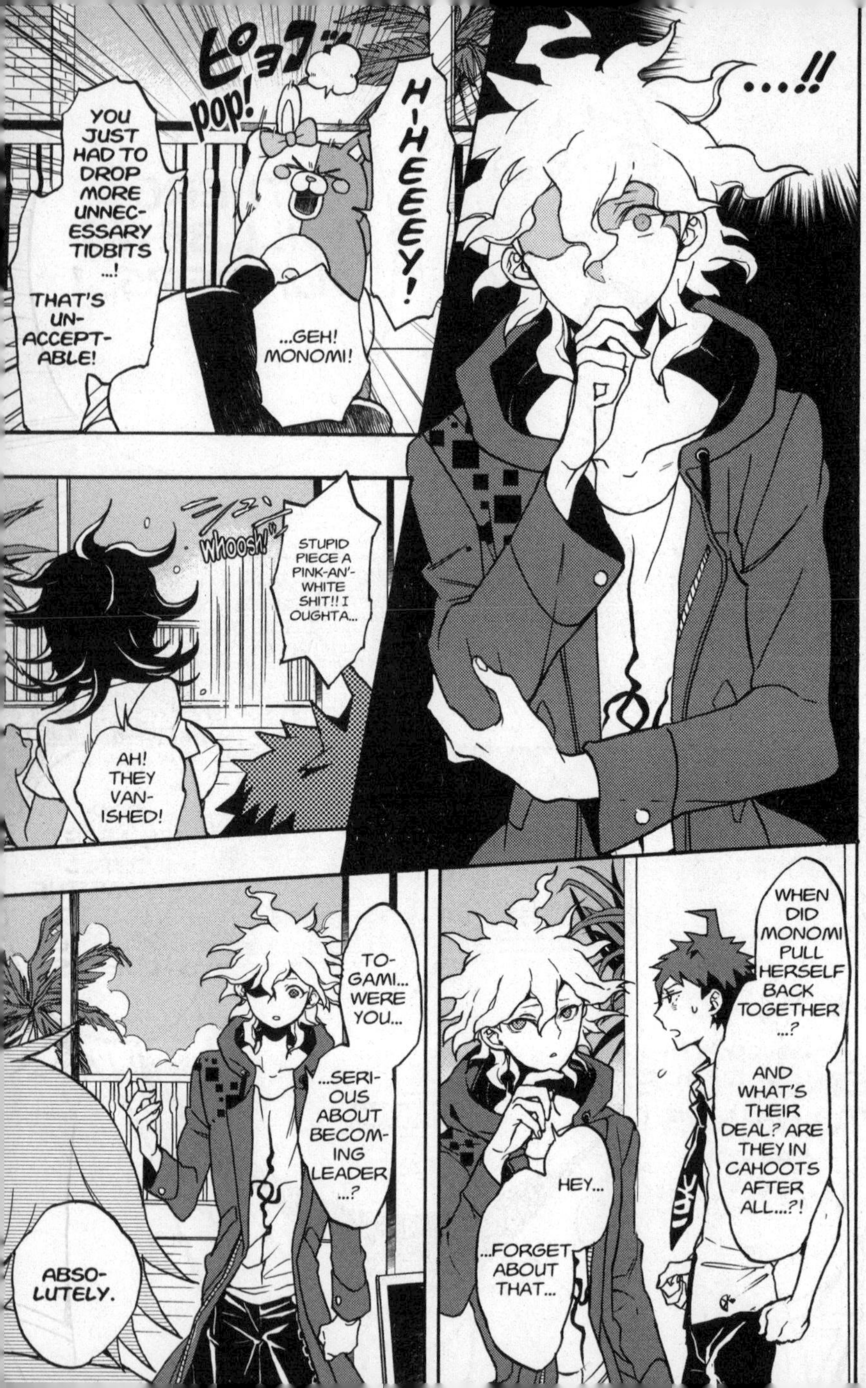
...!!
ピョコッ
pop!
H-HEEEEY!
...GEH! MONOMI!
YOU JUST HAD TO DROP MORE UNNECESSARY TIDBITS ...!
THAT'S UNACCEPTABLE!
ニュッ
whoosh!
STUPID PIECE A PINK-AN'-WHITE SHIT!! I OUGHTA...
AH! THEY VANISHED!
WHEN DID MONOMI PULL HERSELF BACK TOGETHER ...?
AND WHAT'S THEIR DEAL? ARE THEY IN CAHOOTS AFTER ALL...?!
HEY...
...FORGET ABOUT THAT...
TOGAMI... WERE YOU...
...SERIOUS ABOUT BECOMING LEADER ...?
ABSOLUTELY.

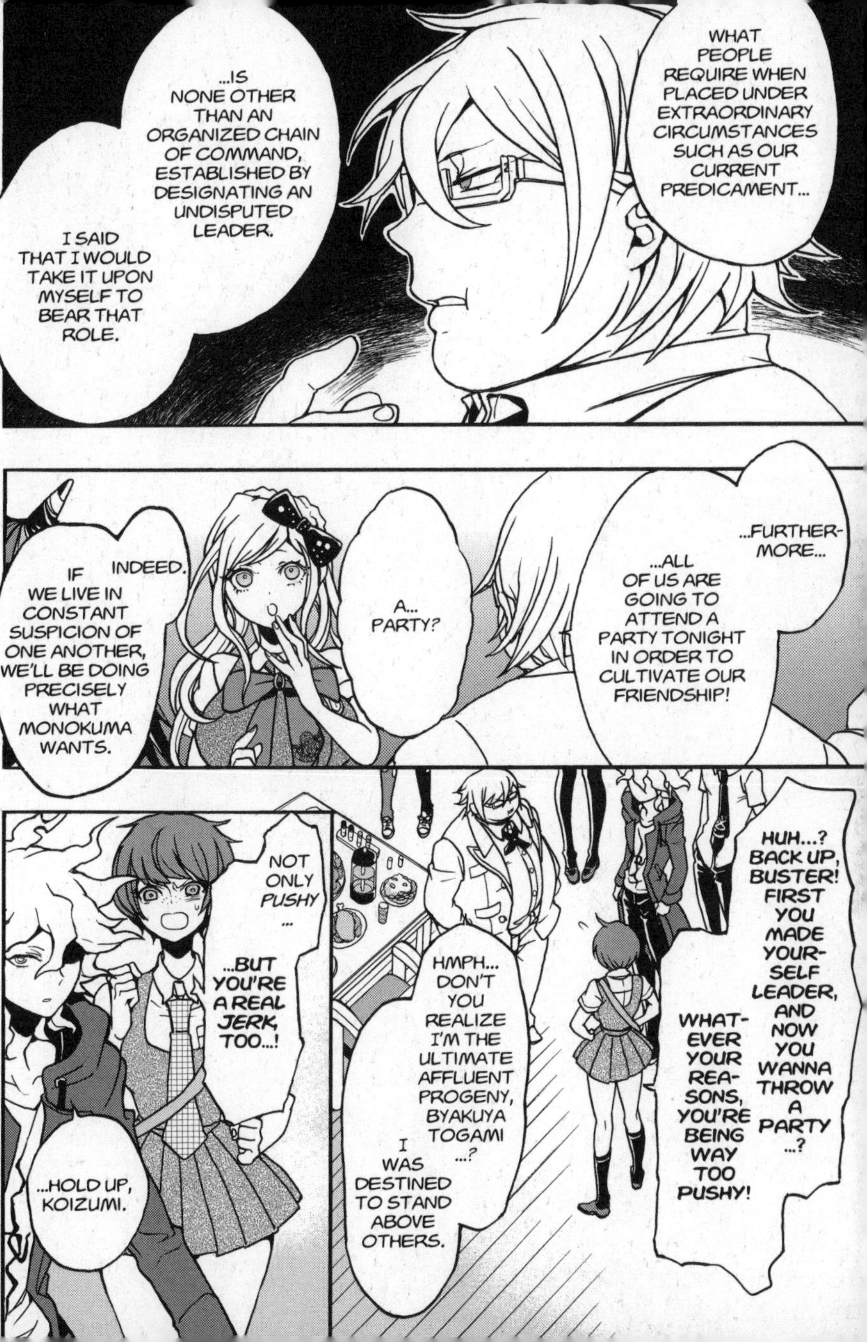
WHAT PEOPLE REQUIRE WHEN PLACED UNDER EXTRAORDINARY CIRCUMSTANCES SUCH AS OUR CURRENT PREDICAMENT...
...IS NONE OTHER THAN AN ORGANIZED CHAIN OF COMMAND, ESTABLISHED BY DESIGNATING AN UNDISPUTED LEADER.
I SAID THAT I WOULD TAKE IT UPON MYSELF TO BEAR THAT ROLE.
...FURTHER-MORE...
...ALL OF US ARE GOING TO ATTEND A PARTY TONIGHT IN ORDER TO CULTIVATE OUR FRIENDSHIP!
A... PARTY?
INDEED.
IF WE LIVE IN CONSTANT SUSPICION OF ONE ANOTHER, WE'LL BE DOING PRECISELY WHAT MONOKUMA WANTS.
HUH...? BACK UP, BUSTER! FIRST YOU MADE YOUR-SELF LEADER, AND NOW YOU WANNA THROW A PARTY ...?
WHAT-EVER YOUR REA-SONS, YOU'RE BEING WAY TOO PUSHY!
HMPH... DON'T YOU REALIZE I'M THE ULTIMATE AFFLUENT PROGENY, BYAKUYA TOGAMI ...?
I WAS DESTINED TO STAND ABOVE OTHERS.
NOT ONLY PUSHY ...
...BUT YOU'RE A REAL JERK, TOO...!
...HOLD UP, KOIZUMI.

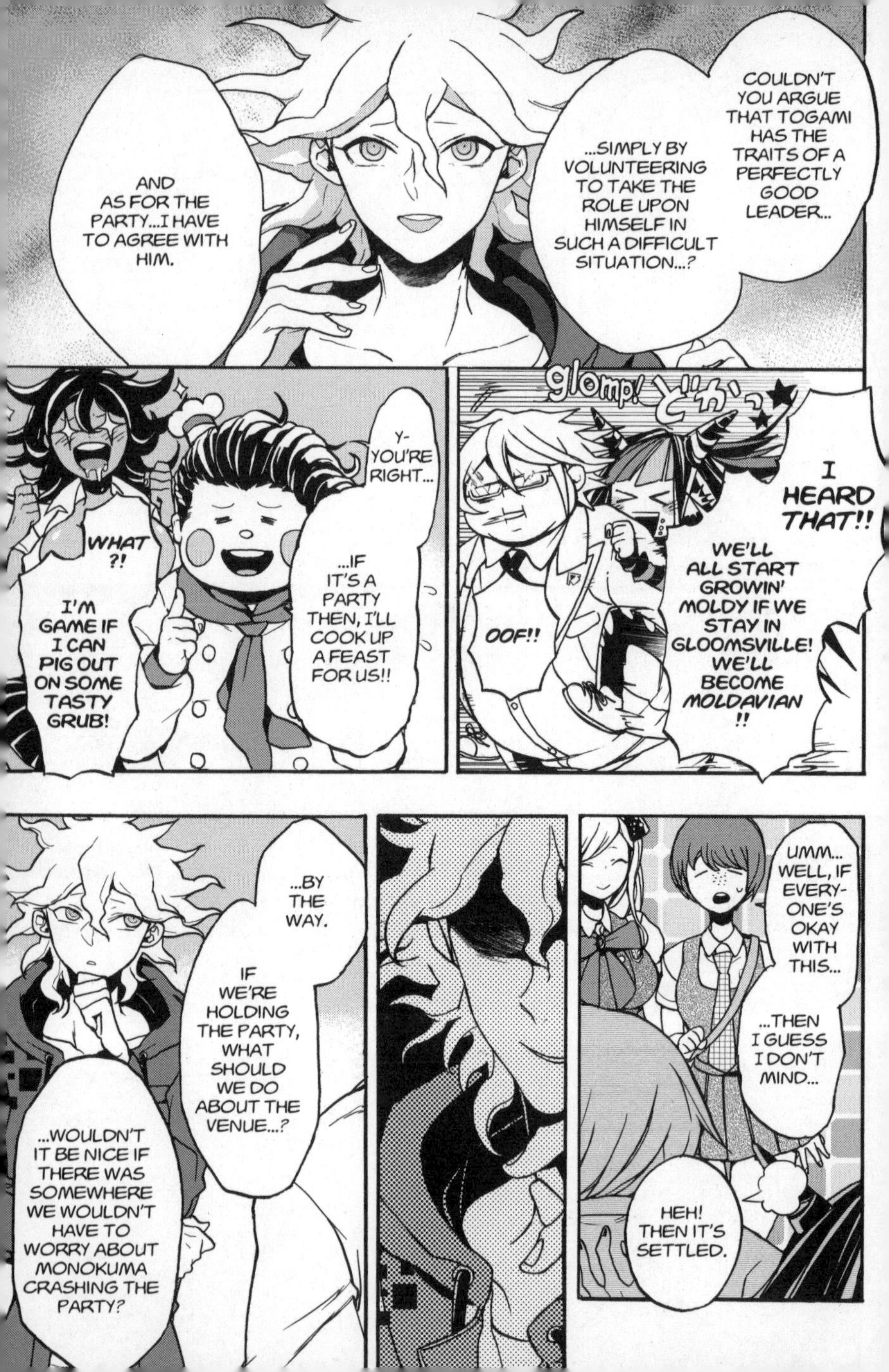
COULDN'T YOU ARGUE THAT TOGAMI HAS THE TRAITS OF A PERFECTLY GOOD LEADER...
...SIMPLY BY VOLUNTEERING TO TAKE THE ROLE UPON HIMSELF IN SUCH A DIFFICULT SITUATION...?
AND AS FOR THE PARTY...I HAVE TO AGREE WITH HIM.
glomp!
どかっ
I HEARD THAT!!
WE'LL ALL START GROWIN' MOLDY IF WE STAY IN GLOOMSVILLE! WE'LL BECOME MOLDAVIAN!!
OOF!!
Y-YOU'RE RIGHT...
...IF IT'S A PARTY THEN, I'LL COOK UP A FEAST FOR US!!
WHAT?!
I'M GAME IF I CAN PIG OUT ON SOME TASTY GRUB!
UMM... WELL, IF EVERYONE'S OKAY WITH THIS...
...THEN I GUESS I DON'T MIND...
HEH! THEN IT'S SETTLED.
...BY THE WAY.
IF WE'RE HOLDING THE PARTY, WHAT SHOULD WE DO ABOUT THE VENUE...?
...WOULDN'T IT BE NICE IF THERE WAS SOMEWHERE WE WOULDN'T HAVE TO WORRY ABOUT MONOKUMA CRASHING THE PARTY?

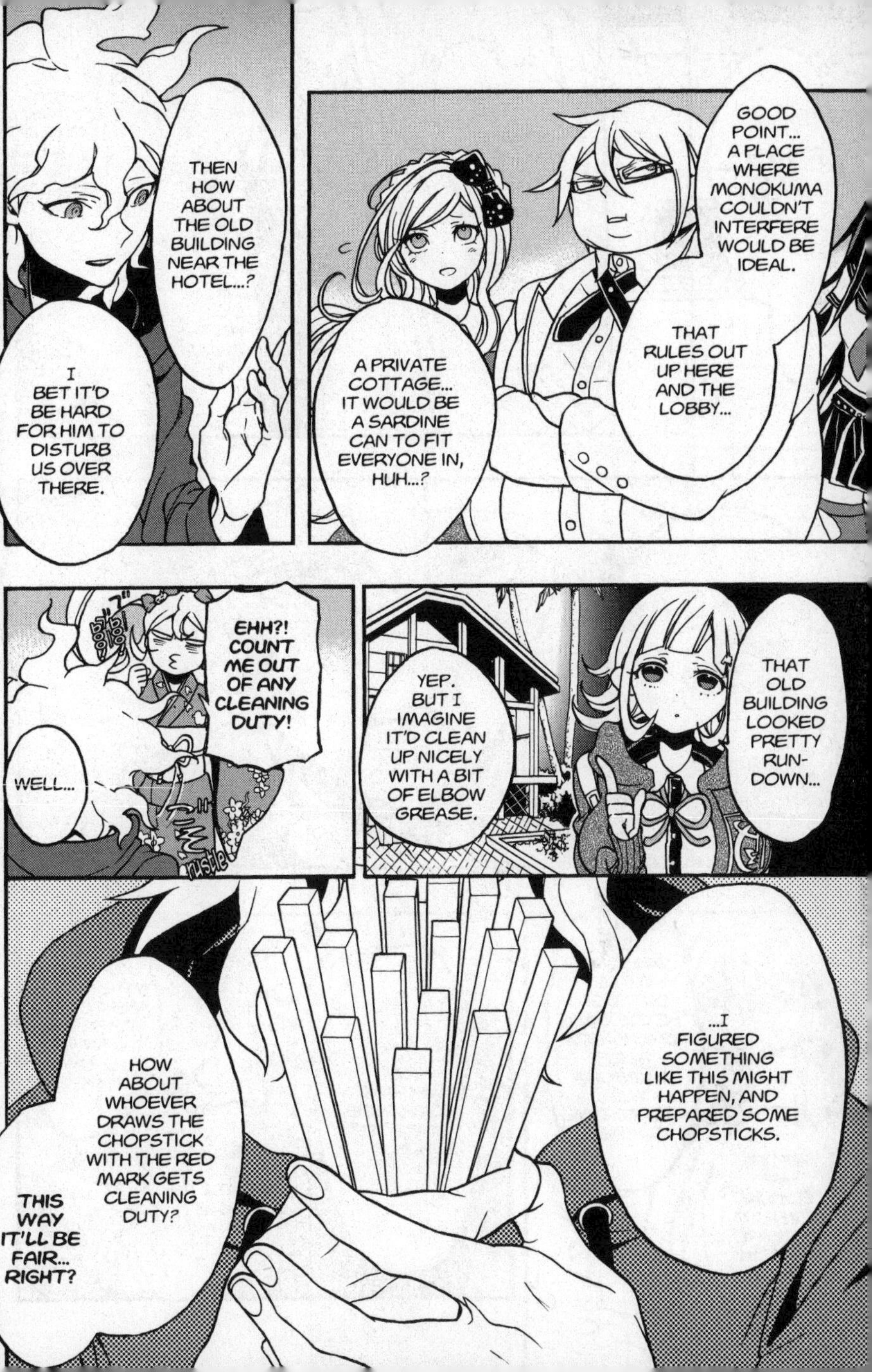
GOOD POINT... A PLACE WHERE MONOKUMA COULDN'T INTERFERE WOULD BE IDEAL.
THAT RULES OUT UP HERE AND THE LOBBY...
A PRIVATE COTTAGE... IT WOULD BE A SARDINE CAN TO FIT EVERYONE IN, HUH...?
THEN HOW ABOUT THE OLD BUILDING NEAR THE HOTEL...?
I BET IT'D BE HARD FOR HIM TO DISTURB US OVER THERE.
THAT OLD BUILDING LOOKED PRETTY RUN-DOWN...
YEP. BUT I IMAGINE IT'D CLEAN UP NICELY WITH A BIT OF ELBOW GREASE.
EHH?! COUNT ME OUT OF ANY CLEANING DUTY!
WELL...
rustle
...I FIGURED SOMETHING LIKE THIS MIGHT HAPPEN, AND PREPARED SOME CHOPSTICKS.
HOW ABOUT WHOEVER DRAWS THE CHOPSTICK WITH THE RED MARK GETS CLEANING DUTY?
THIS WAY IT'LL BE FAIR... RIGHT?

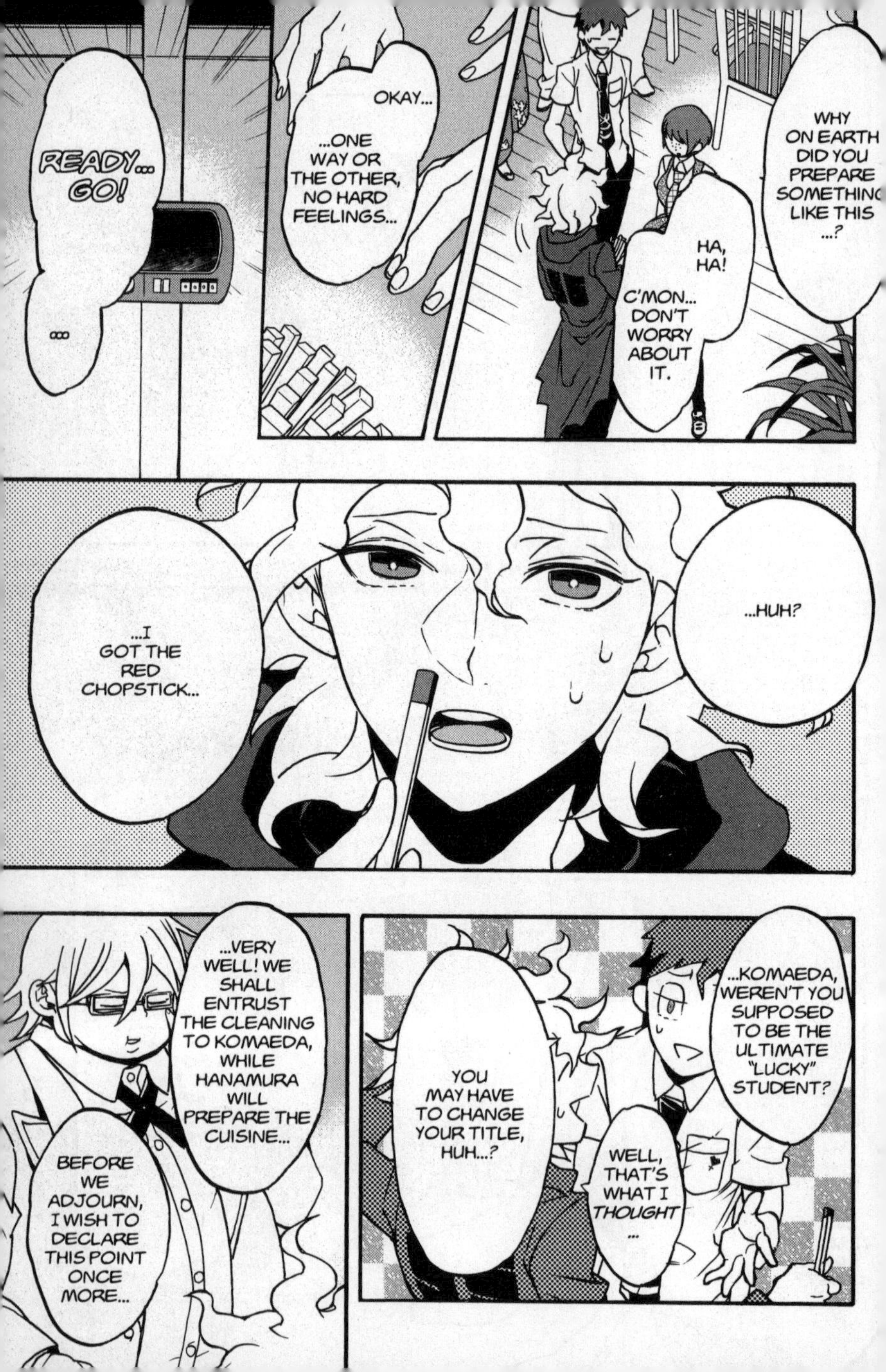
WHY ON EARTH DID YOU PREPARE SOMETHING LIKE THIS ...?
HA, HA!
C'MON... DON'T WORRY ABOUT IT.
OKAY...
...ONE WAY OR THE OTHER, NO HARD FEELINGS...
READY... GO!
...
...HUH?
...I GOT THE RED CHOPSTICK...
...KOMAEDA, WEREN'T YOU SUPPOSED TO BE THE ULTIMATE "LUCKY" STUDENT?
WELL, THAT'S WHAT I *THOUGHT*...
YOU MAY HAVE TO CHANGE YOUR TITLE, HUH...?
...VERY WELL! WE SHALL ENTRUST THE CLEANING TO KOMAEDA, WHILE HANAMURA WILL PREPARE THE CUISINE...
BEFORE WE ADJOURN, I WISH TO DECLARE THIS POINT ONCE MORE...

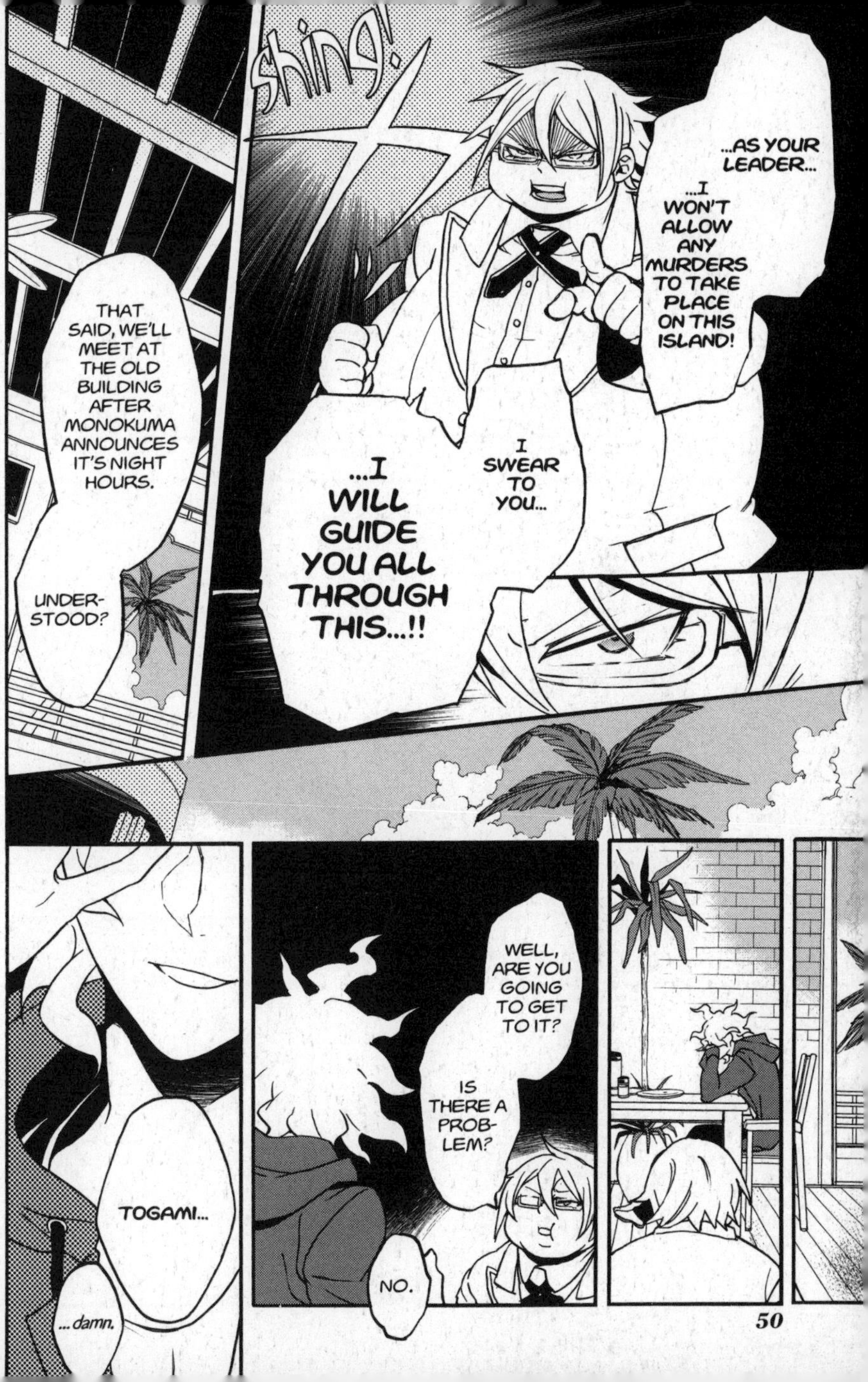
shing!
...AS YOUR LEADER...
...I WON'T ALLOW ANY MURDERS TO TAKE PLACE ON THIS ISLAND!
I SWEAR TO YOU...
...I WILL GUIDE YOU ALL THROUGH THIS...!!
THAT SAID, WE'LL MEET AT THE OLD BUILDING AFTER MONOKUMA ANNOUNCES IT'S NIGHT HOURS.
UNDER-STOOD?
WELL, ARE YOU GOING TO GET TO IT?
IS THERE A PROB-LEM?
NO.
TOGAMI...
...damn.

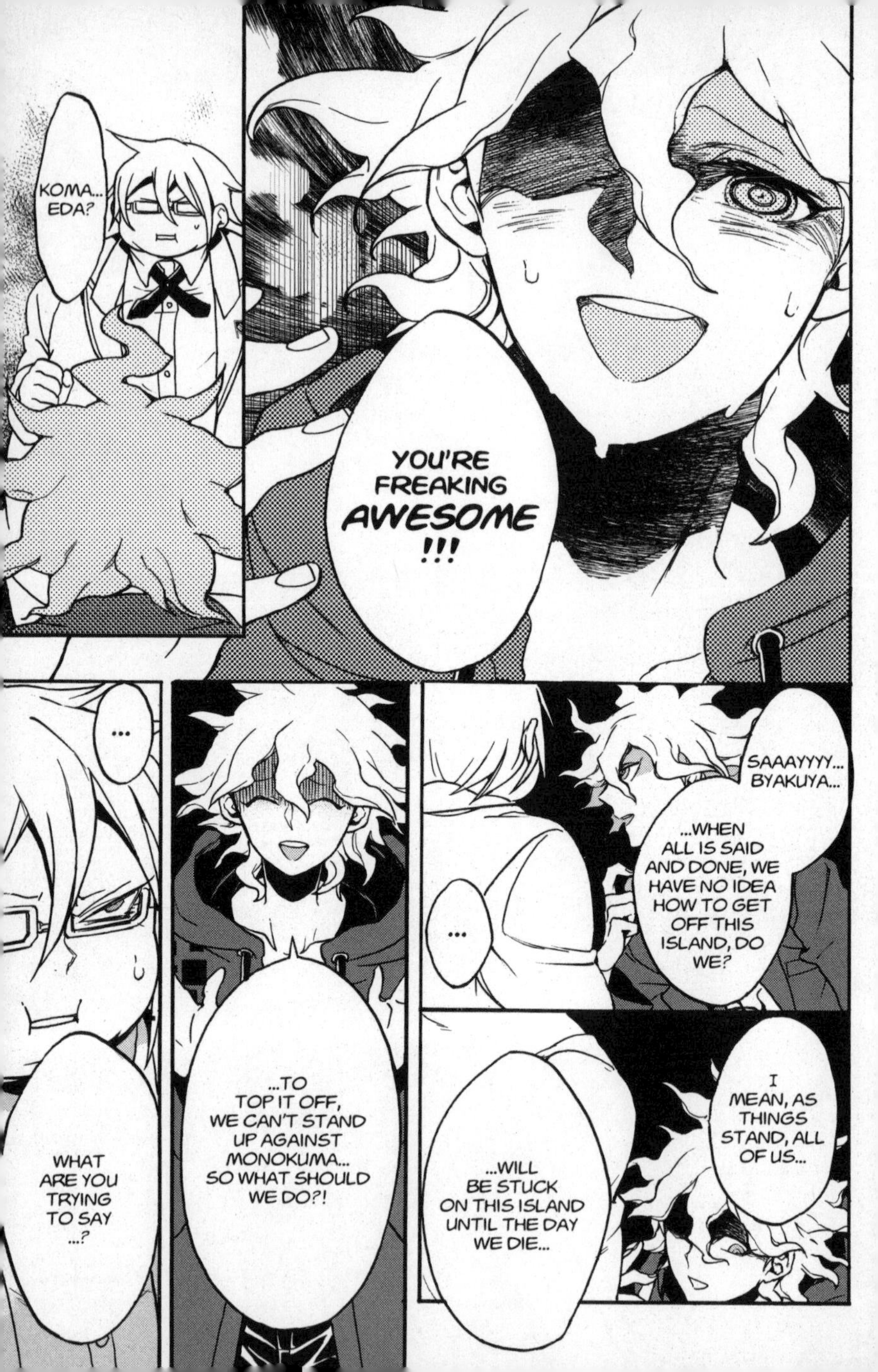
YOU'RE FREAKING AWESOME!!!
KOMA... EDA?
SAAAYYYY... BYAKUYA...
...WHEN ALL IS SAID AND DONE, WE HAVE NO IDEA HOW TO GET OFF THIS ISLAND, DO WE?
...
I MEAN, AS THINGS STAND, ALL OF US...
...WILL BE STUCK ON THIS ISLAND UNTIL THE DAY WE DIE...
...TO TOP IT OFF, WE CAN'T STAND UP AGAINST MONOKUMA... SO WHAT SHOULD WE DO?!
...
WHAT ARE YOU TRYING TO SAY ...?

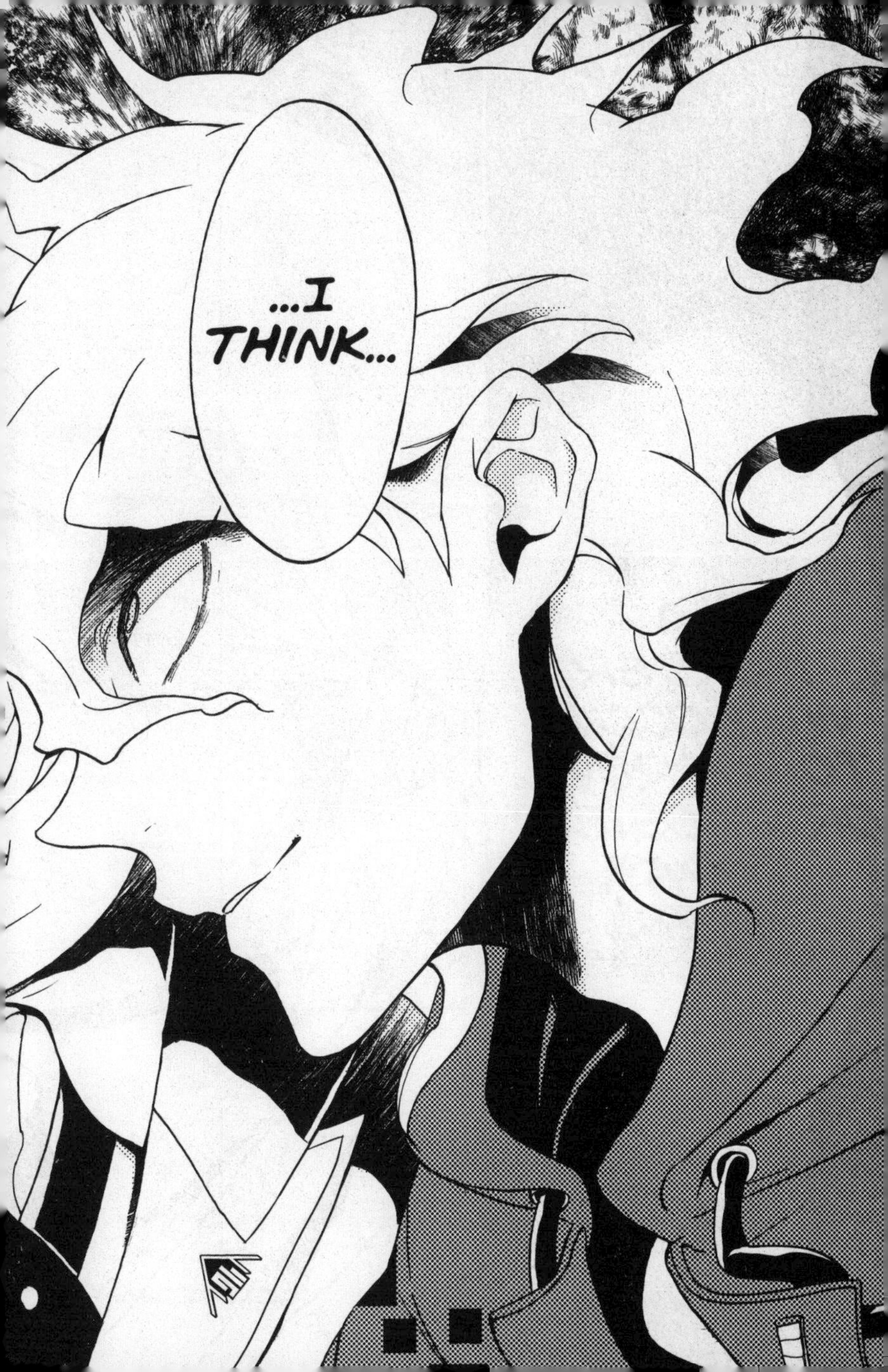
...I THINK...

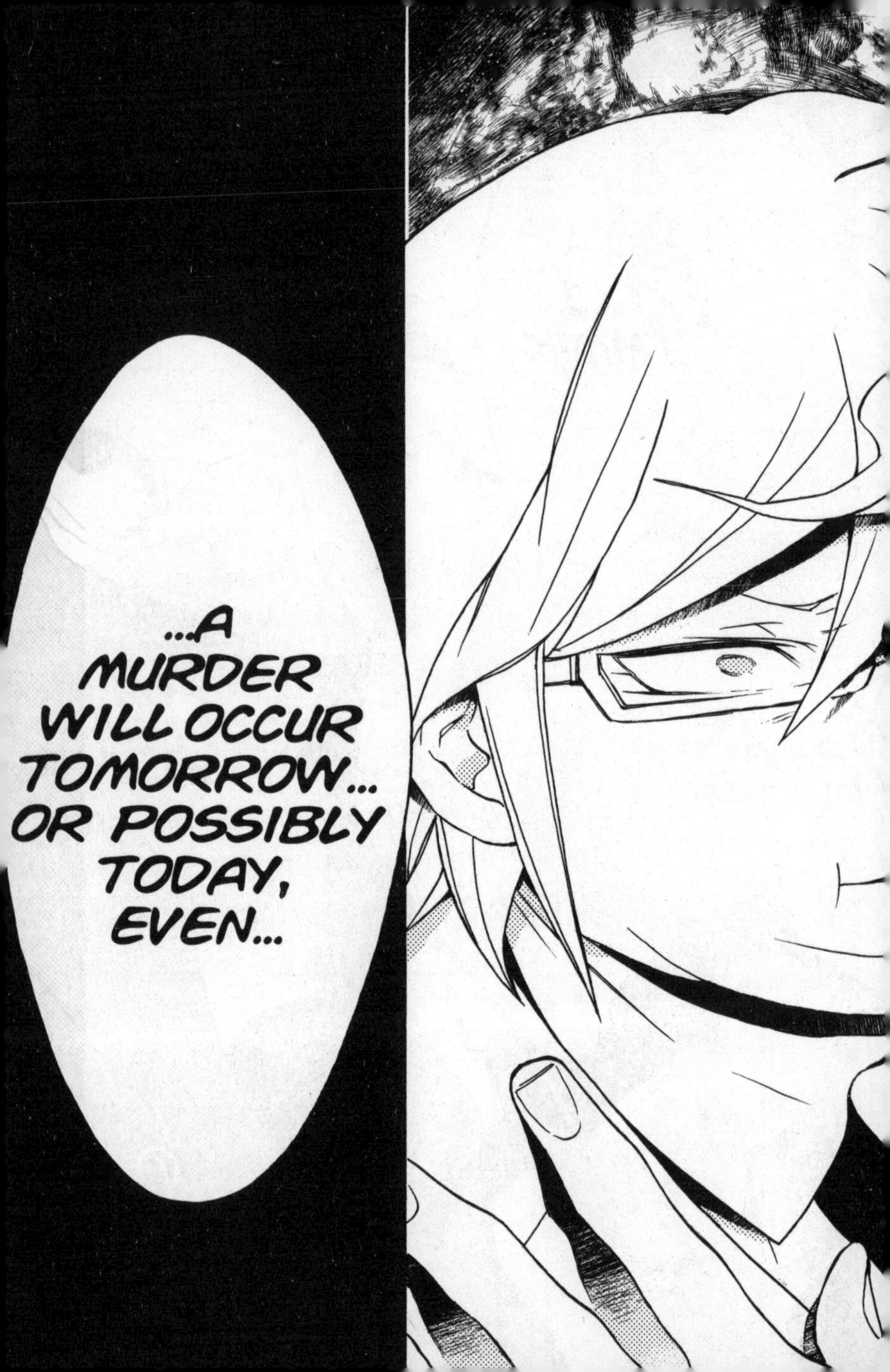
...A MURDER WILL OCCUR TOMORROW... OR POSSIBLY TODAY, EVEN...

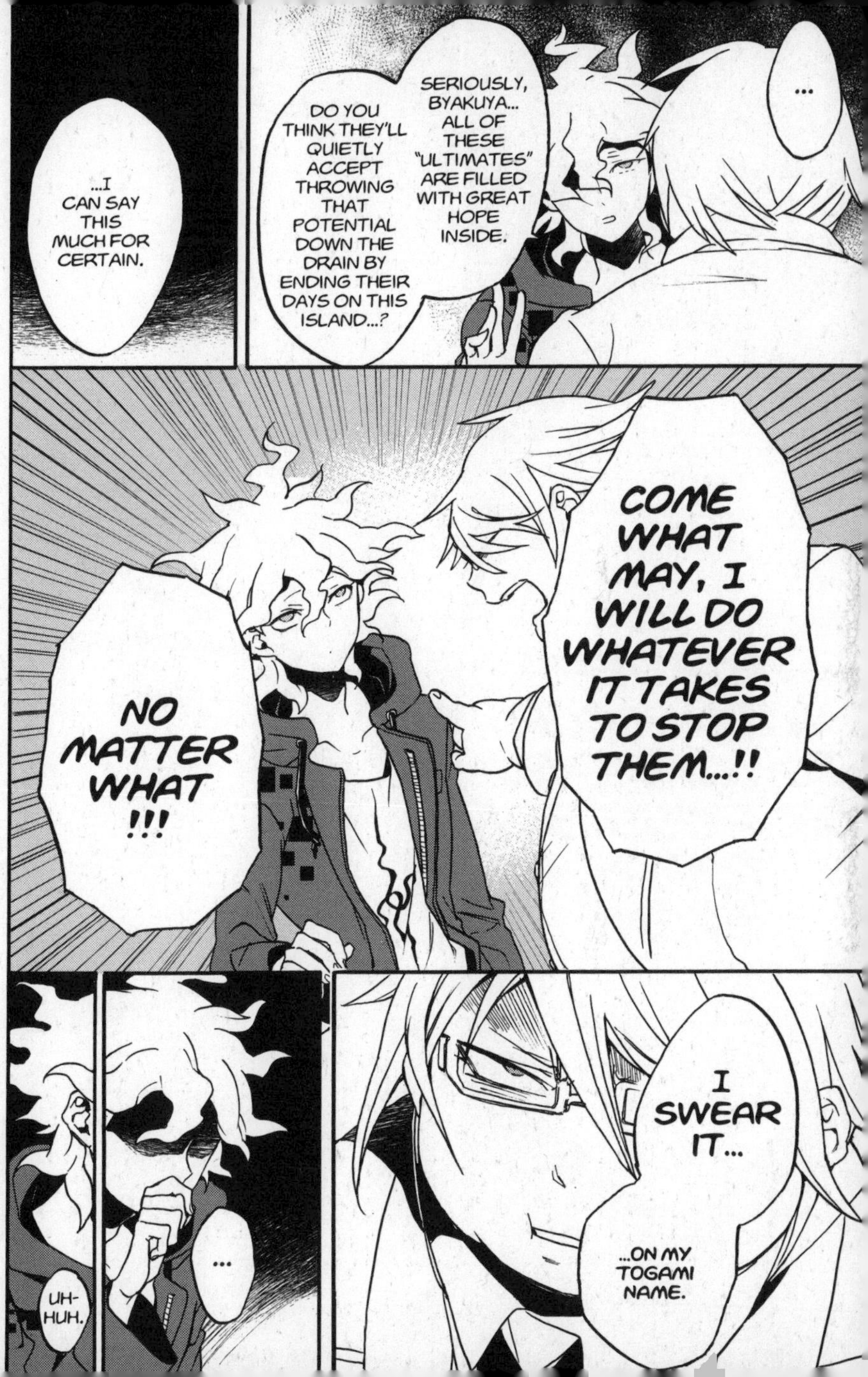
...
SERIOUSLY, BYAKUYA... ALL OF THESE "ULTIMATES" ARE FILLED WITH GREAT HOPE INSIDE.
DO YOU THINK THEY'LL QUIETLY ACCEPT THROWING THAT POTENTIAL DOWN THE DRAIN BY ENDING THEIR DAYS ON THIS ISLAND...?
...I CAN SAY THIS MUCH FOR CERTAIN.
COME WHAT MAY, I WILL DO WHATEVER IT TAKES TO STOP THEM...!!
NO MATTER WHAT!!!
I SWEAR IT...
...ON MY TOGAMI NAME.
...
UH-HUH.

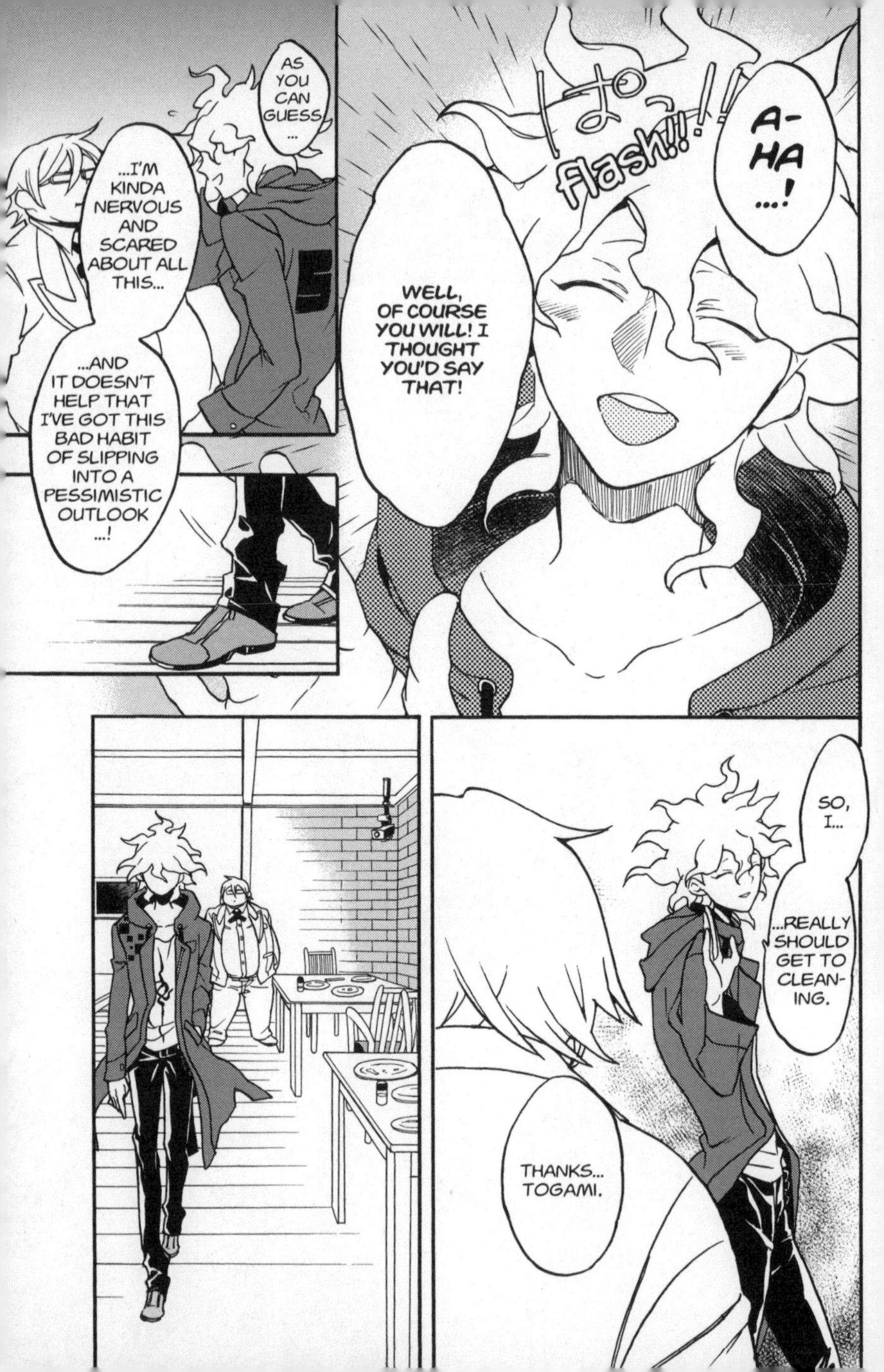
A-HA...!
はっ!!
Flash!!!
WELL, OF COURSE YOU WILL! I THOUGHT YOU'D SAY THAT!
AS YOU CAN GUESS...
...I'M KINDA NERVOUS AND SCARED ABOUT ALL THIS...
...AND IT DOESN'T HELP THAT I'VE GOT THIS BAD HABIT OF SLIPPING INTO A PESSIMISTIC OUTLOOK...!
SO, I...
...REALLY SHOULD GET TO CLEANING.
THANKS... TOGAMI.

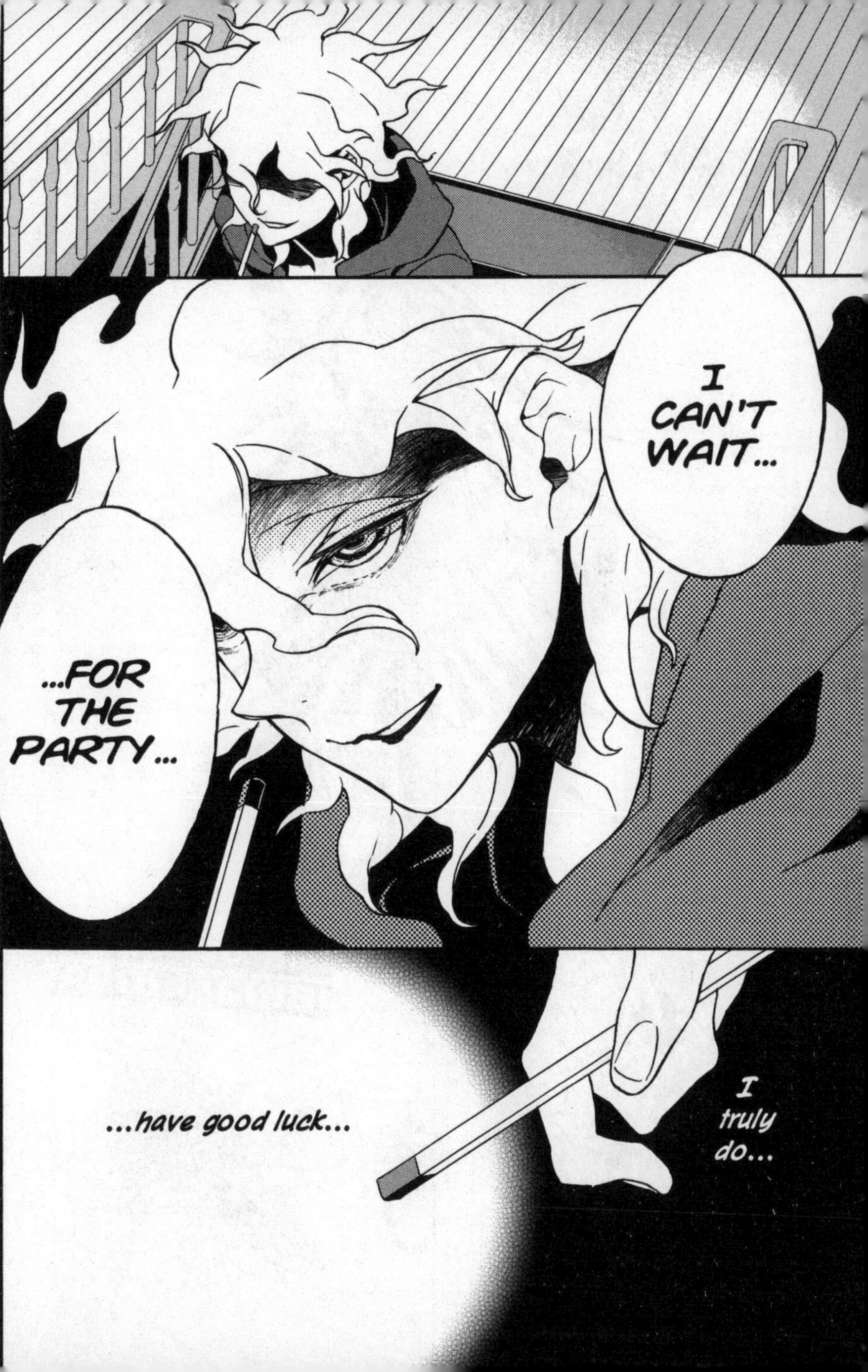
I CAN'T WAIT...
...FOR THE PARTY...
I truly do...
...have good luck...

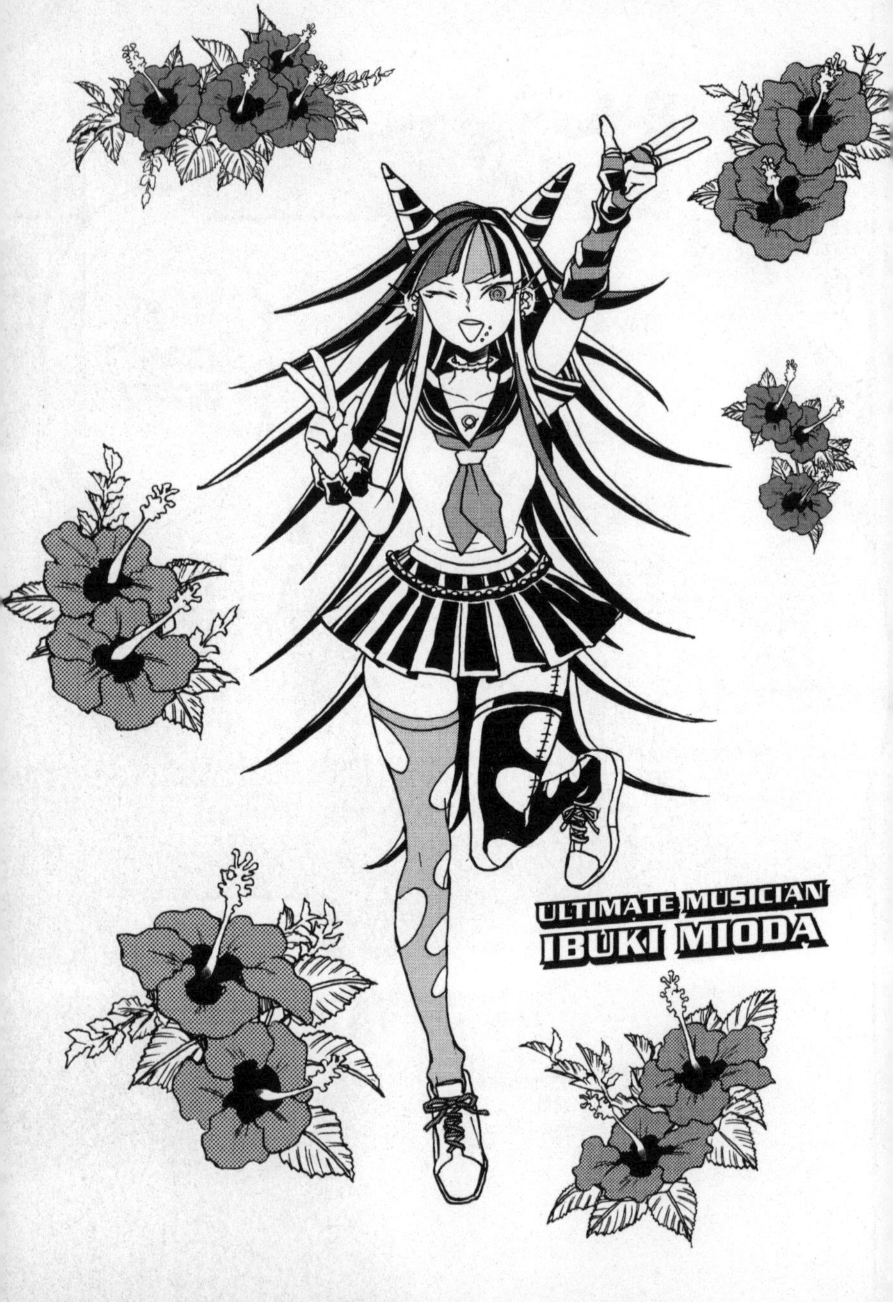
ULTIMATE MUSICIAN
IBUKI MIODA

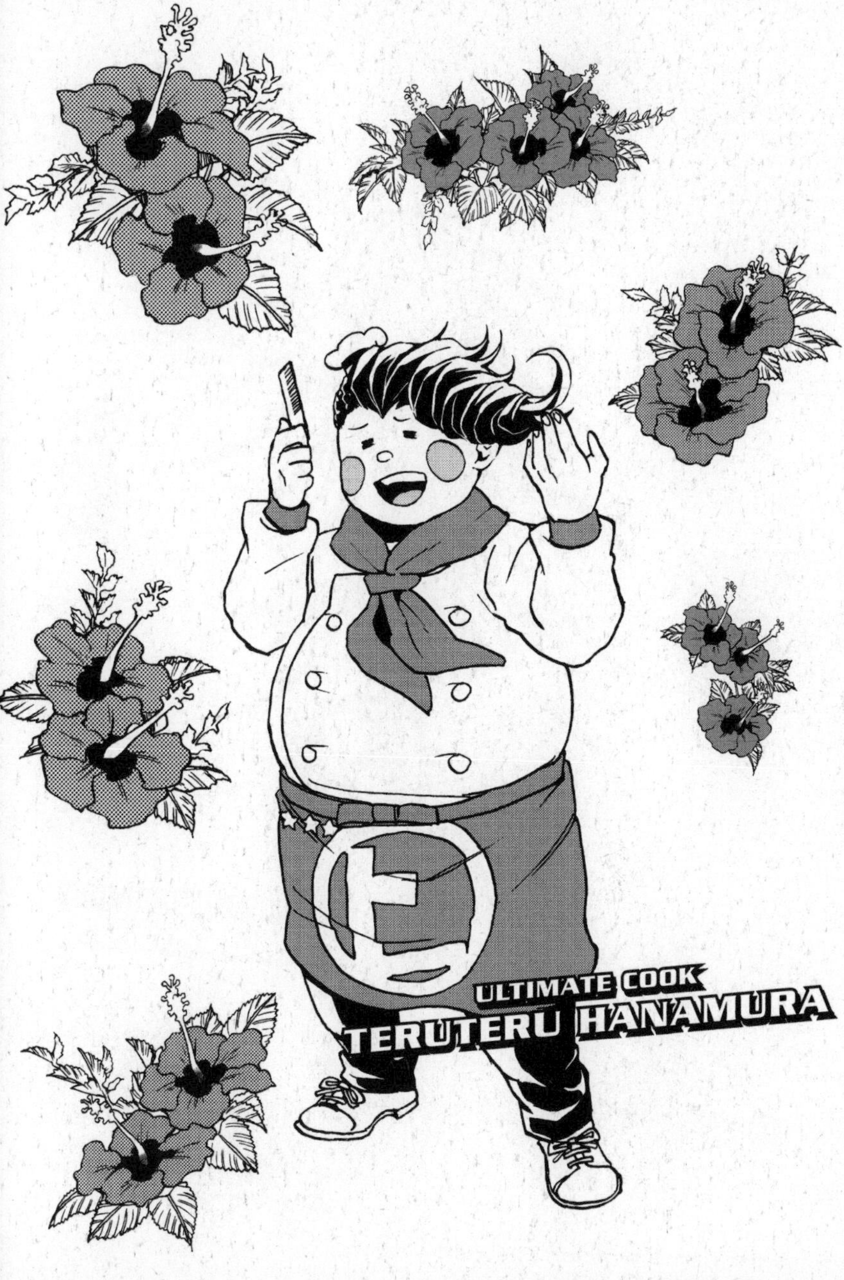
ULTIMATE COOK
TERUTERU HANAMURA

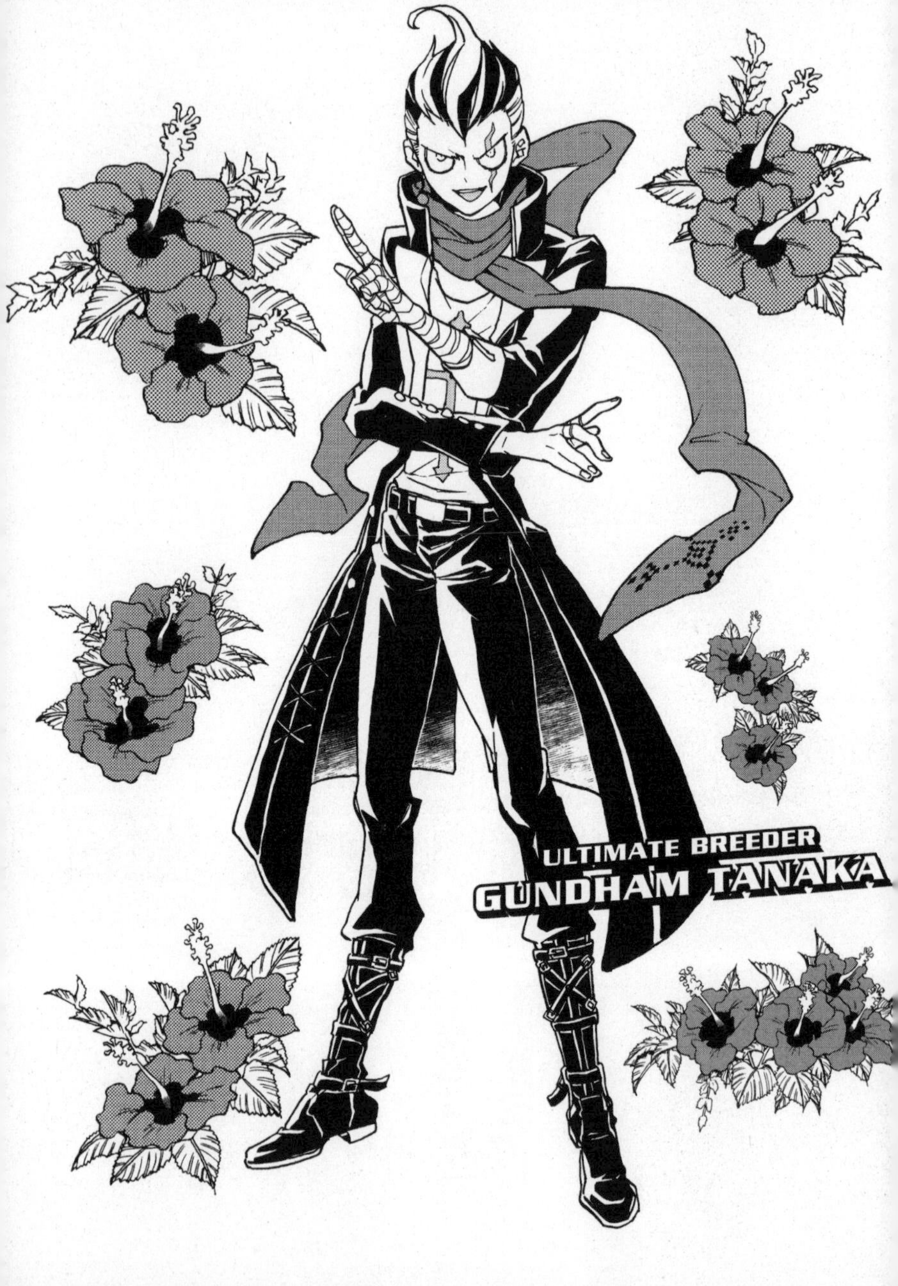
ULTIMATE BREEDER
GUNDHAM TANAKA

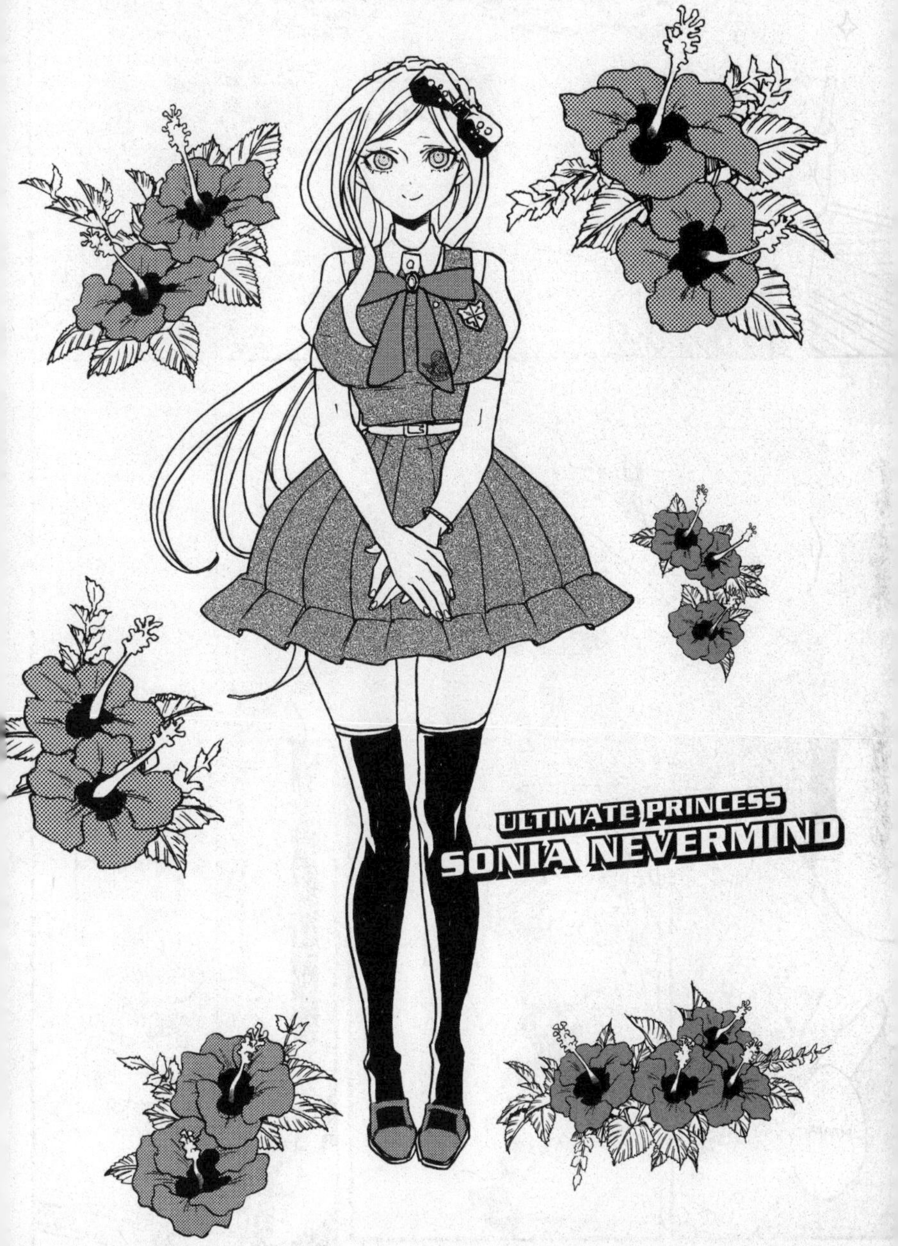
ULTIMATE PRINCESS
SONIA NEVERMIND

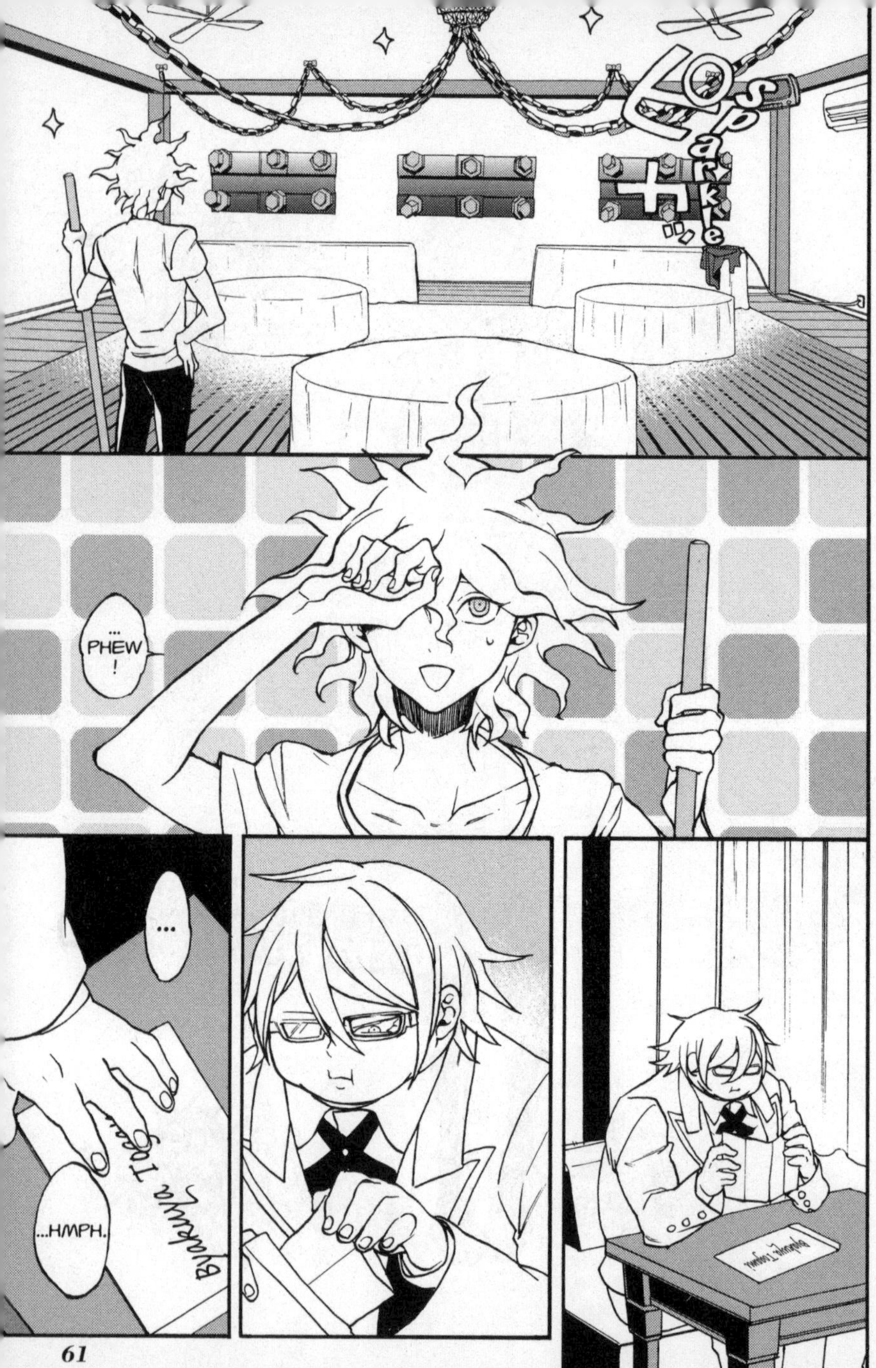
sparkle
...PHEW!
...
...HMPH.
Byakuya Togami

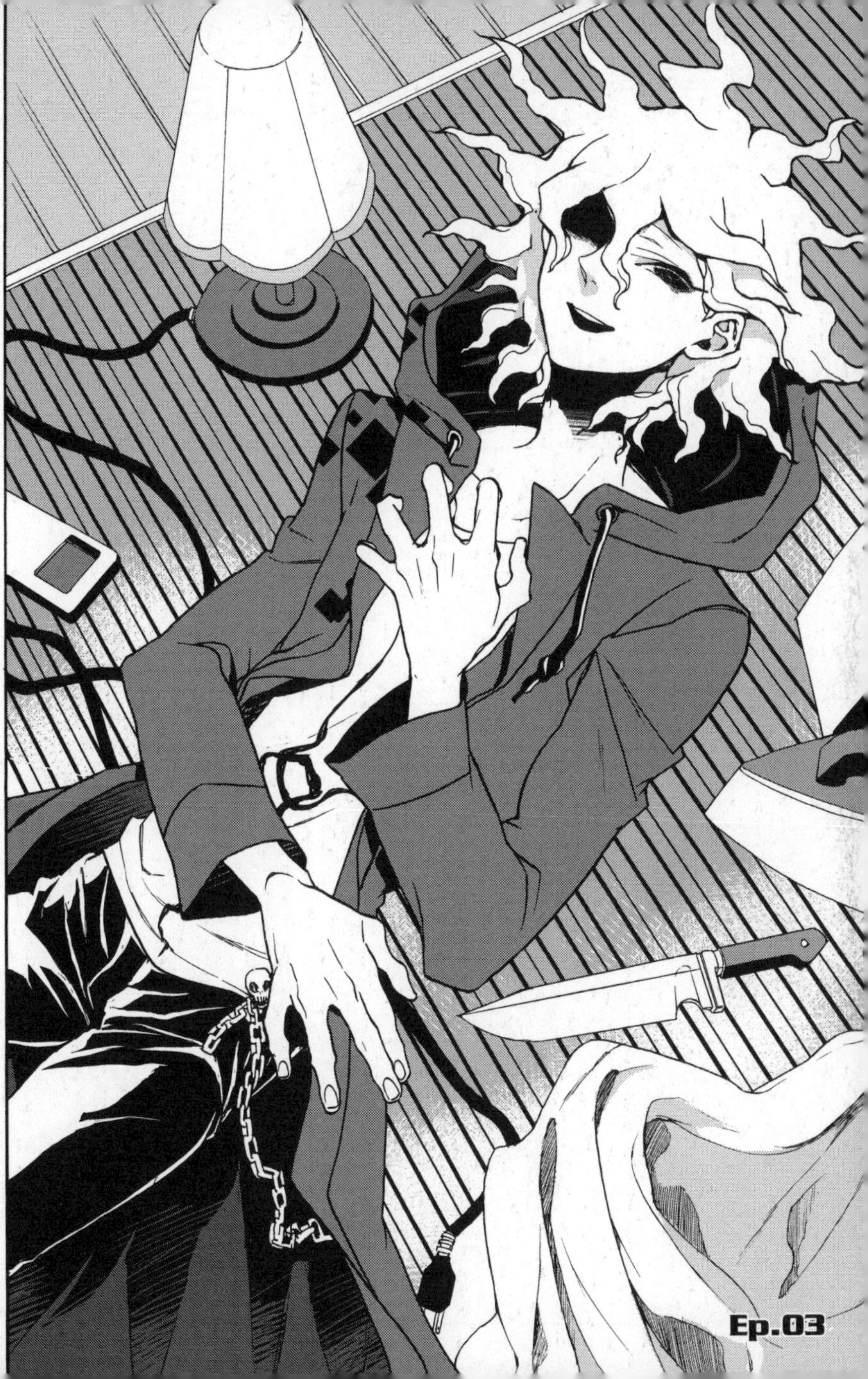
Ep.03

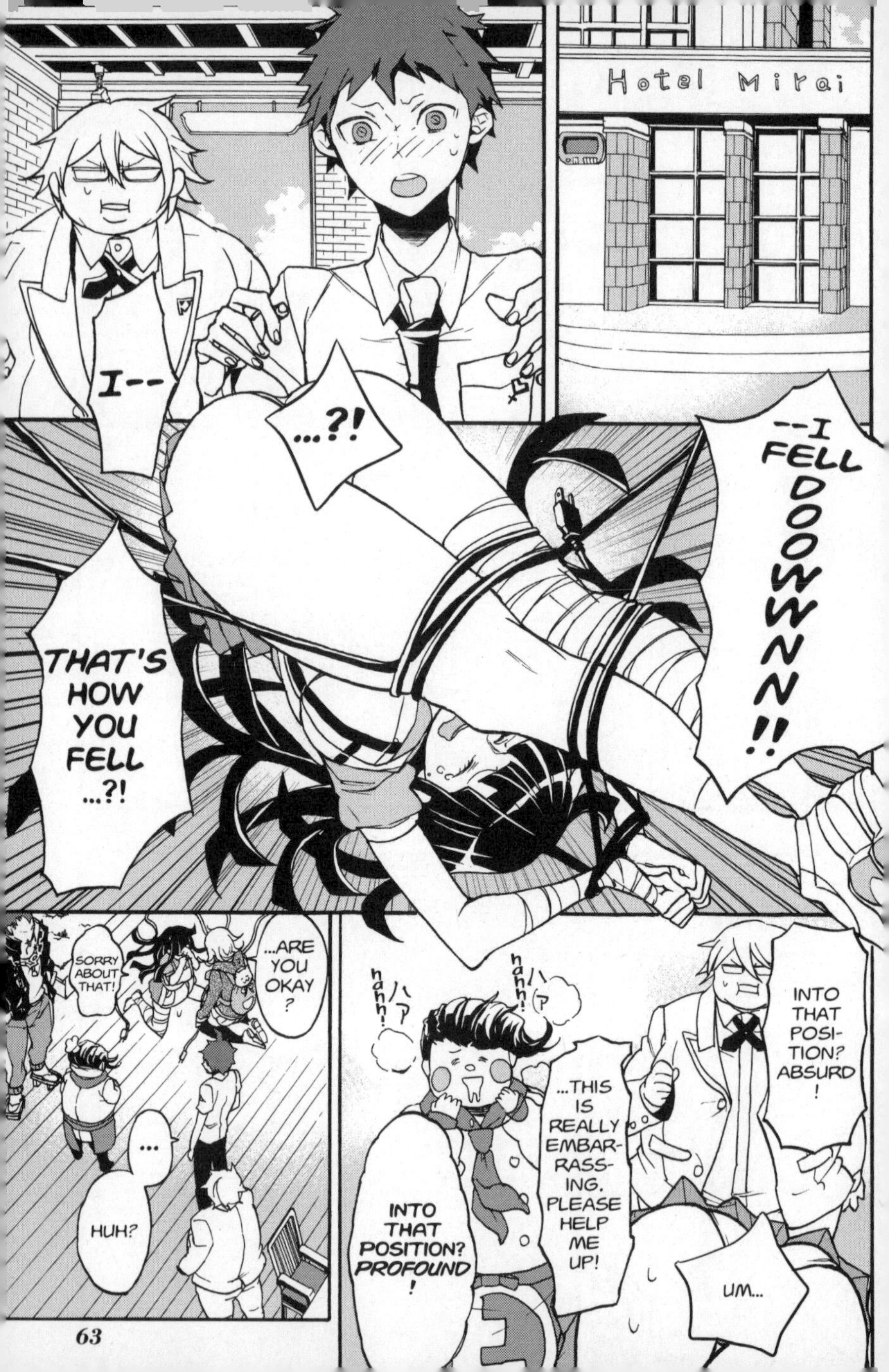
Hotel Mirai
I--
...?!
--I FELL DOOOWWNNN!!
THAT'S HOW YOU FELL ...?!
ハァ hahh!
ハァ hahh!
INTO THAT POSITION? ABSURD!
...THIS IS REALLY EMBARRASSING. PLEASE HELP ME UP!
INTO THAT POSITION? PROFOUND!
UM...
...ARE YOU OKAY?
SORRY ABOUT THAT!
...
HUH?

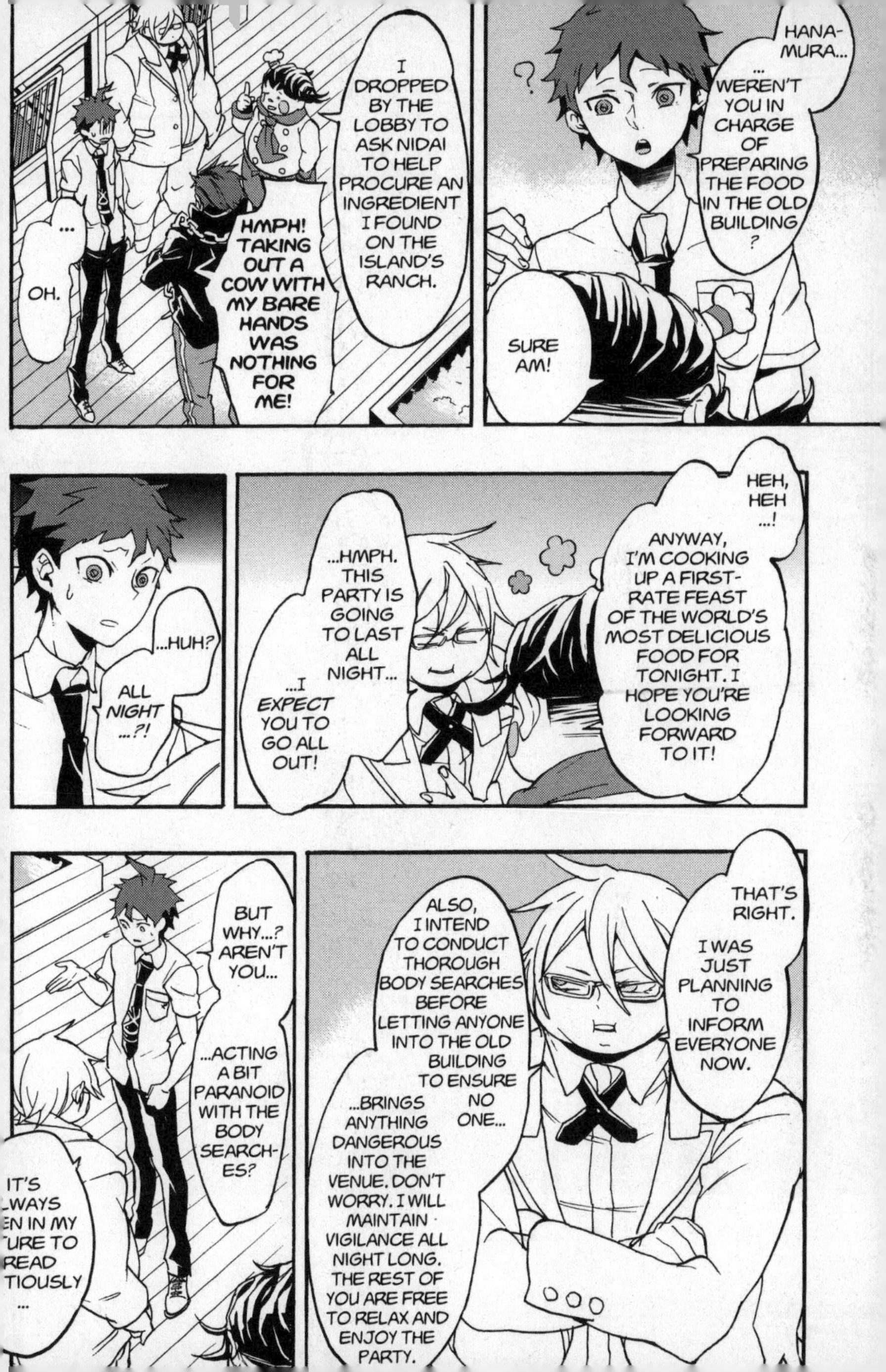

HANA-MURA... ...WEREN'T YOU IN CHARGE OF PREPARING THE FOOD IN THE OLD BUILDING?
SURE AM!
I DROPPED BY THE LOBBY TO ASK NIDAI TO HELP PROCURE AN INGREDIENT I FOUND ON THE ISLAND'S RANCH.
HMPH! TAKING OUT A COW WITH MY BARE HANDS WAS NOTHING FOR ME!
... OH.
HEH, HEH ...!
ANYWAY, I'M COOKING UP A FIRST-RATE FEAST OF THE WORLD'S MOST DELICIOUS FOOD FOR TONIGHT. I HOPE YOU'RE LOOKING FORWARD TO IT!
...HMPH. THIS PARTY IS GOING TO LAST ALL NIGHT...
...I EXPECT YOU TO GO ALL OUT!
...HUH?
ALL NIGHT ...?!
THAT'S RIGHT.
I WAS JUST PLANNING TO INFORM EVERYONE NOW.
ALSO, I INTEND TO CONDUCT THOROUGH BODY SEARCHES BEFORE LETTING ANYONE INTO THE OLD BUILDING TO ENSURE NO ONE...
...BRINGS ANYTHING DANGEROUS INTO THE VENUE. DON'T WORRY. I WILL MAINTAIN VIGILANCE ALL NIGHT LONG. THE REST OF YOU ARE FREE TO RELAX AND ENJOY THE PARTY.
BUT WHY...? AREN'T YOU...
...ACTING A BIT PARANOID WITH THE BODY SEARCH-ES?
IT'S LWAYS EN IN MY TURE TO READ TIOUSLY ...

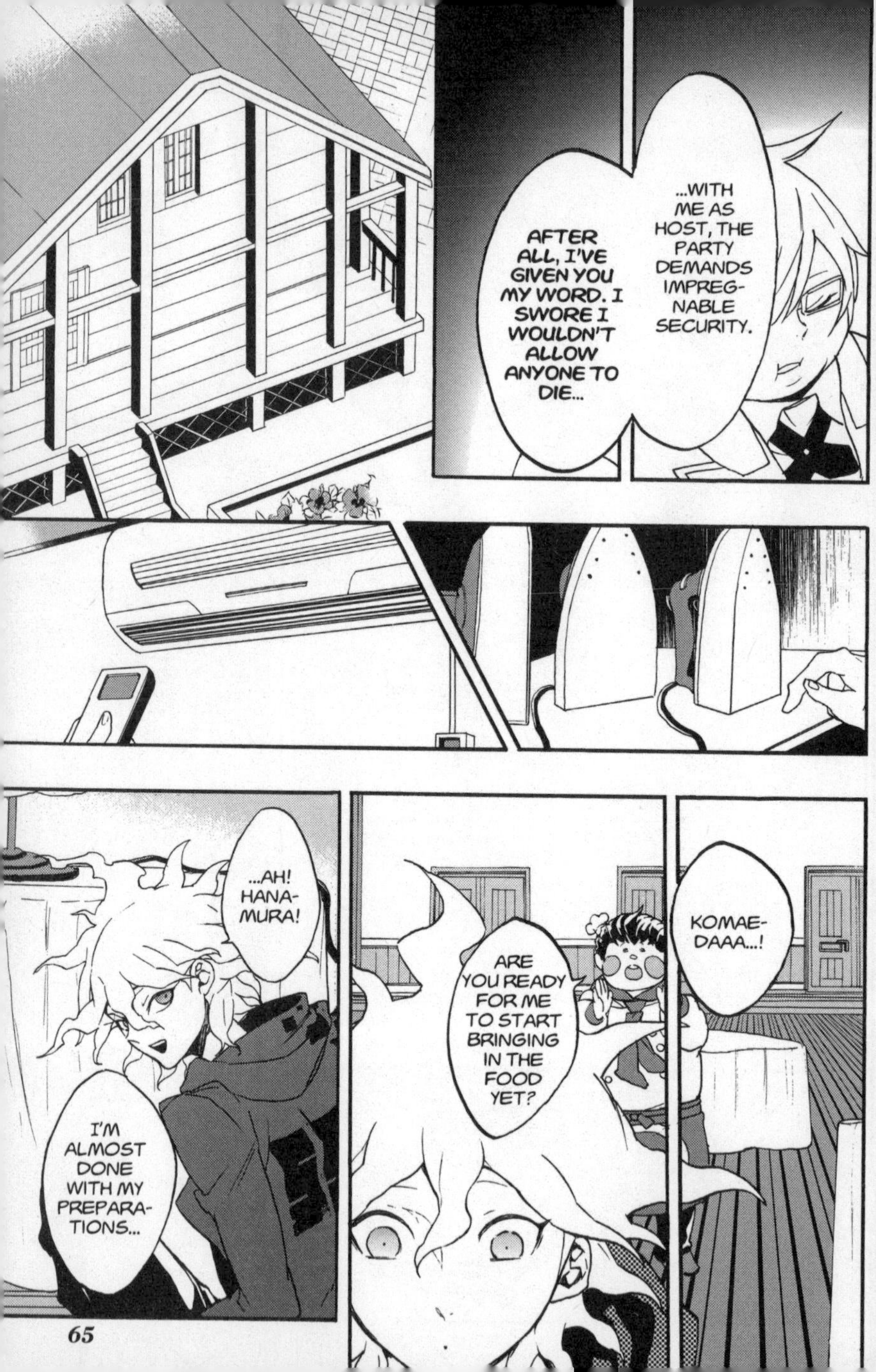
...WITH ME AS HOST, THE PARTY DEMANDS IMPREG-NABLE SECURITY.
AFTER ALL, I'VE GIVEN YOU MY WORD. I SWORE I WOULDN'T ALLOW ANYONE TO DIE...
KOMAE-DAAA...!
ARE YOU READY FOR ME TO START BRINGING IN THE FOOD YET?
...AH! HANA-MURA!
I'M ALMOST DONE WITH MY PREPARA-TIONS...

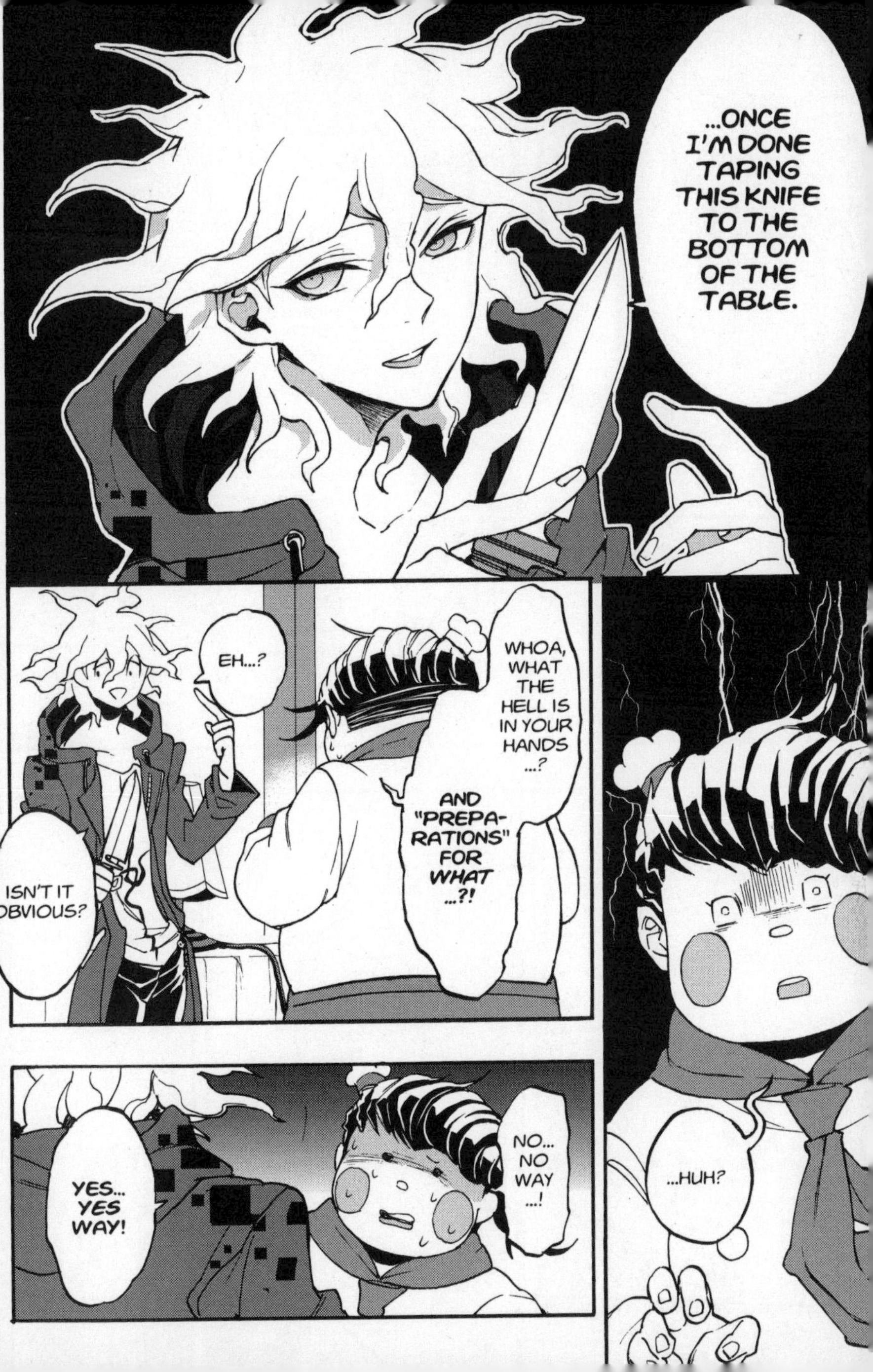
...ONCE I'M DONE TAPING THIS KNIFE TO THE BOTTOM OF THE TABLE.
...HUH?
WHOA, WHAT THE HELL IS IN YOUR HANDS ...?
AND "PREPARATIONS" FOR *WHAT* ...?!
EH...?
ISN'T IT OBVIOUS?
NO... NO WAY ...!
YES... YES WAY!

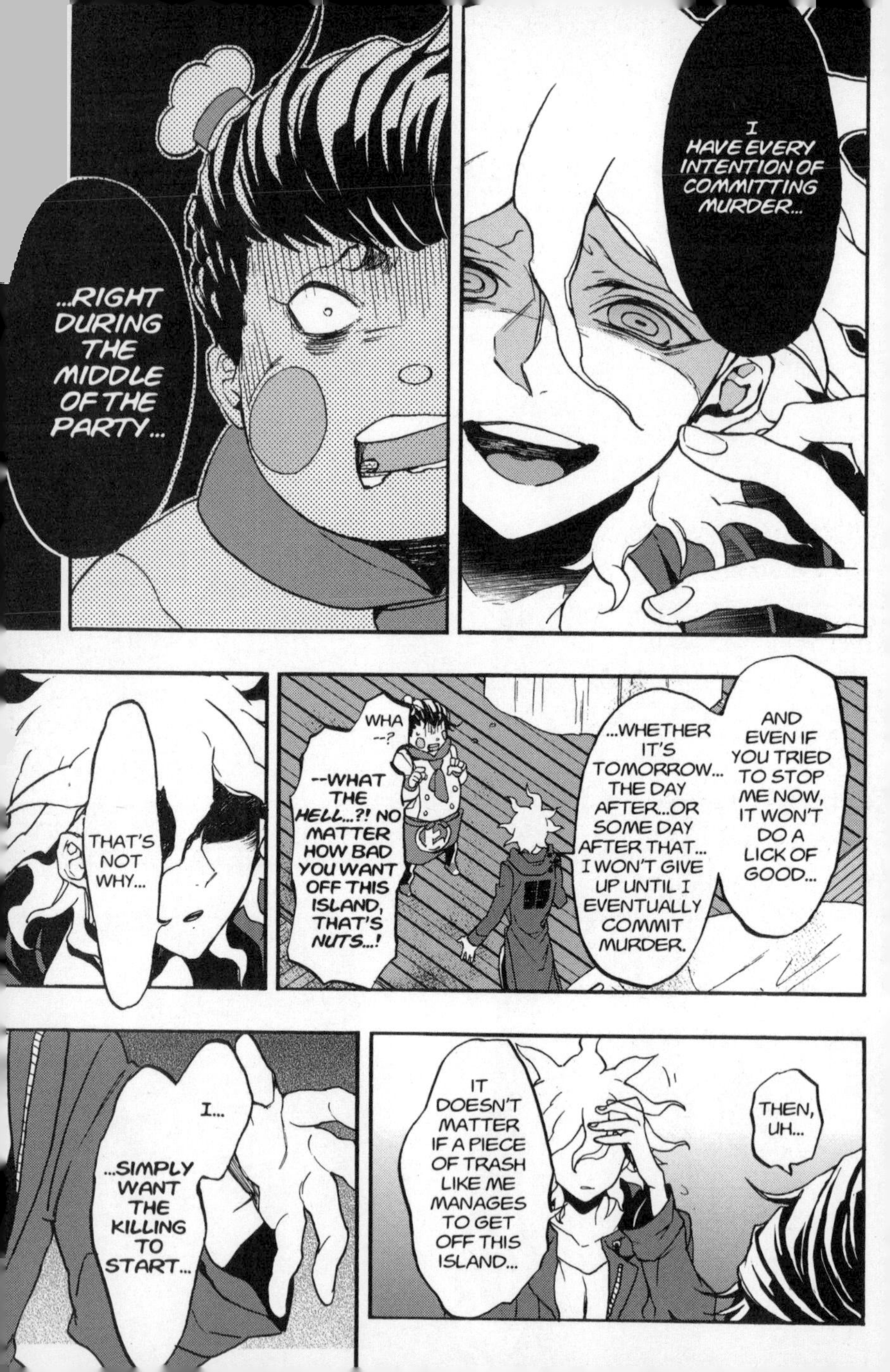
I HAVE EVERY INTENTION OF COMMITTING MURDER...
...RIGHT DURING THE MIDDLE OF THE PARTY...
AND EVEN IF YOU TRIED TO STOP ME NOW, IT WON'T DO A LICK OF GOOD...
...WHETHER IT'S TOMORROW... THE DAY AFTER...OR SOME DAY AFTER THAT... I WON'T GIVE UP UNTIL I EVENTUALLY COMMIT MURDER.
WHA--?
--WHAT THE *HELL*...?! NO MATTER HOW BAD YOU WANT OFF THIS ISLAND, THAT'S *NUTS*...!
THAT'S NOT WHY...
THEN, UH...
IT DOESN'T MATTER IF A PIECE OF TRASH LIKE ME MANAGES TO GET OFF THIS ISLAND...
I...
...SIMPLY WANT THE KILLING TO START...

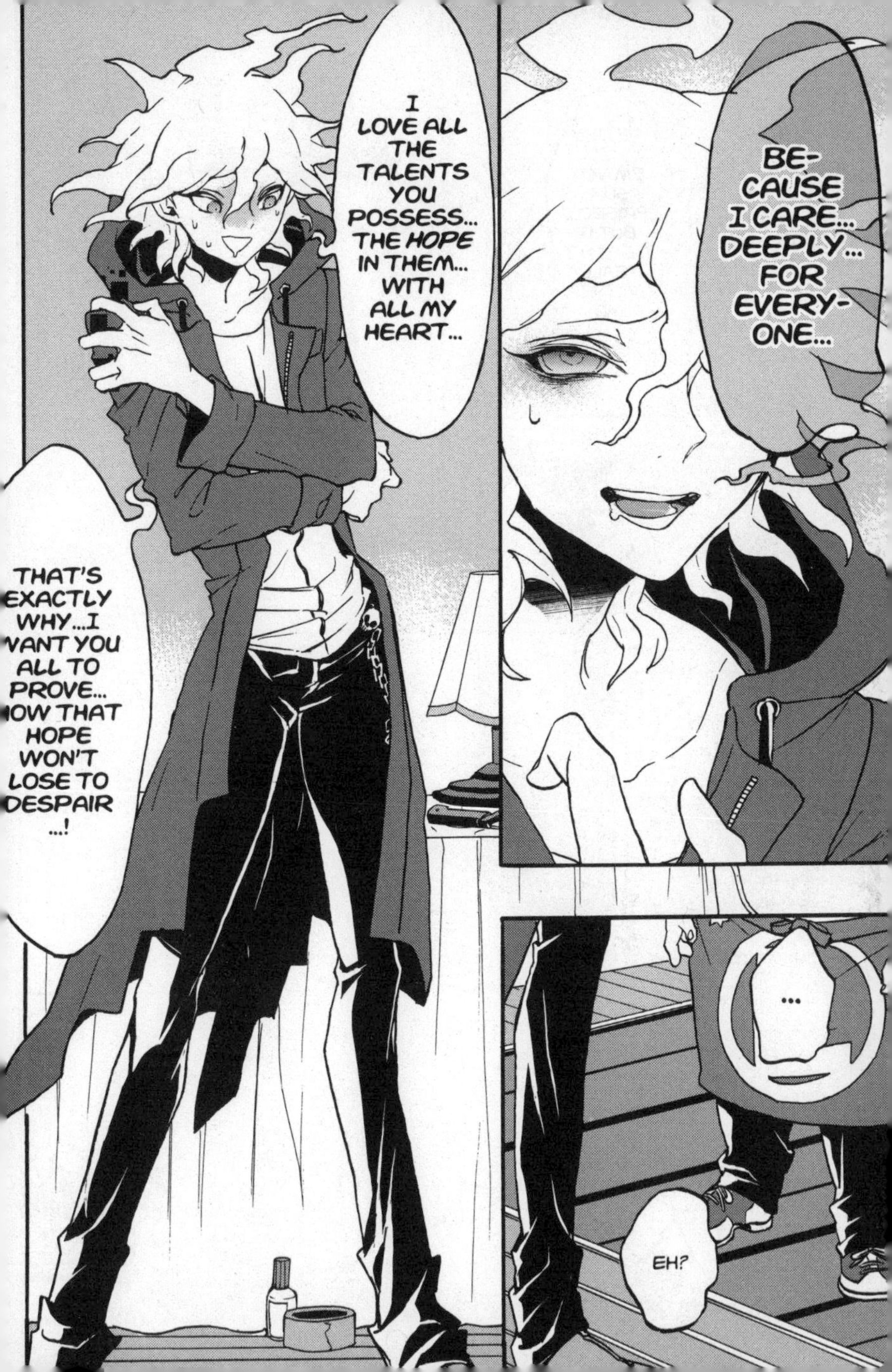
BE-CAUSE I CARE... DEEPLY... FOR EVERY-ONE...
...
EH?
I LOVE ALL THE TALENTS YOU POSSESS... THE *HOPE* IN THEM... WITH ALL MY HEART...
THAT'S EXACTLY WHY...I VANT YOU ALL TO PROVE... OW THAT HOPE WON'T LOSE TO DESPAIR ...!

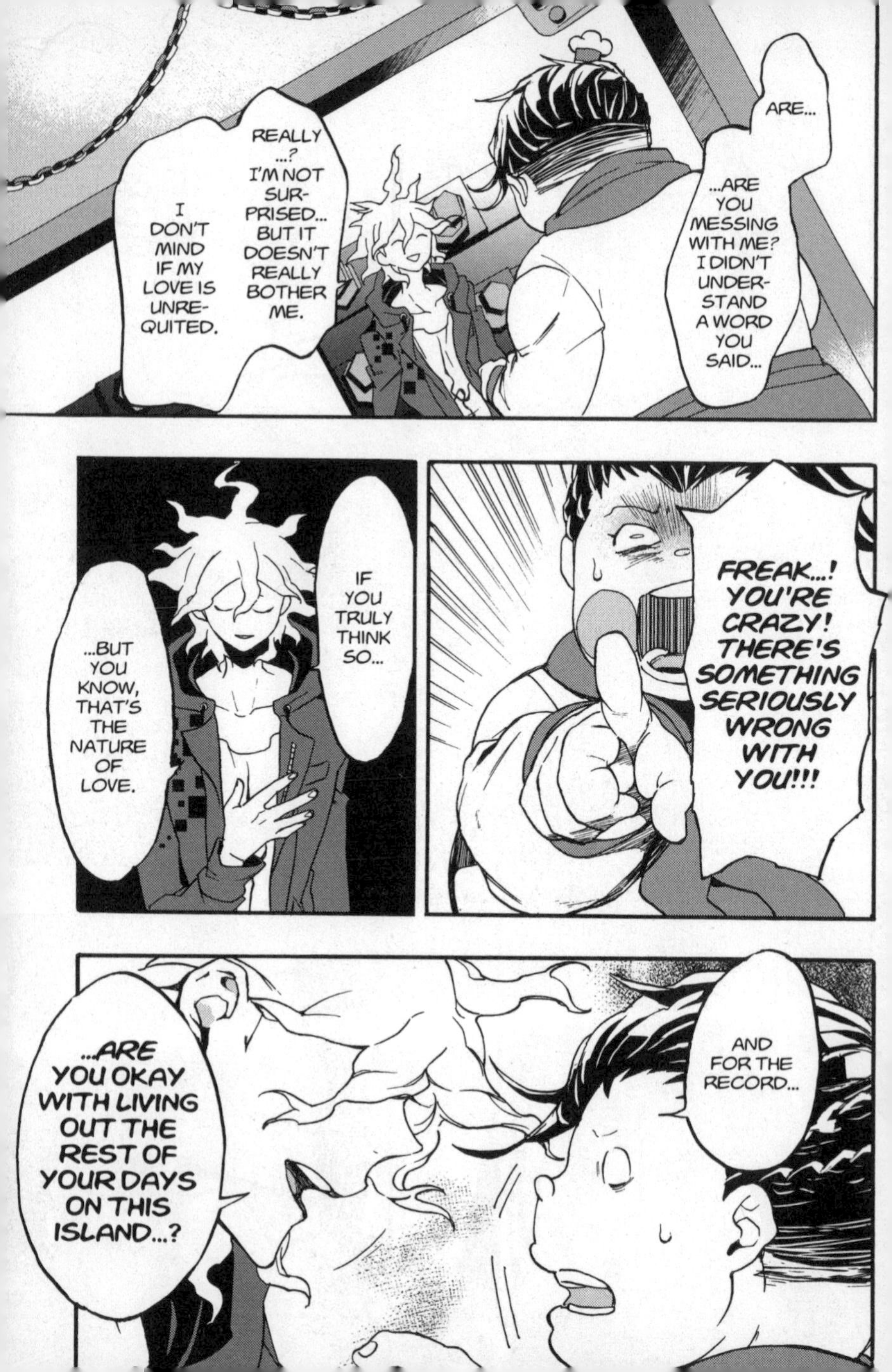
ARE...
...ARE YOU MESSING WITH ME? I DIDN'T UNDERSTAND A WORD YOU SAID...
REALLY ...? I'M NOT SURPRISED... BUT IT DOESN'T REALLY BOTHER ME.
I DON'T MIND IF MY LOVE IS UNREQUITED.
FREAK...! YOU'RE CRAZY! THERE'S SOMETHING SERIOUSLY WRONG WITH YOU!!!
IF YOU TRULY THINK SO...
...BUT YOU KNOW, THAT'S THE NATURE OF LOVE.
AND FOR THE RECORD...
...ARE YOU OKAY WITH LIVING OUT THE REST OF YOUR DAYS ON THIS ISLAND...?

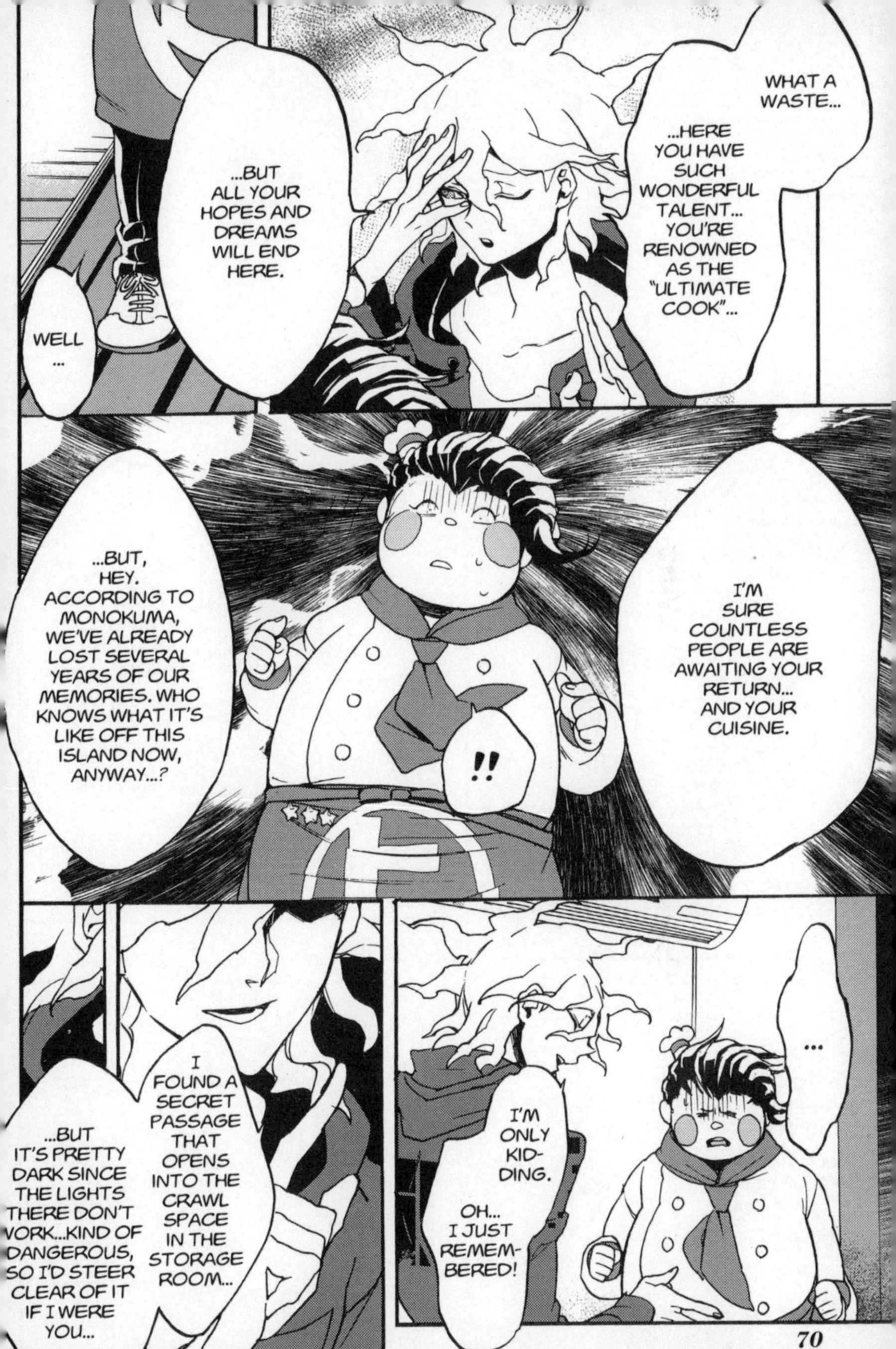
WHAT A WASTE...
...HERE YOU HAVE SUCH WONDERFUL TALENT... YOU'RE RENOWNED AS THE "ULTIMATE COOK"...
...BUT ALL YOUR HOPES AND DREAMS WILL END HERE.
WELL ...
I'M SURE COUNTLESS PEOPLE ARE AWAITING YOUR RETURN... AND YOUR CUISINE.
!!
...BUT, HEY. ACCORDING TO MONOKUMA, WE'VE ALREADY LOST SEVERAL YEARS OF OUR MEMORIES. WHO KNOWS WHAT IT'S LIKE OFF THIS ISLAND NOW, ANYWAY...?
...
I'M ONLY KIDDING.
OH... I JUST REMEMBERED!
I FOUND A SECRET PASSAGE THAT OPENS INTO THE CRAWL SPACE IN THE STORAGE ROOM...
...BUT IT'S PRETTY DARK SINCE THE LIGHTS THERE DON'T VORK...KIND OF DANGEROUS, SO I'D STEER CLEAR OF IT IF I WERE YOU...

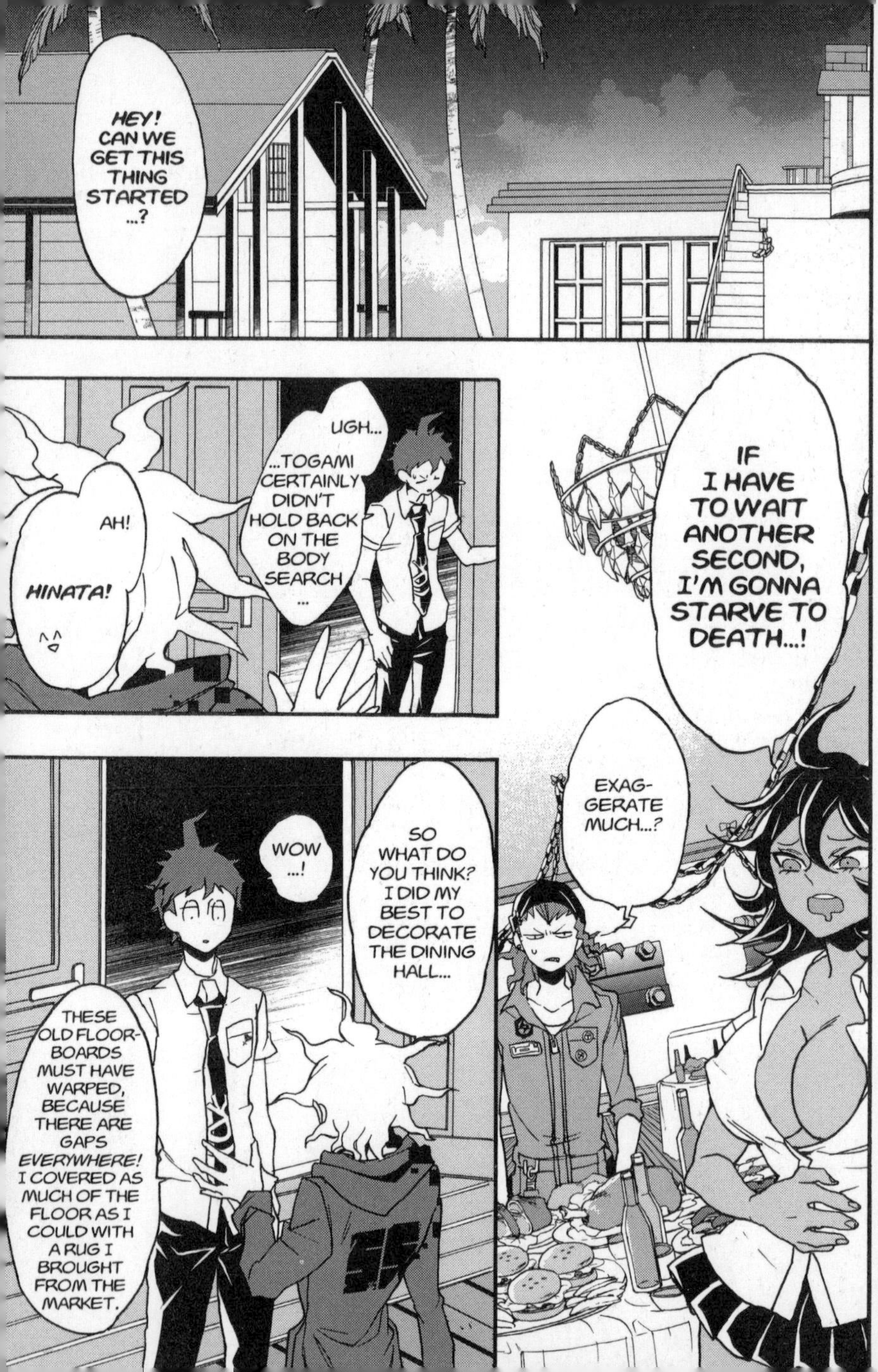
HEY! CAN WE GET THIS THING STARTED ...?
IF I HAVE TO WAIT ANOTHER SECOND, I'M GONNA STARVE TO DEATH...!
EXAG-GERATE MUCH...?
UGH...
...TOGAMI CERTAINLY DIDN'T HOLD BACK ON THE BODY SEARCH ...
AH!
HINATA!
SO WHAT DO YOU THINK? I DID MY BEST TO DECORATE THE DINING HALL...
WOW ...!
THESE OLD FLOOR-BOARDS MUST HAVE WARPED, BECAUSE THERE ARE GAPS EVERYWHERE! I COVERED AS MUCH OF THE FLOOR AS I COULD WITH A RUG I BROUGHT FROM THE MARKET.

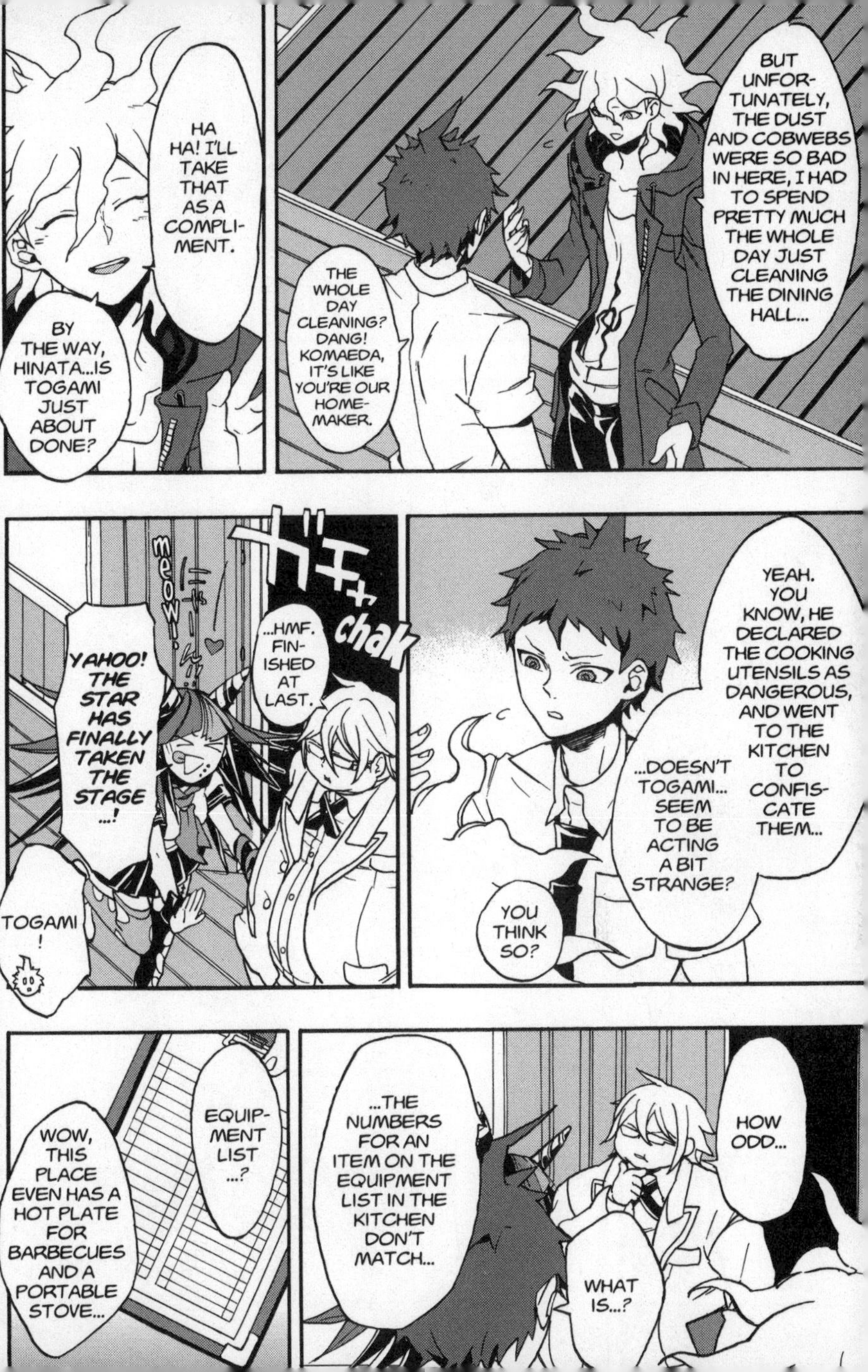
BUT UNFORTUNATELY, THE DUST AND COBWEBS WERE SO BAD IN HERE, I HAD TO SPEND PRETTY MUCH THE WHOLE DAY JUST CLEANING THE DINING HALL...
THE WHOLE DAY CLEANING? DANG! KOMAEDA, IT'S LIKE YOU'RE OUR HOMEMAKER.
HA HA! I'LL TAKE THAT AS A COMPLIMENT.
BY THE WAY, HINATA...IS TOGAMI JUST ABOUT DONE?
YEAH. YOU KNOW, HE DECLARED THE COOKING UTENSILS AS DANGEROUS, AND WENT TO THE KITCHEN TO CONFISCATE THEM...
...DOESN'T TOGAMI... SEEM TO BE ACTING A BIT STRANGE?
YOU THINK SO?
chak
...HMF. FINISHED AT LAST.
meow!!
YAHOO! THE STAR HAS FINALLY TAKEN THE STAGE...!
TOGAMI!
HOW ODD...
...THE NUMBERS FOR AN ITEM ON THE EQUIPMENT LIST IN THE KITCHEN DON'T MATCH...
WHAT IS...?
EQUIPMENT LIST...?
WOW, THIS PLACE EVEN HAS A HOT PLATE FOR BARBECUES AND A PORTABLE STOVE...

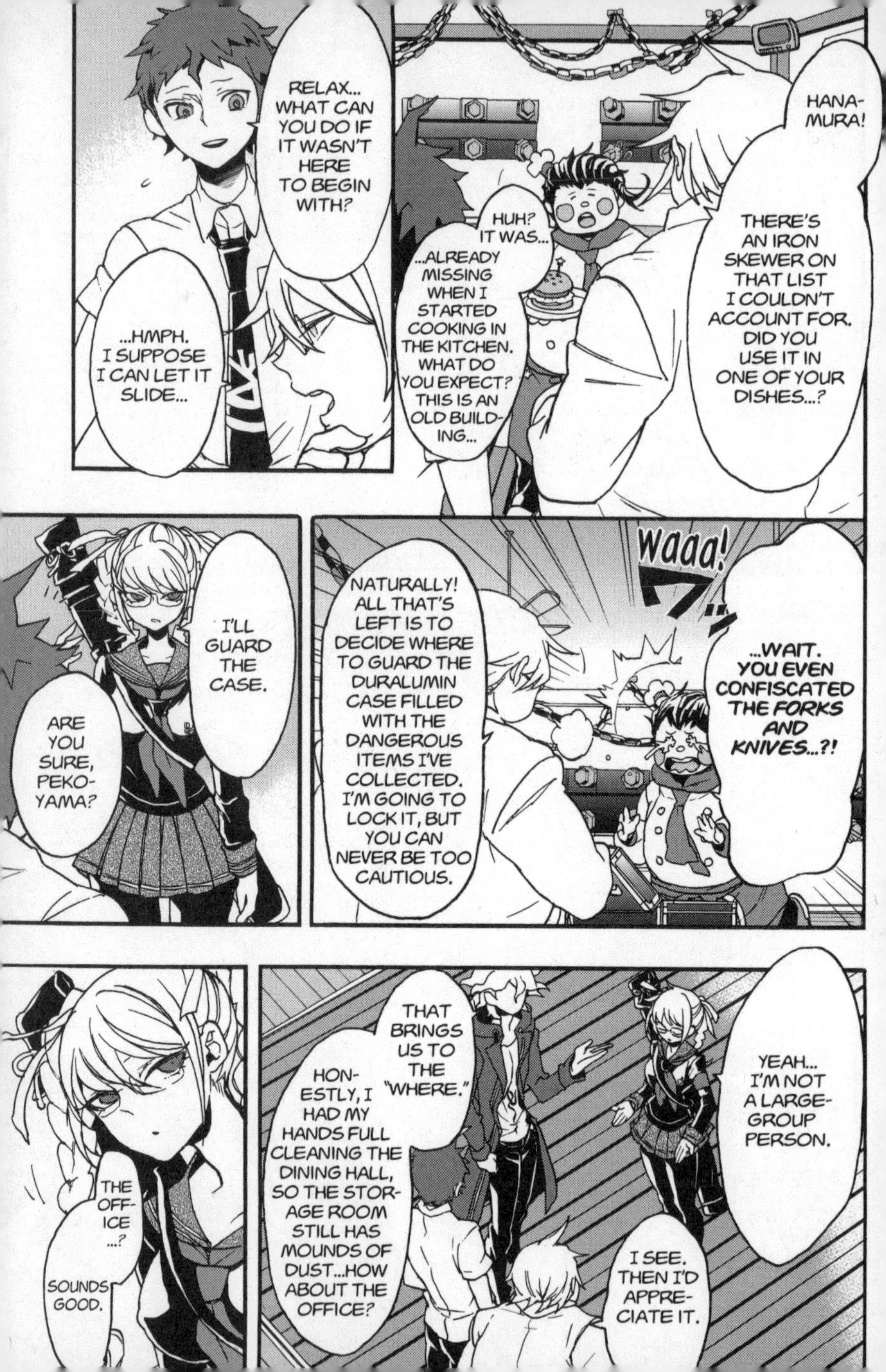
HANAMURA!
THERE'S AN IRON SKEWER ON THAT LIST I COULDN'T ACCOUNT FOR. DID YOU USE IT IN ONE OF YOUR DISHES...?
HUH? IT WAS...
...ALREADY MISSING WHEN I STARTED COOKING IN THE KITCHEN. WHAT DO YOU EXPECT? THIS IS AN OLD BUILDING...
RELAX... WHAT CAN YOU DO IF IT WASN'T HERE TO BEGIN WITH?
...HMPH. I SUPPOSE I CAN LET IT SLIDE...
Waaa!
...WAIT. YOU EVEN CONFISCATED THE *FORKS AND KNIVES*...?!
NATURALLY! ALL THAT'S LEFT IS TO DECIDE WHERE TO GUARD THE DURALUMIN CASE FILLED WITH THE DANGEROUS ITEMS I'VE COLLECTED. I'M GOING TO LOCK IT, BUT YOU CAN NEVER BE TOO CAUTIOUS.
I'LL GUARD THE CASE.
ARE YOU SURE, PEKOYAMA?
YEAH... I'M NOT A LARGE-GROUP PERSON.
THAT BRINGS US TO THE "WHERE."
HONESTLY, I HAD MY HANDS FULL CLEANING THE DINING HALL, SO THE STORAGE ROOM STILL HAS MOUNDS OF DUST...HOW ABOUT THE OFFICE?
I SEE. THEN I'D APPRECIATE IT.
THE OFFICE...?
SOUNDS GOOD.

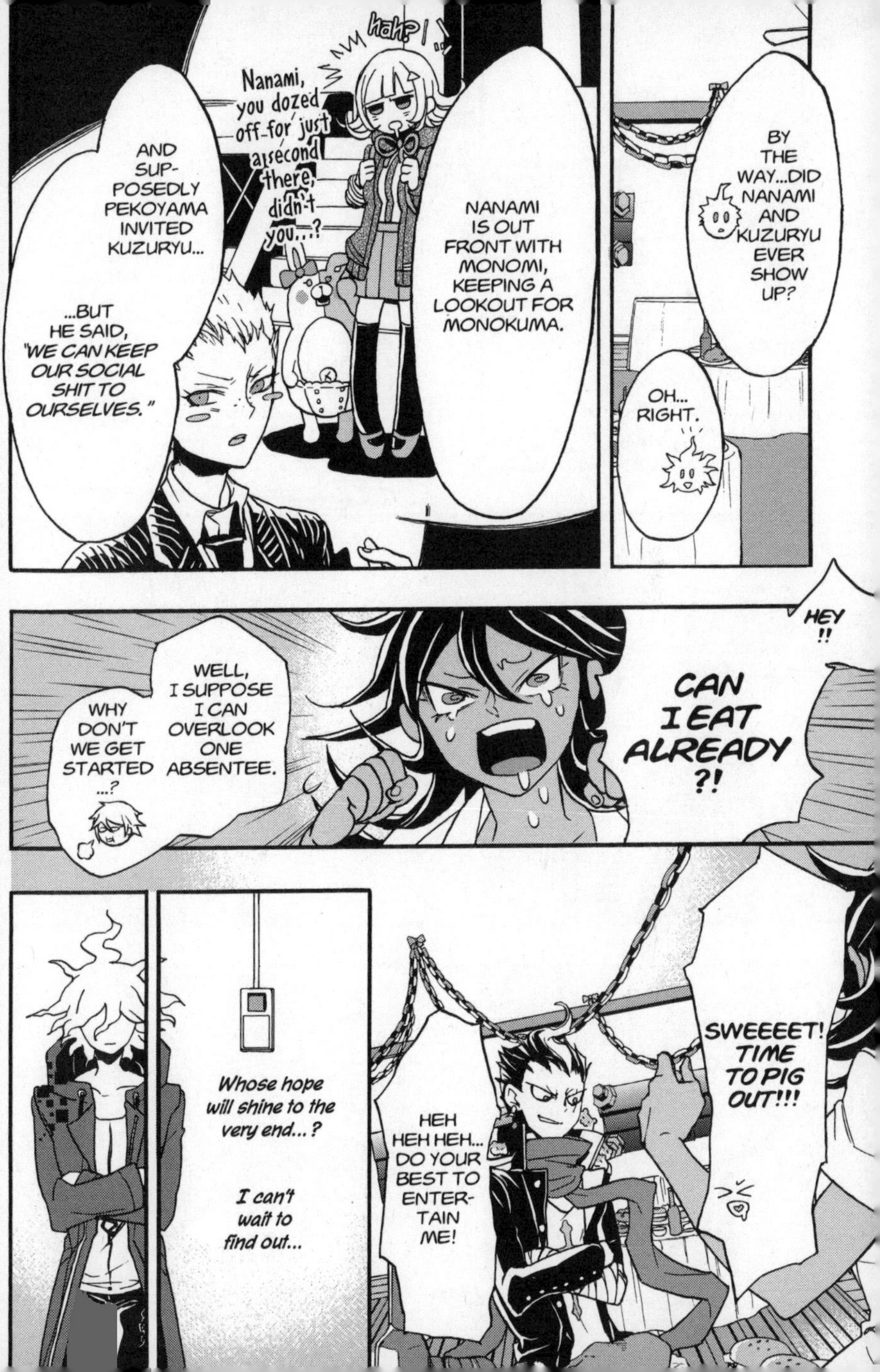
BY THE WAY...DID NANAMI AND KUZURYU EVER SHOW UP?
OH... RIGHT.
NANAMI IS OUT FRONT WITH MONOMI, KEEPING A LOOKOUT FOR MONOKUMA.
hah?!
Nanami, you dozed off for just a second there, didn't you...?
AND SUPPOSEDLY PEKOYAMA INVITED KUZURYU...
...BUT HE SAID, "WE CAN KEEP OUR SOCIAL SHIT TO OURSELVES."
HEY!!
CAN I EAT ALREADY?!
WELL, I SUPPOSE I CAN OVERLOOK ONE ABSENTEE.
WHY DON'T WE GET STARTED...?
SWEEEET! TIME TO PIG OUT!!!
HEH HEH HEH... DO YOUR BEST TO ENTERTAIN ME!
Whose hope will shine to the very end...?
I can't wait to find out...

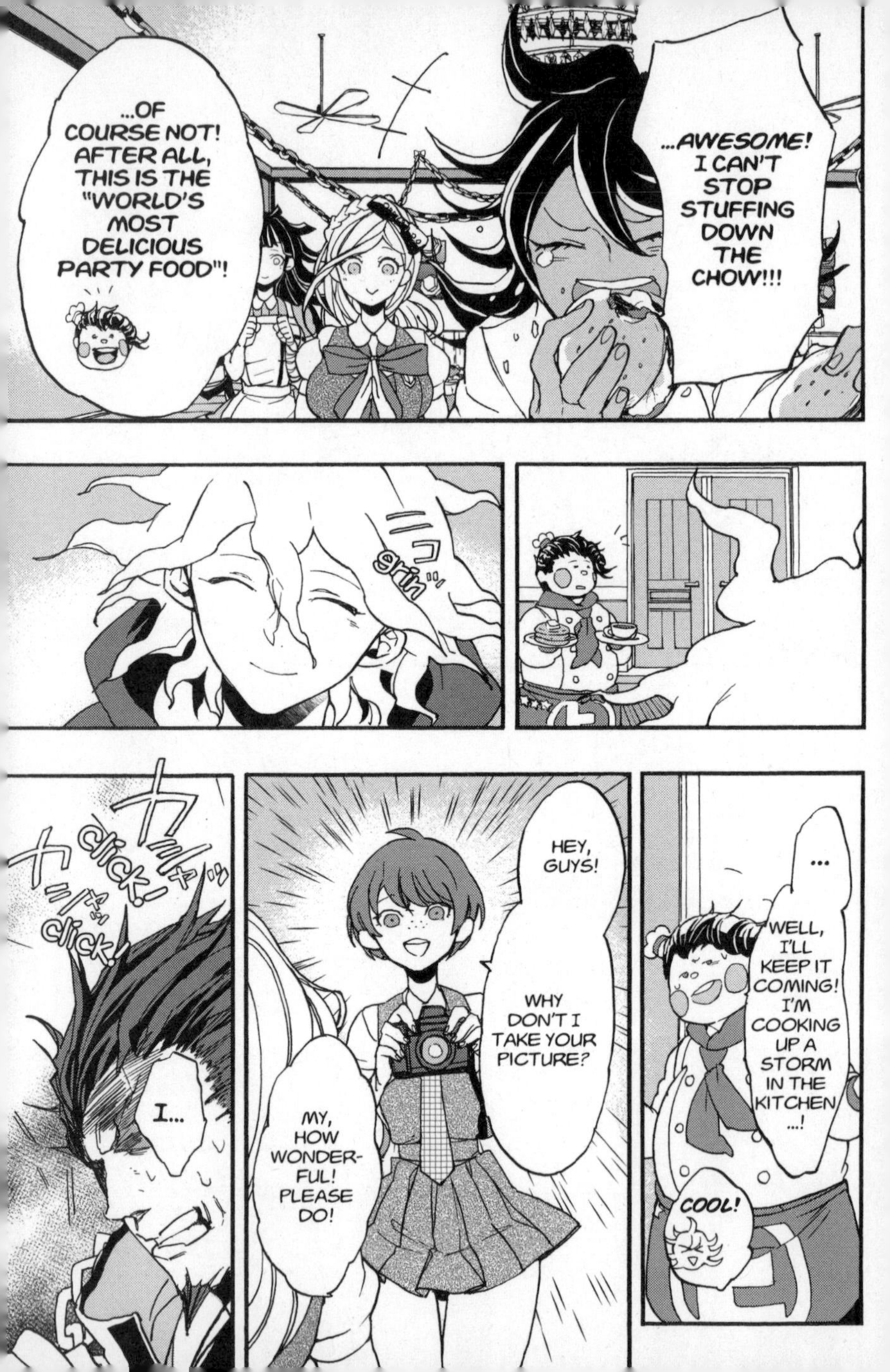
...AWESOME! I CAN'T STOP STUFFING DOWN THE CHOW!!!
...OF COURSE NOT! AFTER ALL, THIS IS THE "WORLD'S MOST DELICIOUS PARTY FOOD"!
grin
...
WELL, I'LL KEEP IT COMING! I'M COOKING UP A STORM IN THE KITCHEN...!
COOL!
HEY, GUYS!
WHY DON'T I TAKE YOUR PICTURE?
MY, HOW WONDERFUL! PLEASE DO!
click!
click!
I...

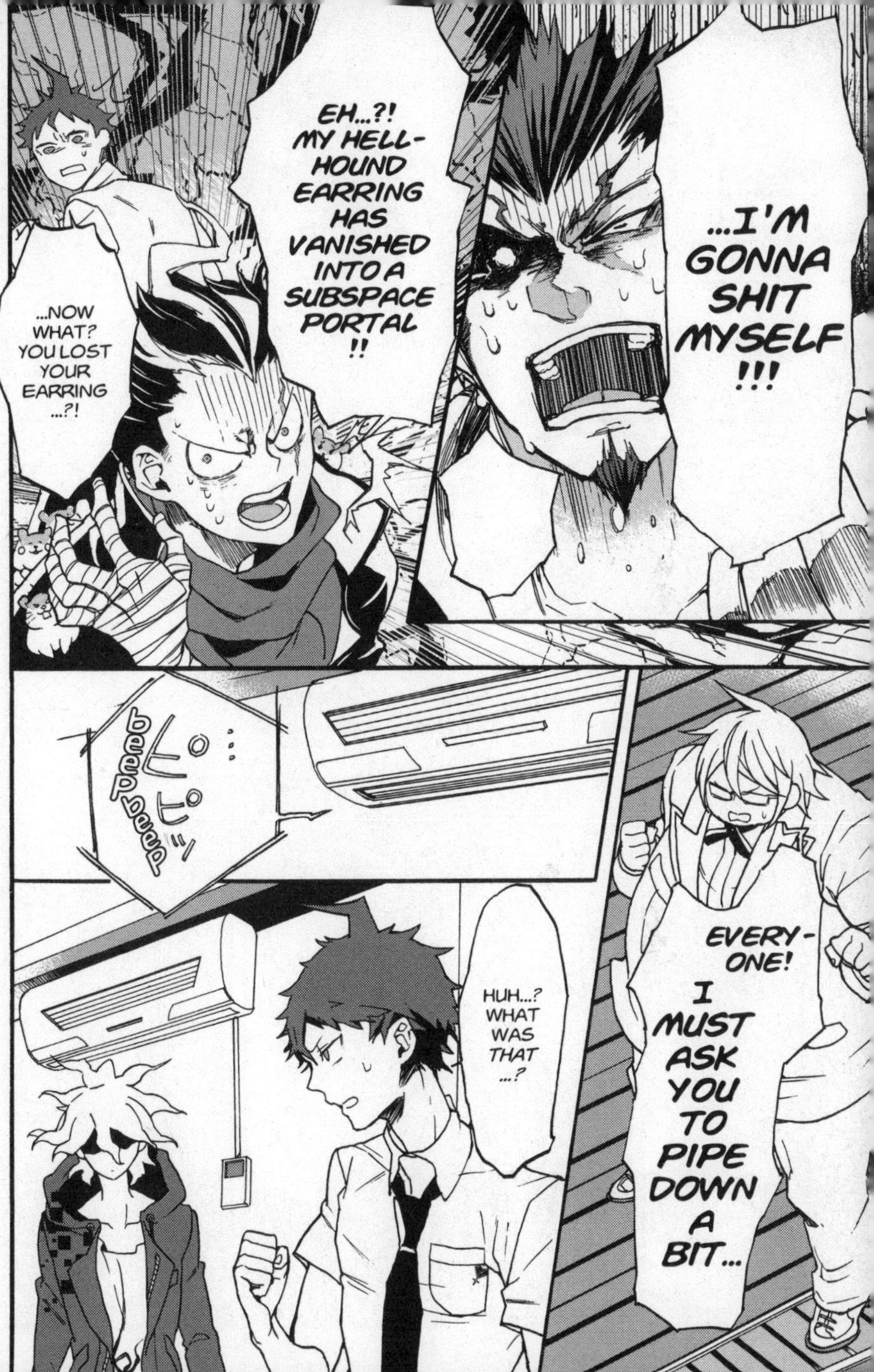
...I'M GONNA SHIT MYSELF!!!
EH...?! MY HELL-HOUND EARRING HAS VANISHED INTO A SUBSPACE PORTAL!!
...NOW WHAT? YOU LOST YOUR EARRING...?!
EVERY-ONE! I MUST ASK YOU TO PIPE DOWN A BIT...
ピピッ
beep beep
HUH...? WHAT WAS THAT...?

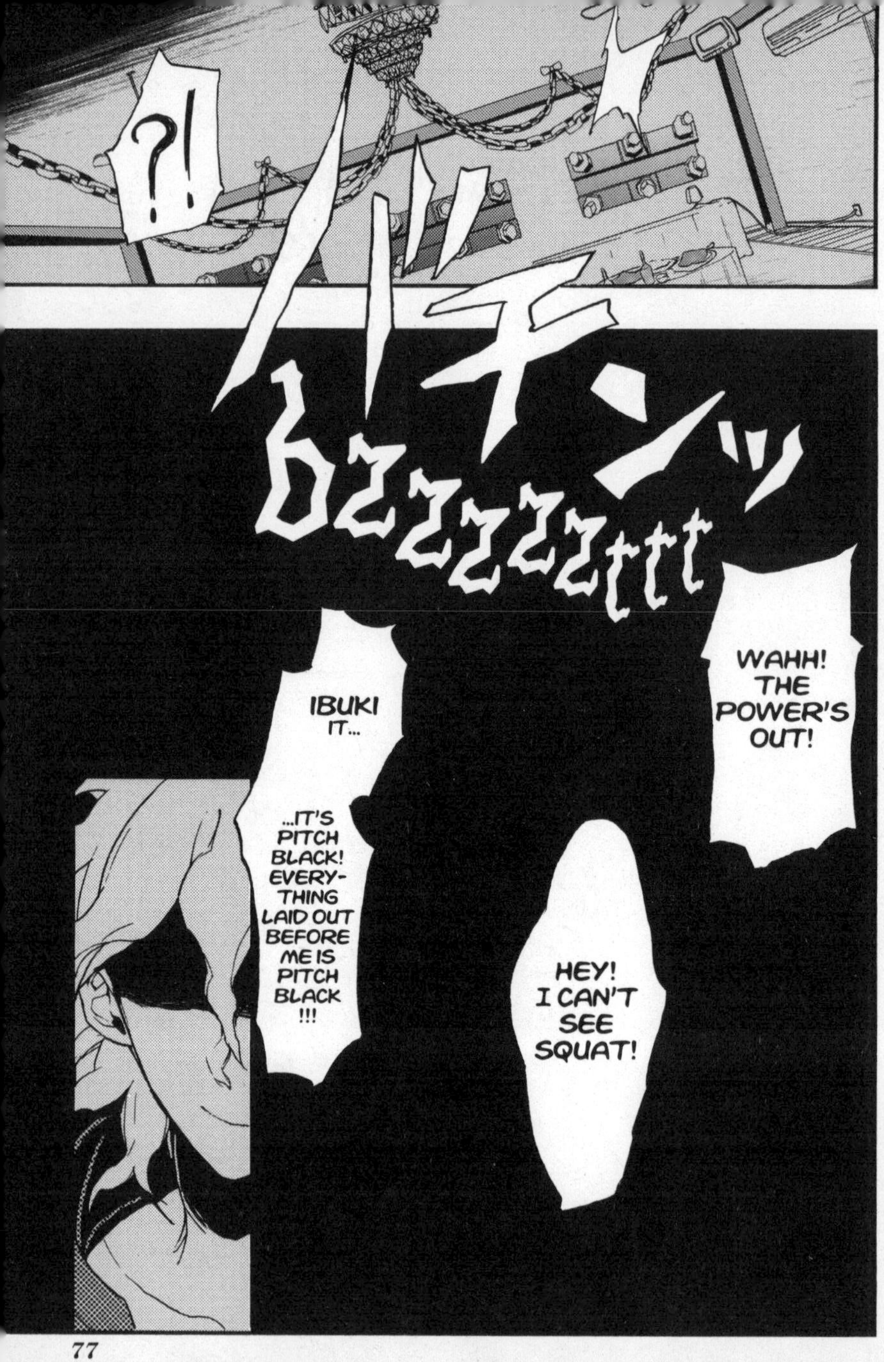
?!
bzzzzzzttt
WAHH! THE POWER'S OUT!
HEY! I CAN'T SEE SQUAT!
IBUKI IT...
...IT'S PITCH BLACK! EVERY-THING LAID OUT BEFORE ME IS PITCH BLACK !!!

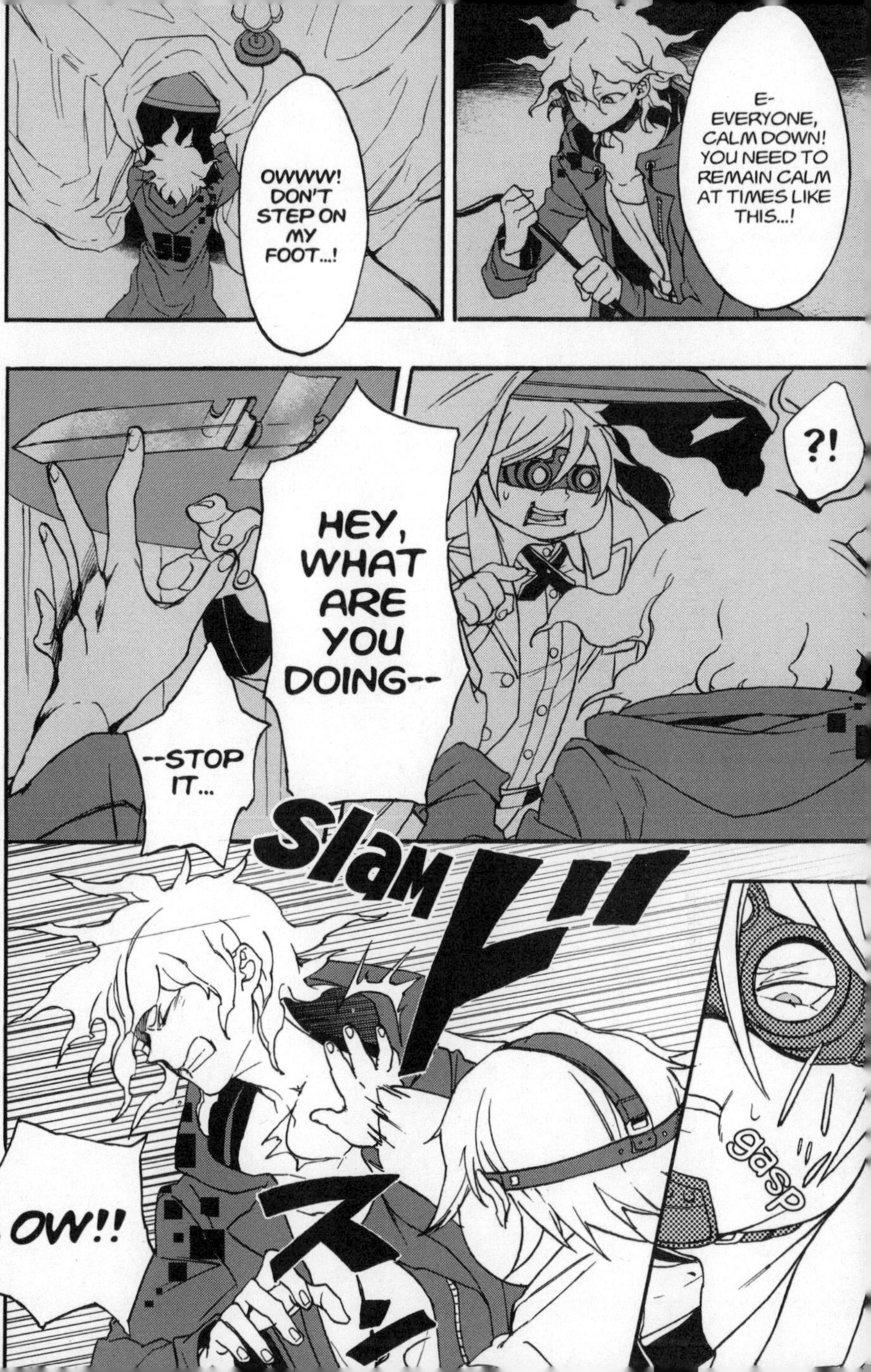
E- EVERYONE, CALM DOWN! YOU NEED TO REMAIN CALM AT TIMES LIKE THIS...!
OWWW! DON'T STEP ON MY FOOT...!
?!
HEY, WHAT ARE YOU DOING--
--STOP IT...
gasp
SLAM!!
OW!!

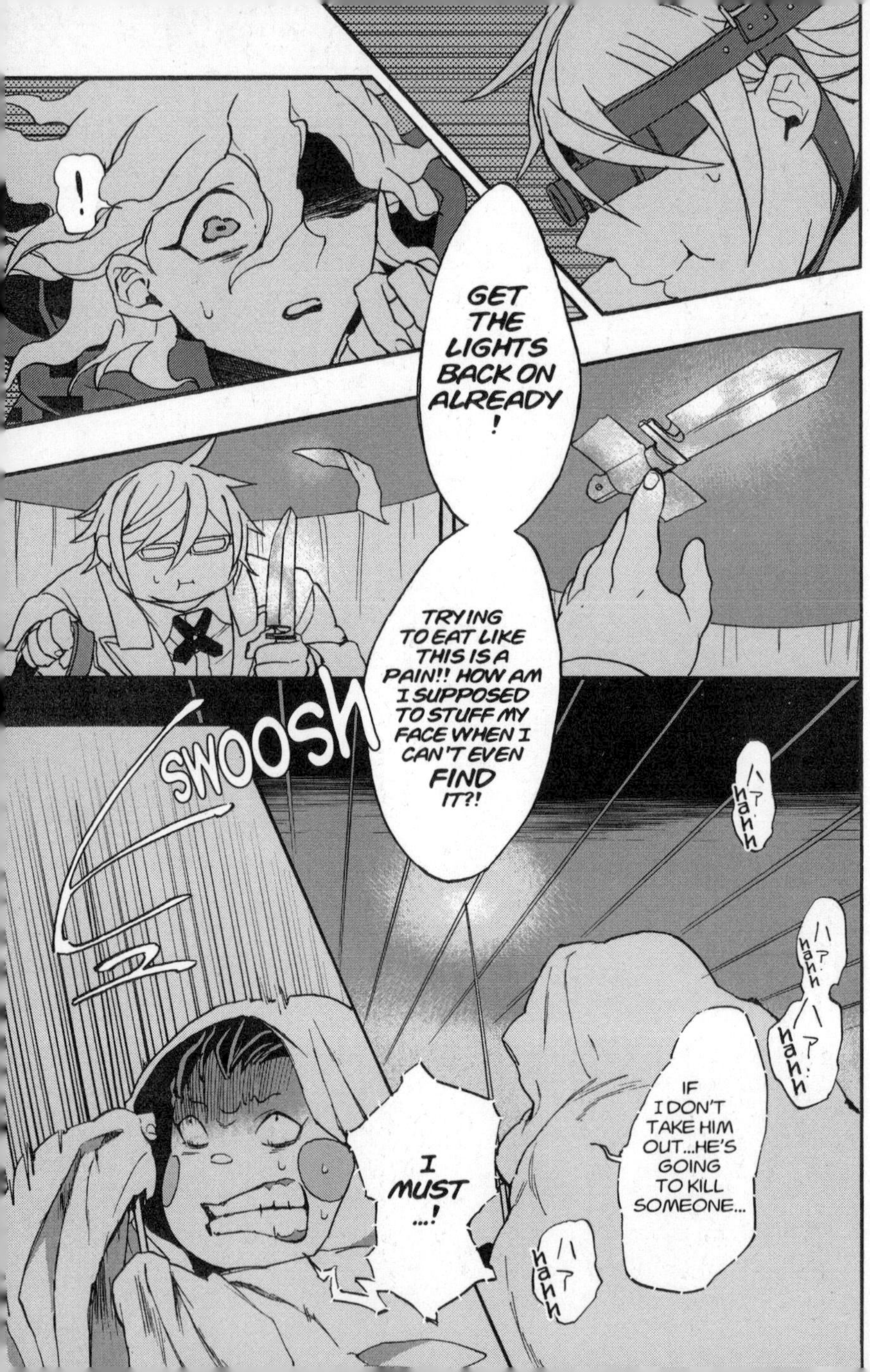
GET THE LIGHTS BACK ON ALREADY!
!
TRYING TO EAT LIKE THIS IS A PAIN!! HOW AM I SUPPOSED TO STUFF MY FACE WHEN I CAN'T EVEN FIND IT?!
SWOOSH
hahh
hahh hahh
IF I DON'T TAKE HIM OUT...HE'S GOING TO KILL SOMEONE...
I MUST...!
hahh

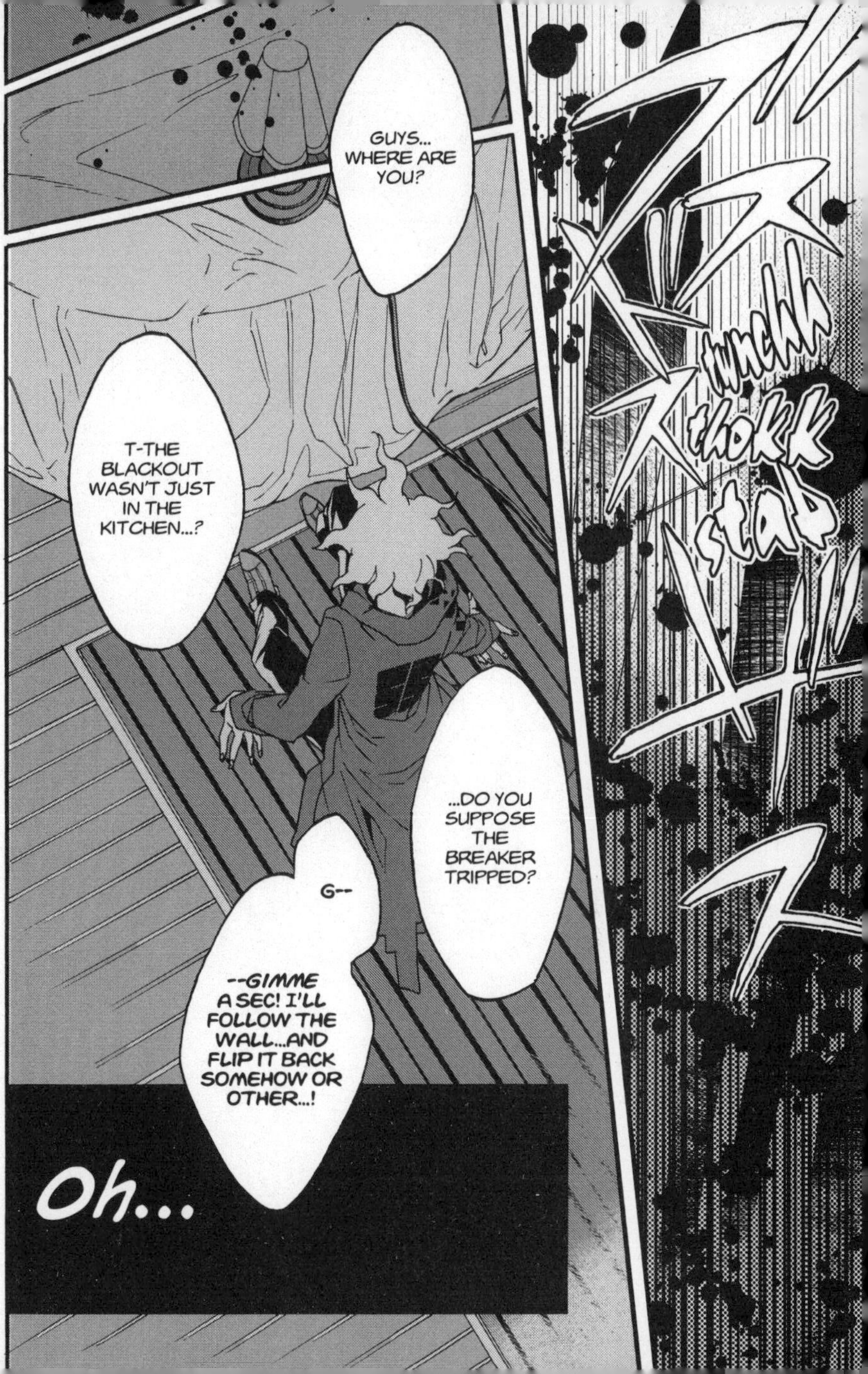
twunchh
thokk
stab
GUYS... WHERE ARE YOU?
T-THE BLACKOUT WASN'T JUST IN THE KITCHEN...?
...DO YOU SUPPOSE THE BREAKER TRIPPED?
G--
--GIMME A SEC! I'LL FOLLOW THE WALL...AND FLIP IT BACK SOMEHOW OR OTHER...!
Oh...

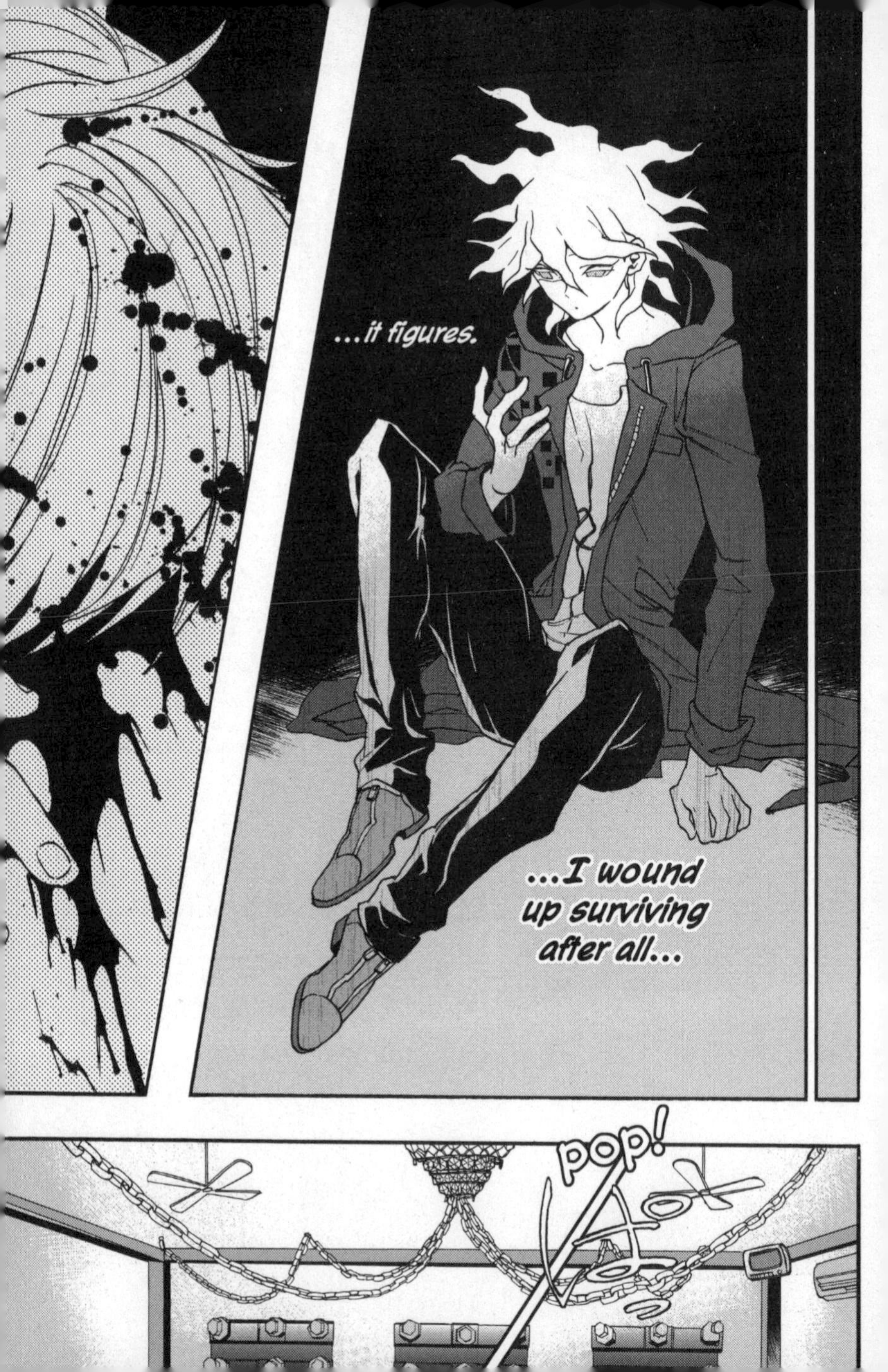
...it figures.
...I wound up surviving after all...
pop!

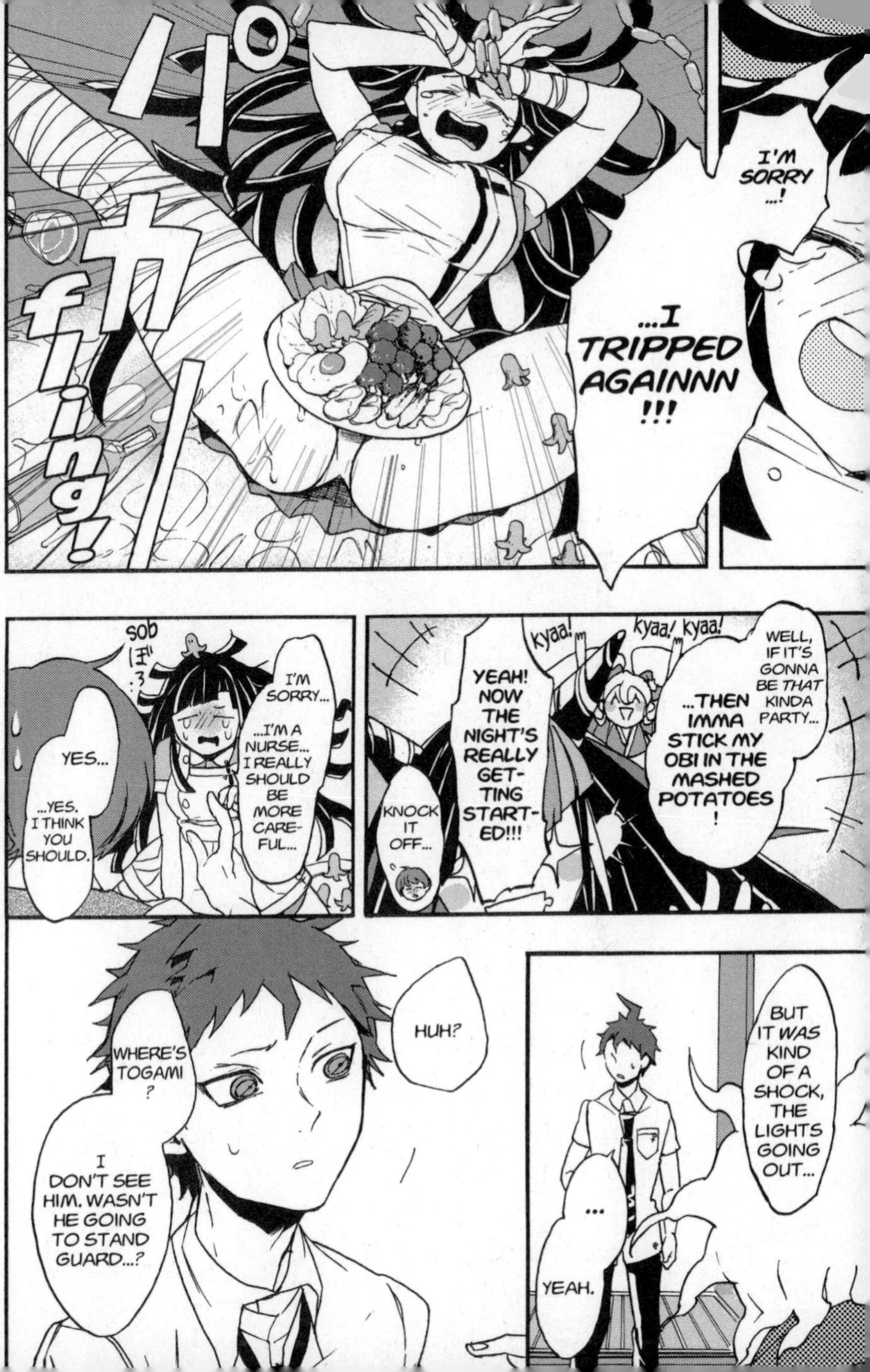
I'M SORRY ...!
...I TRIPPED AGAINNN!!!
パ
カ
fling!
WELL, IF IT'S GONNA BE *THAT* KINDA PARTY...
...THEN IMMA STICK MY OBI IN THE MASHED POTATOES!
kyaa! kyaa! kyaa!
YEAH! NOW THE NIGHT'S REALLY GETTING STARTED!!!
KNOCK IT OFF...
sob
I'M SORRY...
...I'M A NURSE... I REALLY SHOULD BE MORE CAREFUL...
YES...
...YES. I THINK YOU SHOULD.
BUT IT *WAS* KIND OF A SHOCK, THE LIGHTS GOING OUT...
...
YEAH.
HUH?
WHERE'S TOGAMI?
I DON'T SEE HIM. WASN'T HE GOING TO STAND GUARD...?

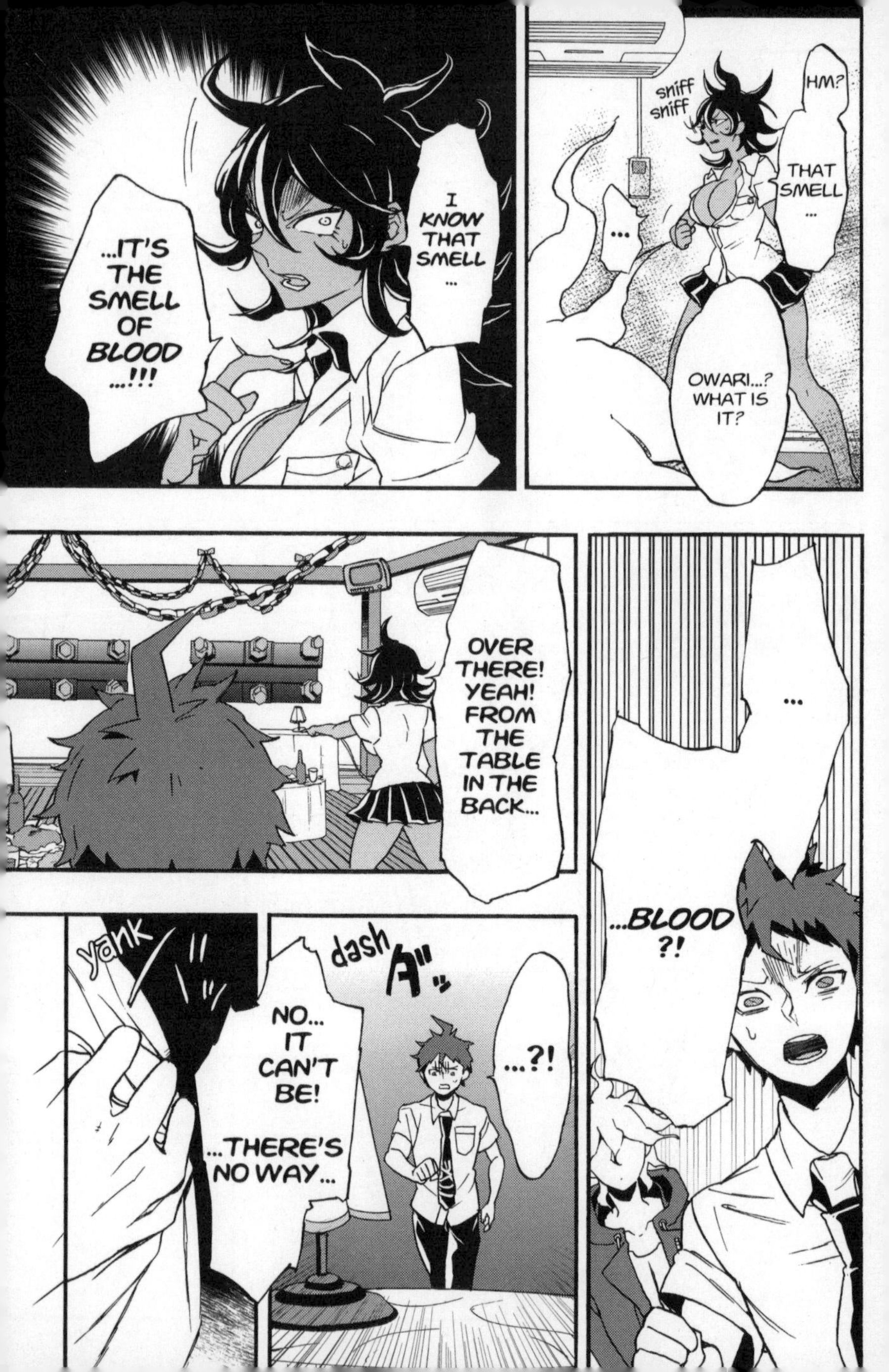
HM?
sniff sniff
THAT SMELL ...
...
OWARI...? WHAT IS IT?
I KNOW THAT SMELL ...
...IT'S THE SMELL OF BLOOD ...!!!
...
...BLOOD ?!
OVER THERE! YEAH! FROM THE TABLE IN THE BACK...
dash
...?!
yank
NO... IT CAN'T BE!
...THERE'S NO WAY...

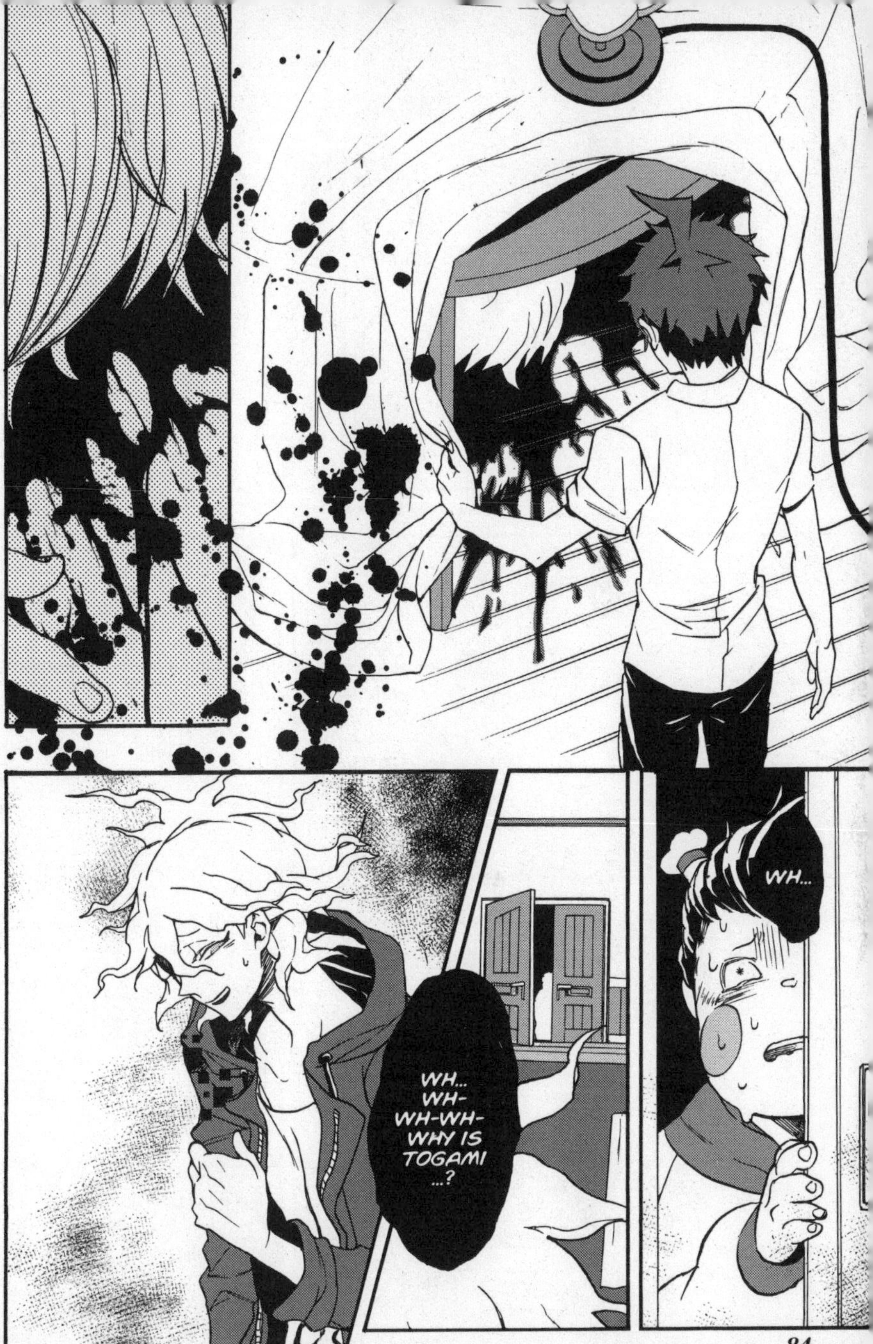
WH...
WH... WH- WH-WH- WHY IS TOGAMI ...?

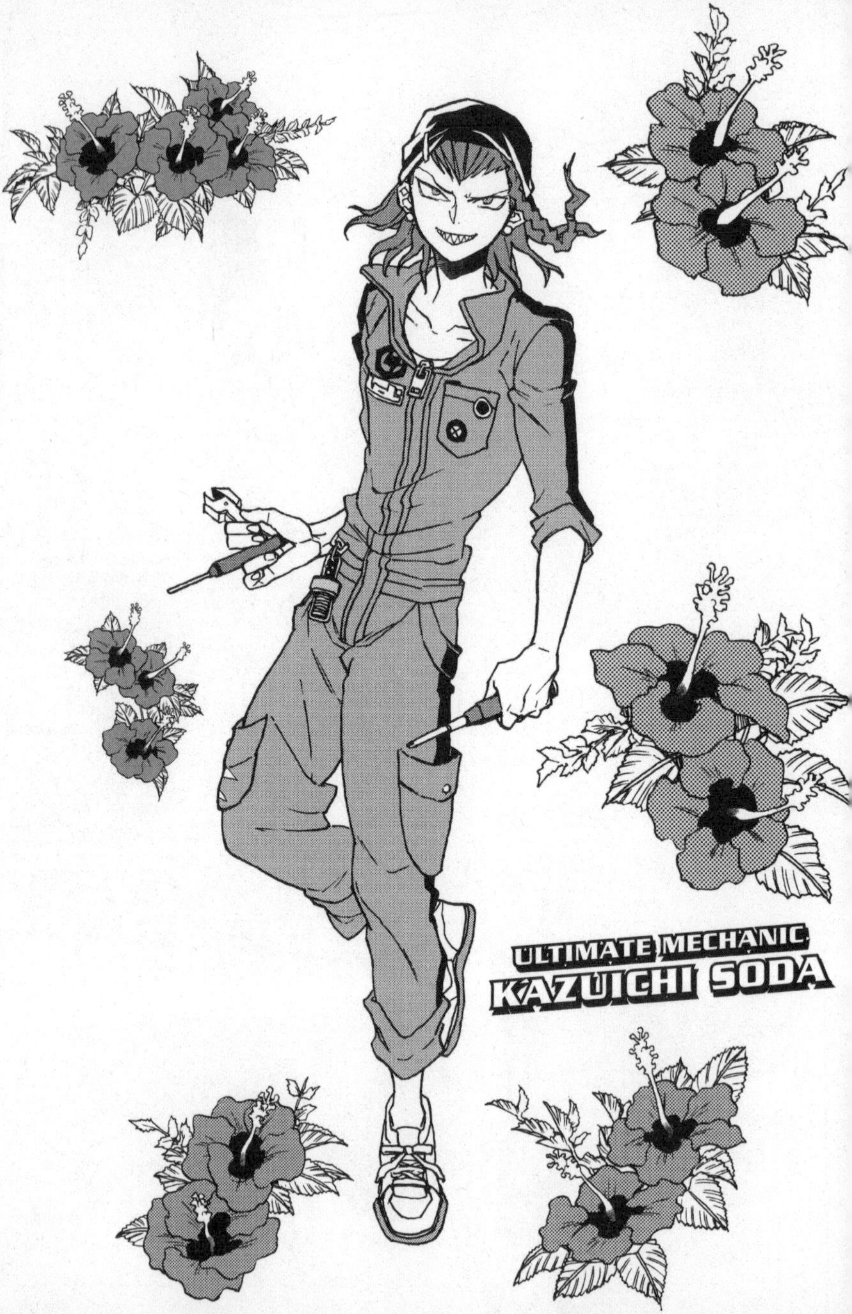
ULTIMATE MECHANIC
KAZUICHI SODA

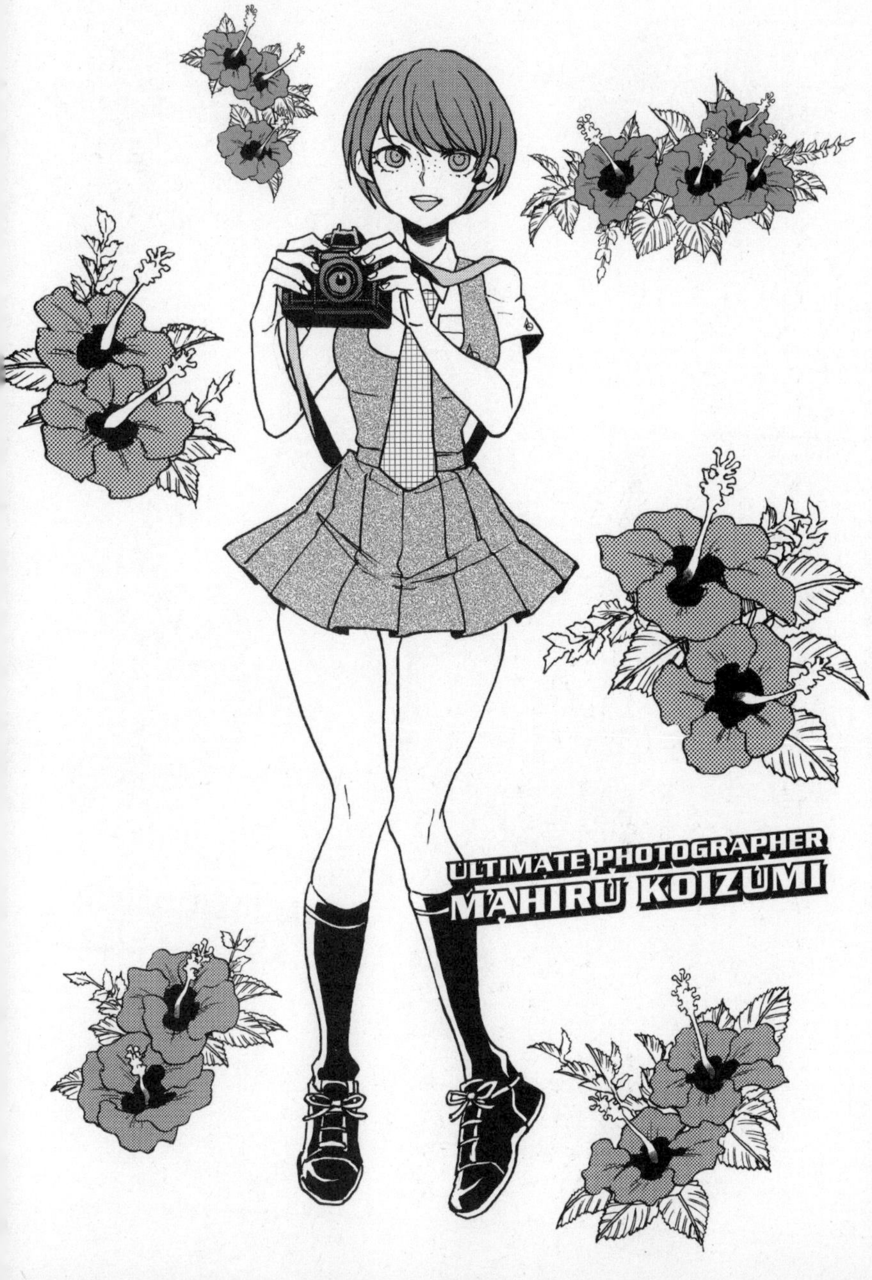
ULTIMATE PHOTOGRAPHER
MAHIRU KOIZUMI

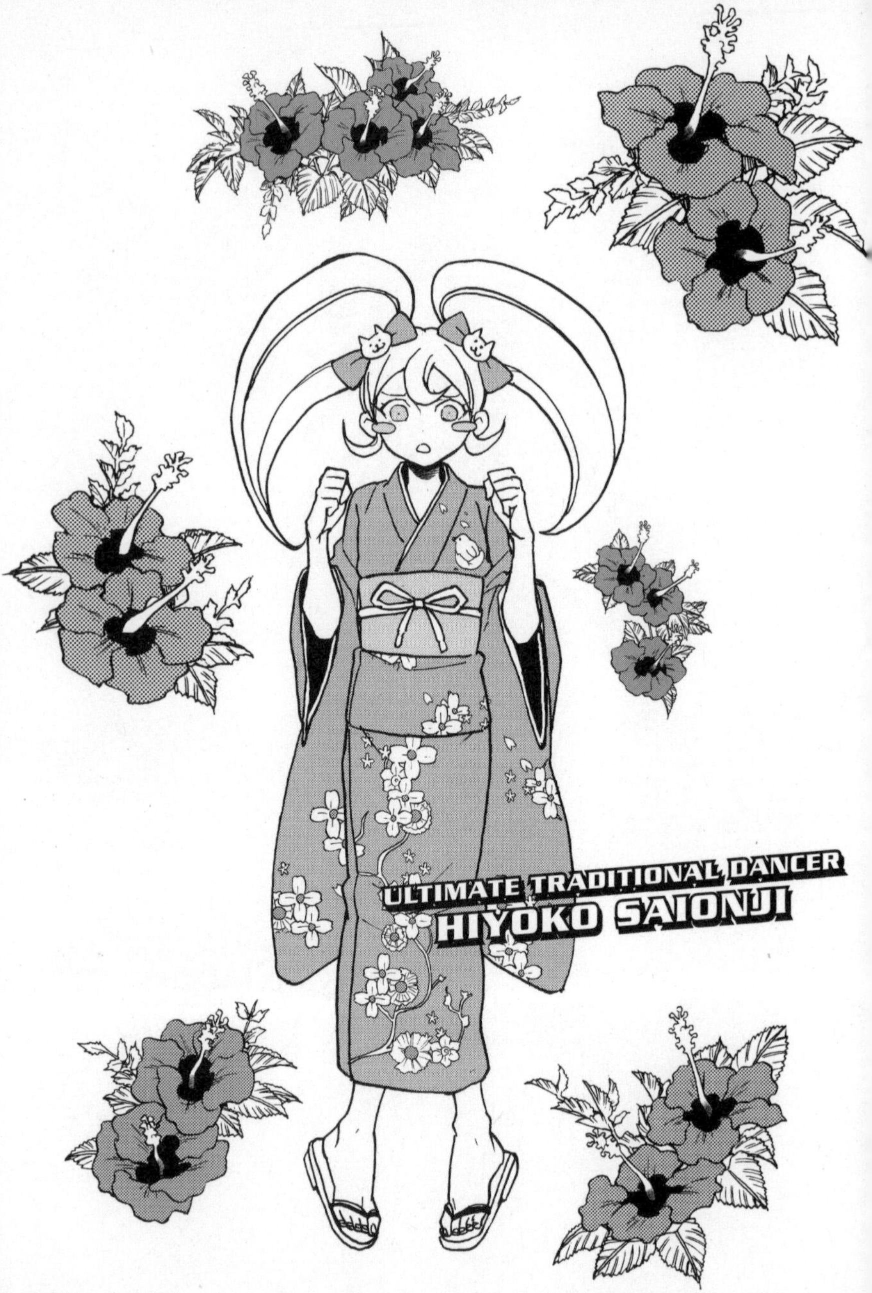
ULTIMATE TRADITIONAL DANCER
HIYOKO SAIONJI

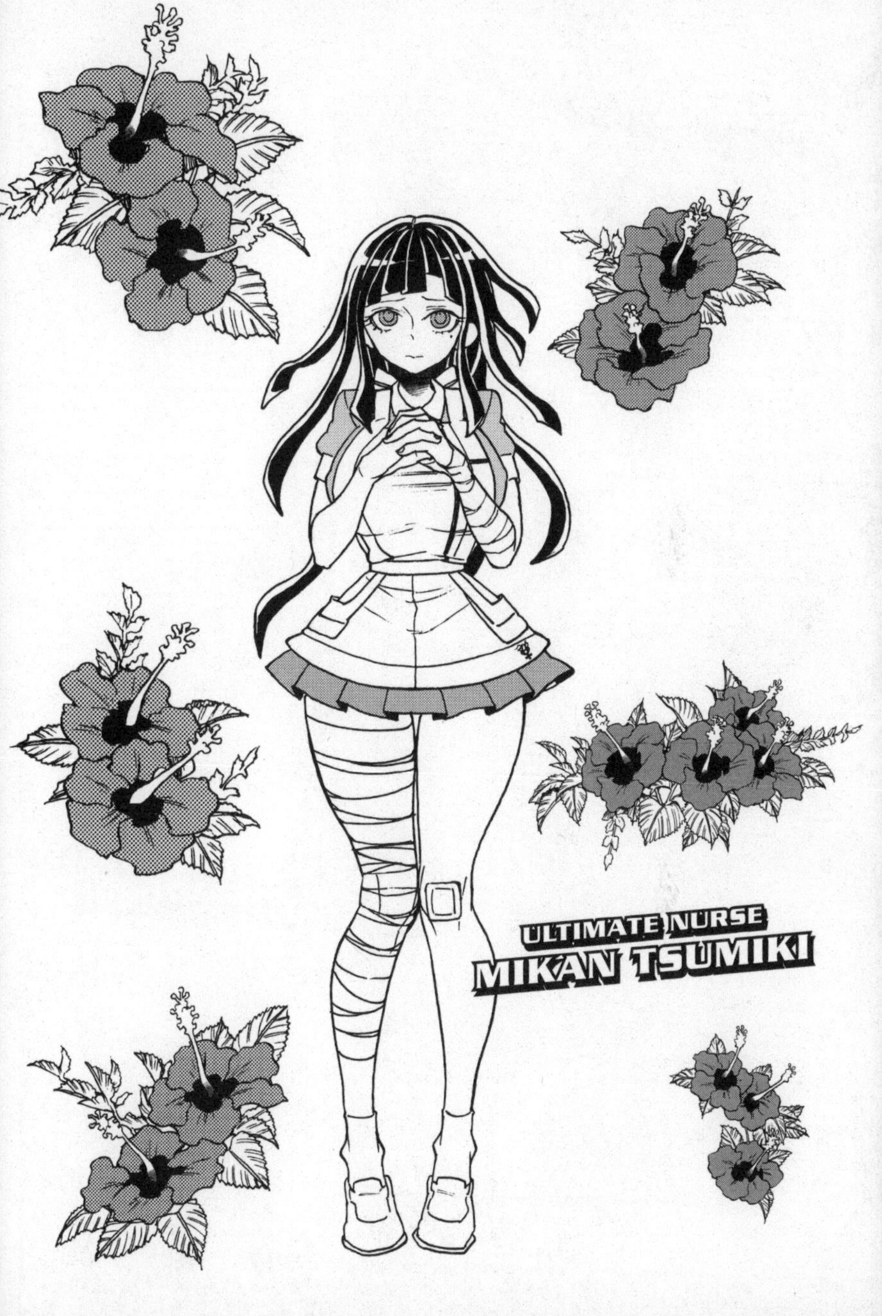
ULTIMATE NURSE
MIKAN TSUMIKI

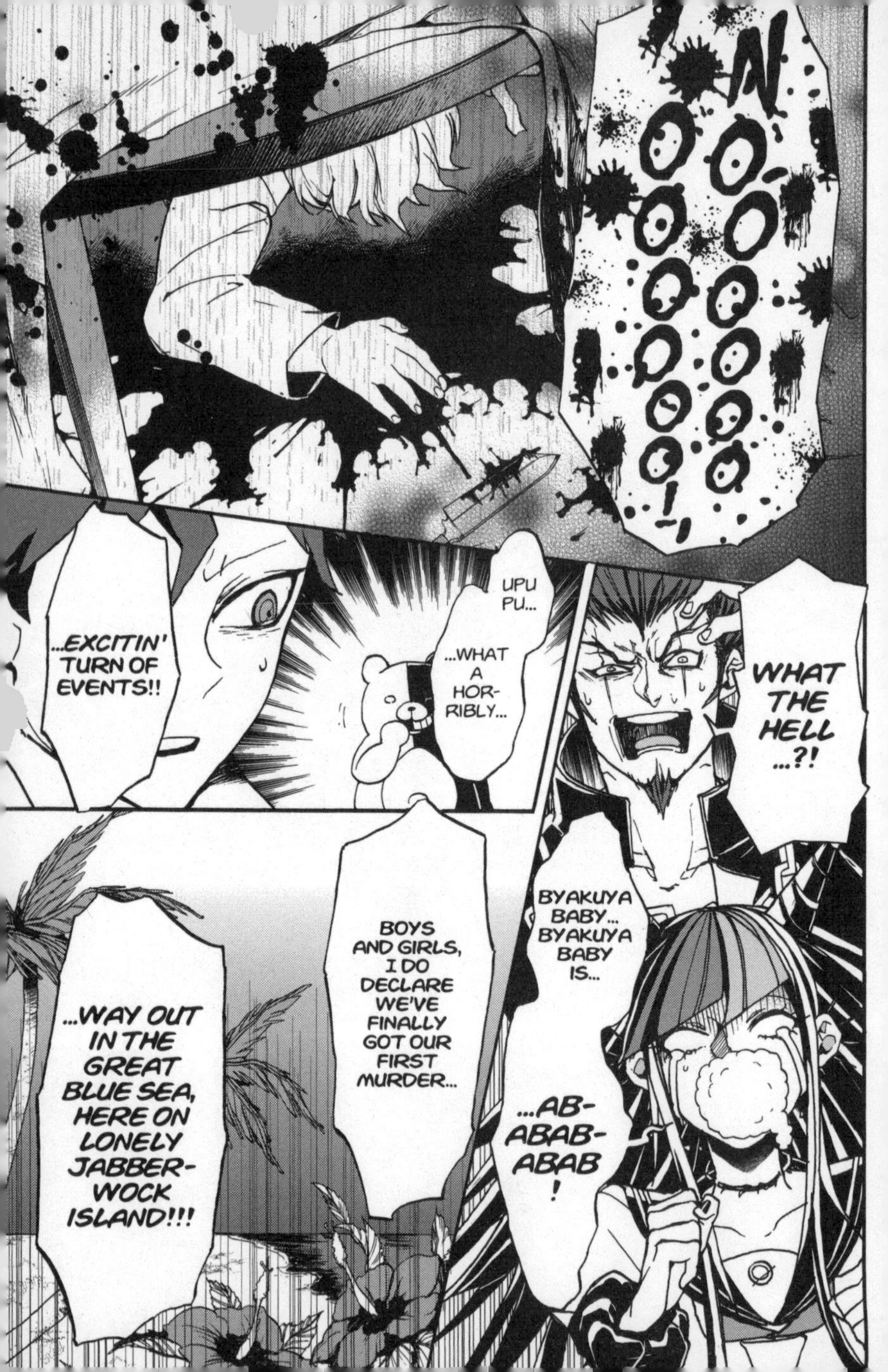
NOOOOOOOOOOOOOOO-!
WHAT THE HELL ...?!
UPU PU...
...WHAT A HORRIBLY...
...EXCITIN' TURN OF EVENTS!!
BYAKUYA BABY... BYAKUYA BABY IS...
...AB-ABAB-ABAB!
BOYS AND GIRLS, I DO DECLARE WE'VE FINALLY GOT OUR FIRST MURDER...
...WAY OUT IN THE GREAT BLUE SEA, HERE ON LONELY JABBERWOCK ISLAND!!!

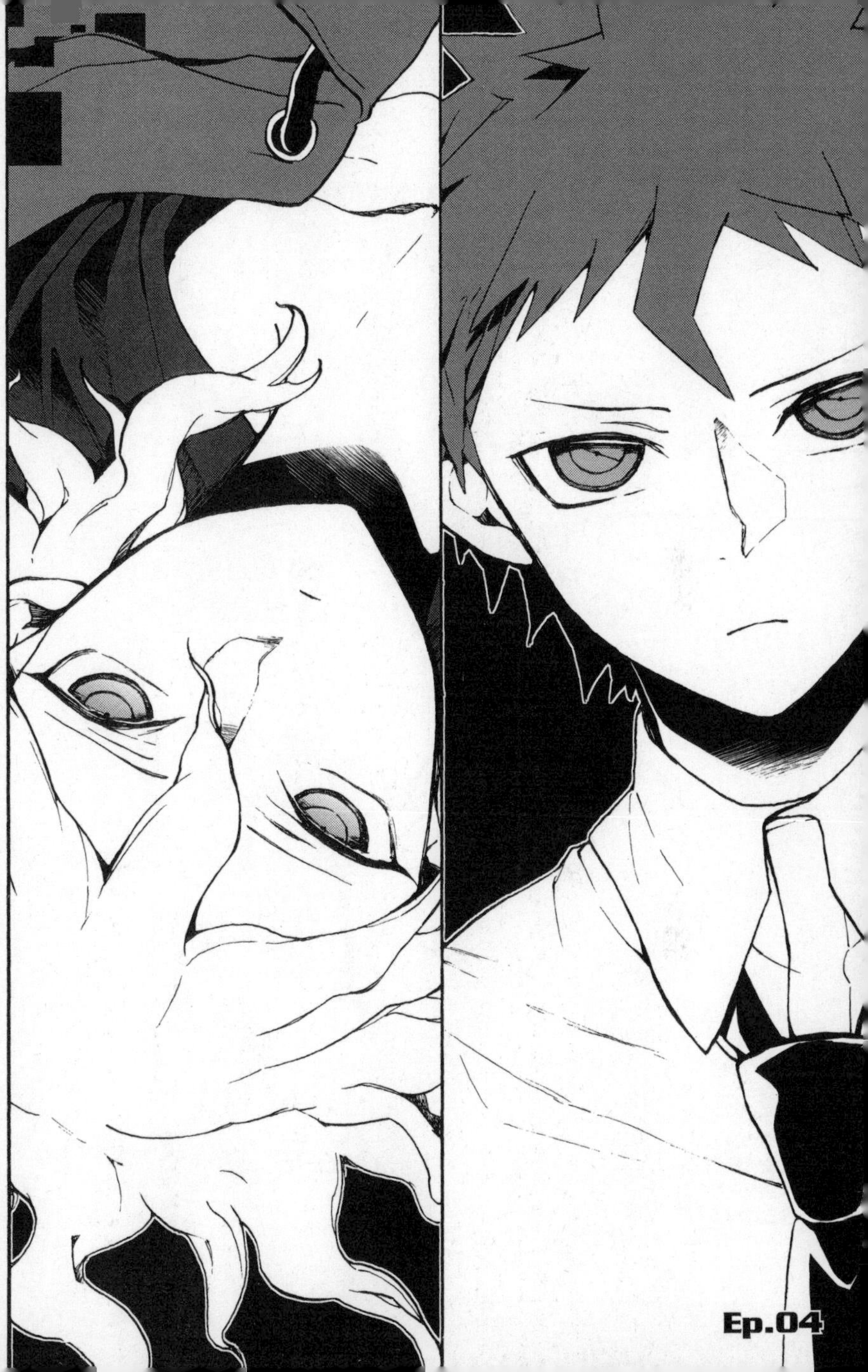
Ep.04

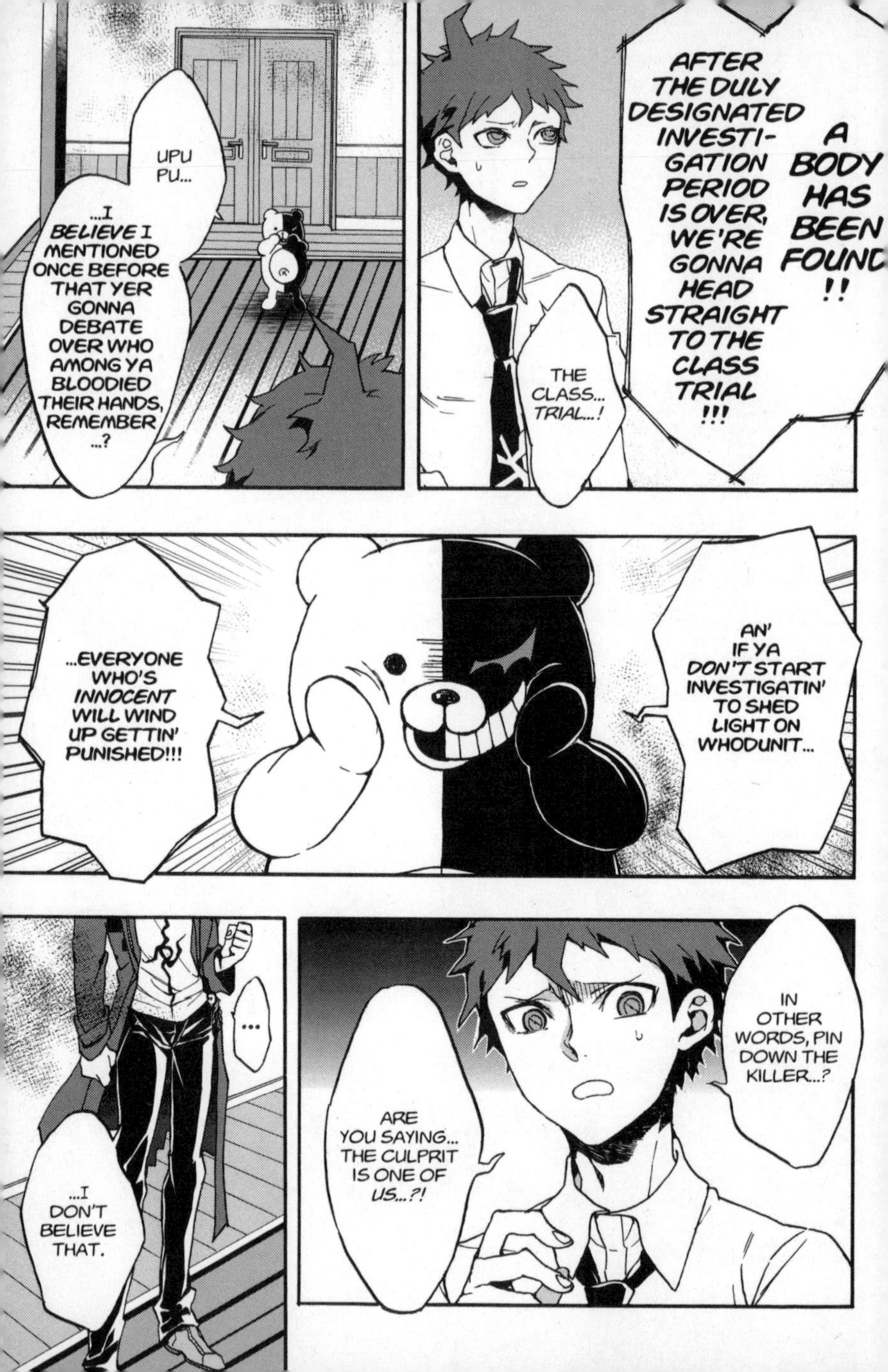
A BODY HAS BEEN FOUND!!
AFTER THE DULY DESIGNATED INVESTIGATION PERIOD IS OVER, WE'RE GONNA HEAD STRAIGHT TO THE CLASS TRIAL!!!
THE CLASS... TRIAL...!
UPU PU...
...I BELIEVE I MENTIONED ONCE BEFORE THAT YER GONNA DEBATE OVER WHO AMONG YA BLOODIED THEIR HANDS, REMEMBER...?
AN' IF YA DON'T START INVESTIGATIN' TO SHED LIGHT ON WHODUNIT...
...EVERYONE WHO'S INNOCENT WILL WIND UP GETTIN' PUNISHED!!!
IN OTHER WORDS, PIN DOWN THE KILLER...?
ARE YOU SAYING... THE CULPRIT IS ONE OF US...?!
...
...I DON'T BELIEVE THAT.

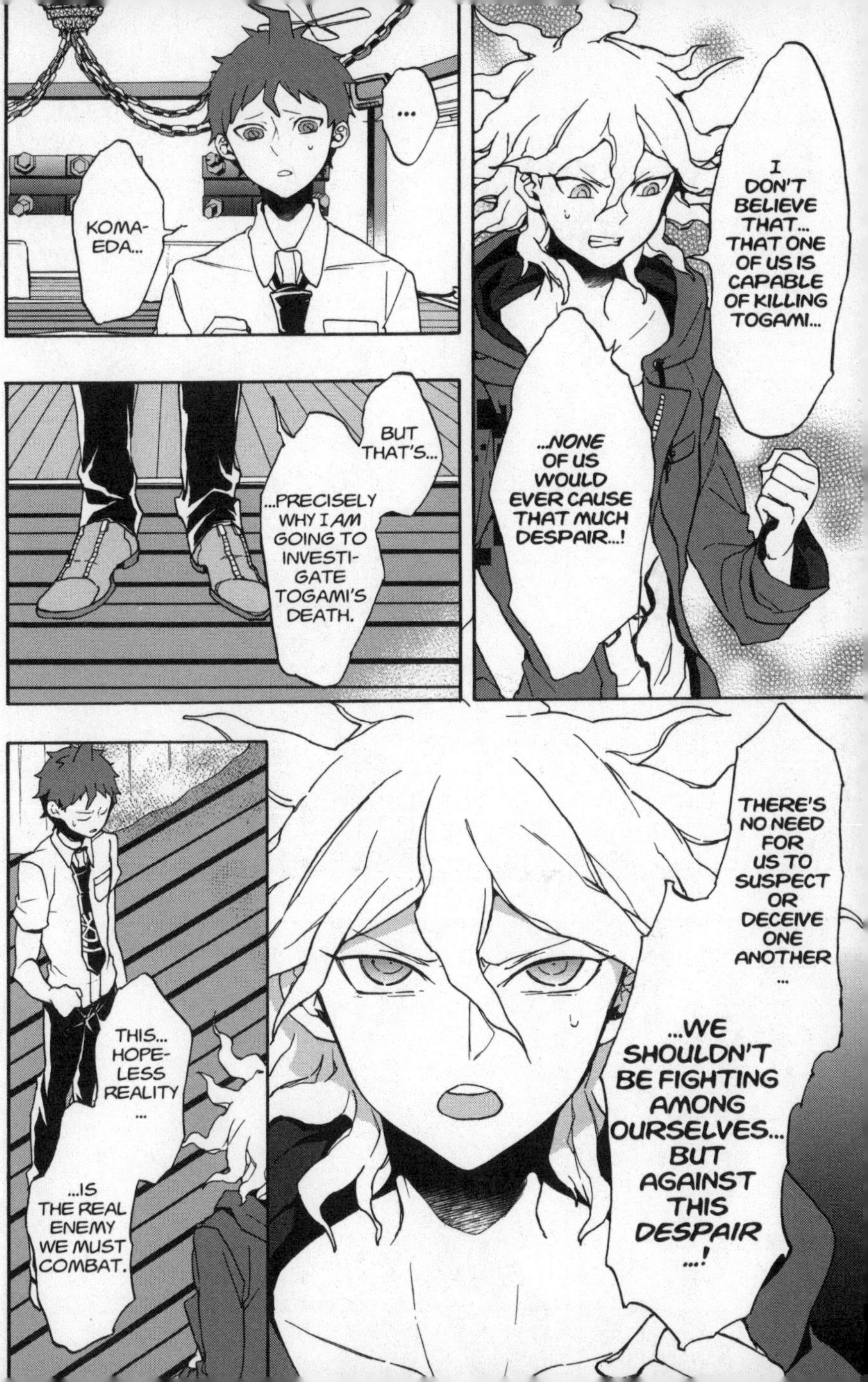
I DON'T BELIEVE THAT... THAT ONE OF US IS CAPABLE OF KILLING TOGAMI...
...NONE OF US WOULD EVER CAUSE THAT MUCH DESPAIR...!
...
KOMA-EDA...
BUT THAT'S...
...PRECISELY WHY I AM GOING TO INVESTI-GATE TOGAMI'S DEATH.
THERE'S NO NEED FOR US TO SUSPECT OR DECEIVE ONE ANOTHER...
...WE SHOULDN'T BE FIGHTING AMONG OURSELVES... BUT AGAINST THIS DESPAIR...!
THIS... HOPE-LESS REALITY...
...IS THE REAL ENEMY WE MUST COMBAT.

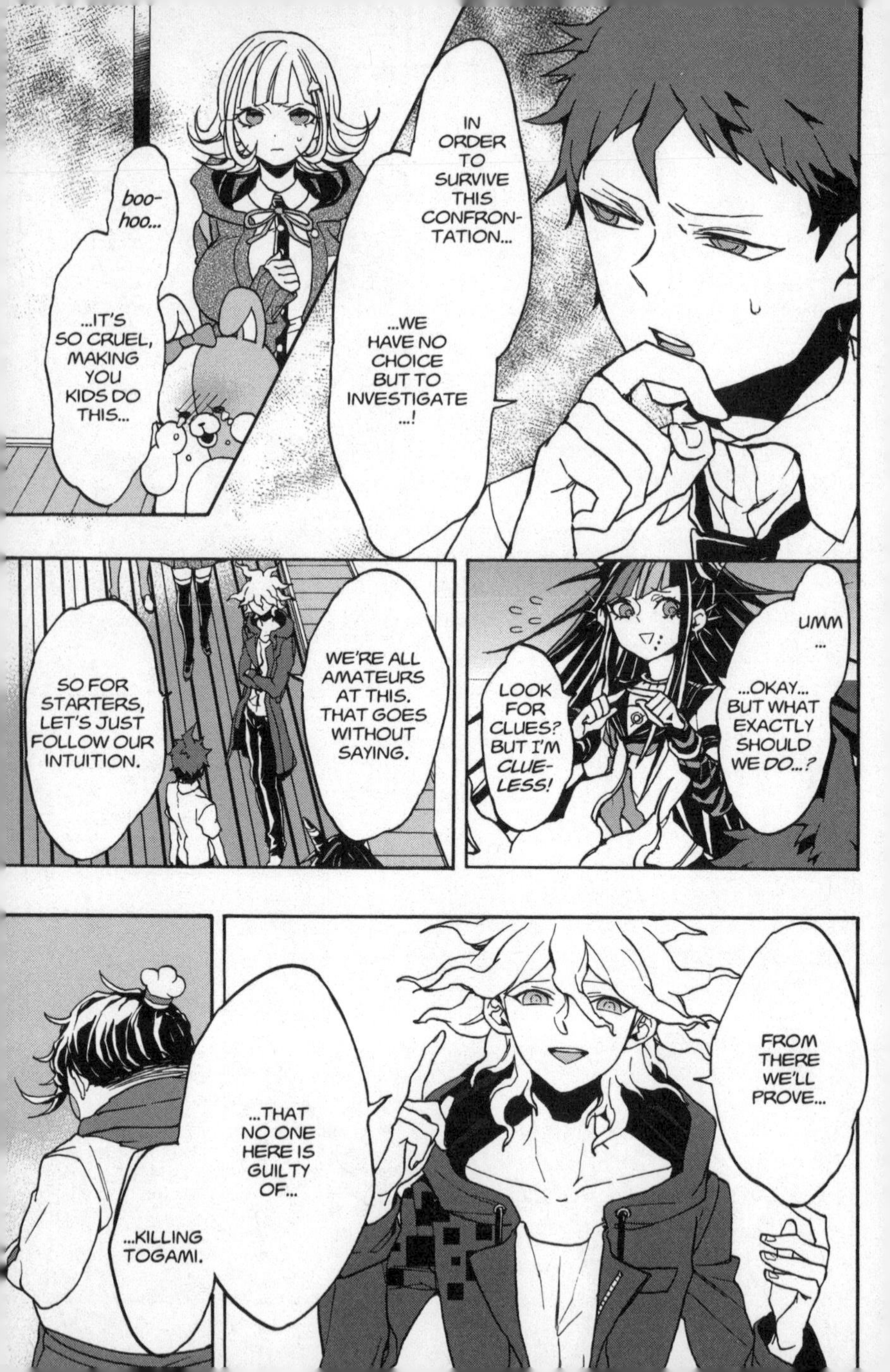
IN ORDER TO SURVIVE THIS CONFRONTATION...
...WE HAVE NO CHOICE BUT TO INVESTIGATE ...!
boo-hoo...
...IT'S SO CRUEL, MAKING YOU KIDS DO THIS...
UMM ...
...OKAY... BUT WHAT EXACTLY SHOULD WE DO...?
LOOK FOR CLUES? BUT I'M CLUELESS!
WE'RE ALL AMATEURS AT THIS. THAT GOES WITHOUT SAYING.
SO FOR STARTERS, LET'S JUST FOLLOW OUR INTUITION.
FROM THERE WE'LL PROVE...
...THAT NO ONE HERE IS GUILTY OF...
...KILLING TOGAMI.

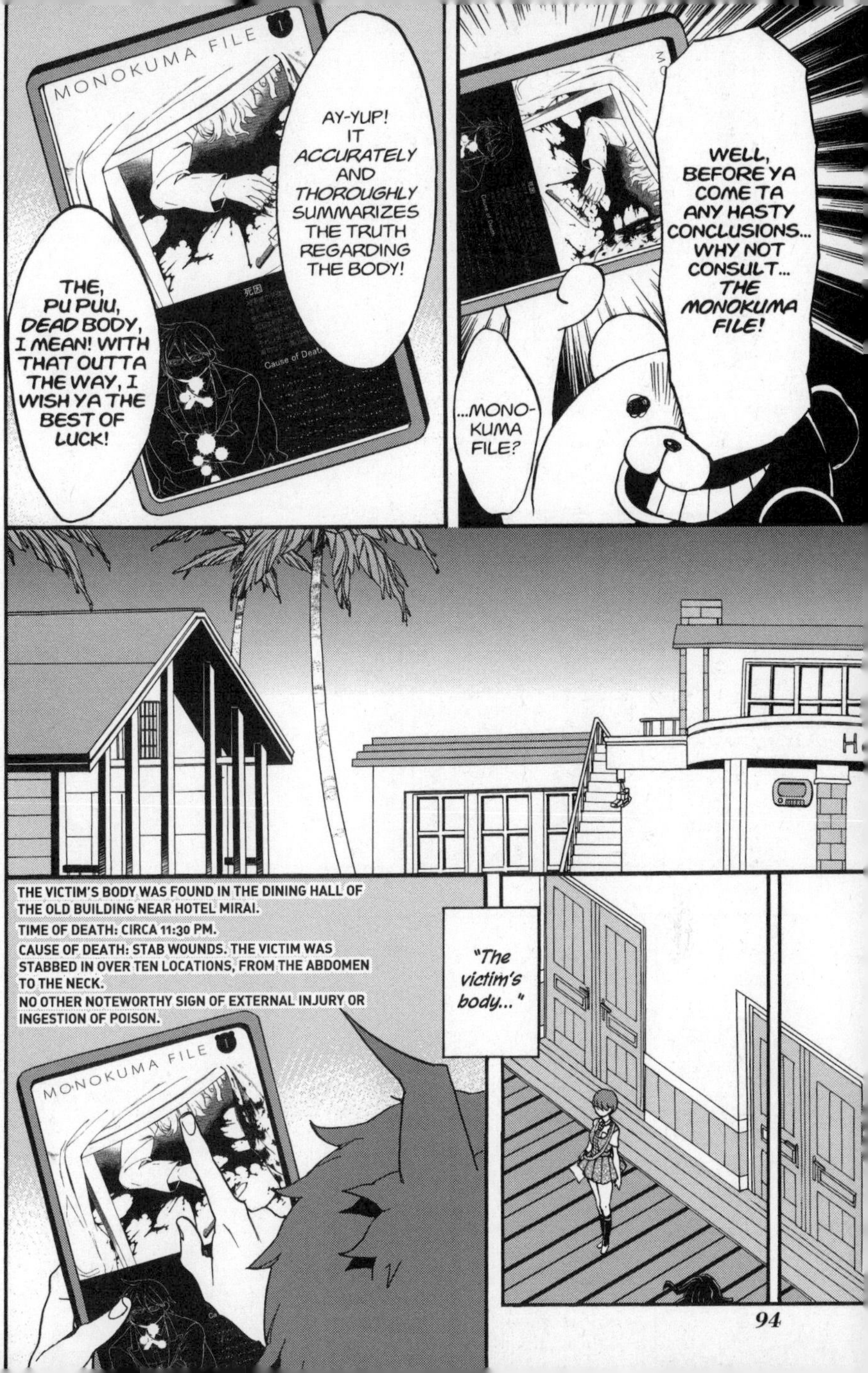

WELL, BEFORE YA COME TA ANY HASTY CONCLUSIONS... WHY NOT CONSULT... *THE MONOKUMA FILE!*
...MONO-KUMA FILE?
MONOKUMA FILE
AY-YUP! IT *ACCURATELY* AND *THOROUGHLY* SUMMARIZES THE TRUTH REGARDING THE BODY!
THE, PU PUU, *DEAD BODY,* I MEAN! WITH THAT OUTTA THE WAY, I WISH YA THE BEST OF LUCK!
"The victim's body..."
THE VICTIM'S BODY WAS FOUND IN THE DINING HALL OF THE OLD BUILDING NEAR HOTEL MIRAI.
TIME OF DEATH: CIRCA 11:30 PM.
CAUSE OF DEATH: STAB WOUNDS. THE VICTIM WAS STABBED IN OVER TEN LOCATIONS, FROM THE ABDOMEN TO THE NECK.
NO OTHER NOTEWORTHY SIGN OF EXTERNAL INJURY OR INGESTION OF POISON.
MONOKUMA FILE

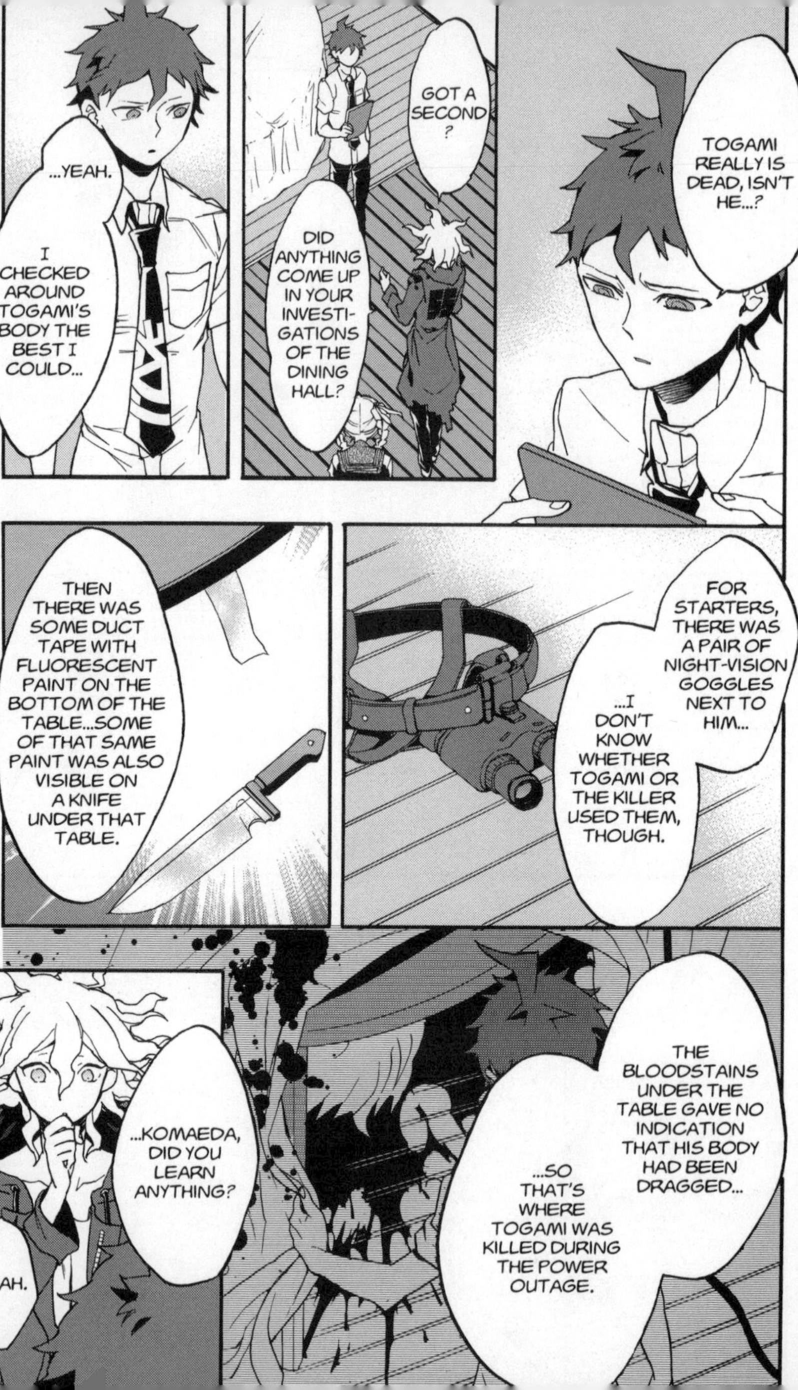
TOGAMI REALLY IS DEAD, ISN'T HE...?
GOT A SECOND?
DID ANYTHING COME UP IN YOUR INVESTIGATIONS OF THE DINING HALL?
...YEAH.
I CHECKED AROUND TOGAMI'S BODY THE BEST I COULD...
FOR STARTERS, THERE WAS A PAIR OF NIGHT-VISION GOGGLES NEXT TO HIM...
...I DON'T KNOW WHETHER TOGAMI OR THE KILLER USED THEM, THOUGH.
THEN THERE WAS SOME DUCT TAPE WITH FLUORESCENT PAINT ON THE BOTTOM OF THE TABLE...SOME OF THAT SAME PAINT WAS ALSO VISIBLE ON A KNIFE UNDER THAT TABLE.
THE BLOODSTAINS UNDER THE TABLE GAVE NO INDICATION THAT HIS BODY HAD BEEN DRAGGED...
...SO THAT'S WHERE TOGAMI WAS KILLED DURING THE POWER OUTAGE.
...KOMAEDA, DID YOU LEARN ANYTHING?
...YEAH.

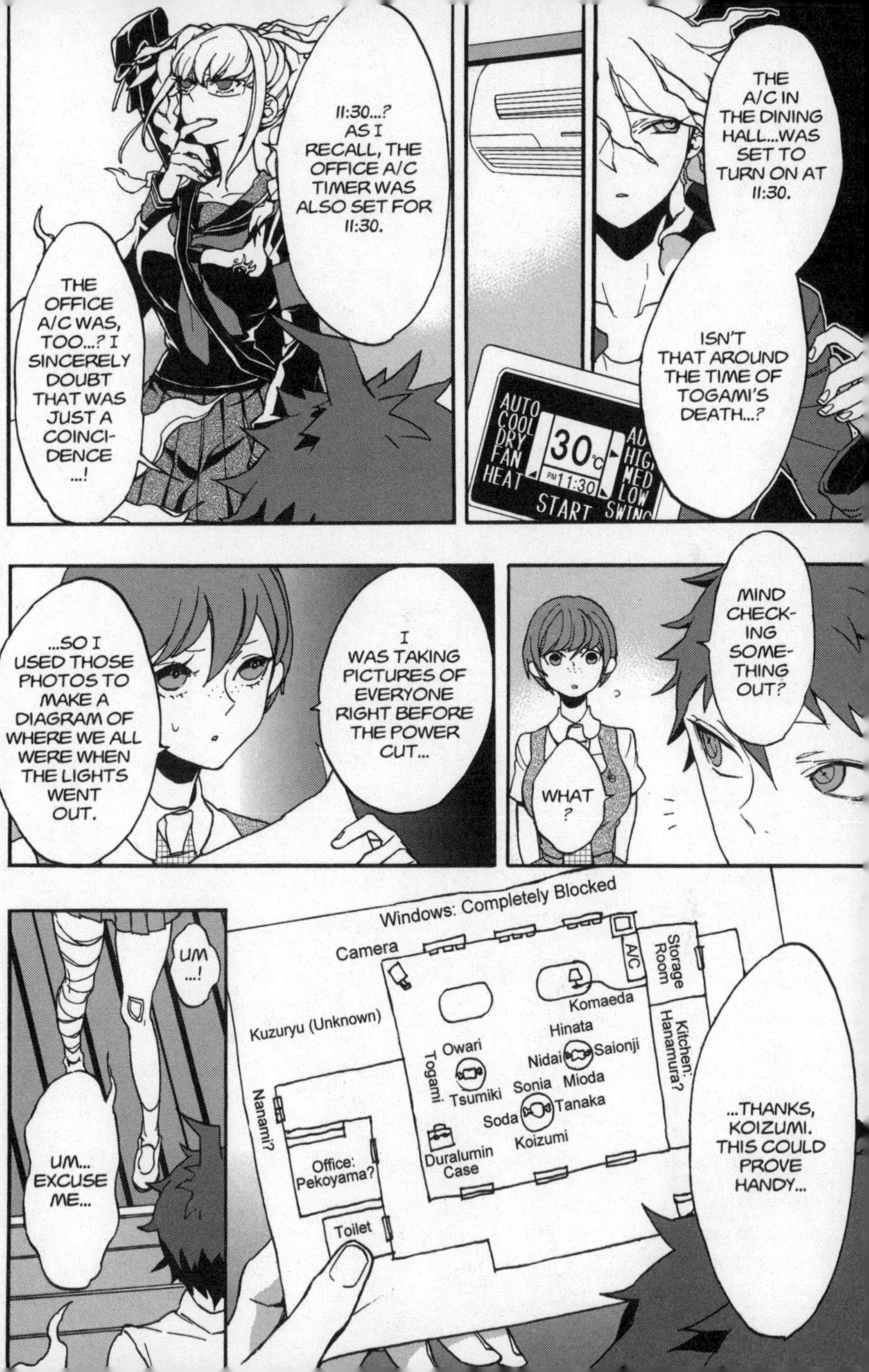
THE A/C IN THE DINING HALL...WAS SET TO TURN ON AT 11:30.
AUTO COOL DRY FAN HEAT
30°C
PM 11:30
START
ISN'T THAT AROUND THE TIME OF TOGAMI'S DEATH...?
11:30...? AS I RECALL, THE OFFICE A/C TIMER WAS ALSO SET FOR 11:30.
THE OFFICE A/C WAS, TOO...? I SINCERELY DOUBT THAT WAS JUST A COINCIDENCE...!
MIND CHECKING SOMETHING OUT?
WHAT?
I WAS TAKING PICTURES OF EVERYONE RIGHT BEFORE THE POWER CUT...
...SO I USED THOSE PHOTOS TO MAKE A DIAGRAM OF WHERE WE ALL WERE WHEN THE LIGHTS WENT OUT.
...THANKS, KOIZUMI. THIS COULD PROVE HANDY...
Windows: Completely Blocked
Camera
A/C
Storage Room
Komaeda
Kitchen: Hanamura?
Kuzuryu (Unknown)
Hinata
Owari
Nidai
Saionji
Togami
Tsumiki
Sonia
Mioda
Tanaka
Soda
Koizumi
Nanami?
Duralumin Case
Office: Pekoyama?
Toilet
UM...!
UM... EXCUSE ME...

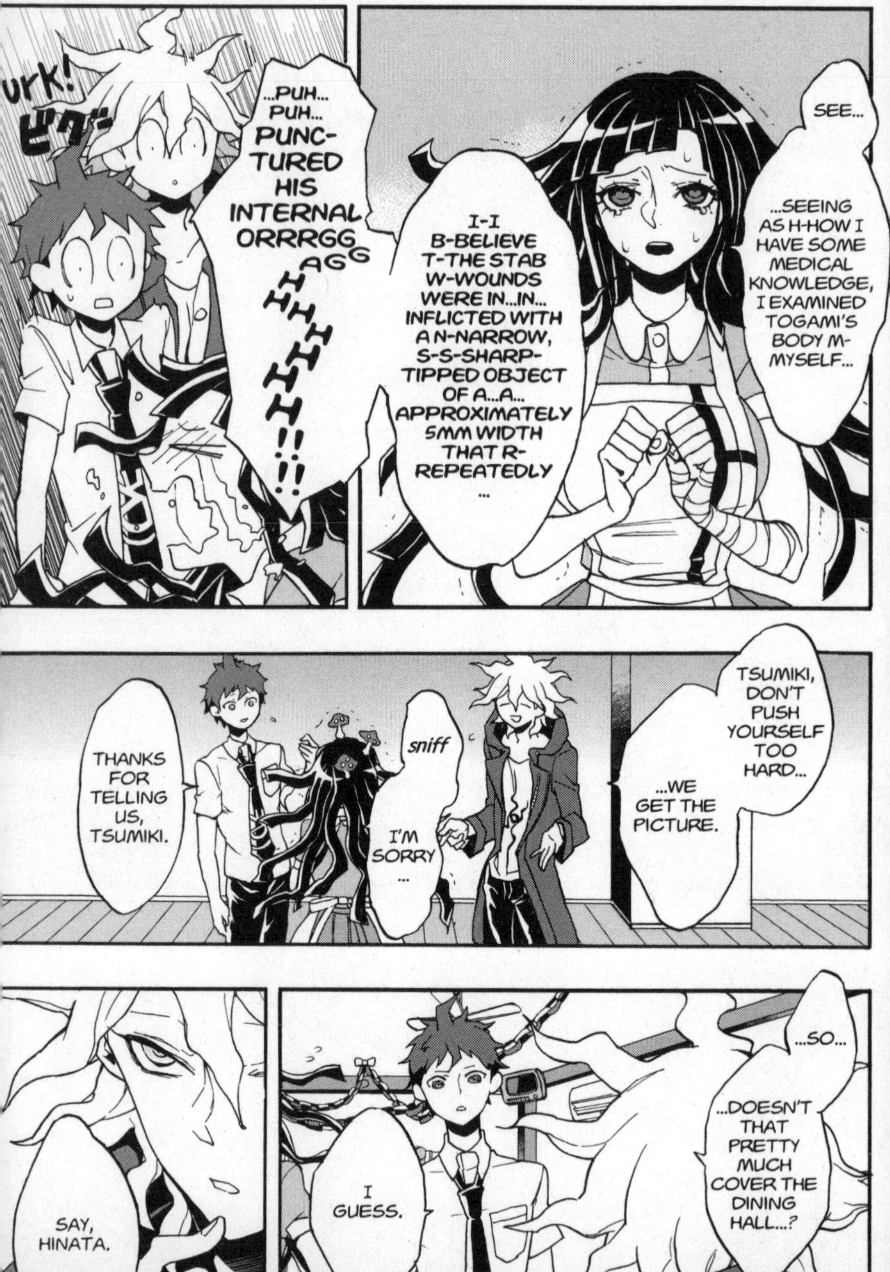
SEE...
...SEEING AS H-HOW I HAVE SOME MEDICAL KNOWLEDGE, I EXAMINED TOGAMI'S BODY M-MYSELF...
I-I B-BELIEVE T-THE STAB W-WOUNDS WERE IN...IN... INFLICTED WITH A N-NARROW, S-S-SHARP-TIPPED OBJECT OF A...A... APPROXIMATELY 5MM WIDTH THAT R-REPEATEDLY ...
...PUH... PUH... PUNCTURED HIS INTERNAL ORRRGGGAGHHHHHHH!!!
urk!
TSUMIKI, DON'T PUSH YOURSELF TOO HARD...
...WE GET THE PICTURE.
sniff
I'M SORRY ...
THANKS FOR TELLING US, TSUMIKI.
...SO...
...DOESN'T THAT PRETTY MUCH COVER THE DINING HALL...?
I GUESS.
SAY, HINATA.

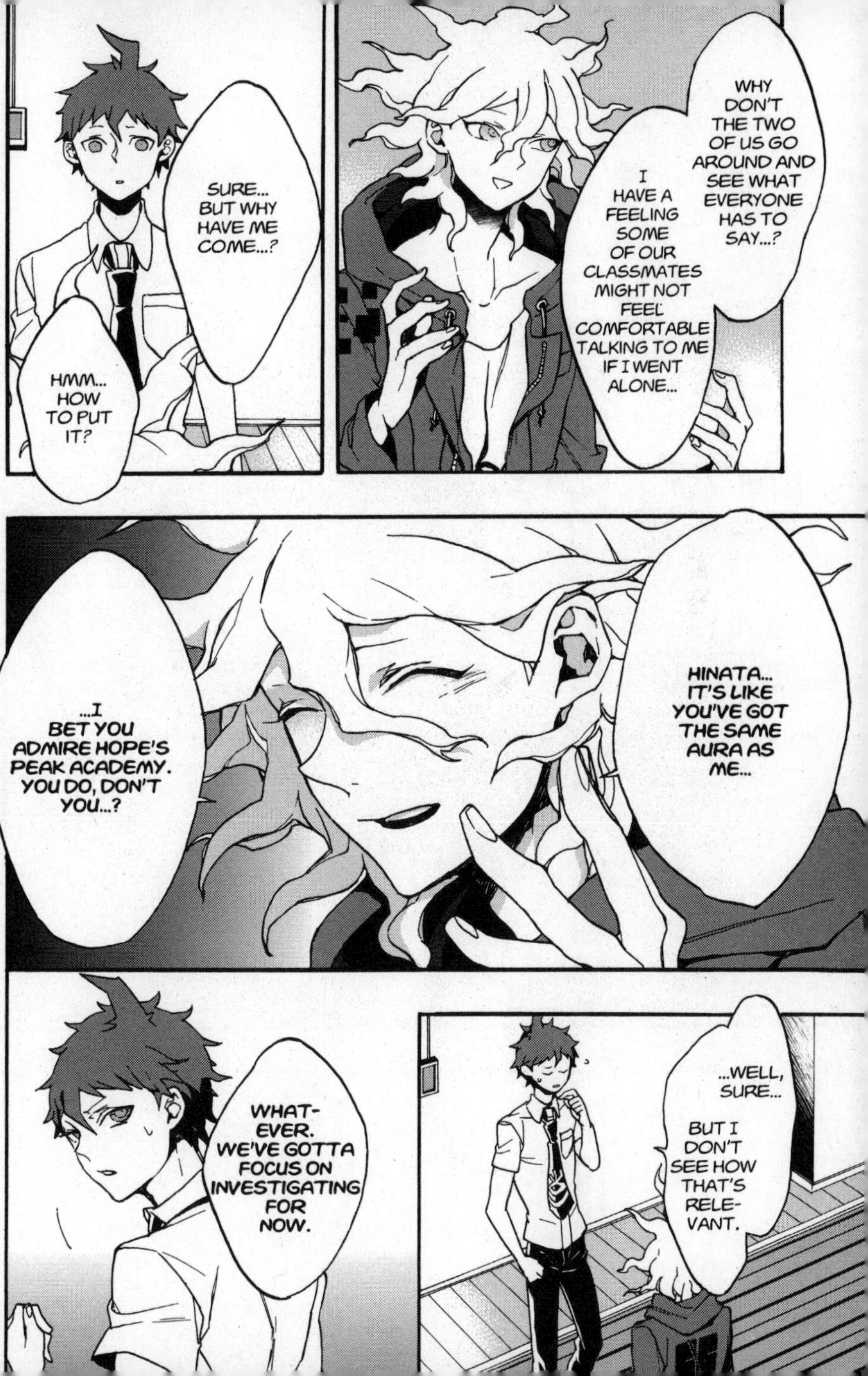
WHY DON'T THE TWO OF US GO AROUND AND SEE WHAT EVERYONE HAS TO SAY...?
I HAVE A FEELING SOME OF OUR CLASSMATES MIGHT NOT FEEL COMFORTABLE TALKING TO ME IF I WENT ALONE...
SURE... BUT WHY HAVE ME COME...?
HMM... HOW TO PUT IT?
HINATA... IT'S LIKE YOU'VE GOT THE SAME AURA AS ME...
...I BET YOU ADMIRE HOPE'S PEAK ACADEMY. YOU DO, DON'T YOU...?
...WELL, SURE...
BUT I DON'T SEE HOW THAT'S RELEVANT.
WHAT-EVER. WE'VE GOTTA FOCUS ON INVESTIGATING FOR NOW.

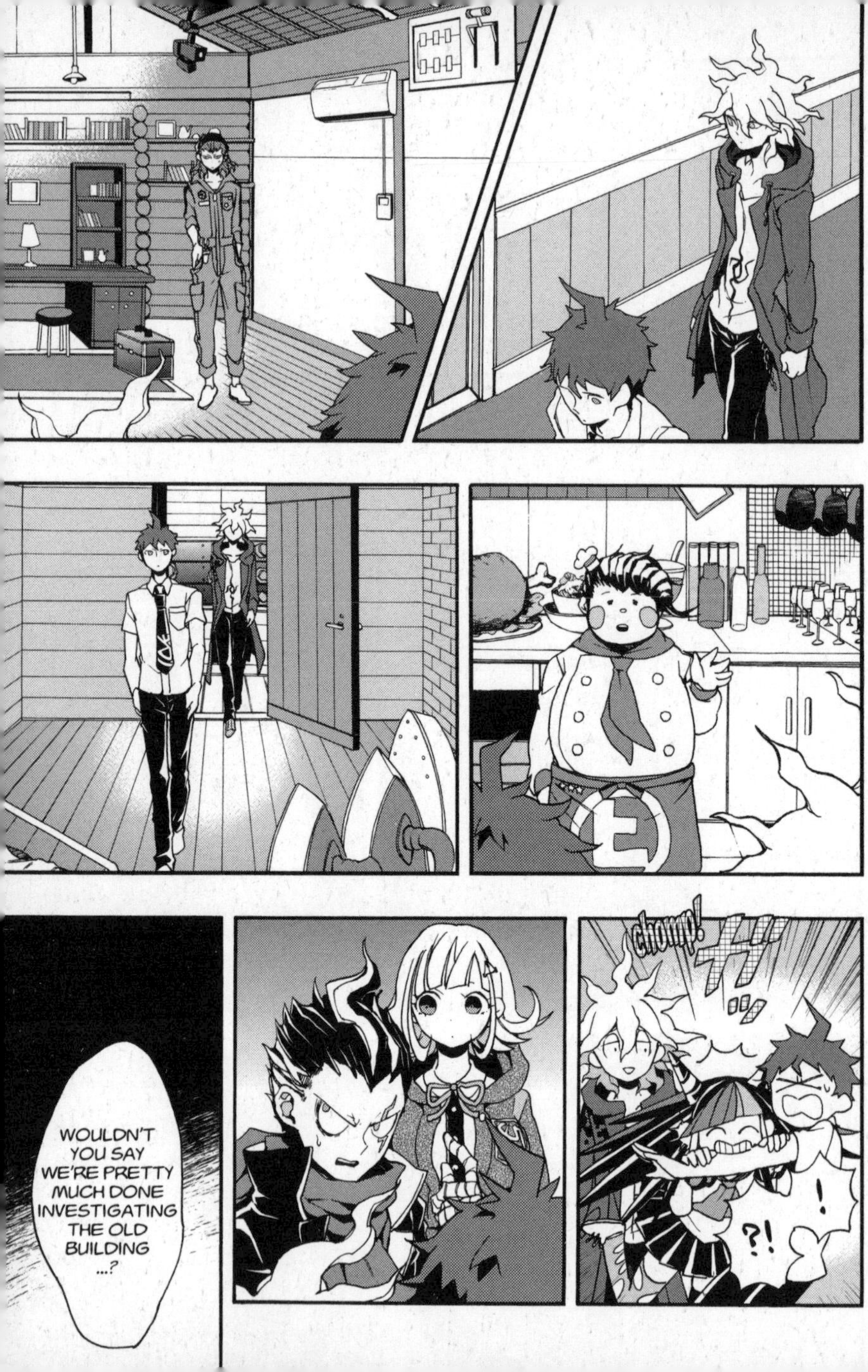
chomp!
!
?!
WOULDN'T YOU SAY WE'RE PRETTY MUCH DONE INVESTIGATING THE OLD BUILDING ...?

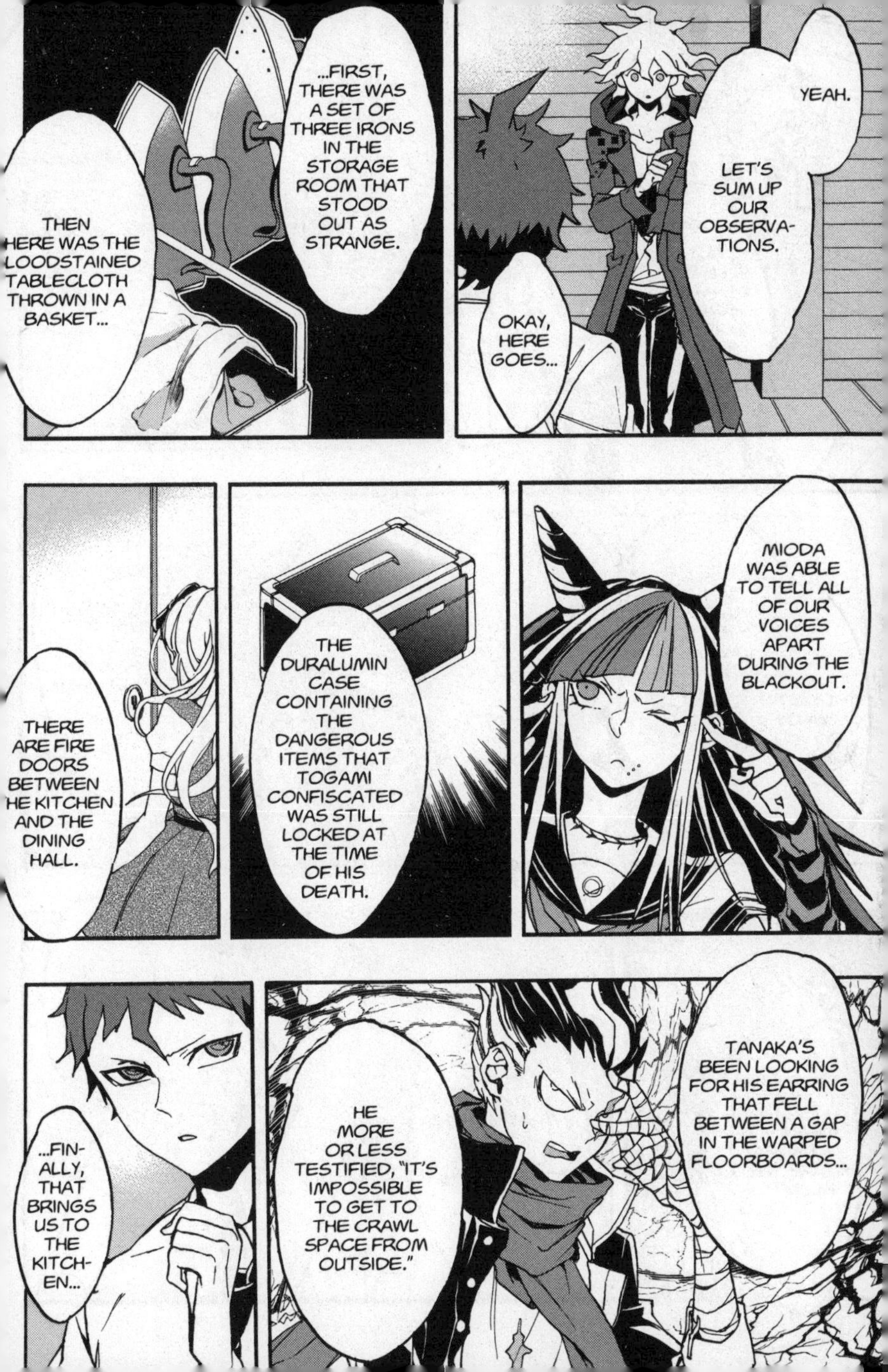
YEAH.
LET'S SUM UP OUR OBSERVA-TIONS.
OKAY, HERE GOES...
...FIRST, THERE WAS A SET OF THREE IRONS IN THE STORAGE ROOM THAT STOOD OUT AS STRANGE.
THEN HERE WAS THE LOODSTAINED TABLECLOTH THROWN IN A BASKET...
MIODA WAS ABLE TO TELL ALL OF OUR VOICES APART DURING THE BLACKOUT.
THE DURALUMIN CASE CONTAINING THE DANGEROUS ITEMS THAT TOGAMI CONFISCATED WAS STILL LOCKED AT THE TIME OF HIS DEATH.
THERE ARE FIRE DOORS BETWEEN HE KITCHEN AND THE DINING HALL.
TANAKA'S BEEN LOOKING FOR HIS EARRING THAT FELL BETWEEN A GAP IN THE WARPED FLOORBOARDS...
HE MORE OR LESS TESTIFIED, "IT'S IMPOSSIBLE TO GET TO THE CRAWL SPACE FROM OUTSIDE."
...FIN-ALLY, THAT BRINGS US TO THE KITCH-EN...

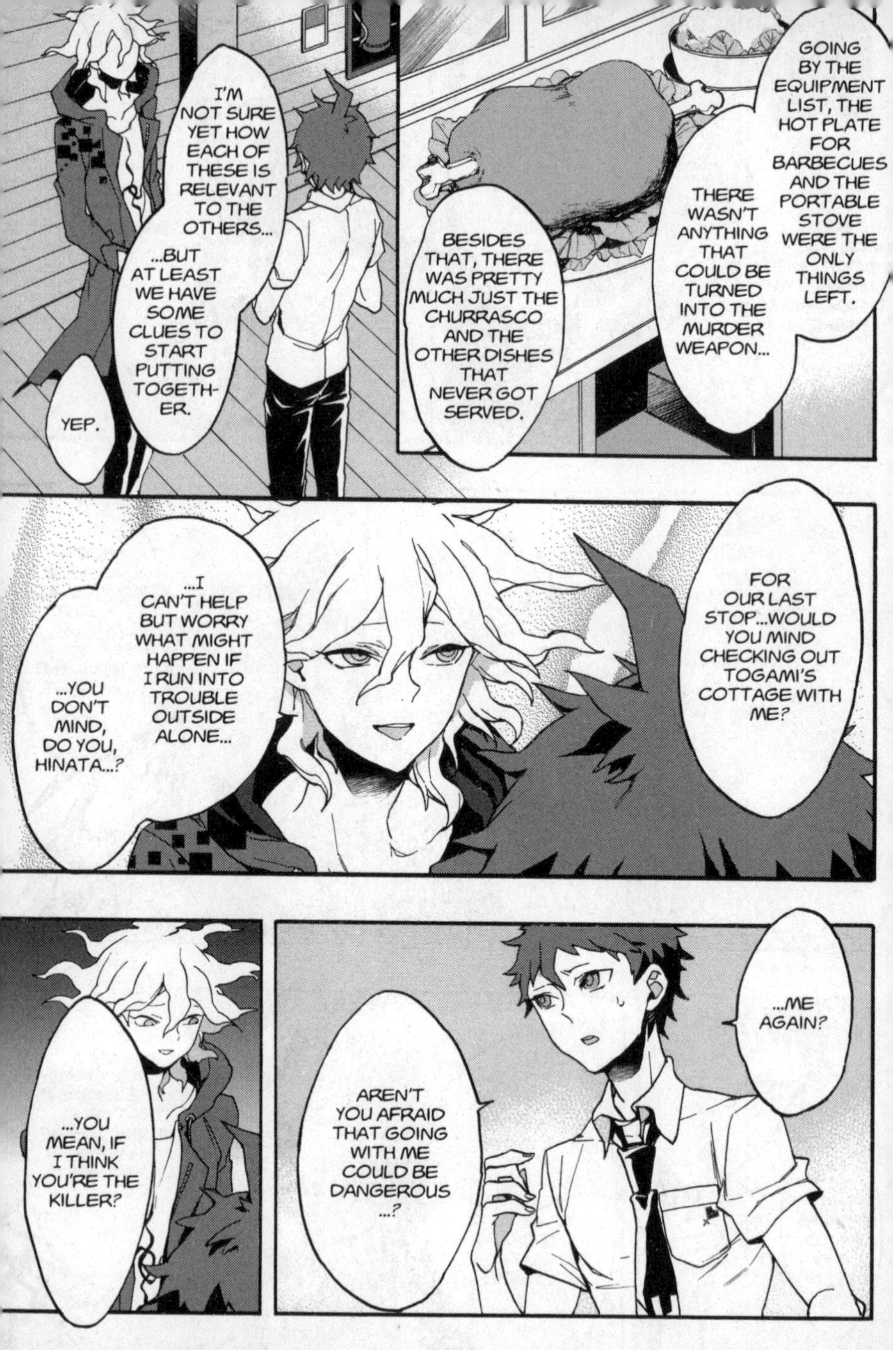
GOING BY THE EQUIPMENT LIST, THE HOT PLATE FOR BARBECUES AND THE PORTABLE STOVE WERE THE ONLY THINGS LEFT.
THERE WASN'T ANYTHING THAT COULD BE TURNED INTO THE MURDER WEAPON...
BESIDES THAT, THERE WAS PRETTY MUCH JUST THE CHURRASCO AND THE OTHER DISHES THAT NEVER GOT SERVED.
I'M NOT SURE YET HOW EACH OF THESE IS RELEVANT TO THE OTHERS...
...BUT AT LEAST WE HAVE SOME CLUES TO START PUTTING TOGETH-ER.
YEP.
FOR OUR LAST STOP...WOULD YOU MIND CHECKING OUT TOGAMI'S COTTAGE WITH ME?
...I CAN'T HELP BUT WORRY WHAT MIGHT HAPPEN IF I RUN INTO TROUBLE OUTSIDE ALONE...
...YOU DON'T MIND, DO YOU, HINATA...?
...ME AGAIN?
AREN'T YOU AFRAID THAT GOING WITH ME COULD BE DANGEROUS ...?
...YOU MEAN, IF I THINK YOU'RE THE KILLER?

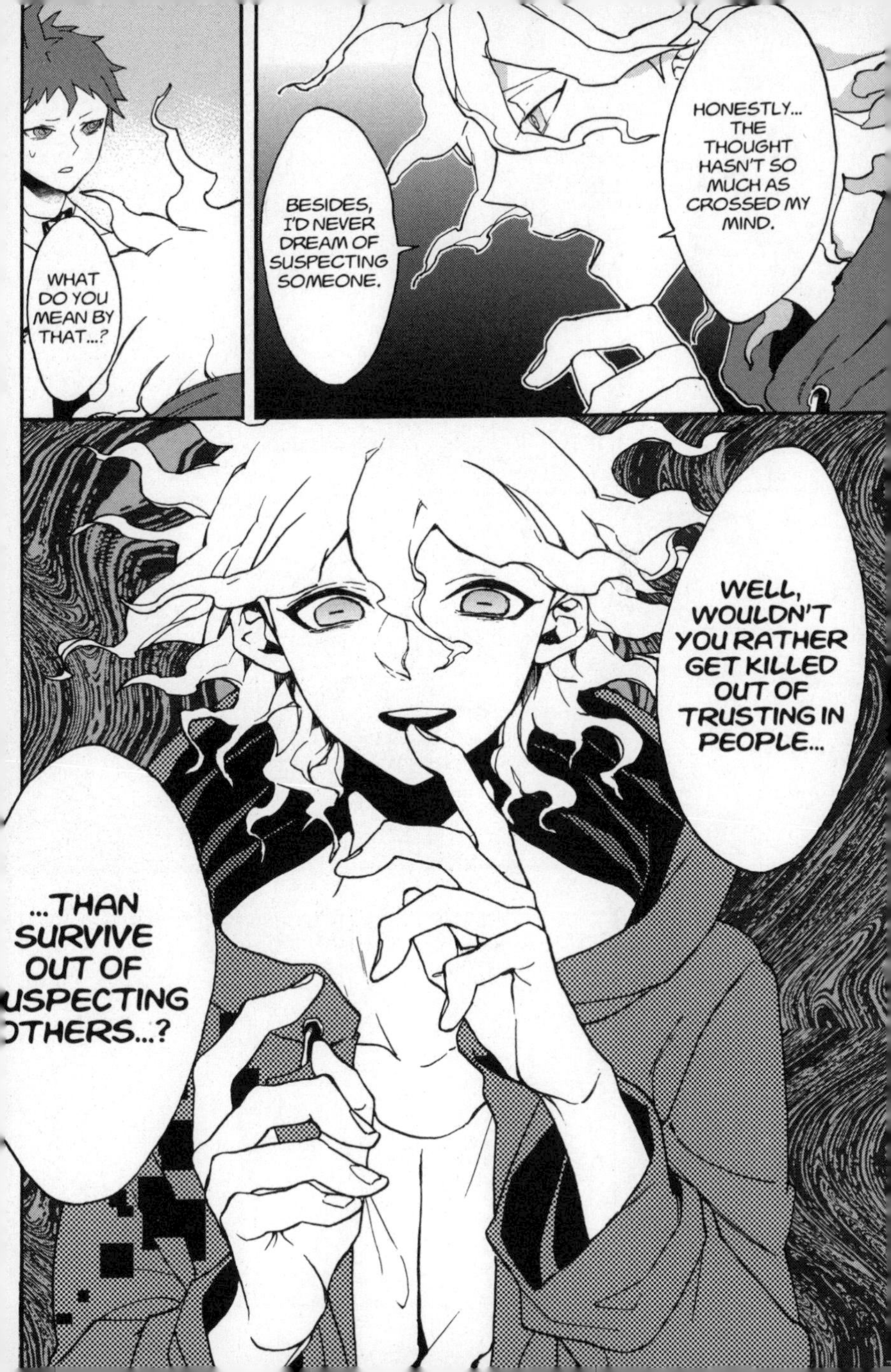
HONESTLY... THE THOUGHT HASN'T SO MUCH AS CROSSED MY MIND.
BESIDES, I'D NEVER DREAM OF SUSPECTING SOMEONE.
WHAT DO YOU MEAN BY THAT...?
WELL, WOULDN'T YOU RATHER GET KILLED OUT OF TRUSTING IN PEOPLE...
...THAN SURVIVE OUT OF USPECTING OTHERS...?

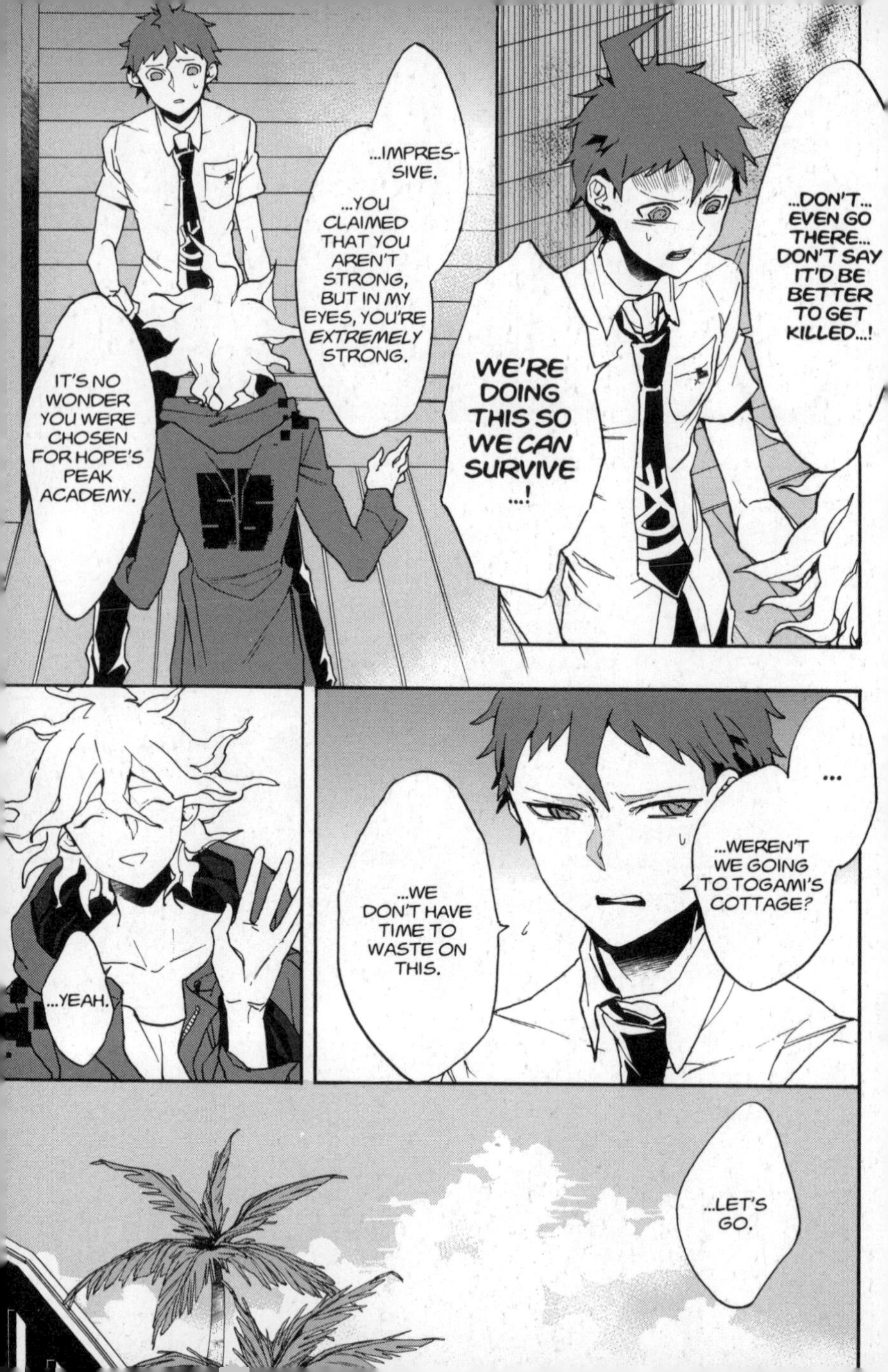
...DON'T... EVEN GO THERE... DON'T SAY IT'D BE BETTER TO GET KILLED...!
WE'RE DOING THIS SO WE CAN SURVIVE ...!
...IMPRES-SIVE.
...YOU CLAIMED THAT YOU AREN'T STRONG, BUT IN MY EYES, YOU'RE *EXTREMELY* STRONG.
IT'S NO WONDER YOU WERE CHOSEN FOR HOPE'S PEAK ACADEMY.
...
...WEREN'T WE GOING TO TOGAMI'S COTTAGE?
...WE DON'T HAVE TIME TO WASTE ON THIS.
...YEAH.
...LET'S GO.

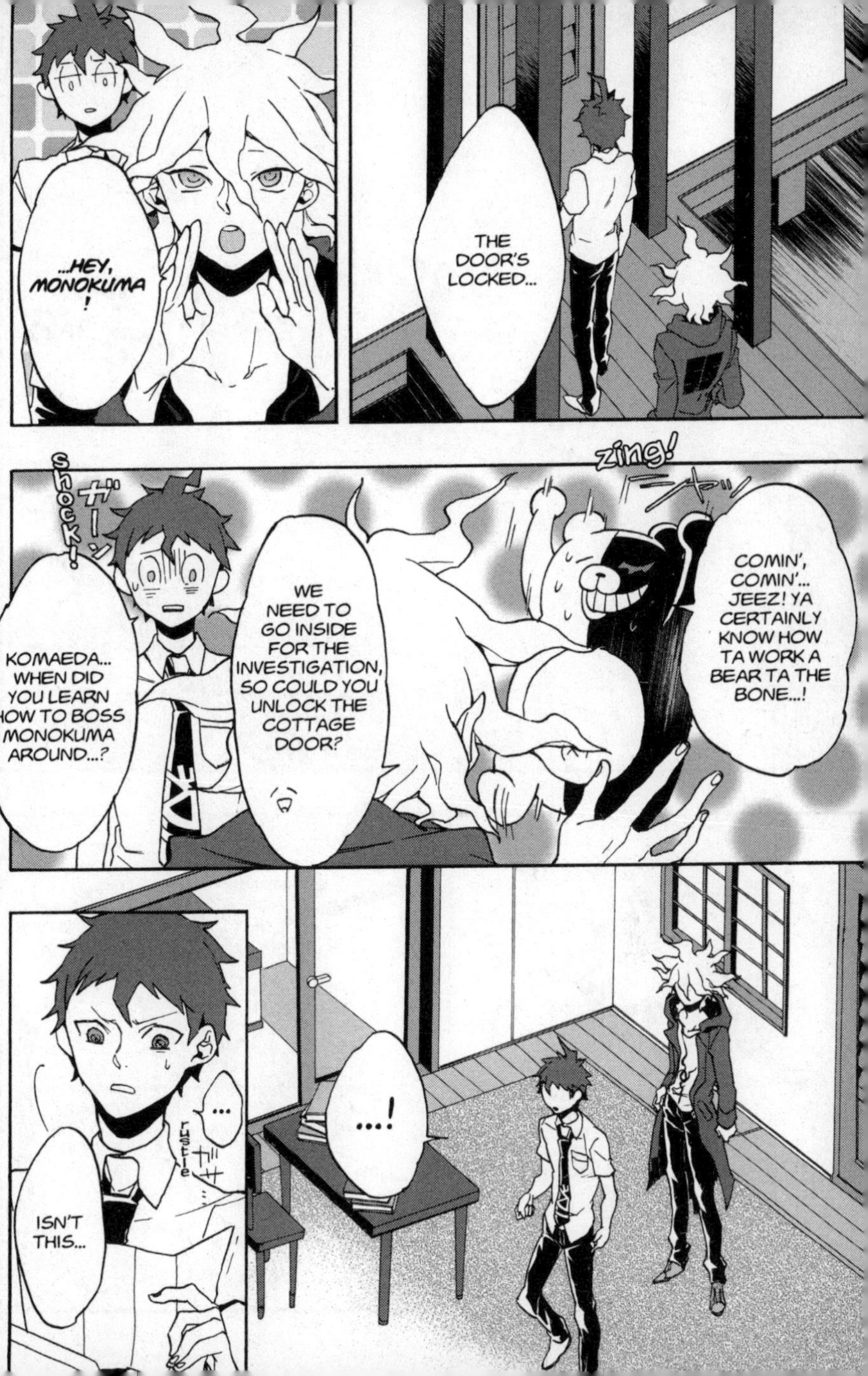
THE DOOR'S LOCKED...
...HEY, MONOKUMA!
zing!
COMIN', COMIN'... JEEZ! YA CERTAINLY KNOW HOW TA WORK A BEAR TA THE BONE...!
WE NEED TO GO INSIDE FOR THE INVESTIGATION, SO COULD YOU UNLOCK THE COTTAGE DOOR?
shock!
KOMAEDA... WHEN DID YOU LEARN HOW TO BOSS MONOKUMA AROUND...?
...!
...
rustle
ISN'T THIS...

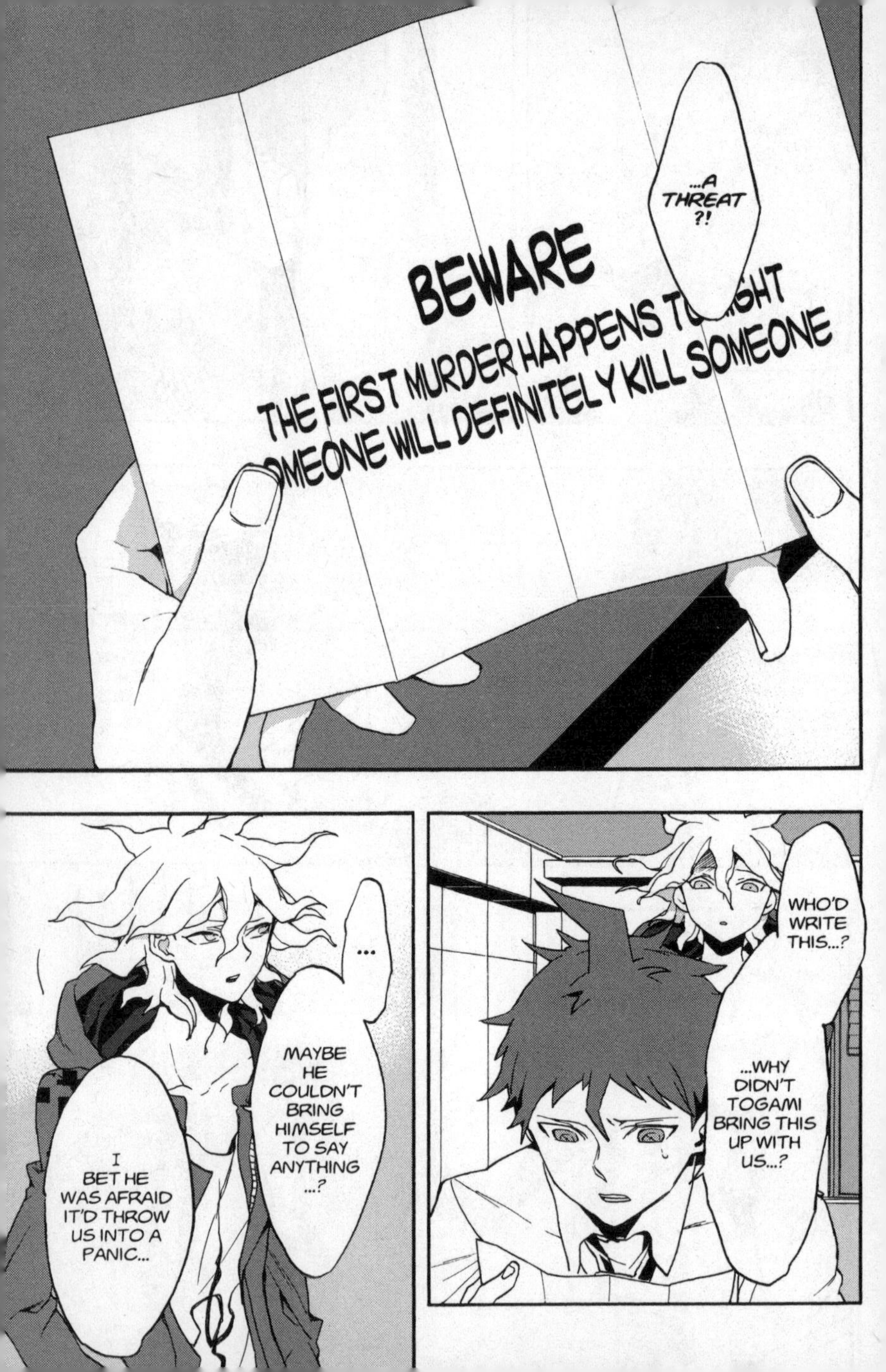
...A THREAT ?!
BEWARE
THE FIRST MURDER HAPPENS TO IGHT
OMEONE WILL DEFINITELY KILL SOMEONE
WHO'D WRITE THIS...?
...WHY DIDN'T TOGAMI BRING THIS UP WITH US...?
...
MAYBE HE COULDN'T BRING HIMSELF TO SAY ANYTHING ...?
I BET HE WAS AFRAID IT'D THROW US INTO A PANIC...

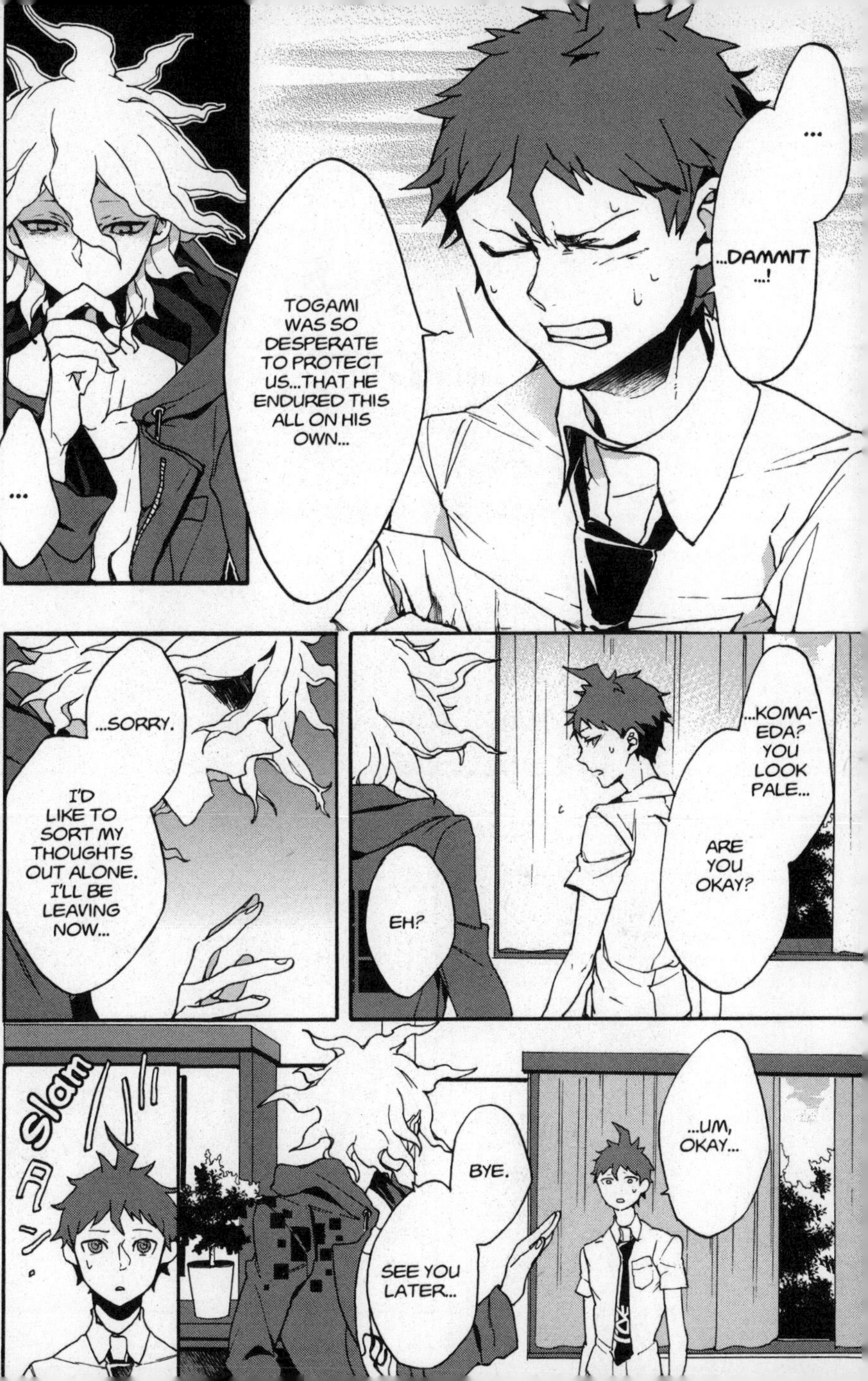
...
...DAMMIT ...!
TOGAMI WAS SO DESPERATE TO PROTECT US...THAT HE ENDURED THIS ALL ON HIS OWN...
...
...KOMA-EDA? YOU LOOK PALE...
ARE YOU OKAY?
EH?
...SORRY.
I'D LIKE TO SORT MY THOUGHTS OUT ALONE. I'LL BE LEAVING NOW...
...UM, OKAY...
BYE.
SEE YOU LATER...
Slam

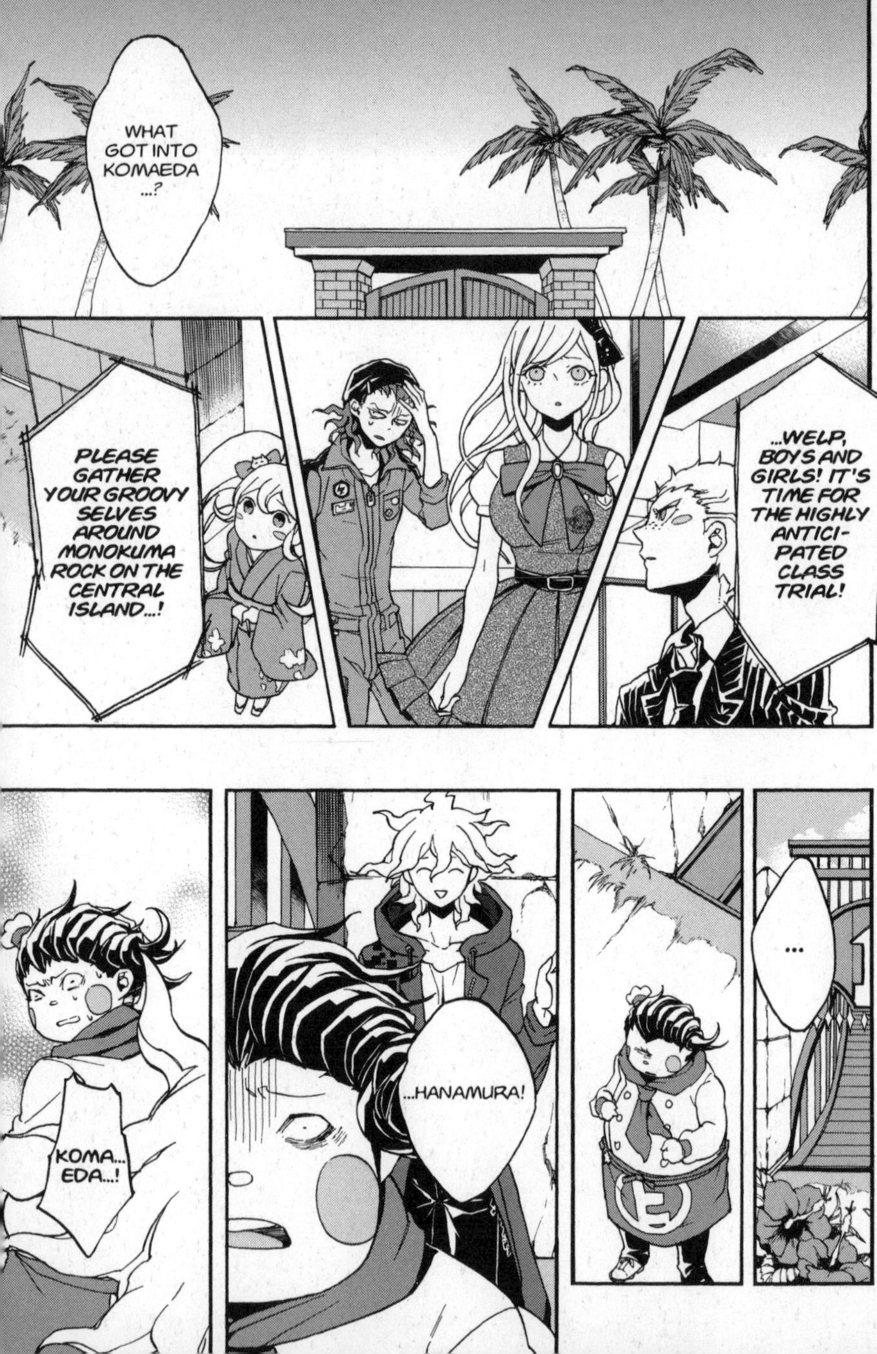
WHAT GOT INTO KOMAEDA ...?
...WELP, BOYS AND GIRLS! IT'S TIME FOR THE HIGHLY ANTICI-PATED CLASS TRIAL!
PLEASE GATHER YOUR GROOVY SELVES AROUND MONOKUMA ROCK ON THE CENTRAL ISLAND...!
...
...HANAMURA!
KOMA... EDA...!

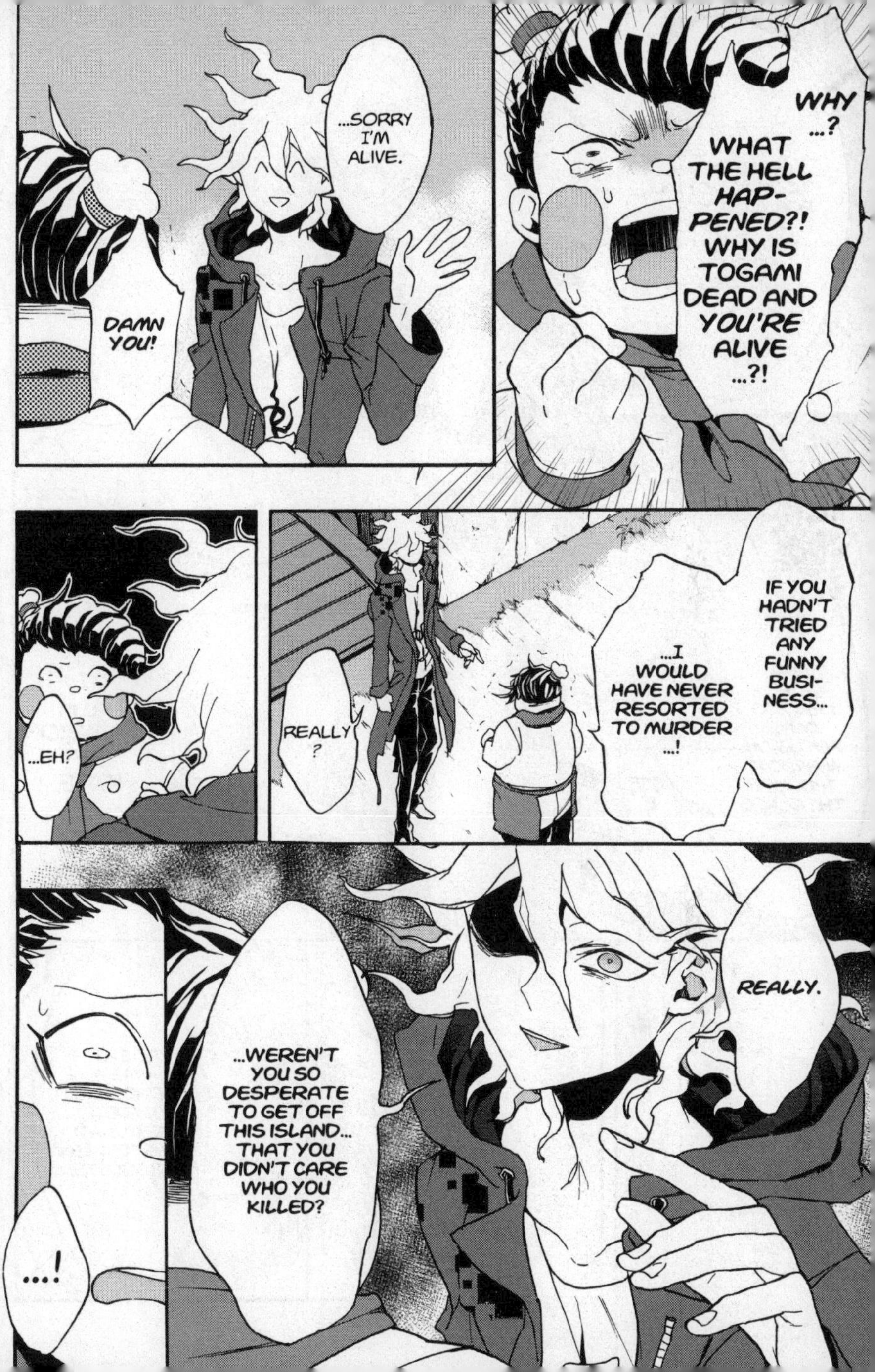
WHY ...?
WHAT THE HELL HAPPENED?! WHY IS TOGAMI DEAD AND YOU'RE ALIVE ...?!
...SORRY I'M ALIVE.
DAMN YOU!
IF YOU HADN'T TRIED ANY FUNNY BUSINESS...
...I WOULD HAVE NEVER RESORTED TO MURDER ...!
REALLY ?
...EH?
REALLY.
...WEREN'T YOU SO DESPERATE TO GET OFF THIS ISLAND... THAT YOU DIDN'T CARE WHO YOU KILLED?
...!

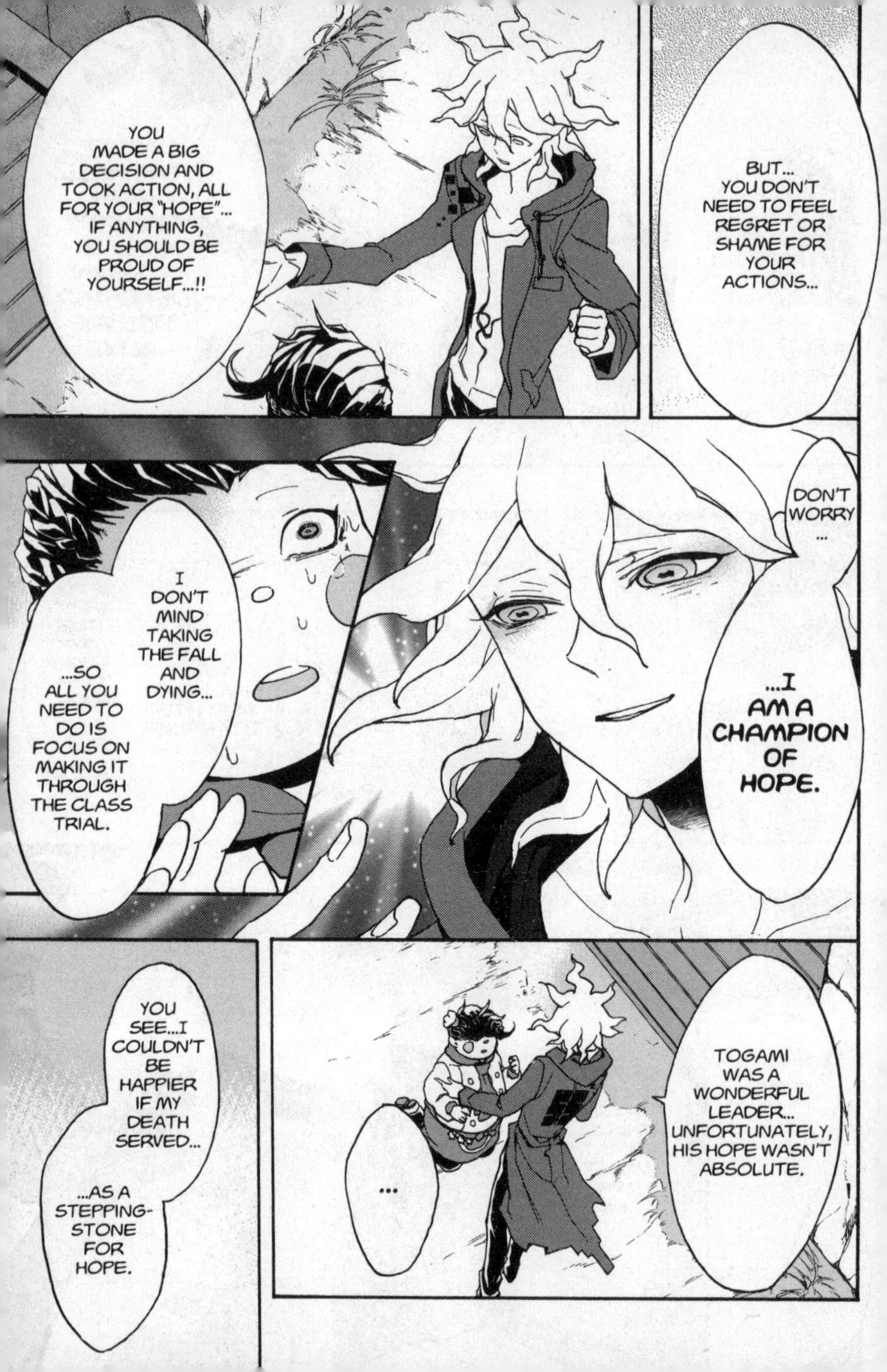
BUT... YOU DON'T NEED TO FEEL REGRET OR SHAME FOR YOUR ACTIONS...
YOU MADE A BIG DECISION AND TOOK ACTION, ALL FOR YOUR "HOPE"... IF ANYTHING, YOU SHOULD BE PROUD OF YOURSELF...!!
DON'T WORRY ...
...I AM A CHAMPION OF HOPE.
I DON'T MIND TAKING THE FALL AND DYING...
...SO ALL YOU NEED TO DO IS FOCUS ON MAKING IT THROUGH THE CLASS TRIAL.
TOGAMI WAS A WONDERFUL LEADER... UNFORTUNATELY, HIS HOPE WASN'T ABSOLUTE.
...
YOU SEE...I COULDN'T BE HAPPIER IF MY DEATH SERVED...
...AS A STEPPING-STONE FOR HOPE.

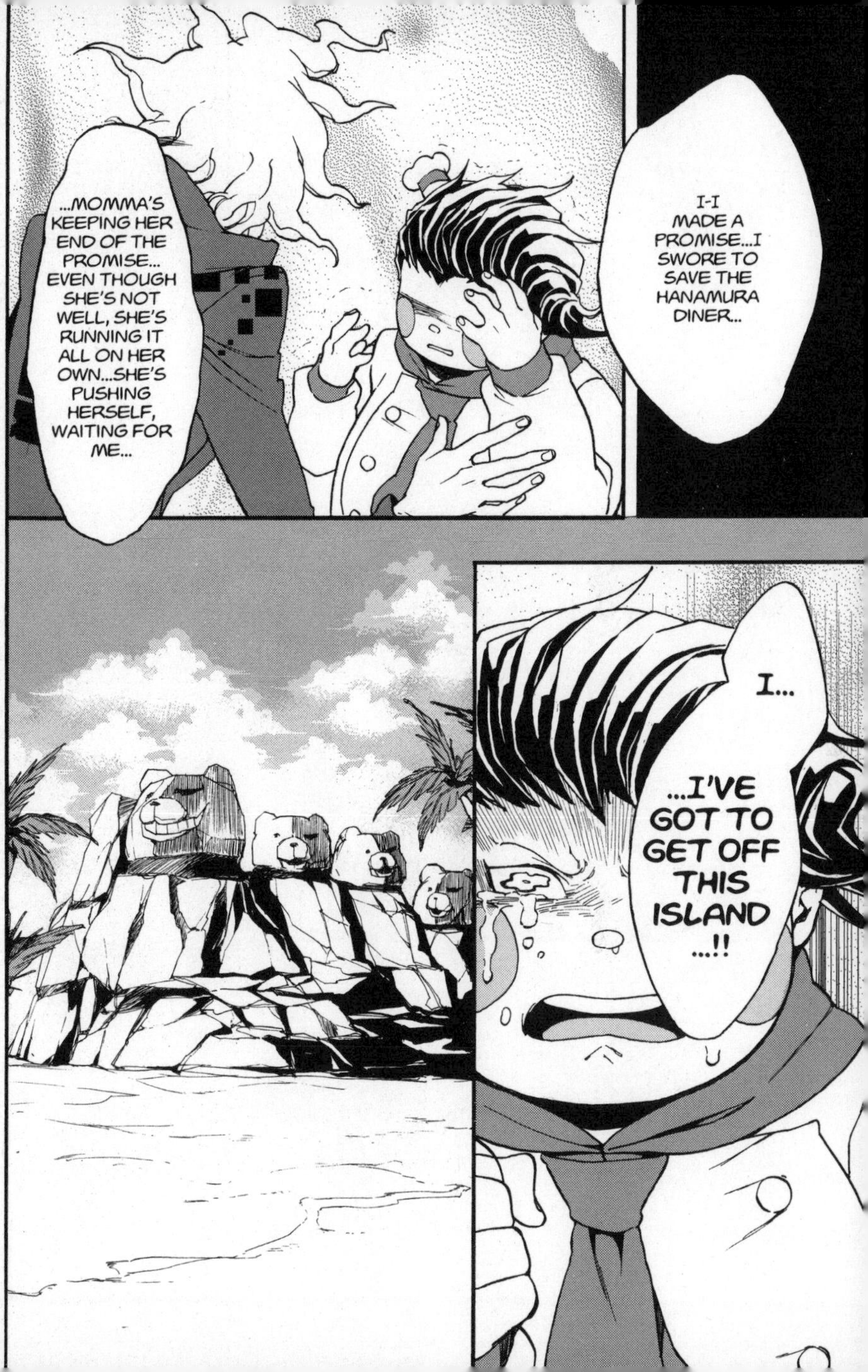
I-I MADE A PROMISE...I SWORE TO SAVE THE HANAMURA DINER...
...MOMMA'S KEEPING HER END OF THE PROMISE... EVEN THOUGH SHE'S NOT WELL, SHE'S RUNNING IT ALL ON HER OWN...SHE'S PUSHING HERSELF, WAITING FOR ME...
I...
...I'VE GOT TO GET OFF THIS ISLAND ...!!

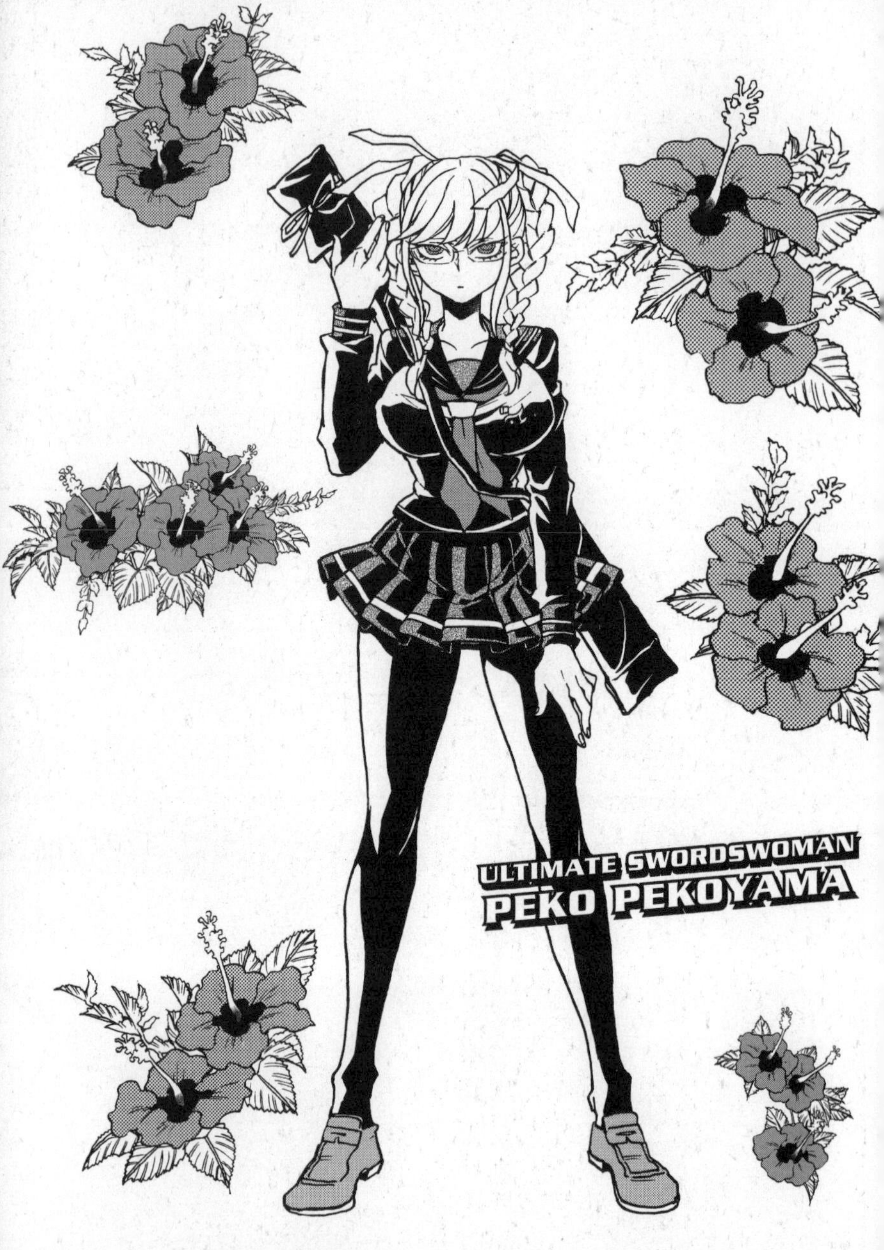
ULTIMATE SWORDSWOMAN
PEKO PEKOYAMA

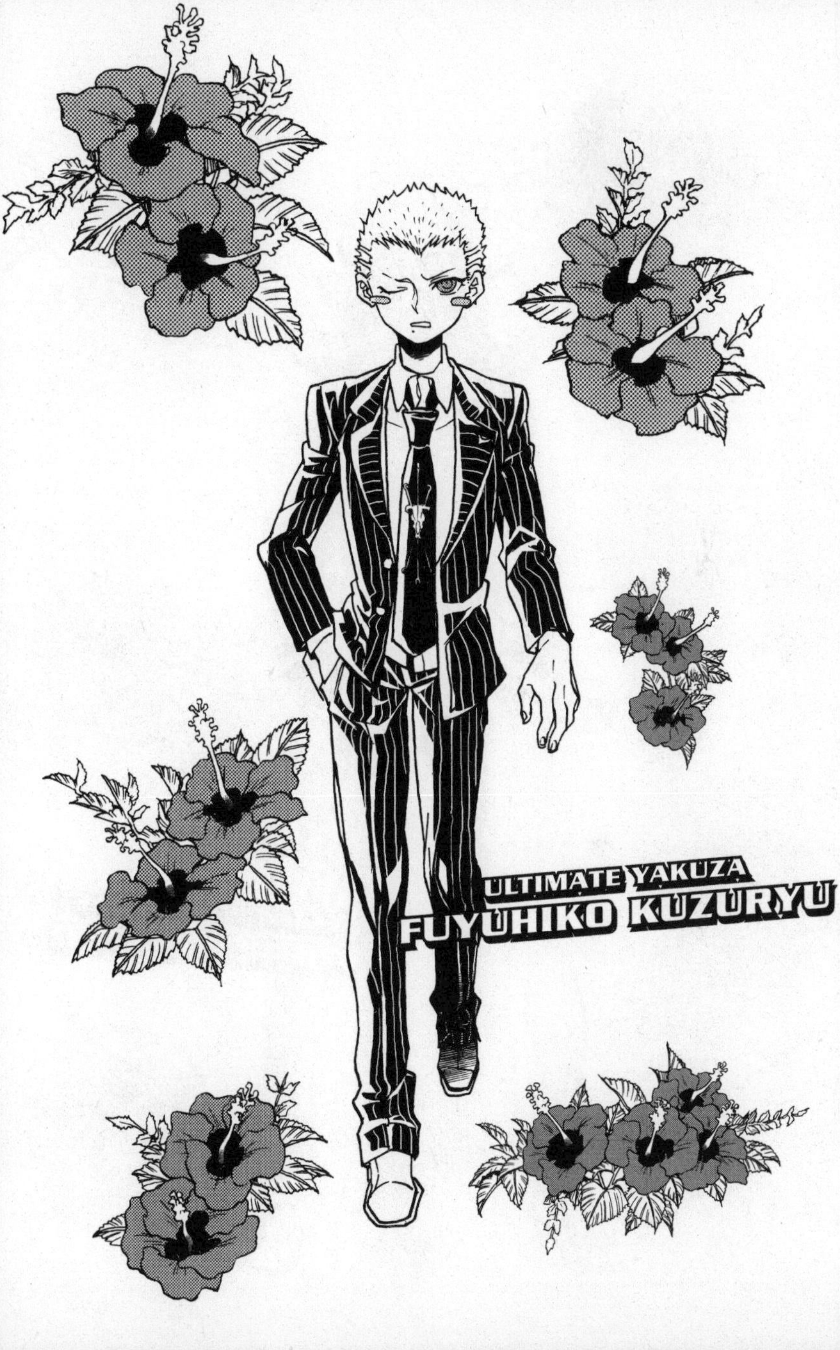
ULTIMATE YAKUZA
FUYUHIKO KUZURYU

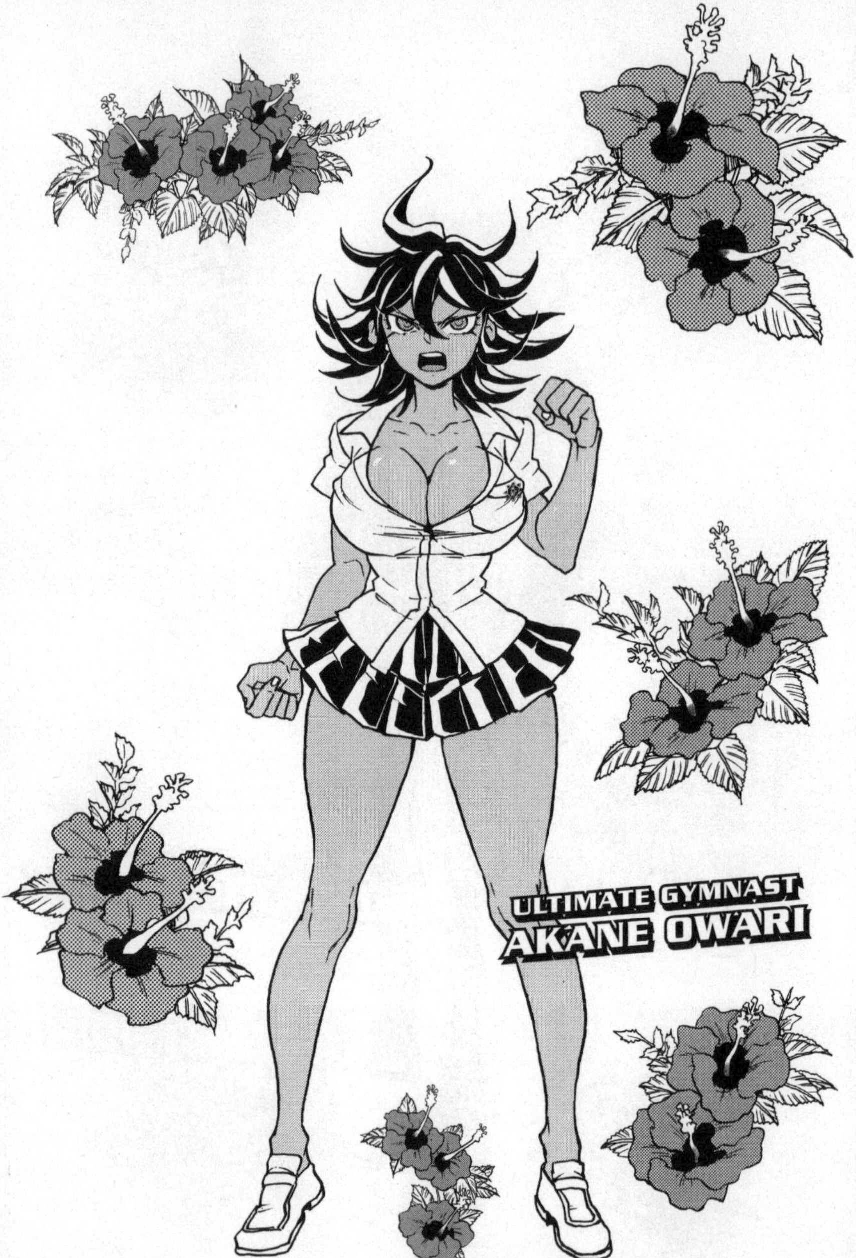
ULTIMATE GYMNAST
AKANE OWARI

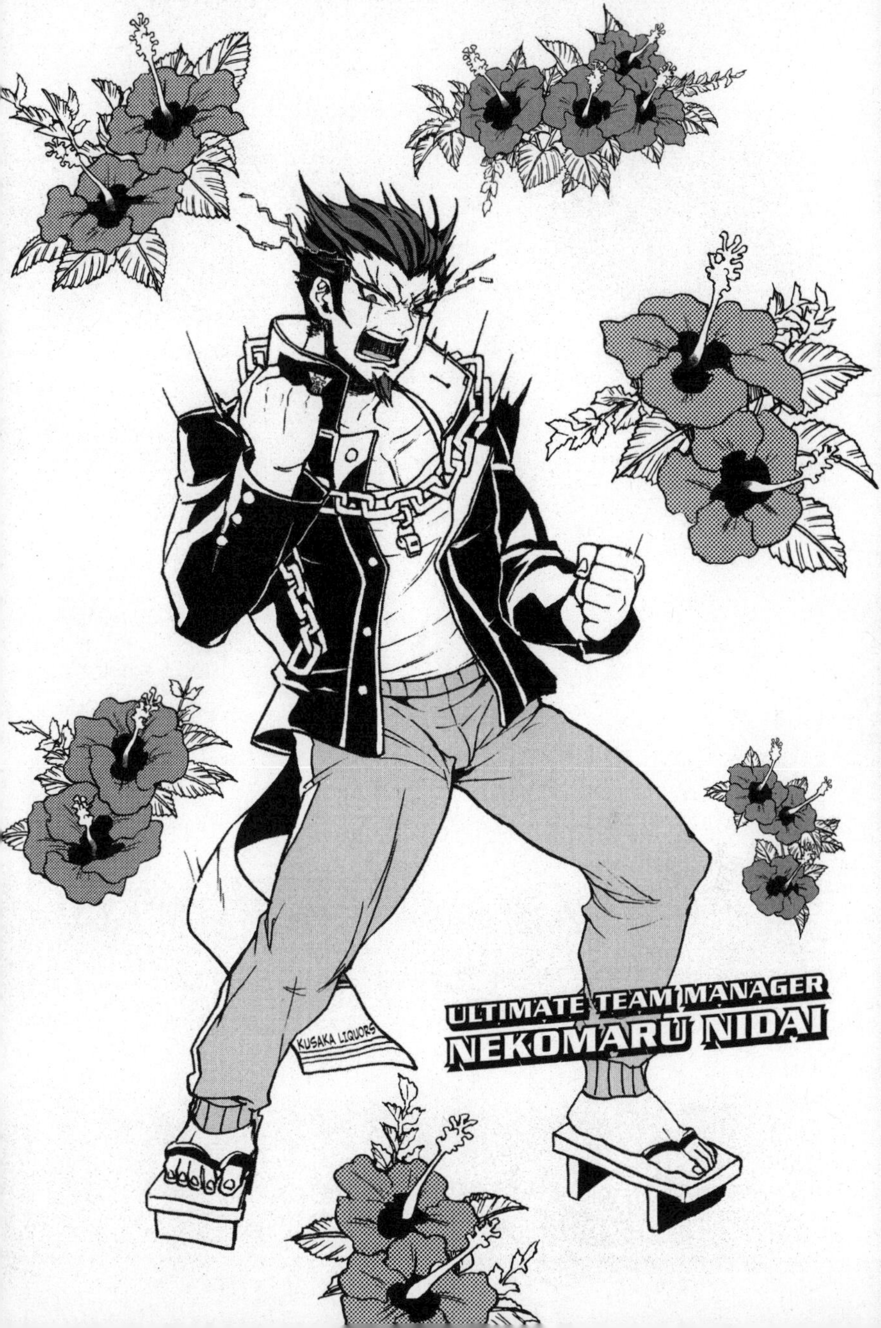
ULTIMATE TEAM MANAGER
NEKOMARU NIDAI
KUSAKA LIQUORS

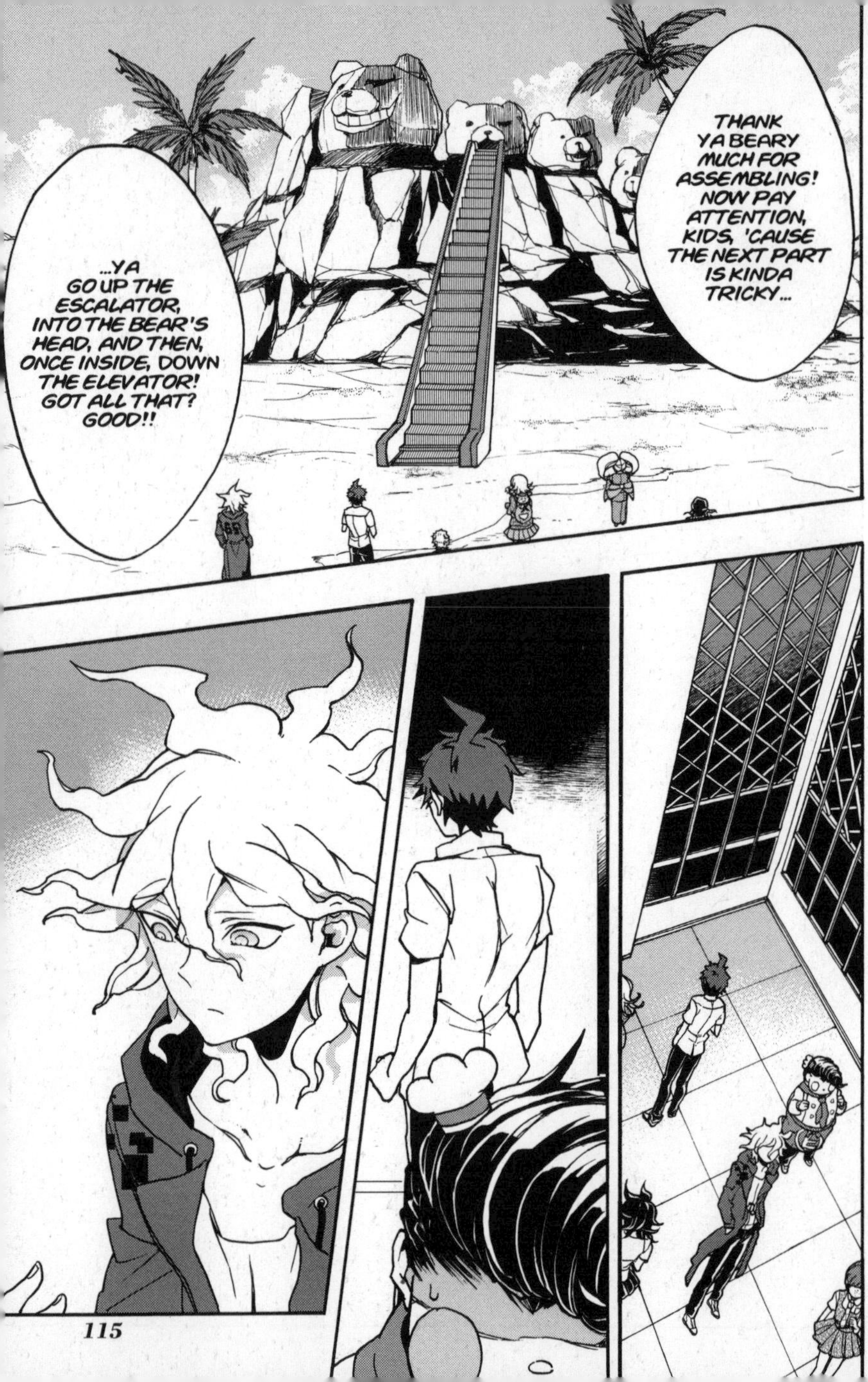
THANK YA BEARY MUCH FOR ASSEMBLING! NOW PAY ATTENTION, KIDS, 'CAUSE THE NEXT PART IS KINDA TRICKY...
...YA GO UP THE ESCALATOR, INTO THE BEAR'S HEAD, AND THEN, ONCE INSIDE, DOWN THE ELEVATOR! GOT ALL THAT? GOOD!!

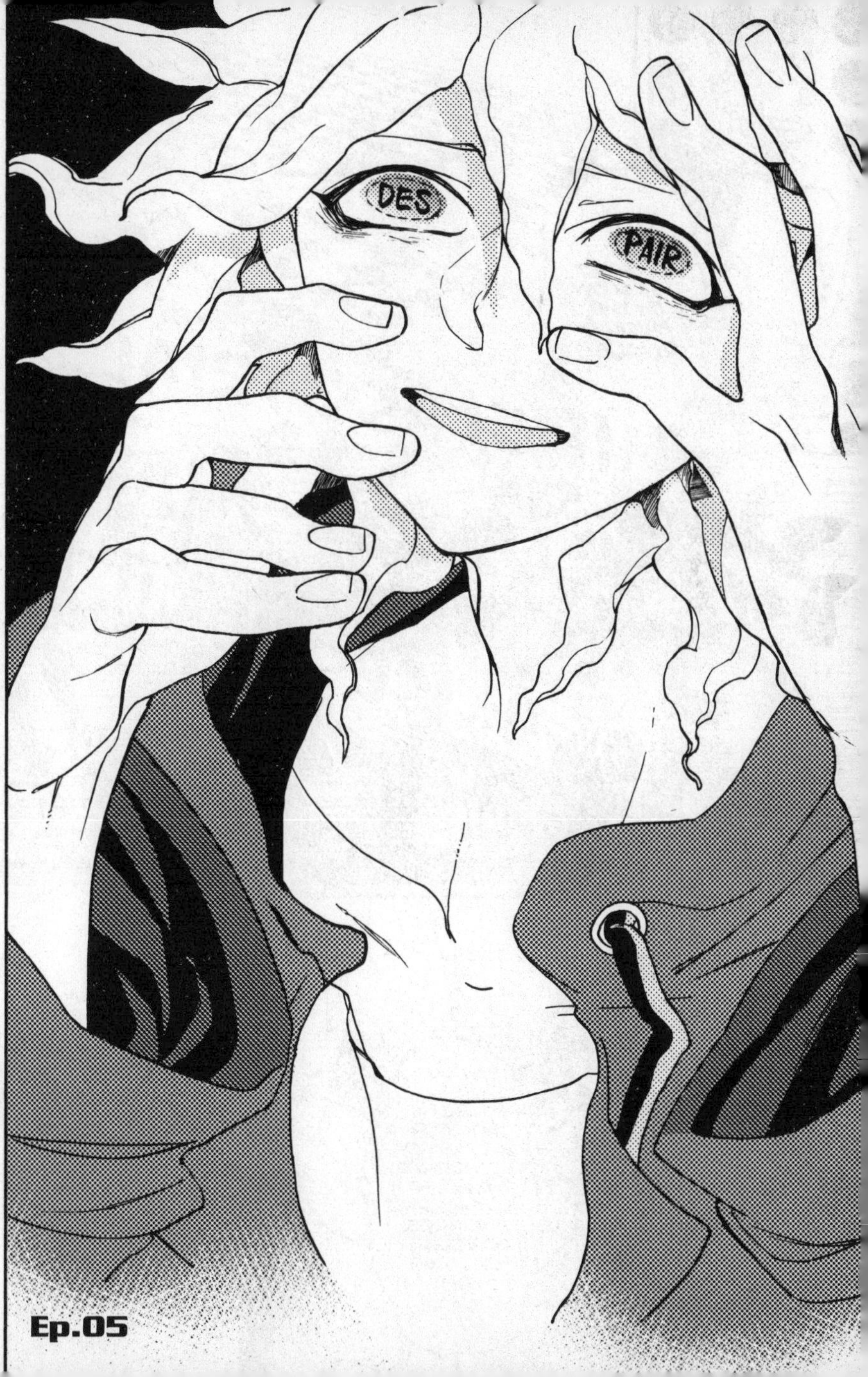
DES
PAIR
Ep.05

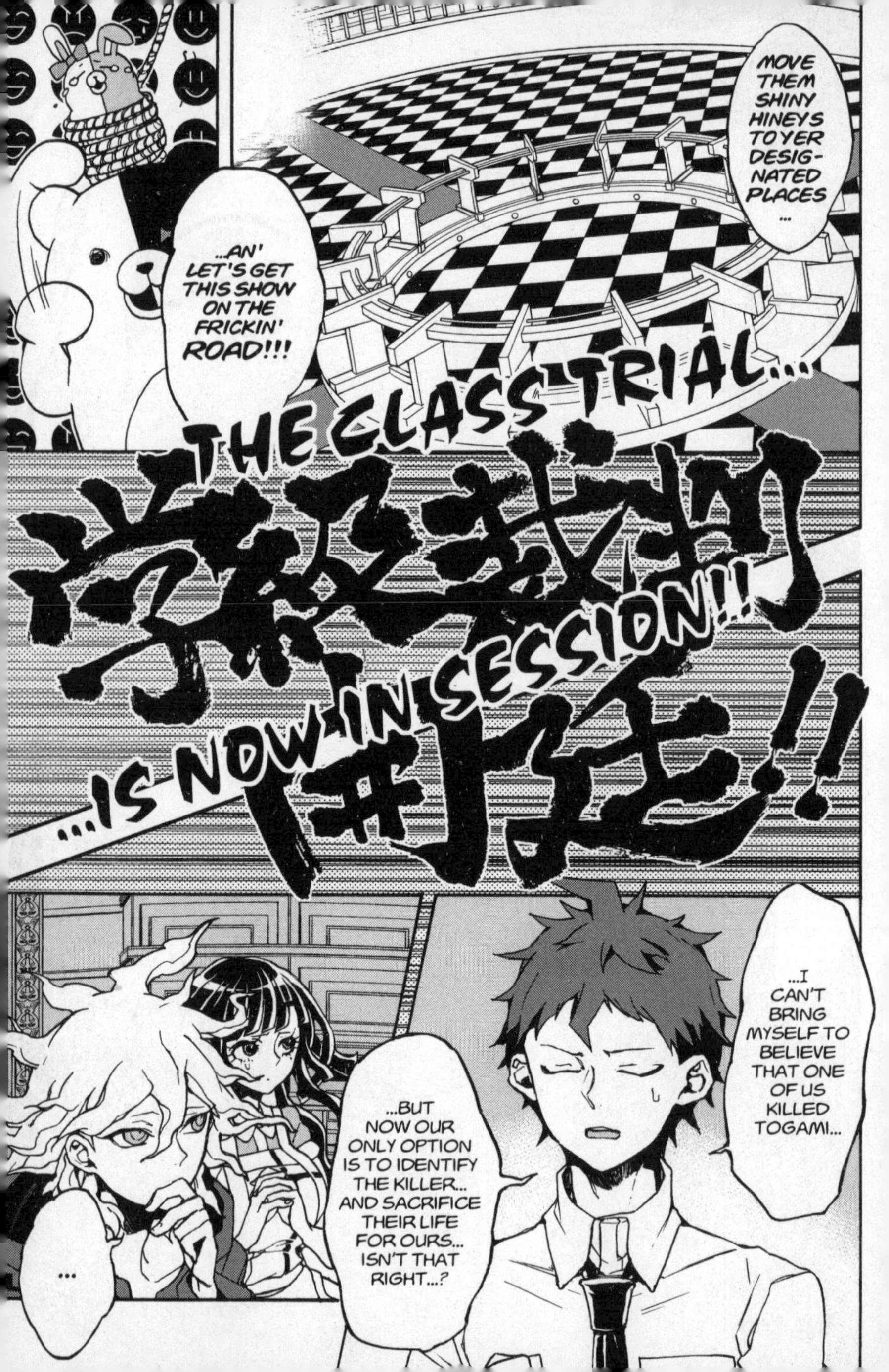

MOVE THEM SHINY HINEYS TO YER DESIG-NATED PLACES ...
...AN' LET'S GET THIS SHOW ON THE FRICKIN' ROAD!!!
THE CLASS TRIAL...
...IS NOW IN SESSION!!
...I CAN'T BRING MYSELF TO BELIEVE THAT ONE OF US KILLED TOGAMI...
...BUT NOW OUR ONLY OPTION IS TO IDENTIFY THE KILLER... AND SACRIFICE THEIR LIFE FOR OURS... ISN'T THAT RIGHT...?
...

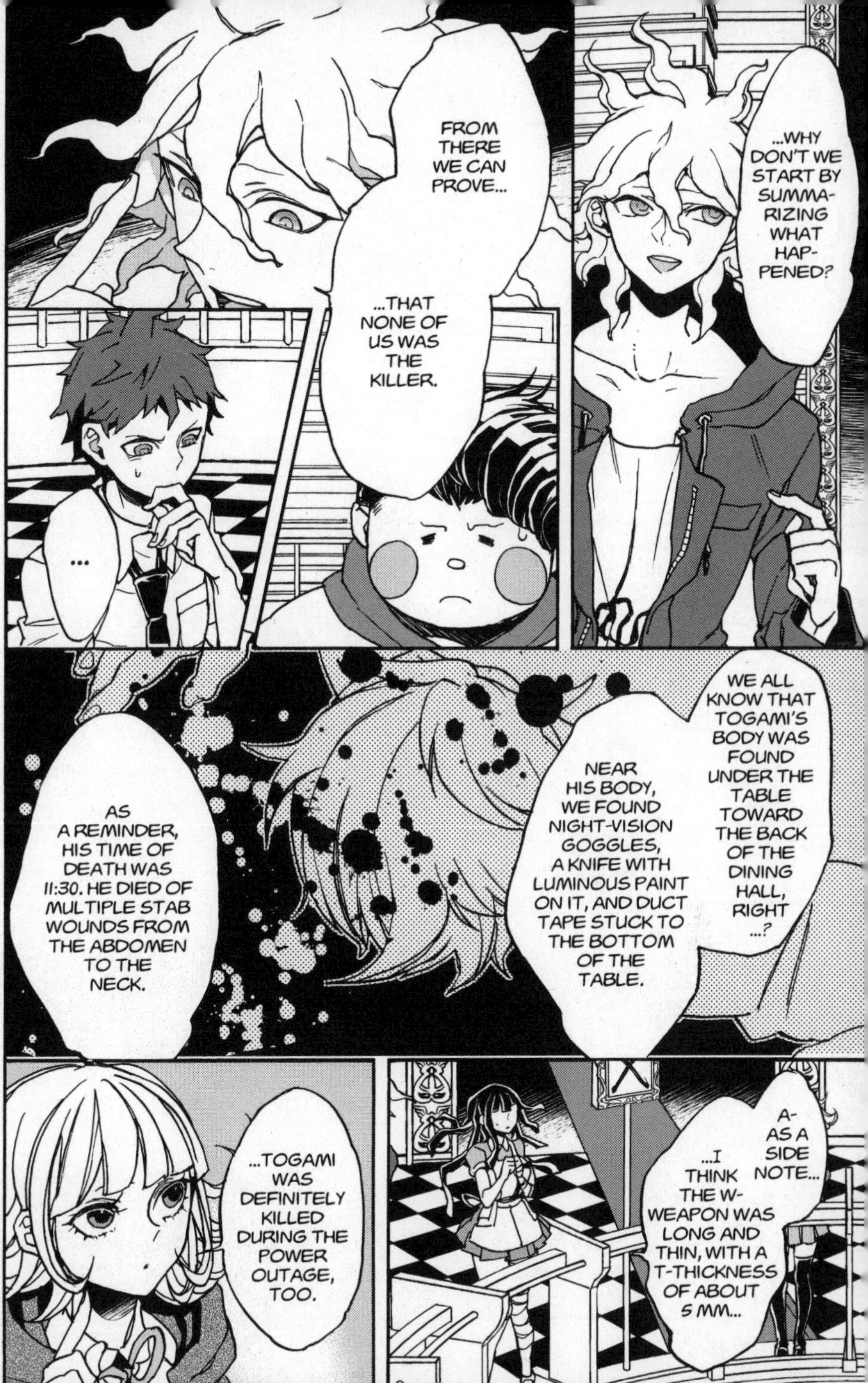
...WHY DON'T WE START BY SUMMA-RIZING WHAT HAP-PENED?
FROM THERE WE CAN PROVE...
...THAT NONE OF US WAS THE KILLER.
...
WE ALL KNOW THAT TOGAMI'S BODY WAS FOUND UNDER THE TABLE TOWARD THE BACK OF THE DINING HALL, RIGHT ...?
NEAR HIS BODY, WE FOUND NIGHT-VISION GOGGLES, A KNIFE WITH LUMINOUS PAINT ON IT, AND DUCT TAPE STUCK TO THE BOTTOM OF THE TABLE.
AS A REMINDER, HIS TIME OF DEATH WAS 11:30. HE DIED OF MULTIPLE STAB WOUNDS FROM THE ABDOMEN TO THE NECK.
A- AS A SIDE NOTE...
...I THINK THE W- WEAPON WAS LONG AND THIN, WITH A T-THICKNESS OF ABOUT 5 MM...
...TOGAMI WAS DEFINITELY KILLED DURING THE POWER OUTAGE, TOO.

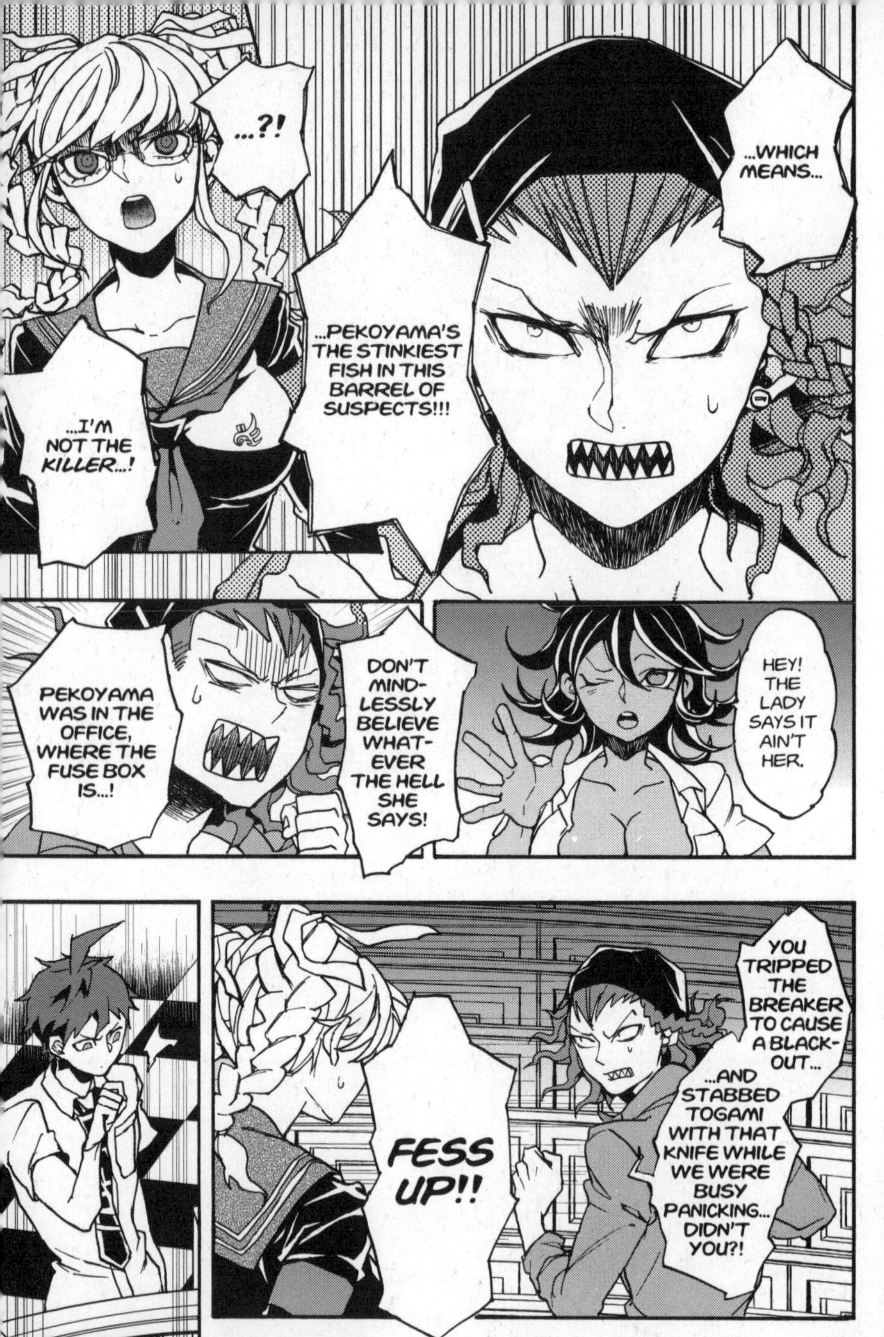
...WHICH MEANS...
...PEKOYAMA'S THE STINKIEST FISH IN THIS BARREL OF SUSPECTS!!!
...?!
...I'M NOT THE KILLER...!
HEY! THE LADY SAYS IT AIN'T HER.
DON'T MINDLESSLY BELIEVE WHATEVER THE HELL SHE SAYS!
PEKOYAMA WAS IN THE OFFICE, WHERE THE FUSE BOX IS...!
YOU TRIPPED THE BREAKER TO CAUSE A BLACKOUT...
...AND STABBED TOGAMI WITH THAT KNIFE WHILE WE WERE BUSY PANICKING... DIDN'T YOU?!
FESS UP!!

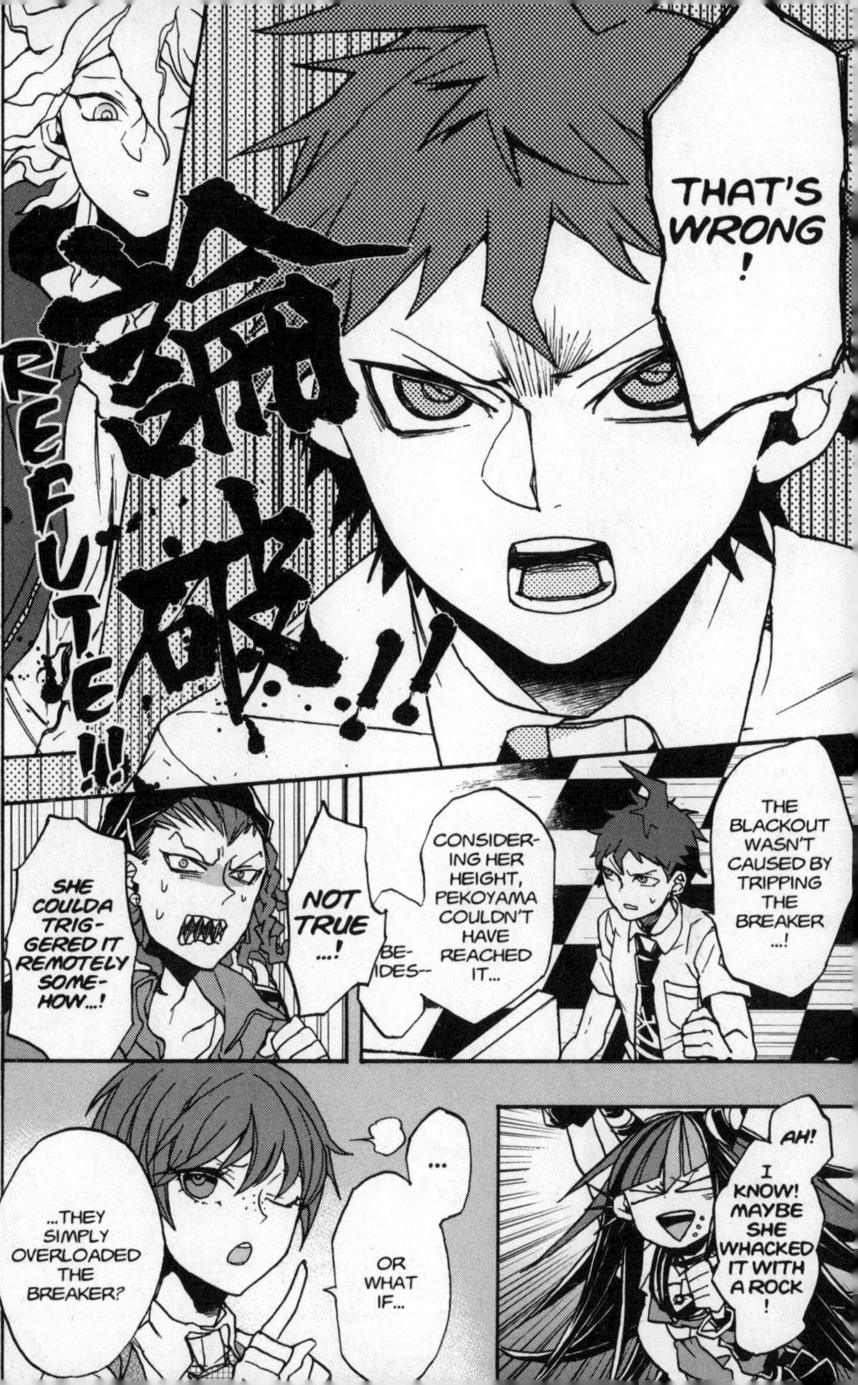
THAT'S WRONG!
論破!!
REFUTE!!
THE BLACKOUT WASN'T CAUSED BY TRIPPING THE BREAKER ...!
CONSIDERING HER HEIGHT, PEKOYAMA COULDN'T HAVE REACHED IT...
BESIDES--
NOT TRUE ...!
SHE COULDA TRIGGERED IT REMOTELY SOMEHOW...!
AH!
I KNOW! MAYBE SHE WHACKED IT WITH A ROCK!
...
OR WHAT IF...
...THEY SIMPLY OVERLOADED THE BREAKER?

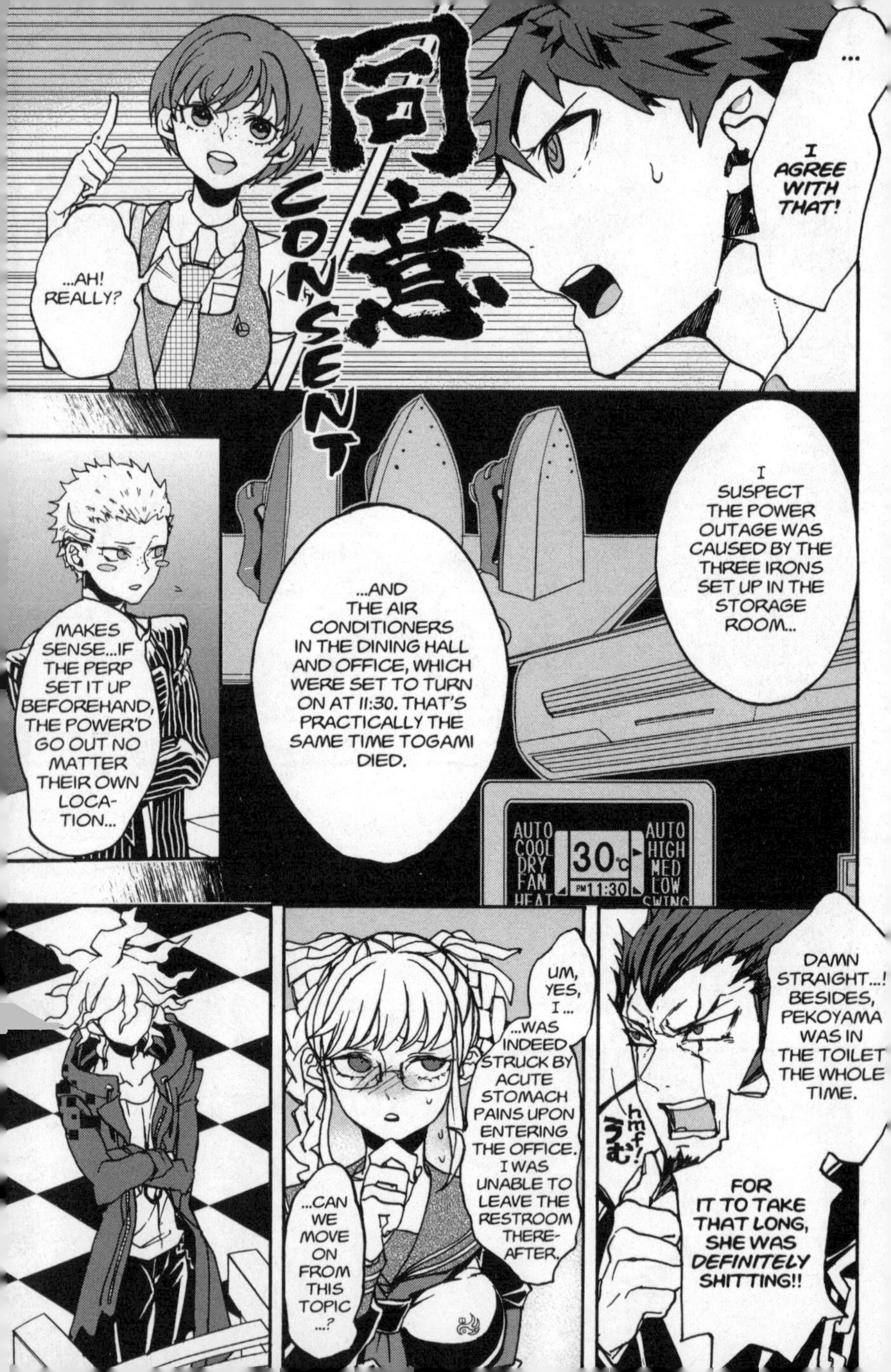
...
I AGREE WITH THAT!
同意
CONSENT
...AH! REALLY?
I SUSPECT THE POWER OUTAGE WAS CAUSED BY THE THREE IRONS SET UP IN THE STORAGE ROOM...
...AND THE AIR CONDITIONERS IN THE DINING HALL AND OFFICE, WHICH WERE SET TO TURN ON AT 11:30. THAT'S PRACTICALLY THE SAME TIME TOGAMI DIED.
AUTO
COOL
DRY
FAN
30℃
PM 11:30
AUTO
HIGH
MED
LOW
MAKES SENSE...IF THE PERP SET IT UP BEFOREHAND, THE POWER'D GO OUT NO MATTER THEIR OWN LOCA-TION...
DAMN STRAIGHT...! BESIDES, PEKOYAMA WAS IN THE TOILET THE WHOLE TIME.
FOR IT TO TAKE THAT LONG, SHE WAS DEFINITELY SHITTING!!
hmf!!
うむ
UM, YES, I... ...WAS INDEED STRUCK BY ACUTE STOMACH PAINS UPON ENTERING THE OFFICE. I WAS UNABLE TO LEAVE THE RESTROOM THERE-AFTER.
...CAN WE MOVE ON FROM THIS TOPIC ...?

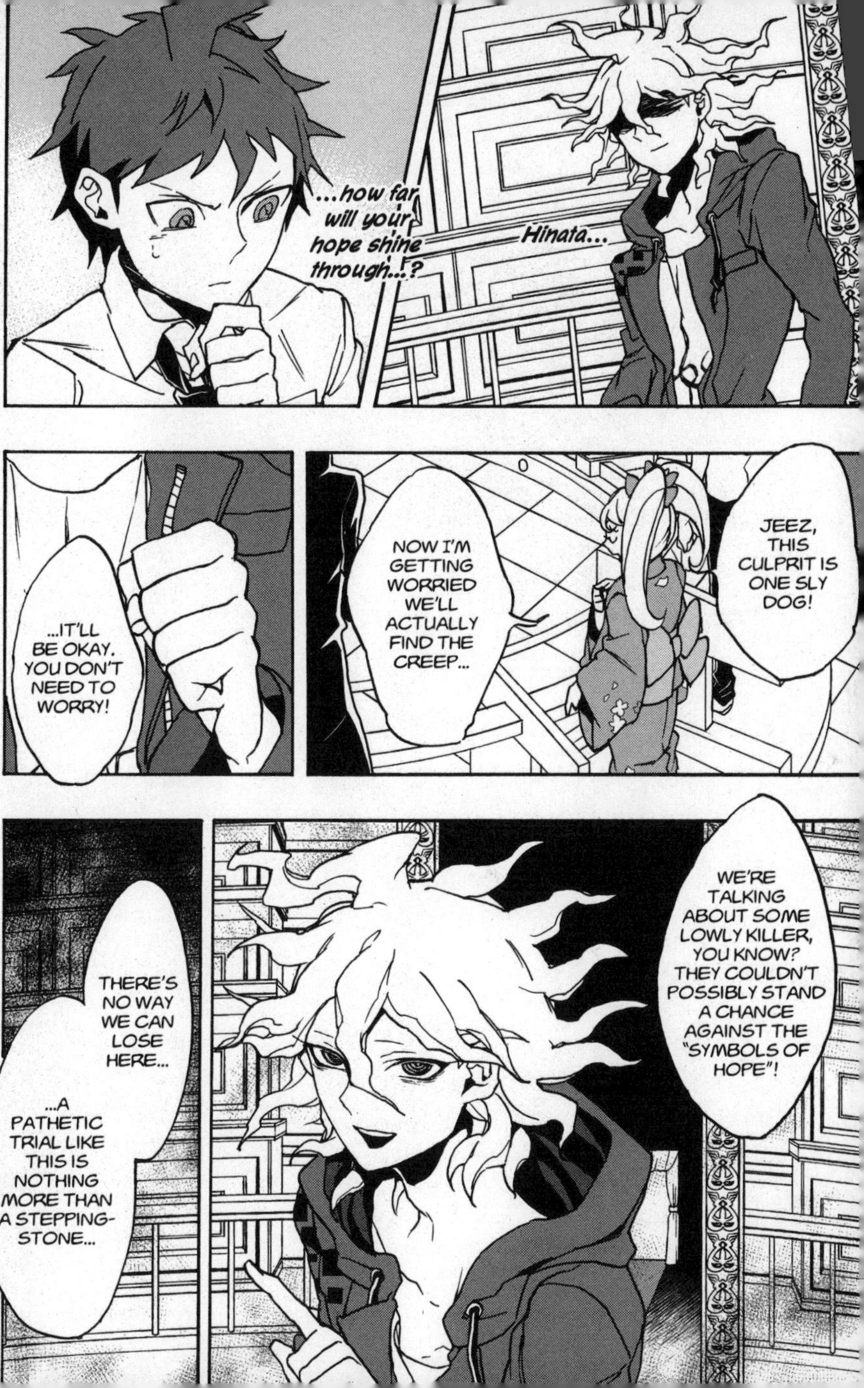
Hinata...
...how far will your hope shine through...?
JEEZ, THIS CULPRIT IS ONE SLY DOG!
NOW I'M GETTING WORRIED WE'LL ACTUALLY FIND THE CREEP...
...IT'LL BE OKAY. YOU DON'T NEED TO WORRY!
WE'RE TALKING ABOUT SOME LOWLY KILLER, YOU KNOW? THEY COULDN'T POSSIBLY STAND A CHANCE AGAINST THE "SYMBOLS OF HOPE"!
THERE'S NO WAY WE CAN LOSE HERE...
...A PATHETIC TRIAL LIKE THIS IS NOTHING MORE THAN A STEPPING-STONE...

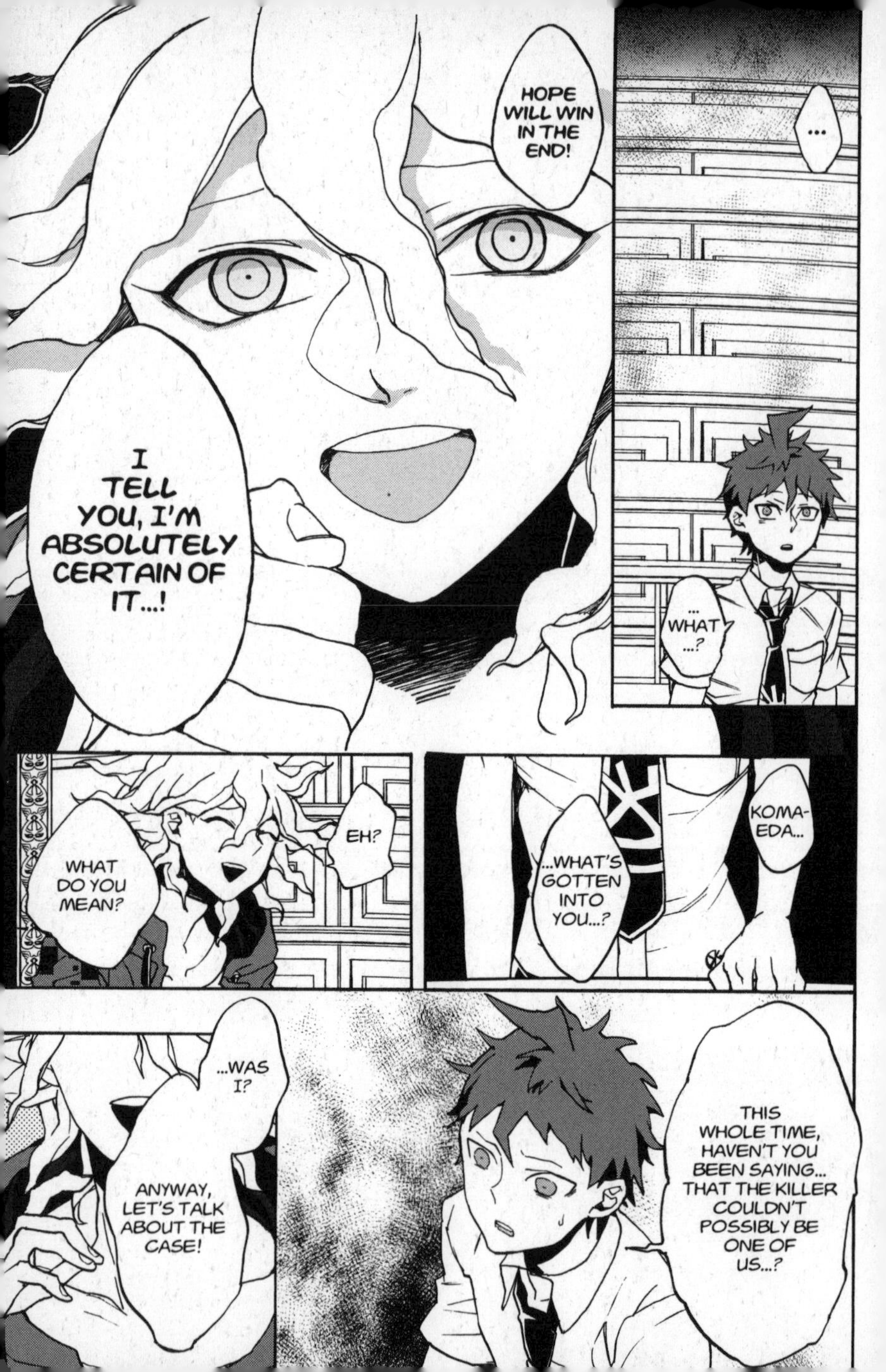
...
... WHAT ...?
HOPE WILL WIN IN THE END!
I TELL YOU, I'M ABSOLUTELY CERTAIN OF IT...!
KOMA-EDA...
...WHAT'S GOTTEN INTO YOU...?
EH?
WHAT DO YOU MEAN?
THIS WHOLE TIME, HAVEN'T YOU BEEN SAYING... THAT THE KILLER COULDN'T POSSIBLY BE ONE OF US...?
...WAS I?
ANYWAY, LET'S TALK ABOUT THE CASE!

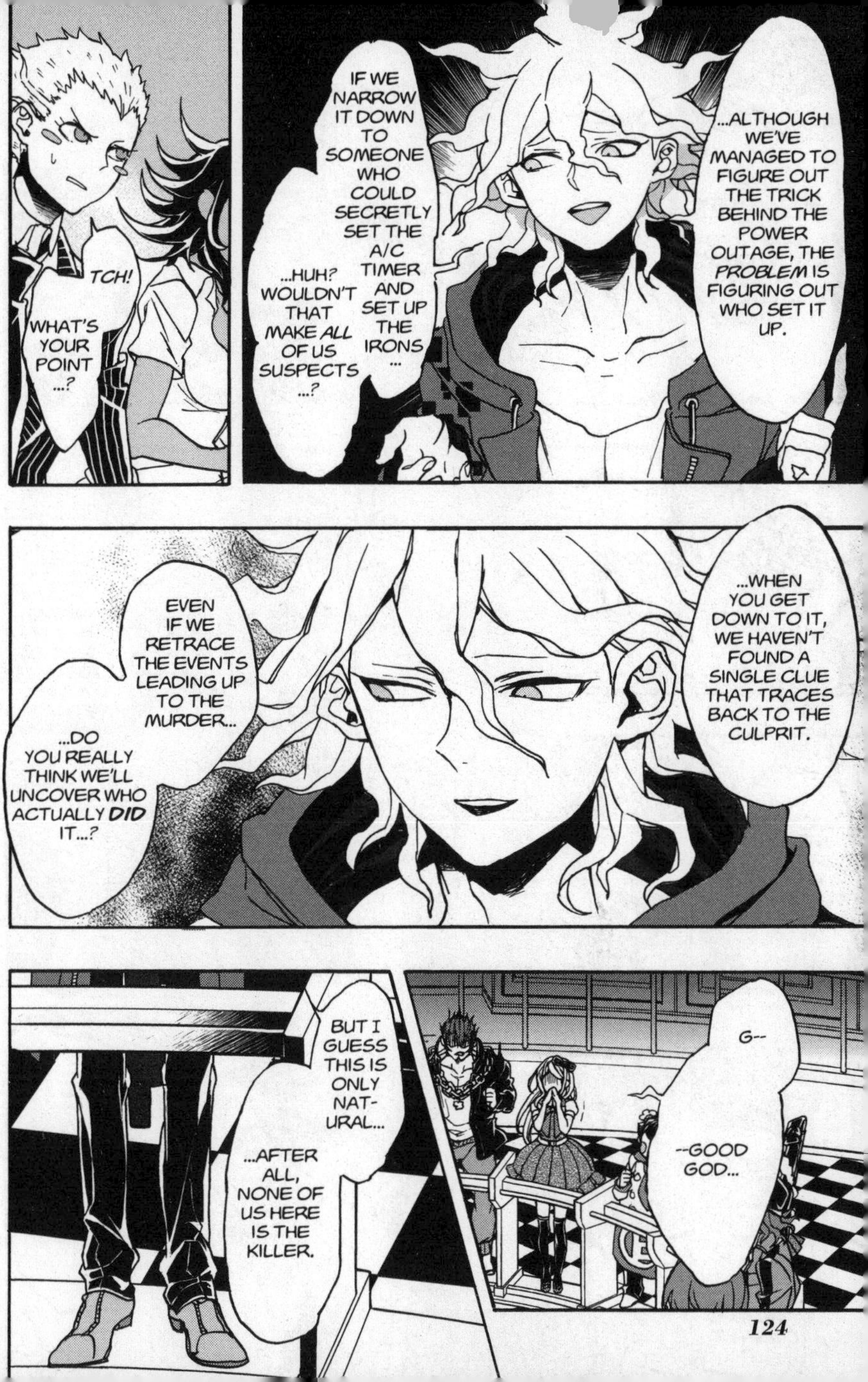
...ALTHOUGH WE'VE MANAGED TO FIGURE OUT THE TRICK BEHIND THE POWER OUTAGE, THE *PROBLEM* IS FIGURING OUT WHO SET IT UP.
IF WE NARROW IT DOWN TO SOMEONE WHO COULD SECRETLY SET THE A/C TIMER AND SET UP THE IRONS...
...HUH? WOULDN'T THAT MAKE *ALL* OF US SUSPECTS...?
TCH!
WHAT'S YOUR POINT...?
...WHEN YOU GET DOWN TO IT, WE HAVEN'T FOUND A SINGLE CLUE THAT TRACES BACK TO THE CULPRIT.
EVEN IF WE RETRACE THE EVENTS LEADING UP TO THE MURDER...
...DO YOU REALLY THINK WE'LL UNCOVER WHO ACTUALLY ***DID*** IT...?
G--
--GOOD GOD...
BUT I GUESS THIS IS ONLY NAT-URAL...
...AFTER ALL, NONE OF US HERE IS THE KILLER.

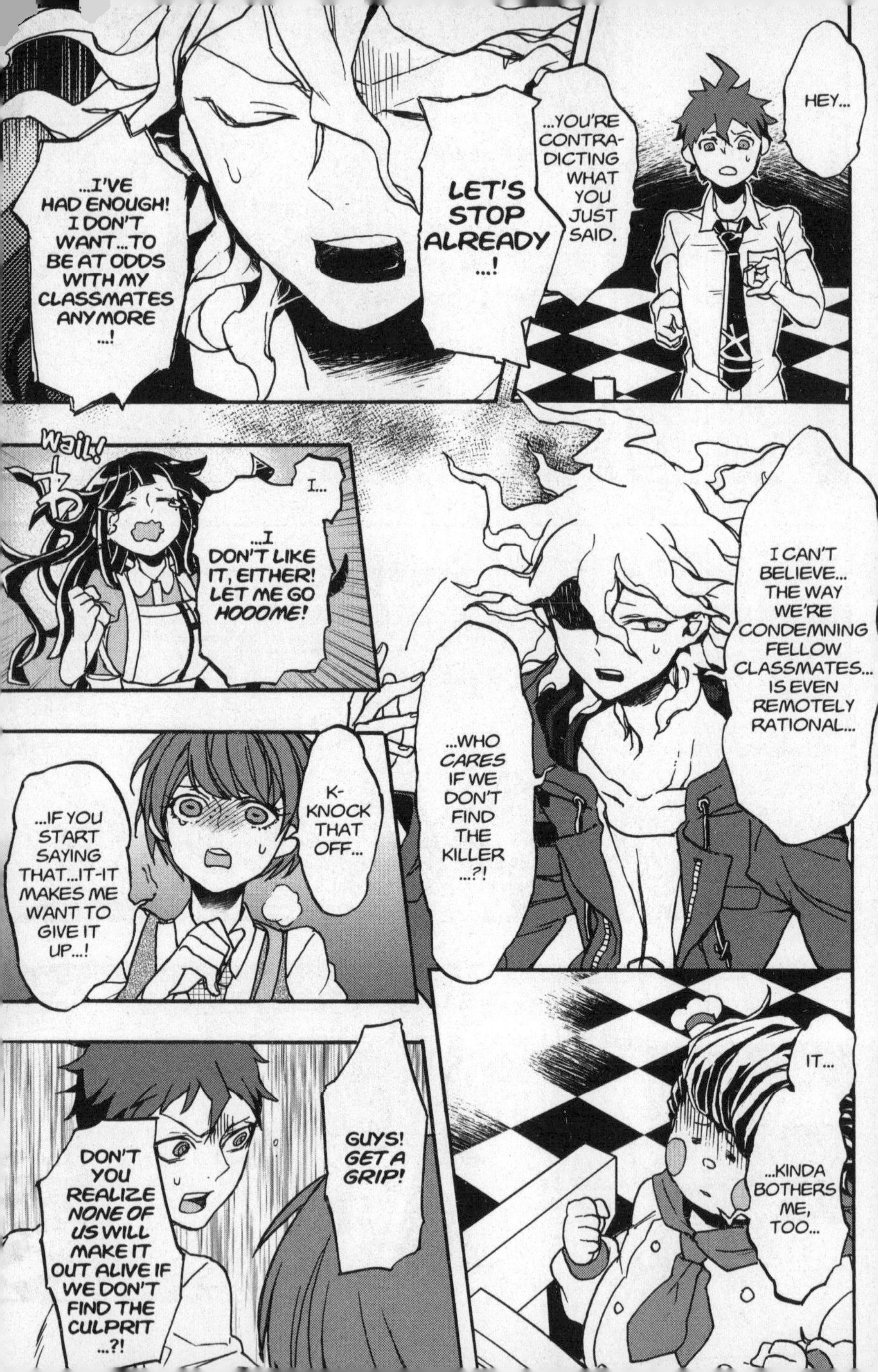
HEY...
...YOU'RE CONTRA-DICTING WHAT YOU JUST SAID.
LET'S STOP ALREADY ...!
...I'VE HAD ENOUGH! I DON'T WANT...TO BE AT ODDS WITH MY CLASSMATES ANYMORE ...!
I CAN'T BELIEVE... THE WAY WE'RE CONDEMNING FELLOW CLASSMATES... IS EVEN REMOTELY RATIONAL...
...WHO CARES IF WE DON'T FIND THE KILLER ...?!
Wail!
I...
...I DON'T LIKE IT, EITHER! LET ME GO HOOOME!
K-KNOCK THAT OFF...
...IF YOU START SAYING THAT...IT-IT MAKES ME WANT TO GIVE IT UP...!
IT...
...KINDA BOTHERS ME, TOO...
GUYS! GET A GRIP!
DON'T YOU REALIZE NONE OF US WILL MAKE IT OUT ALIVE IF WE DON'T FIND THE CULPRIT ...?!

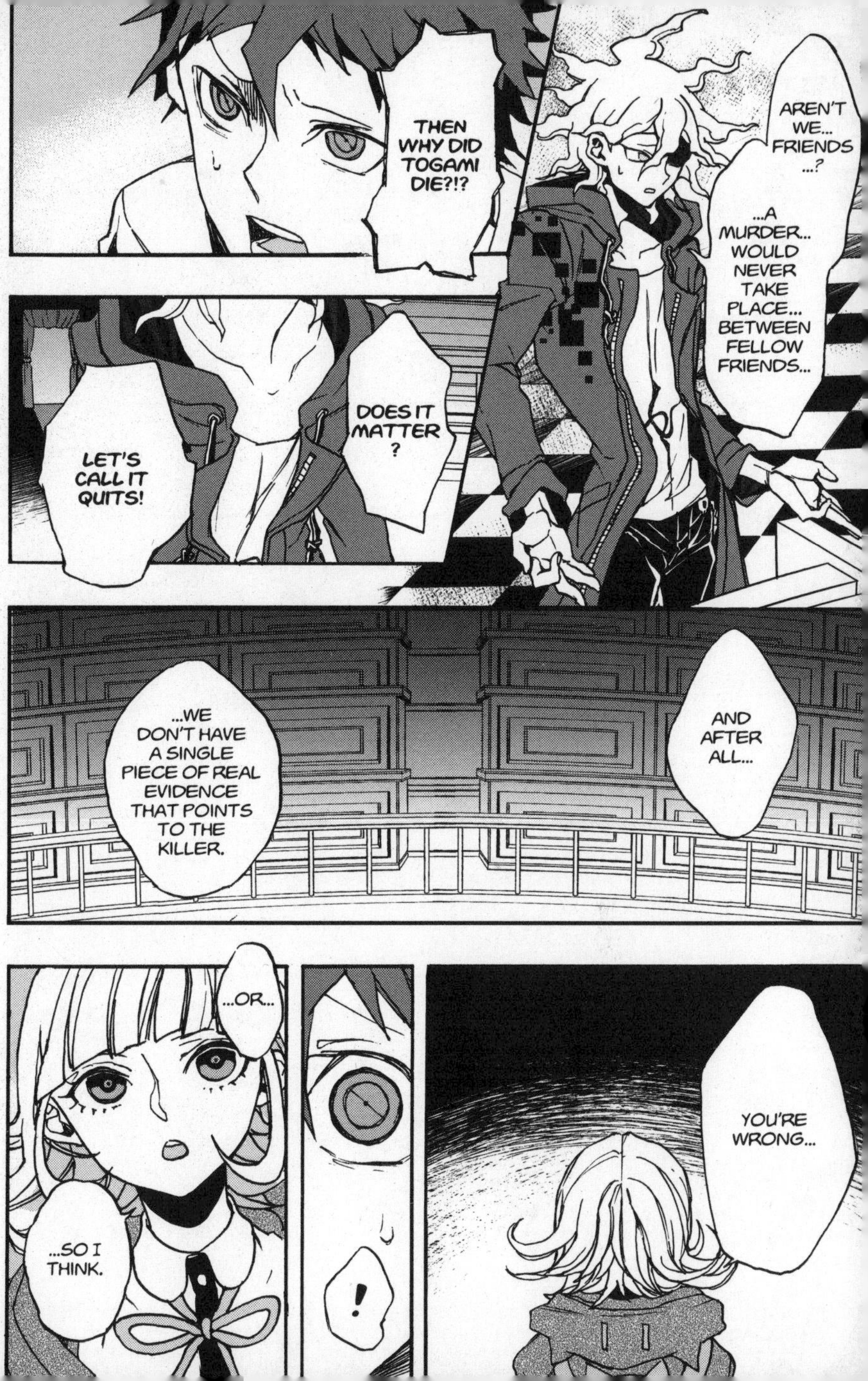
AREN'T WE... FRIENDS ...?
...A MURDER... WOULD NEVER TAKE PLACE... BETWEEN FELLOW FRIENDS...
THEN WHY DID TOGAMI DIE?!?
DOES IT MATTER ?
LET'S CALL IT QUITS!
AND AFTER ALL...
...WE DON'T HAVE A SINGLE PIECE OF REAL EVIDENCE THAT POINTS TO THE KILLER.
YOU'RE WRONG...
!
...OR...
...SO I THINK.

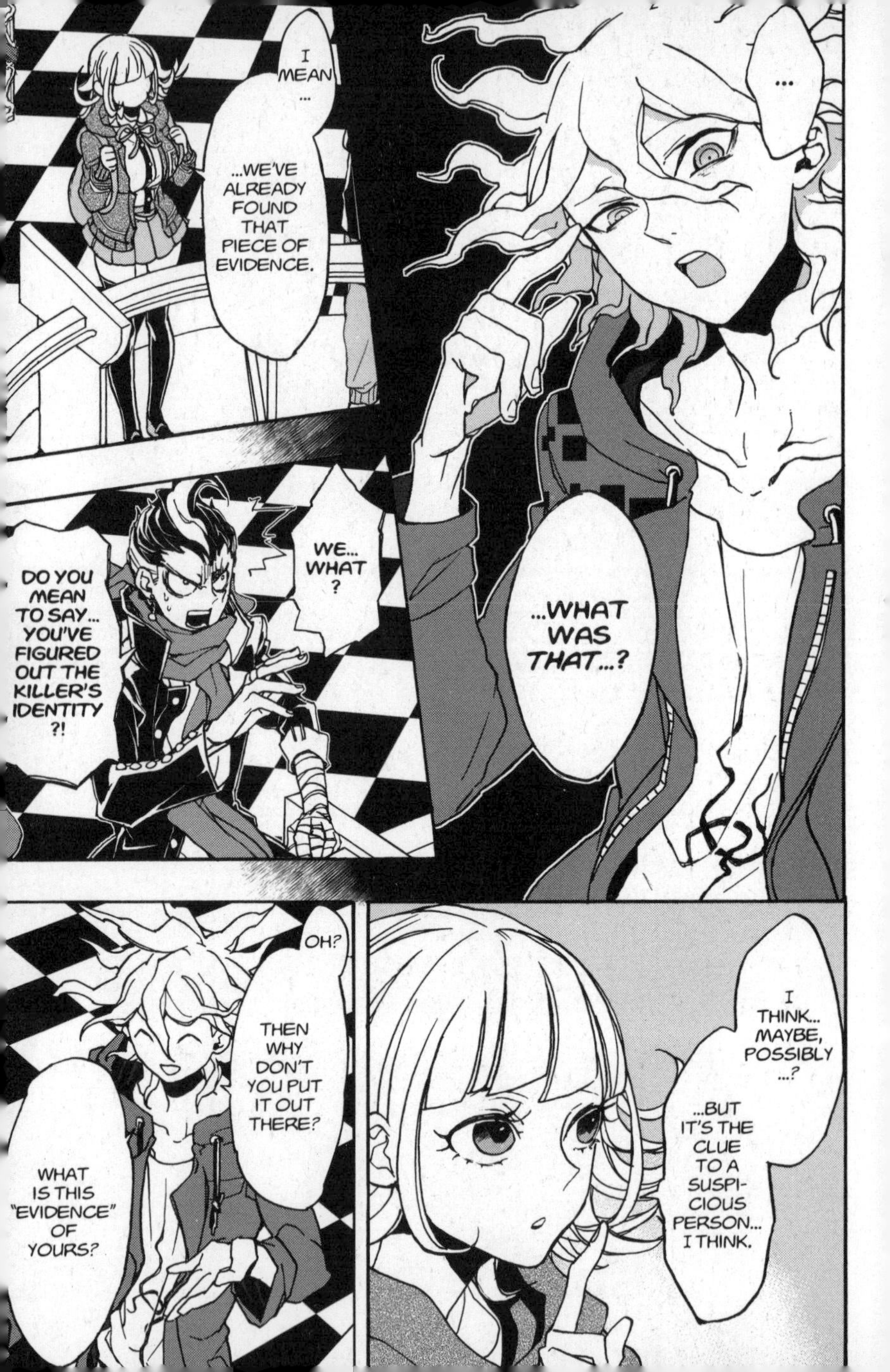
...
...WHAT WAS THAT...?
I MEAN ...
...WE'VE ALREADY FOUND THAT PIECE OF EVIDENCE.
WE... WHAT?
DO YOU MEAN TO SAY... YOU'VE FIGURED OUT THE KILLER'S IDENTITY?!
I THINK... MAYBE, POSSIBLY ...?
...BUT IT'S THE CLUE TO A SUSPICIOUS PERSON... I THINK.
OH?
THEN WHY DON'T YOU PUT IT OUT THERE?
WHAT IS THIS "EVIDENCE" OF YOURS?

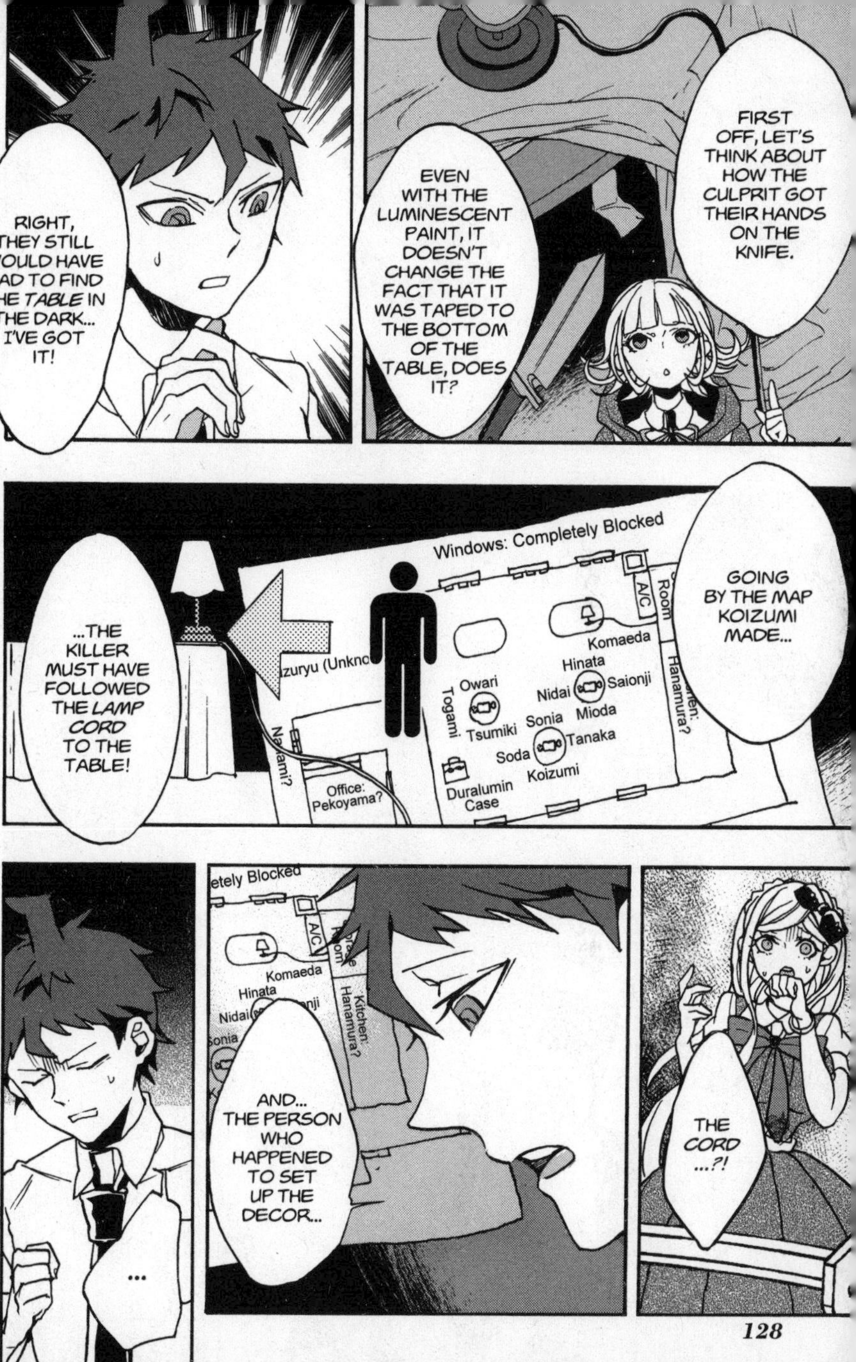
FIRST OFF, LET'S THINK ABOUT HOW THE CULPRIT GOT THEIR HANDS ON THE KNIFE.
EVEN WITH THE LUMINESCENT PAINT, IT DOESN'T CHANGE THE FACT THAT IT WAS TAPED TO THE BOTTOM OF THE TABLE, DOES IT?
RIGHT, THEY STILL WOULD HAVE HAD TO FIND THE *TABLE* IN THE DARK... I'VE GOT IT!
GOING BY THE MAP KOIZUMI MADE...
Windows: Completely Blocked
A/C
Komaeda
Hinata
Owari
Nidai
Saionji
Togami
Sonia
Mioda
Tsumiki
Soda
Tanaka
Koizumi
Duralumin Case
Office: Pekoyama?
Hanamura?
...THE KILLER MUST HAVE FOLLOWED THE *LAMP CORD* TO THE TABLE!
THE *CORD* ...?!
AND... THE PERSON WHO HAPPENED TO SET UP THE DECOR...
...

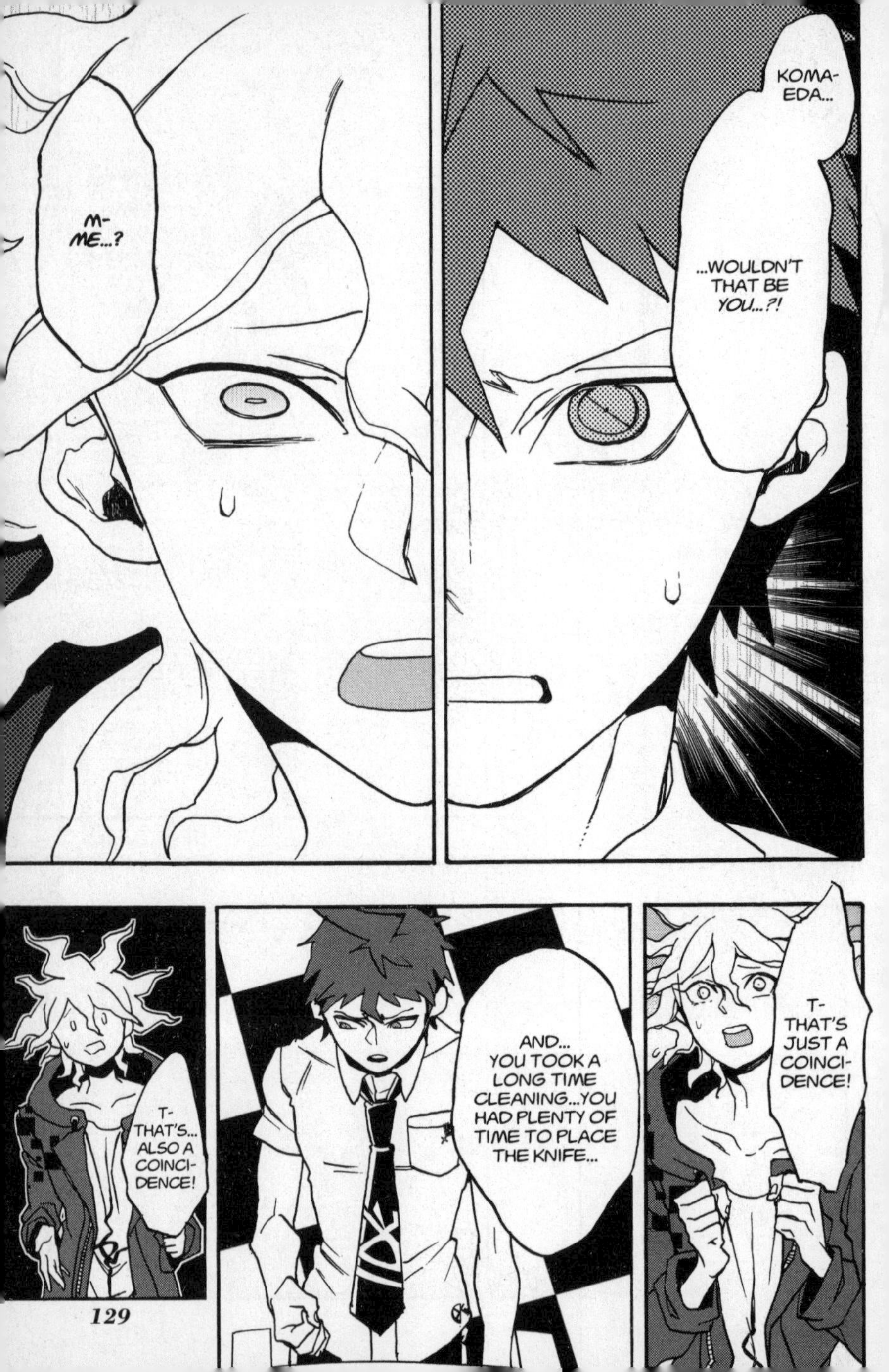
KOMA-EDA...
...WOULDN'T THAT BE *YOU*...?!
M-ME...?
T-THAT'S JUST A COINCI-DENCE!
AND... YOU TOOK A LONG TIME CLEANING...YOU HAD PLENTY OF TIME TO PLACE THE KNIFE...
T-THAT'S... ALSO A COINCI-DENCE!

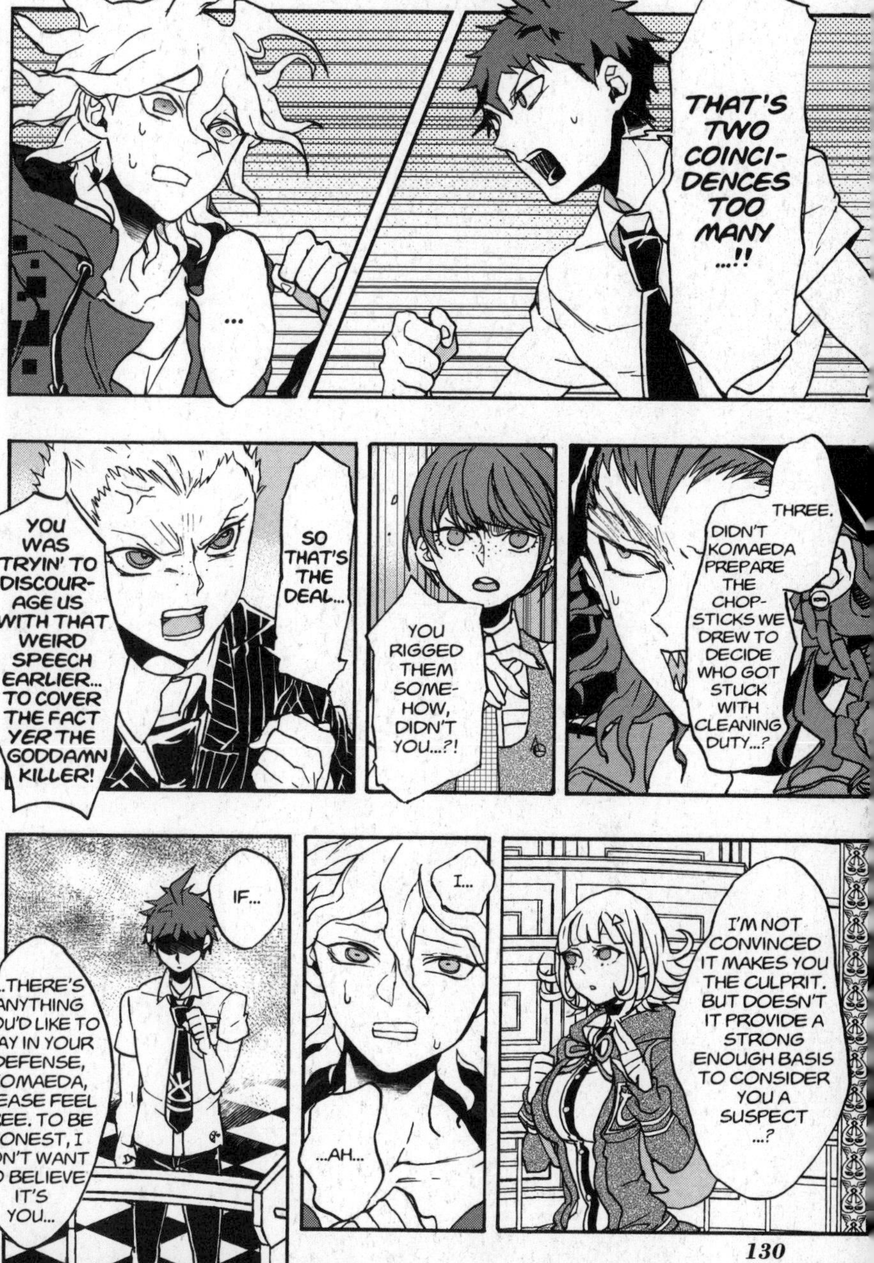
THAT'S TWO COINCIDENCES TOO MANY ...!!
...
THREE. DIDN'T KOMAEDA PREPARE THE CHOPSTICKS WE DREW TO DECIDE WHO GOT STUCK WITH CLEANING DUTY...?
YOU RIGGED THEM SOMEHOW, DIDN'T YOU...?!
SO THAT'S THE DEAL...
YOU WAS TRYIN' TO DISCOURAGE US WITH THAT WEIRD SPEECH EARLIER... TO COVER THE FACT YER THE GODDAMN KILLER!
I'M NOT CONVINCED IT MAKES YOU THE CULPRIT. BUT DOESN'T IT PROVIDE A STRONG ENOUGH BASIS TO CONSIDER YOU A SUSPECT ...?
I...
...AH...
IF...
...THERE'S ANYTHING YOU'D LIKE TO SAY IN YOUR DEFENSE, KOMAEDA, LEASE FEEL REE. TO BE HONEST, I ON'T WANT O BELIEVE IT'S YOU...

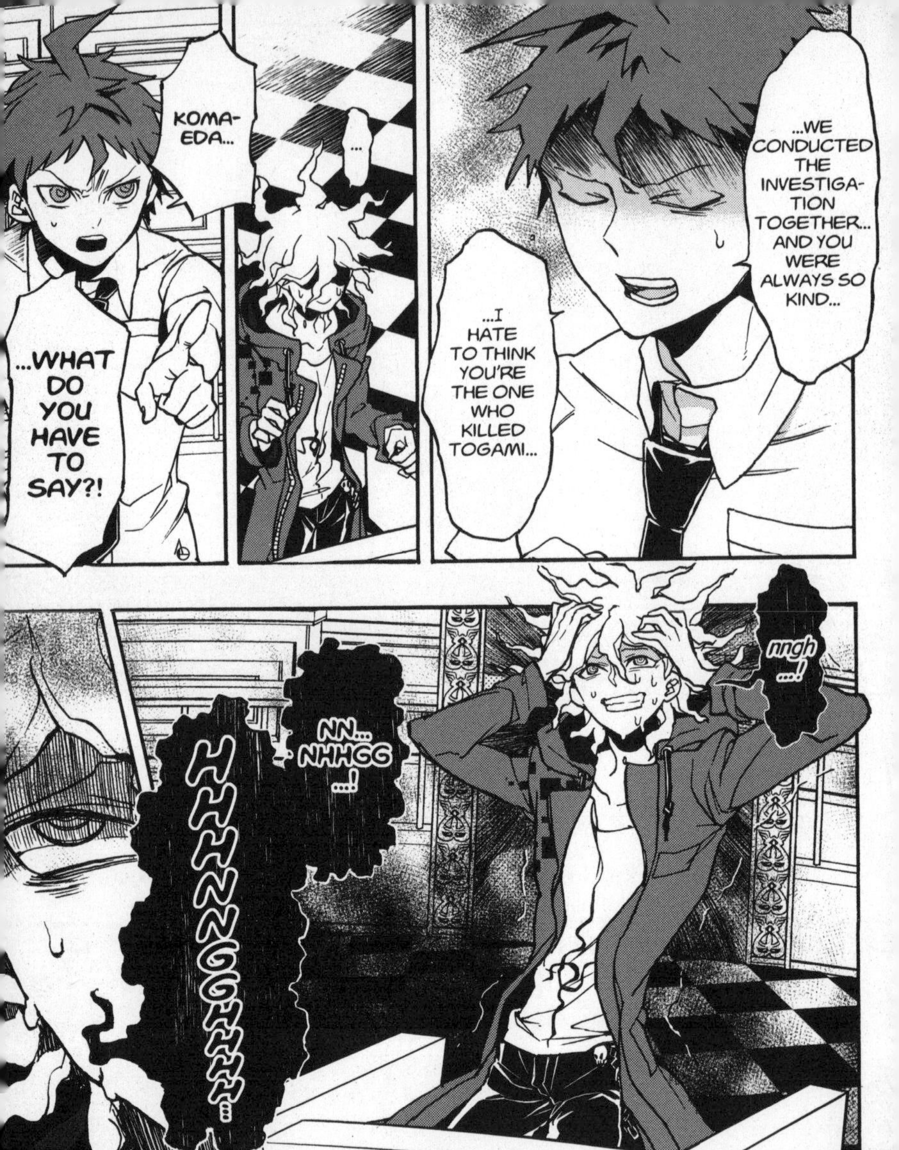
...WE CONDUCTED THE INVESTIGATION TOGETHER... AND YOU WERE ALWAYS SO KIND...
...I HATE TO THINK YOU'RE THE ONE WHO KILLED TOGAMI...
...
KOMA-EDA...
...WHAT DO YOU HAVE TO SAY?!
nngh ...!
NN... NHHGG ...!
HHHNNNGGHHH...

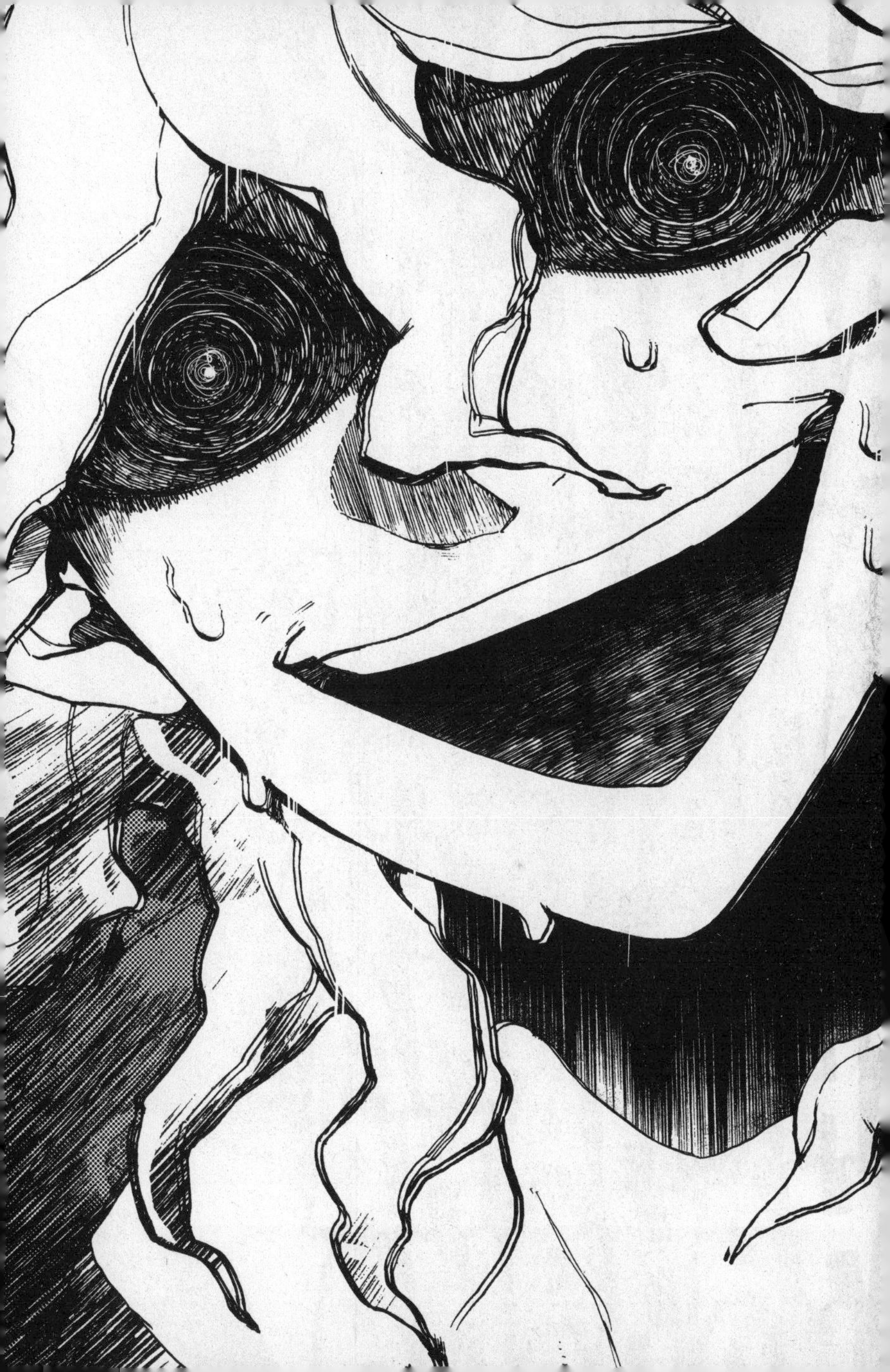

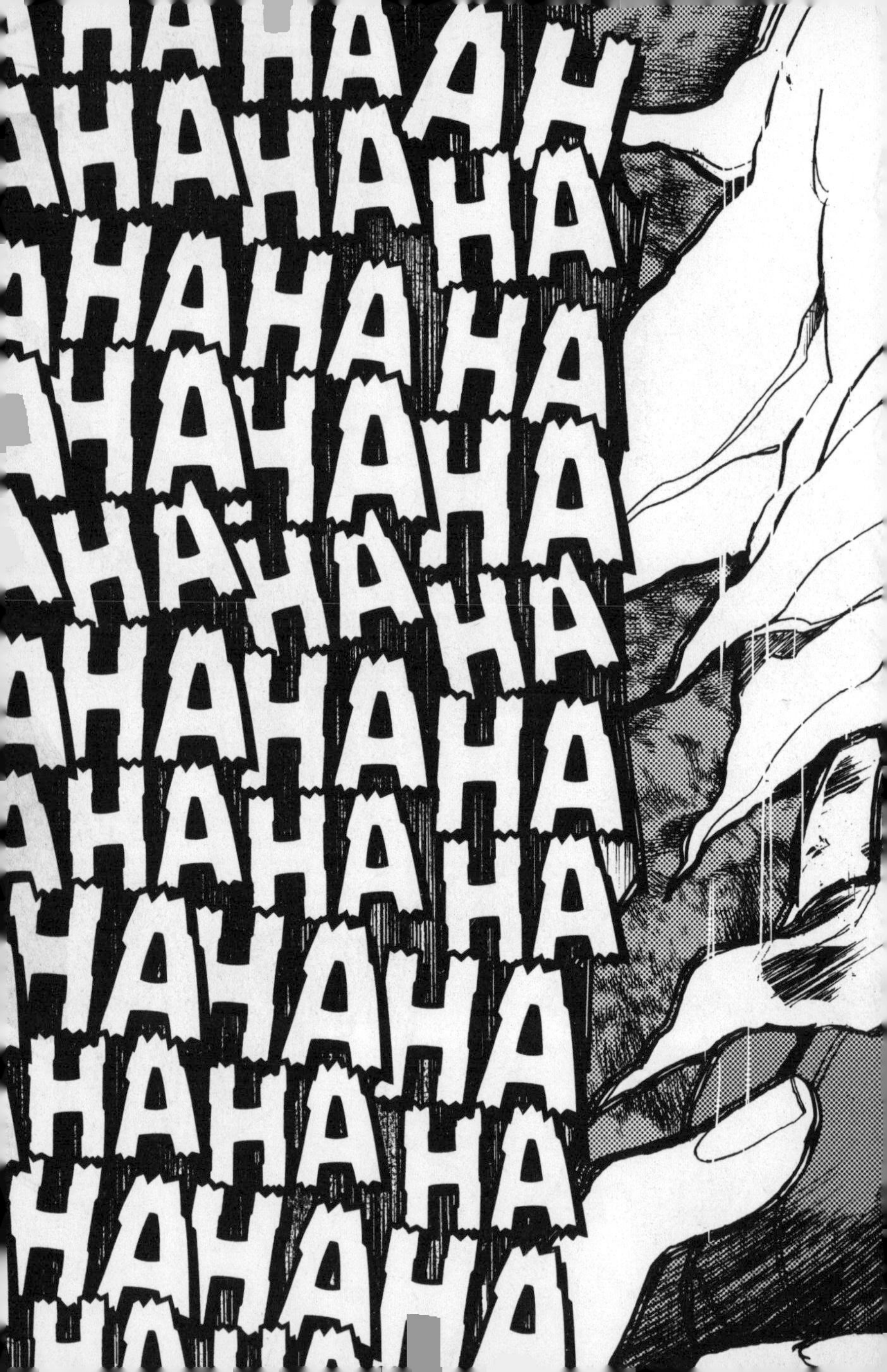

HAHAHAHAHAHAHAHAHAHAHAHAHAHAHAHAHAHAHAHAHAHAHAHAHAHAHAHAHAHAHAHAHAHAHAHAHAHAHA

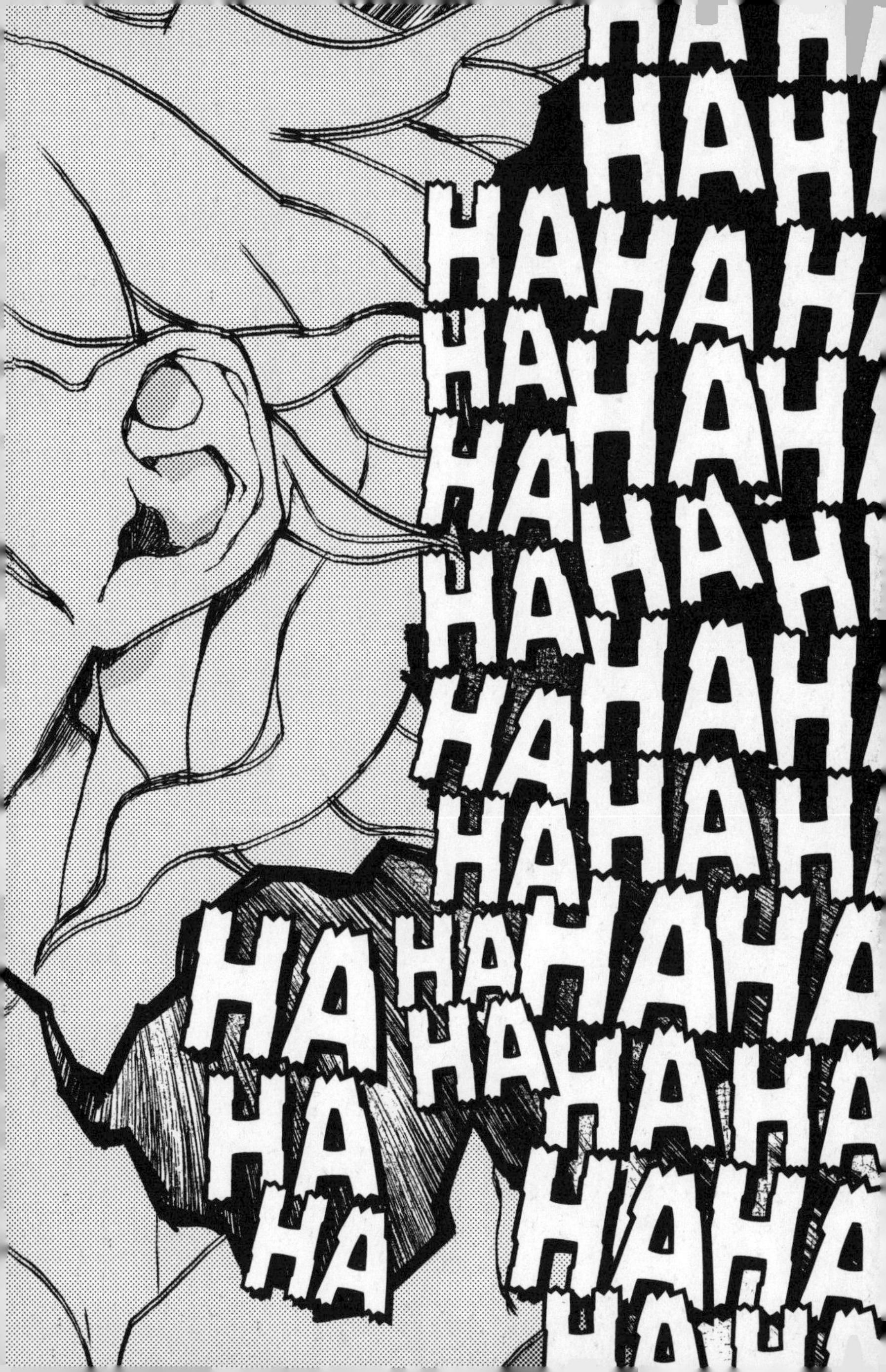
HAHA
HAHA
HAHAH
HAHAH
HAHAH
HAHAH
HAHAH
HAHAH
HAHAH
HAHAH
HA HAHAHA
HA HAHAHA
HA HAHA
HAHA
HAHA

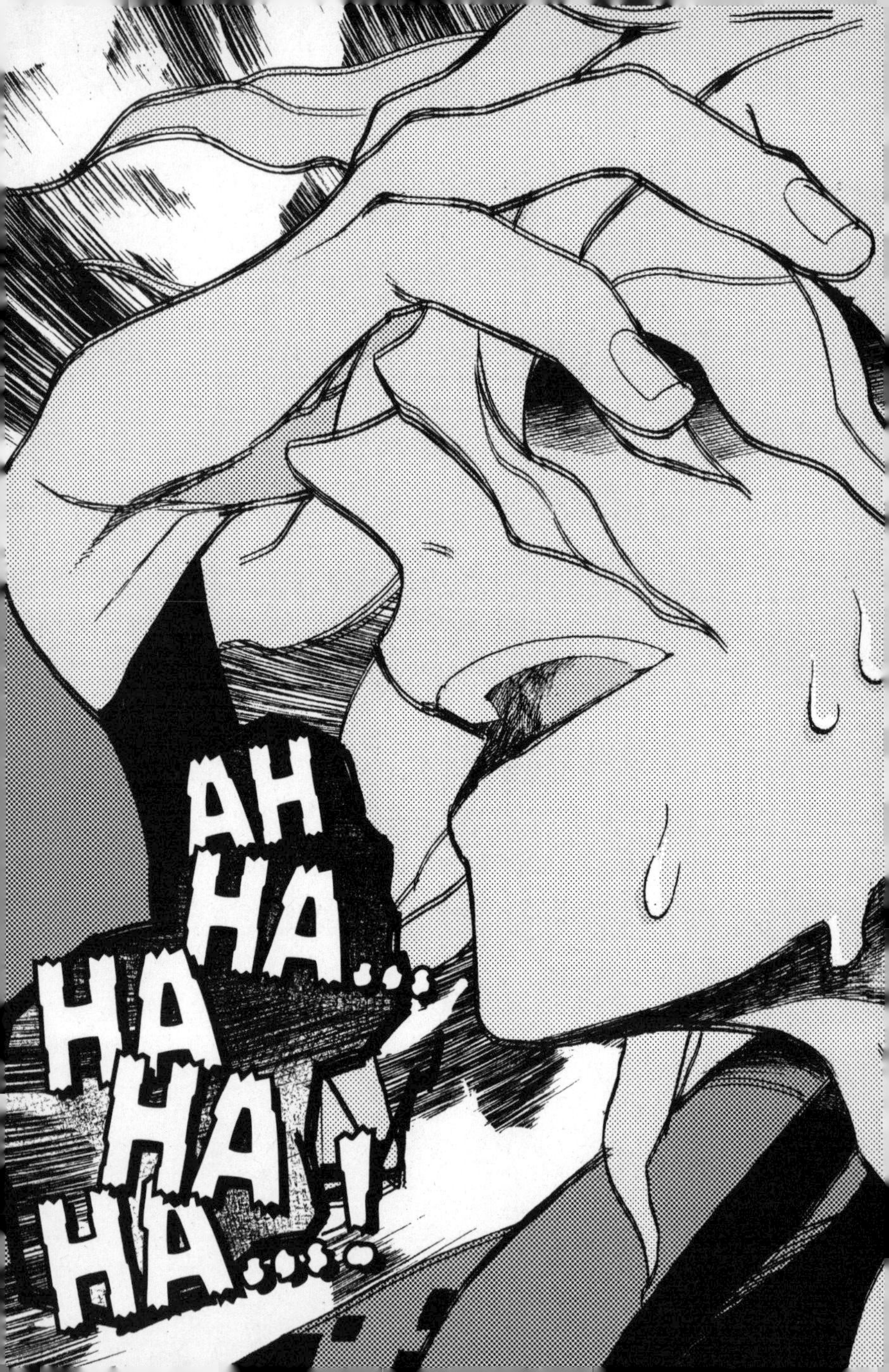
AH HA HA... HA HA HA...!!

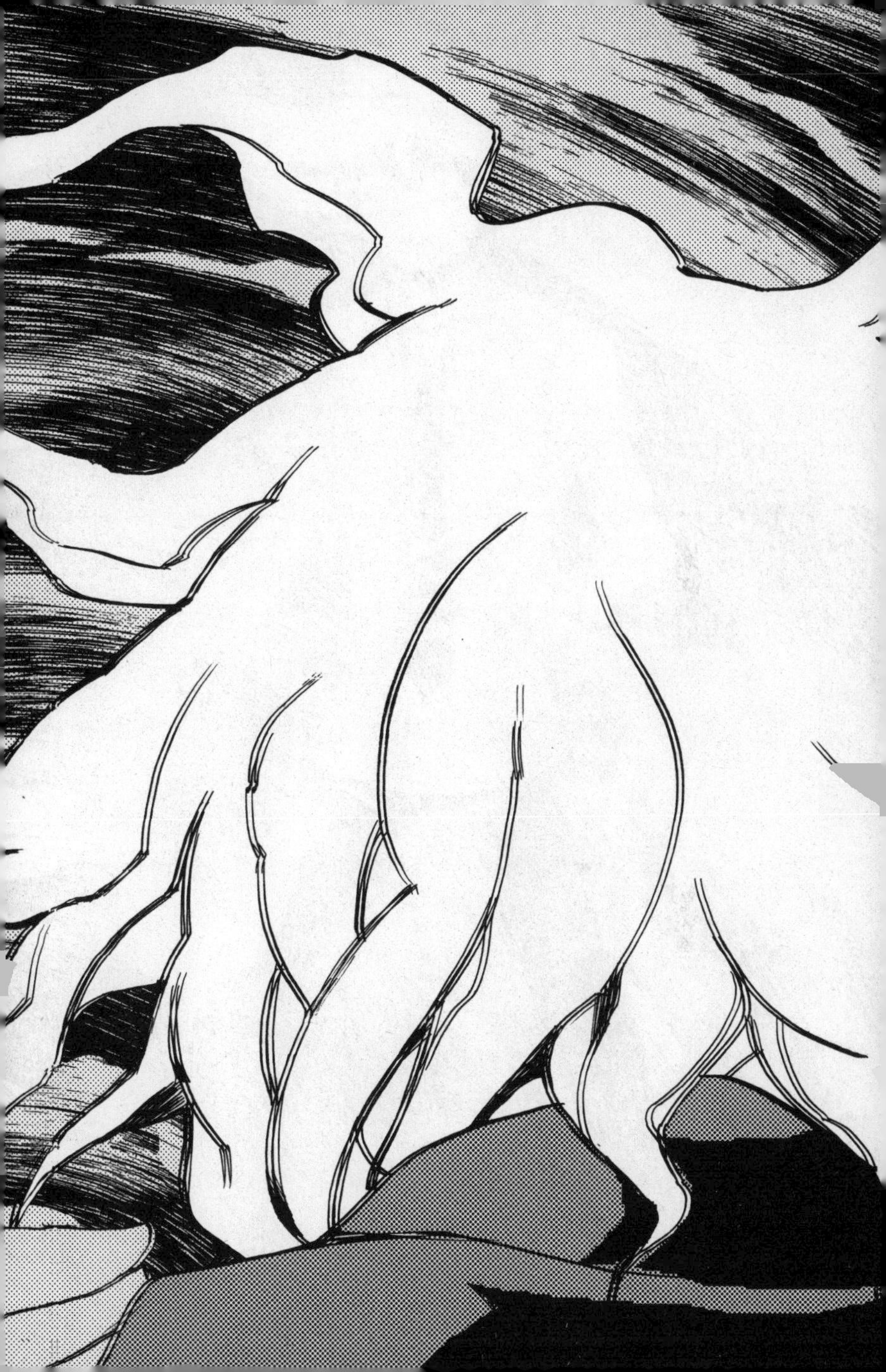

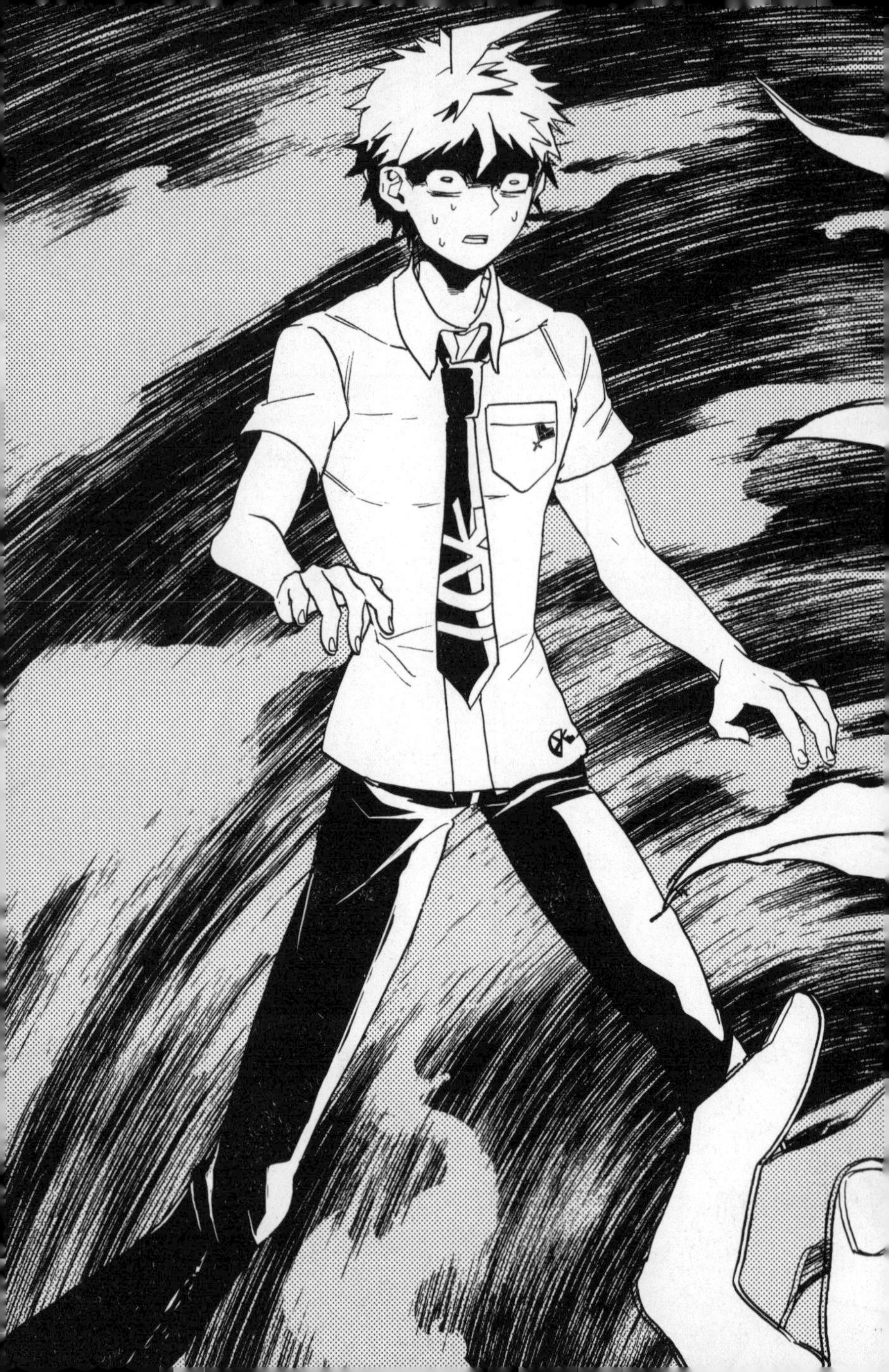

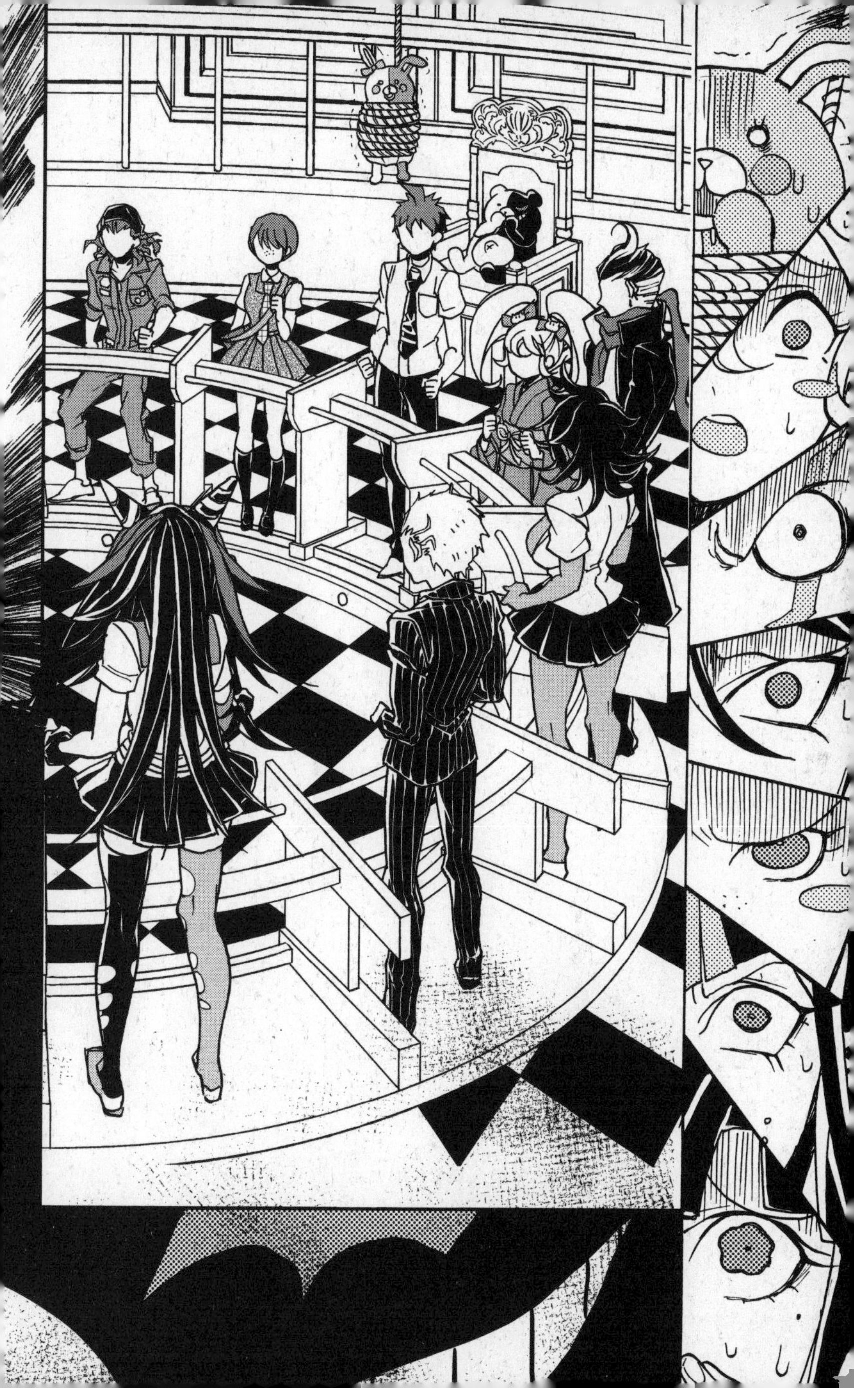

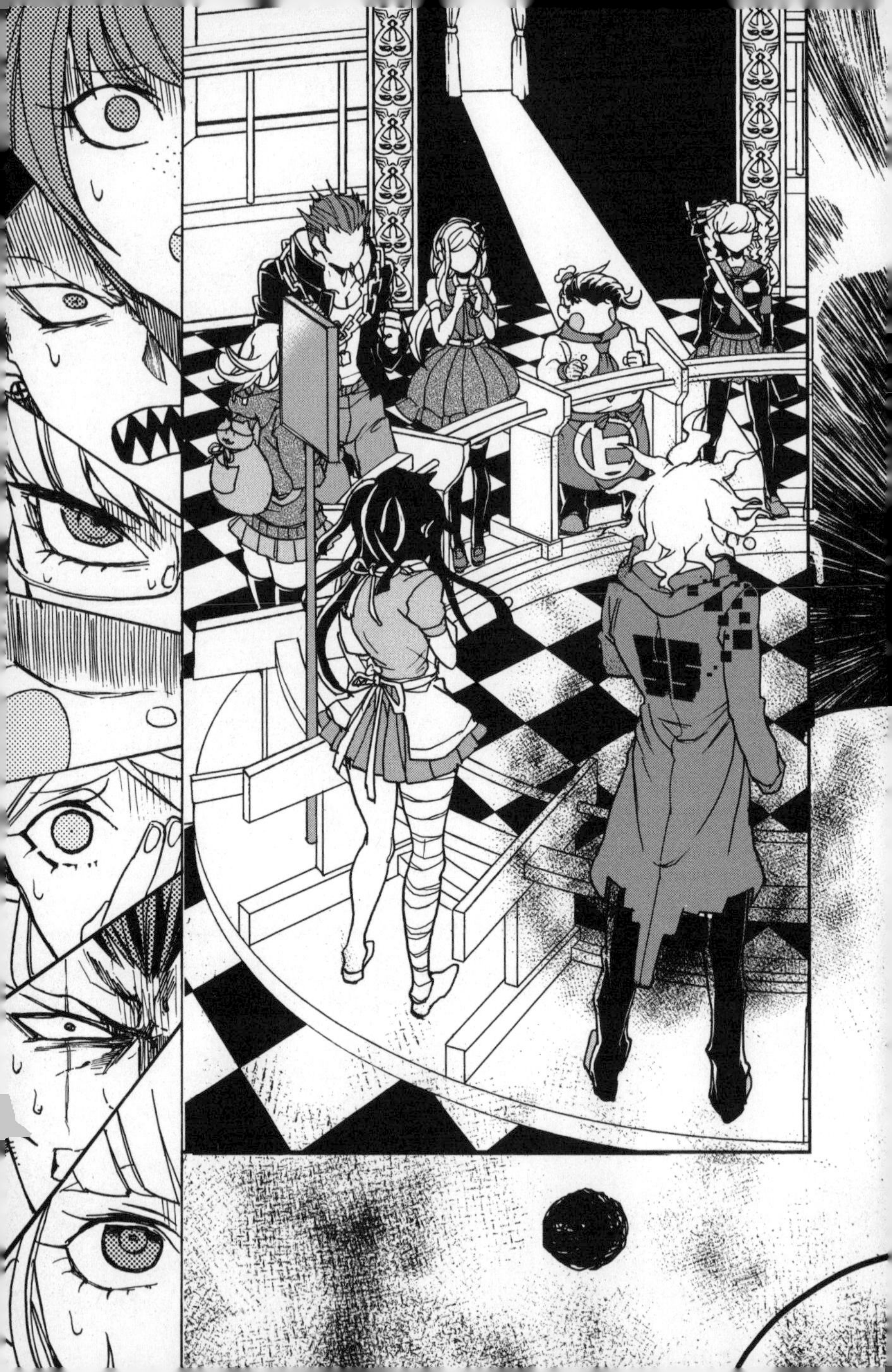

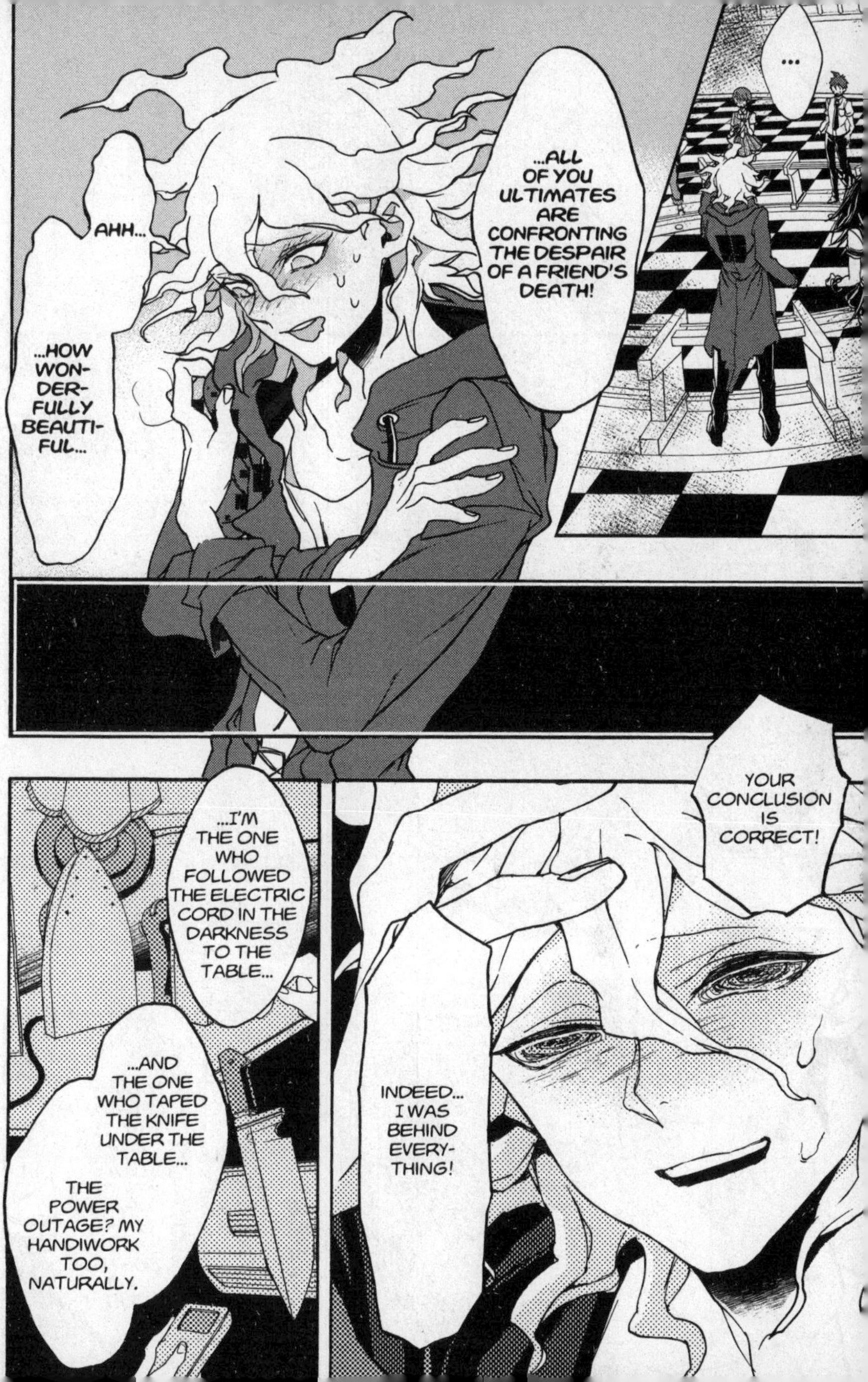
...
...ALL OF YOU ULTIMATES ARE CONFRONTING THE DESPAIR OF A FRIEND'S DEATH!
AHH...
...HOW WONDERFULLY BEAUTIFUL...
YOUR CONCLUSION IS CORRECT!
INDEED... I WAS BEHIND EVERYTHING!
...I'M THE ONE WHO FOLLOWED THE ELECTRIC CORD IN THE DARKNESS TO THE TABLE...
...AND THE ONE WHO TAPED THE KNIFE UNDER THE TABLE...
THE POWER OUTAGE? MY HANDIWORK TOO, NATURALLY.

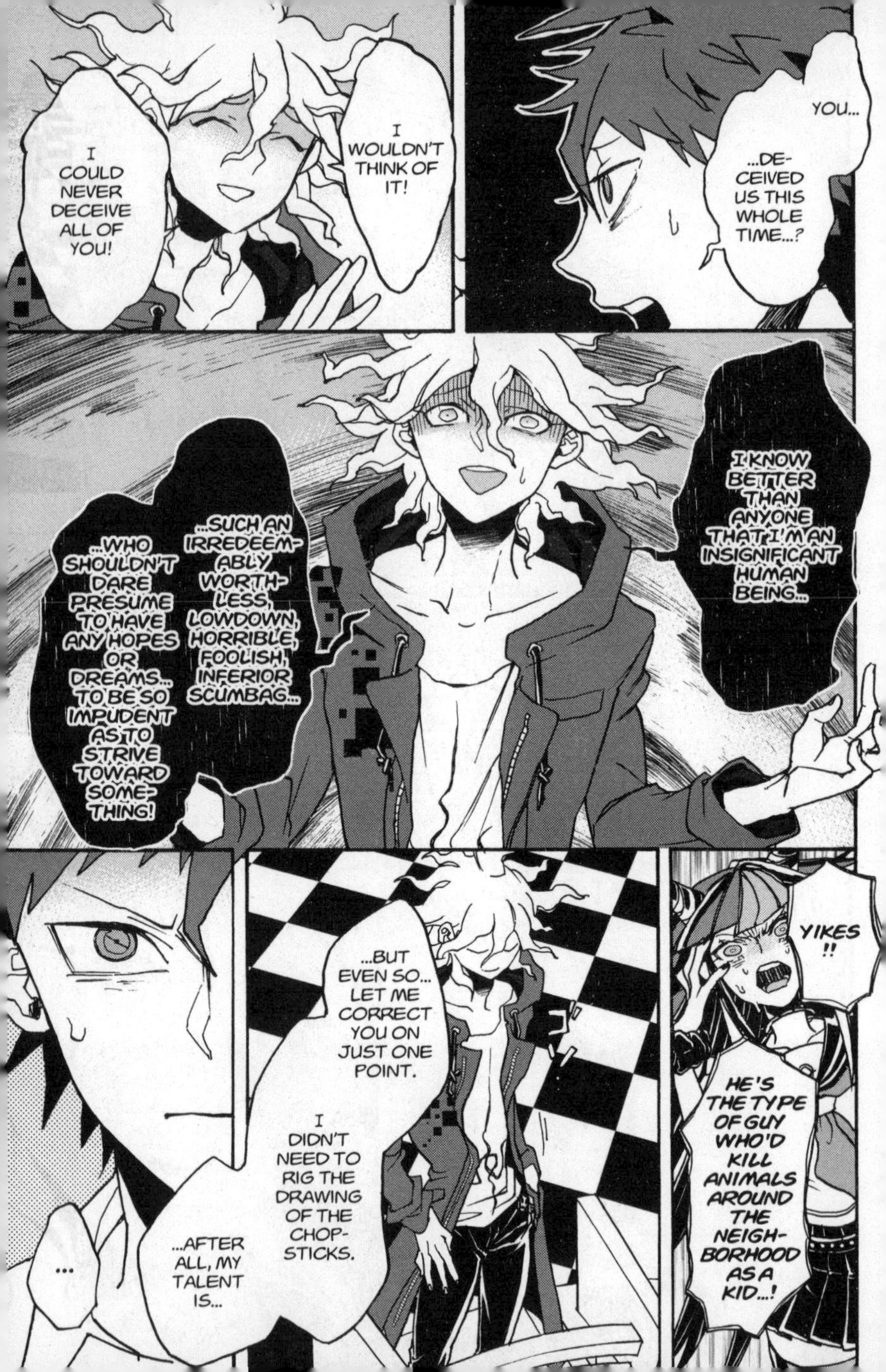
YOU...
...DE-CEIVED US THIS WHOLE TIME...?
I WOULDN'T THINK OF IT!
I COULD NEVER DECEIVE ALL OF YOU!
I KNOW BETTER THAN ANYONE THAT I'M AN INSIGNIFICANT HUMAN BEING...
...SUCH AN IRREDEEMABLY WORTHLESS, LOWDOWN, HORRIBLE, FOOLISH, INFERIOR SCUMBAG...
...WHO SHOULDN'T DARE PRESUME TO HAVE ANY HOPES OR DREAMS... TO BE SO IMPUDENT AS TO STRIVE TOWARD SOMETHING!
YIKES!!
HE'S THE TYPE OF GUY WHO'D KILL ANIMALS AROUND THE NEIGHBORHOOD AS A KID...!
...BUT EVEN SO... LET ME CORRECT YOU ON JUST ONE POINT.
I DIDN'T NEED TO RIG THE DRAWING OF THE CHOPSTICKS.
...AFTER ALL, MY TALENT IS...
...

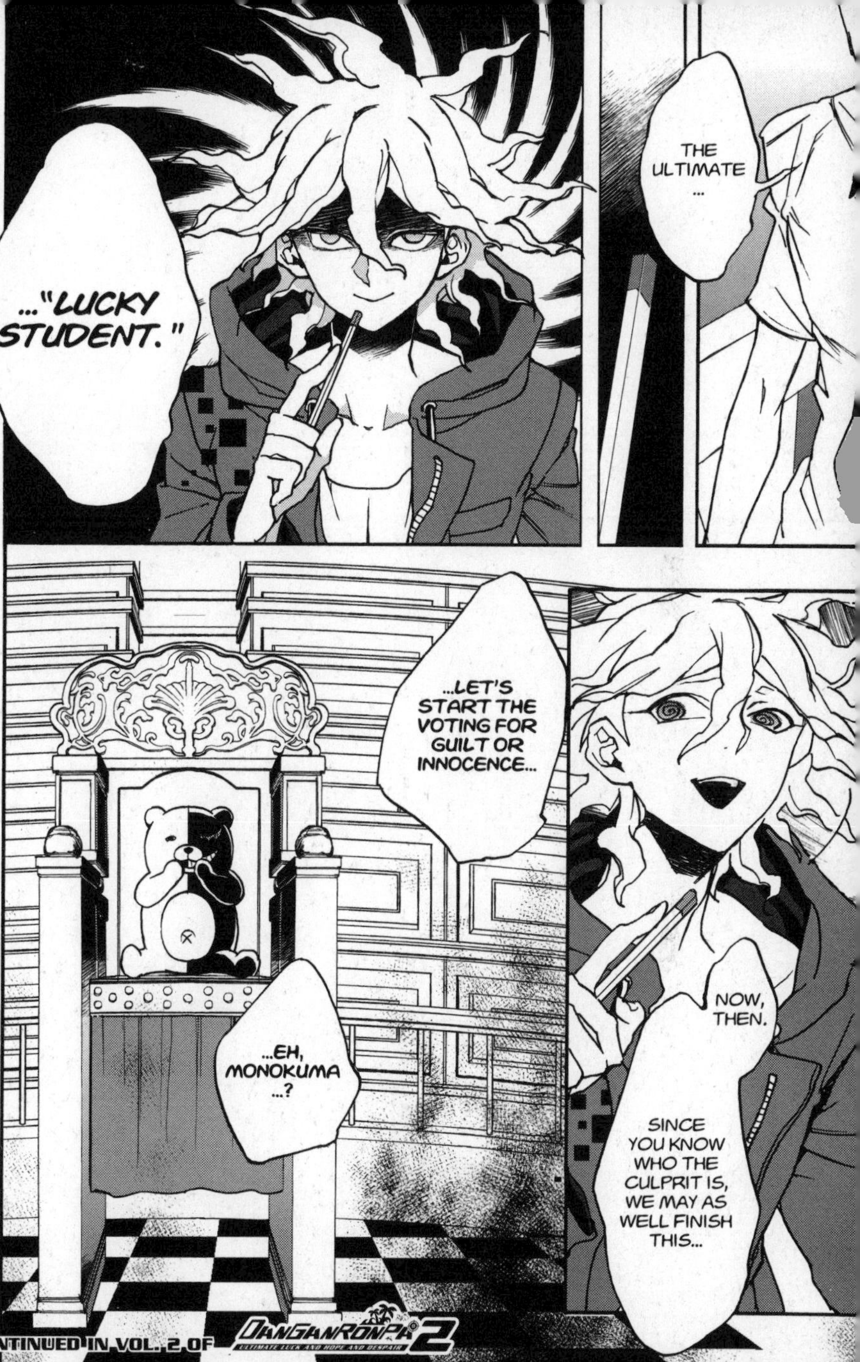
THE ULTIMATE ...
..."LUCKY STUDENT."
NOW, THEN.
SINCE YOU KNOW WHO THE CULPRIT IS, WE MAY AS WELL FINISH THIS...
...LET'S START THE VOTING FOR GUILT OR INNOCENCE...
...EH, MONOKUMA ...?

CONTINUED IN VOL. 2 OF DANGANRONPA 2 ULTIMATE LUCK AND HOPE AND DESPAIR

AFTERWORD:

Hello, I'm Kyousuke Suga. Thank you so much for picking up this copy of **Danganronpa 2: Ultimate Luck and Hope and Despair!**

I'm filled with gratitude for the help and support provided by everyone at Spike Chunsoft, my Japanese editor "W," and all the fans of the game that allowed this manga to take form ...! I've personally been a fan of the original **Danganronpa** game since before it became a big name, so I was thrilled that my first serialized series as a manga pro would be an adaptation of **Danganronpa 2**. It's a greater honor than I deserve.

I know it's far from perfect, but I'd like to devote myself to this manga as I pour my heart into it. If you wouldn't mind, I hope to see you again in the next volume!

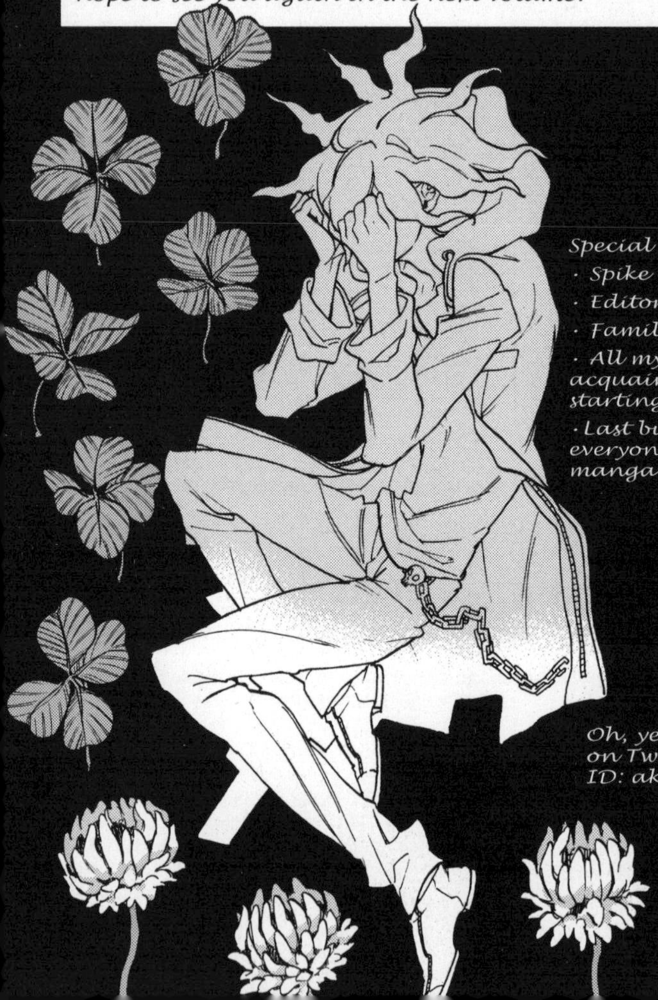

Special Thanks

- Spike Chunsoft
- Editor "W"
- Family and relatives
- All my friends and acquaintances, starting with Ucchi
- Last but not least, everyone reading this manga!

Oh, yeah, I'm on Twitter!
ID: akeri00

president and publisher
MIKE RICHARDSON

designer
SARAH TERRY

ultimate digital art technician
SAMANTHA HUMMER

English-language version produced by Dark Horse Comics

DANGANRONPA 2: ULTIMATE LUCK AND HOPE AND DESPAIR VOLUME 1

Published by
Dark Horse Manga
A division of Dark Horse Comics LLC
10956 SE Main Street | Milwaukie, OR 97222

DarkHorse.com

To find a comics shop in your area, visit comicshoplocator.com.

First edition: October 2018
ISBN 978-1-50670-733-4

8 9 10

Printed in the United States of America

DESPAIR MAIL

c/o Dark Horse Comics | 10956 SE Main St. | Milwaukie, OR 97222 | danganronpa@darkhorse.com

Welcome back to DESPAIR MAIL, the place for Ultimate Danganronpa *Fans! If you'd like to share your thoughts or comments on* Danganronpa *. . . pictures of your* Danganronpa *cosplay . . . or your* Danganronpa *fan art—this is the place for you! Send it to the address or email at the top of the page and remember to use high resolution (300 dpi or better) for your photos or images, so they'll look good in print!*

If this is the first Danganronpa *manga you've picked up from Dark Horse, we say "welcome back" because in 2016–17 we published the four-volume manga series* Danganronpa: The Animation, *which was based on the anime, which was based on the first* Danganronpa *game ^_^ The response was incredible, and still is—just this month, as I write this (in May 2018), vol. 1 of* Danganronpa: The Animation *has gone into its fifth printing! It's great to see how many people are still discovering it.*

A side effect of that popularity :) however, is that we had a lot of letters sent into the manga that we didn't have room to print before Danganronpa: The Animation *concluded with volume 4. However, you are now holding in your hands our NEW* Danganronpa *series, appropriately enough based on the second game.*

Danganronpa 2: Ultimate Luck and Hope and Despair *is going to be three volumes, and we would love to include your reader contributions in DESPAIR MAIL as we go along. But to kick off volume 1, we're going to feature some of those aforementioned letters we didn't have room to print in* Danganronpa: The Animation*! And if you don't see yours here, you may very well see it in the next volume—we thought the fairest way would be to print the contributions in the order we received them, so those who've been waiting the longest get to be first.*

By the way, we know of course that there are other Danganronpa *games and spin-offs in the series, and some of them have manga, too. In fact, some of the games have more than one manga, taking the opportunity that the large cast of characters provides to offer alternative perspectives. What I'm trying to imply here ^_^ is that, yes, we want to release even more* Danganronpa *manga in the future, and hopefully we'll have news about it soon!*

Okay, I've been talking so much about your contributions, so why don't I shut up :) and get to them, starting with the next page . . . ?

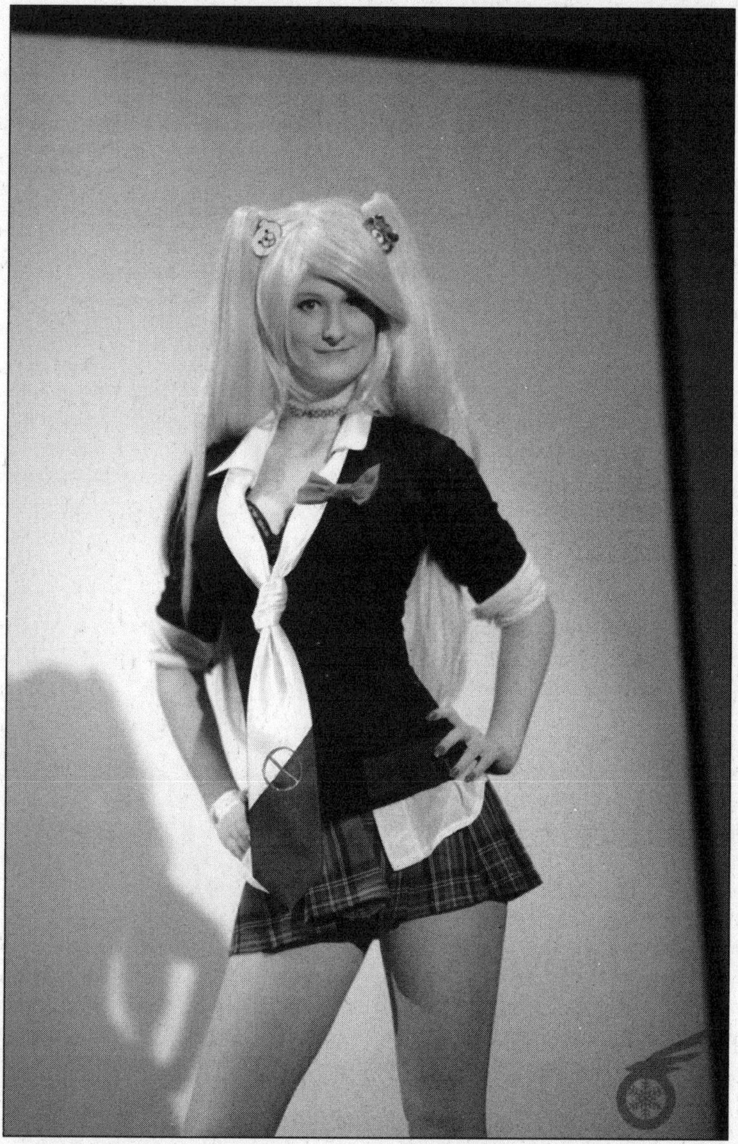

We begin with the most patient of them all—patiently plotting, no doubt, as the mastermind of fashionable despair, Junko Enoshima! This cosplay is from reader Makenna, who wrote in to say: "I've been a huge fan of *Danganronpa* for around 3 years now, and have cosplayed almost all of the female characters from the series, my all-time favorite being Junko! You really feel like the ultimate model up on stage in a costume like that! I thought I would send in a picture of me in cosplay just for fun!"

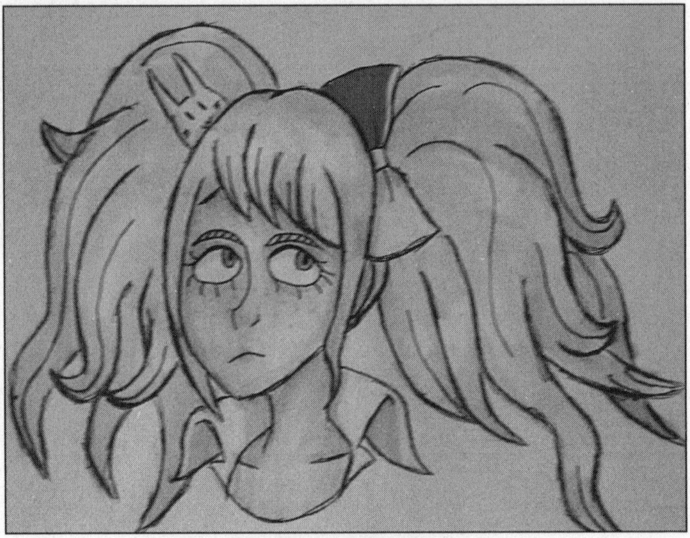

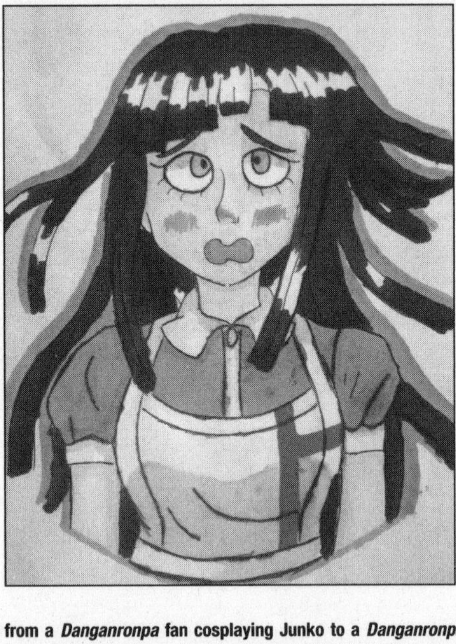

And now we go straight from a *Danganronpa* fan cosplaying Junko to a *Danganronpa* CHARACTER cosplaying Junko! Of course, it's her less-glamorous (but no less dangerous) older twin sister Mukuro Ikusaba, the Ultimate Soldier. Below Mukuro is Mikan Tsumiki, the Ultimate Nurse, and as you can see from vol. 1 of *Danganronpa 2*, the artist of both these pictures, Megan Sullivan, captured her personality very well.

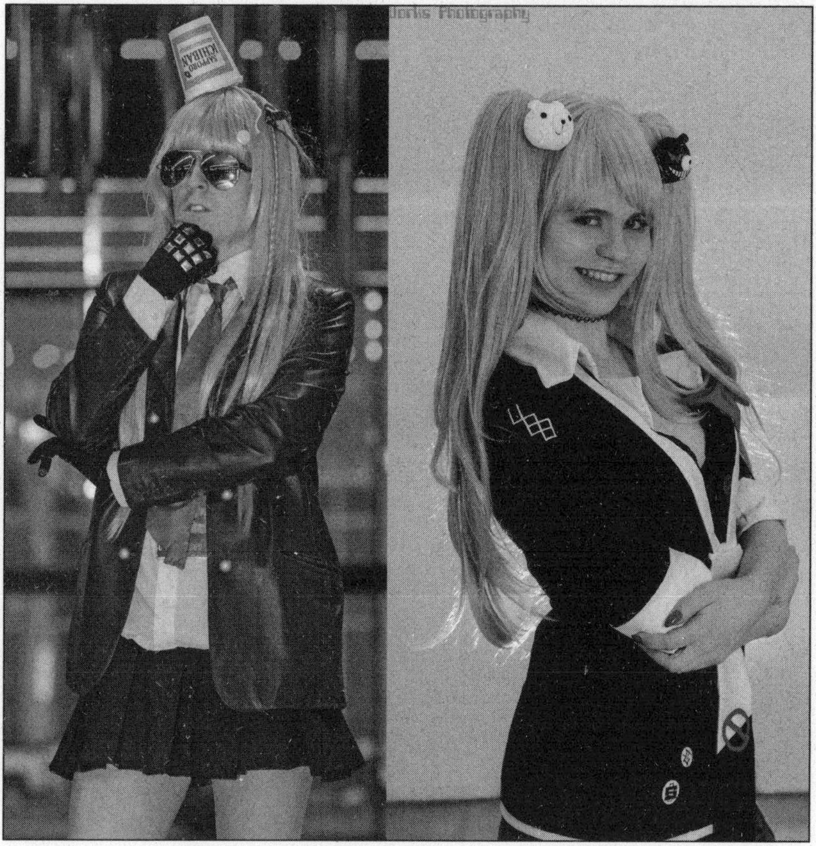

Present with strength on this page and the next is the FunkSoul Cosplay group, who says: "Loving the manga and I've been keeping up to date on the releases so far! It's also totally boss that people can submit things, so that's what I'mma do!" Here we see the ever-popular Junko, plus the person on her trail, Ultimate Detective Kyoko Kirigiri, ratiocinating with ramen on her head (as depicted in vol. 4 of *Danganronpa: The Animation*!).

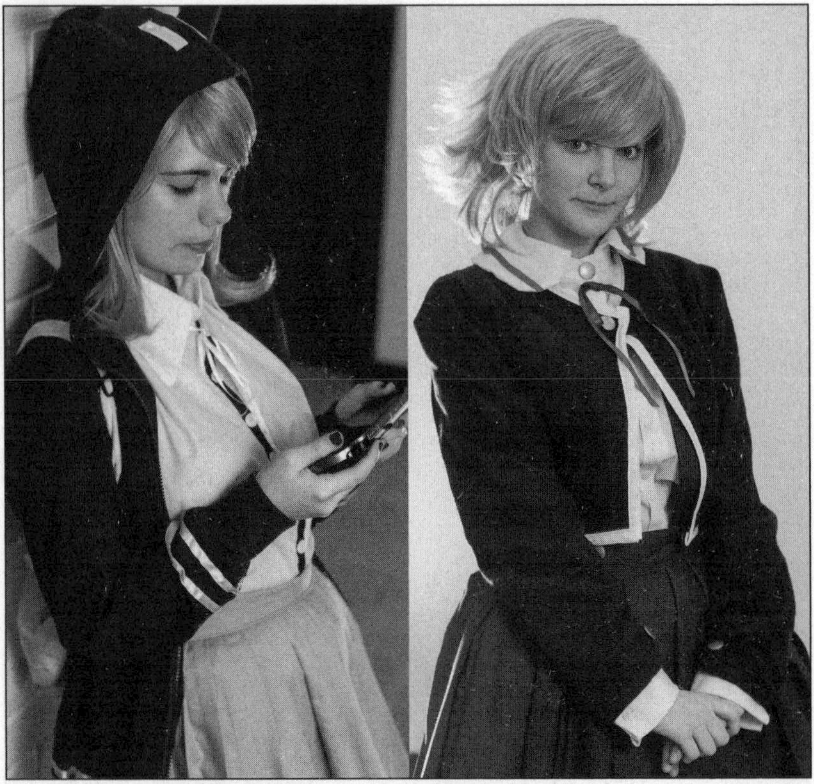

The FunkSoul posse continues to roll with Ultimate Programmer Chihiro Fujisaki, introduced in the first game, plus *Danganronpa 2*'s own Ultimate Gamer, Chiaki Nanami! "We're a cosplay group that has done a few series, *Danganronpa* being one of them. It certainly holds a special place in our hearts. I attached a few images from photoshoots and hopefully they work out for you :) Thanks and a despairy good day!" Y'all as well, FunkSoul!

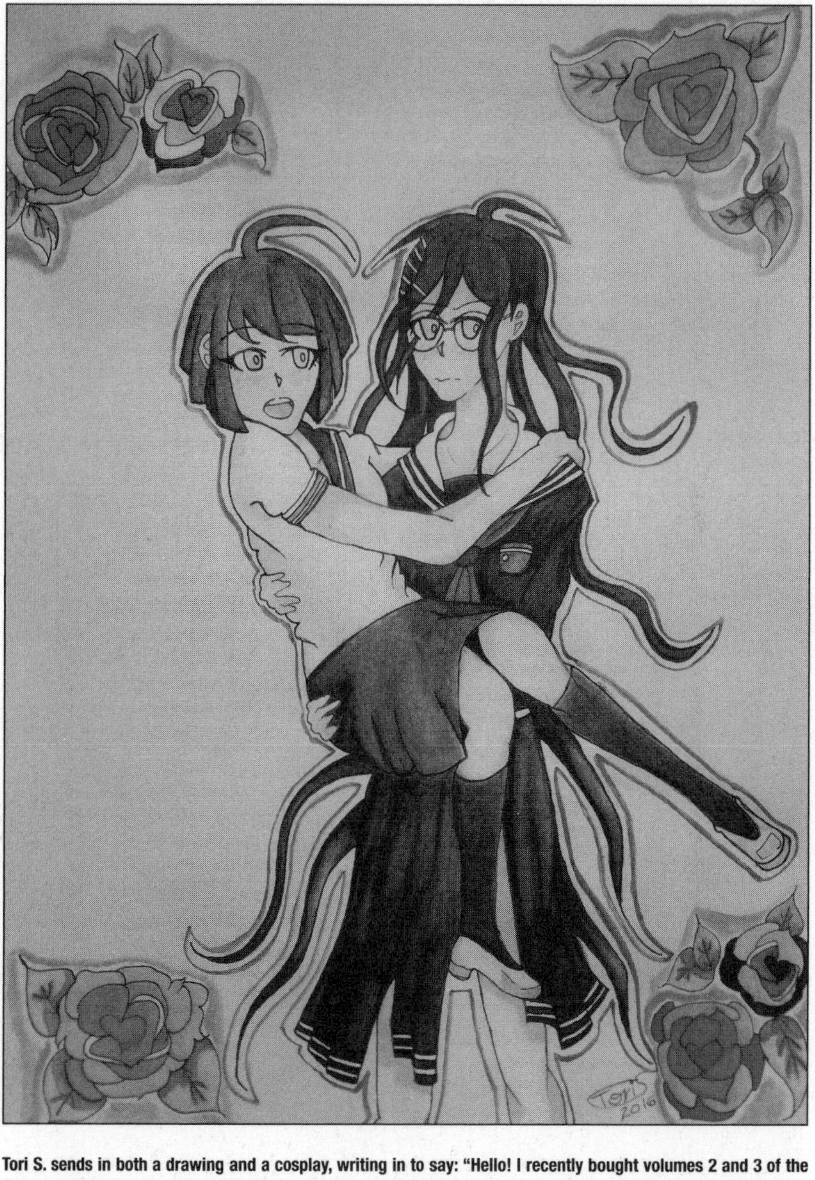
Tori
2016

Tori S. sends in both a drawing and a cosplay, writing in to say: "Hello! I recently bought volumes 2 and 3 of the *Danganronpa* manga and loved both! I'm a cosplayer and I draw as well, so I'd like to submit some of my work for Despair Mail. The first is a watercolor drawing of Toko and Komaru from *Danganronpa Another Episode: Ultra Despair Girls*..."

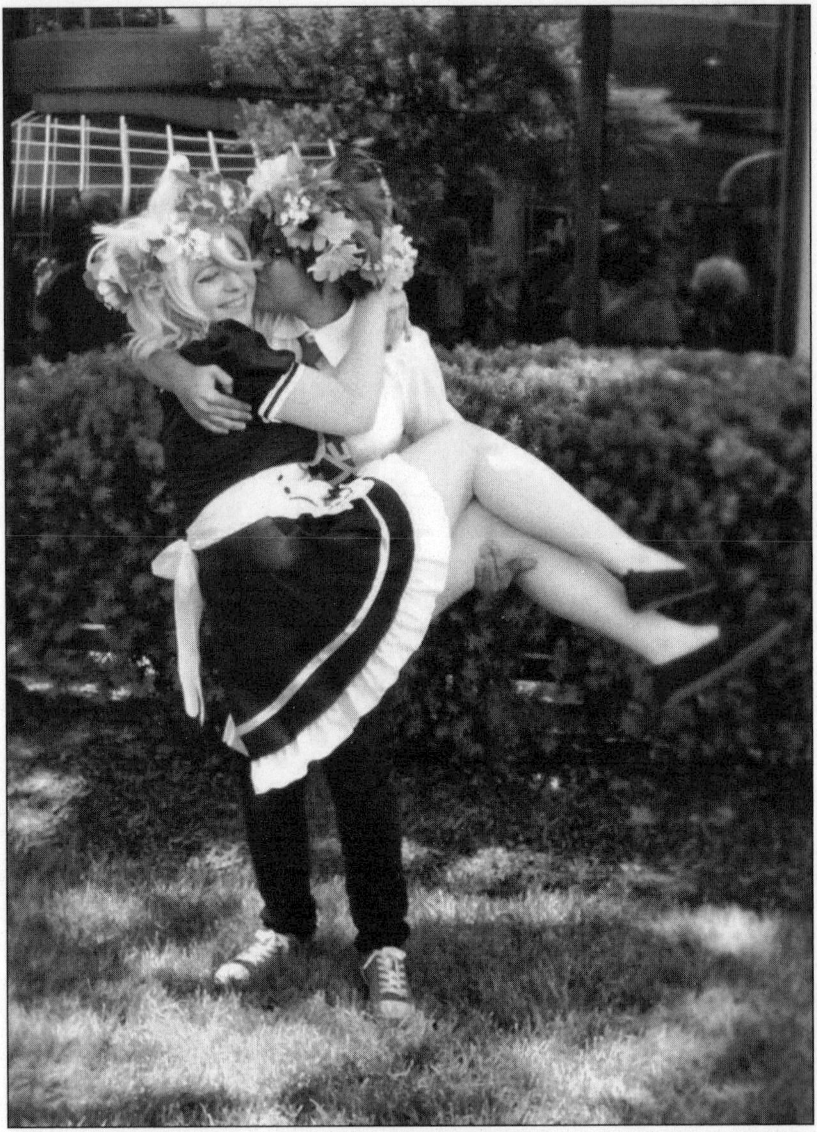

" . . . The second is a picture of my friend Sophia and I cosplaying Maid Komaeda and Hajime at an Anime Midwest photoshoot. I would be so happy and grateful to see one or both of these photos in an upcoming volume! Thank you!" Well, as I mentioned earlier, it's May right now as we put this letter column together . . . the season of flowers and romance. It'll be fall by the time everyone reads this—but keep spring in your hearts!

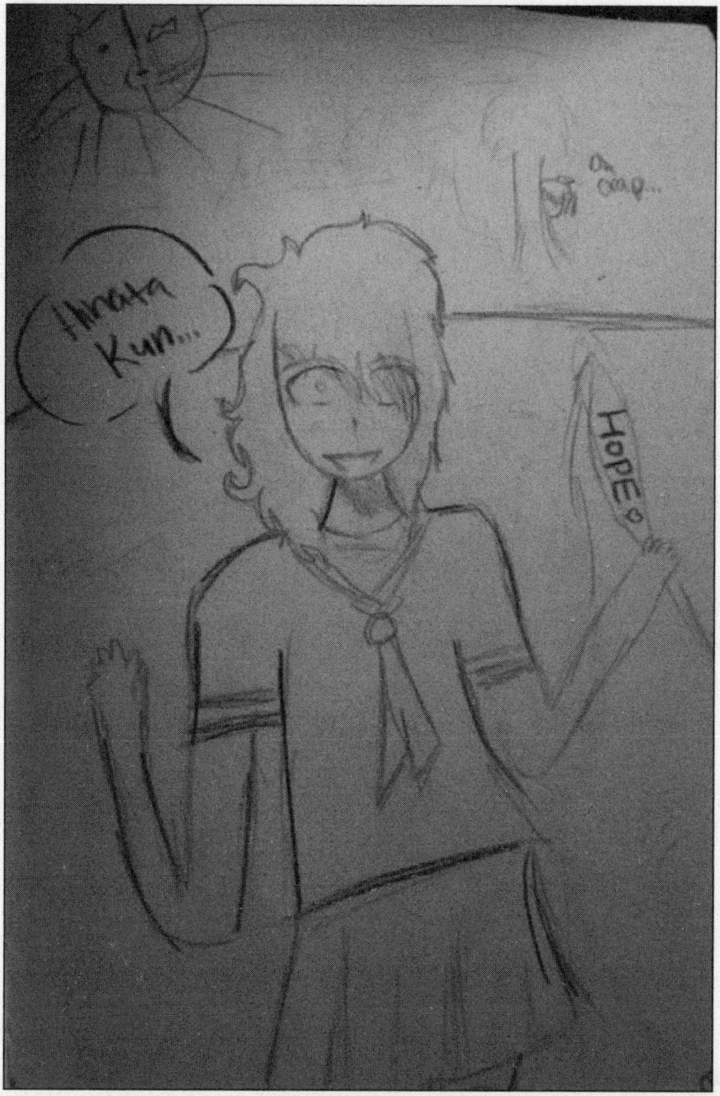
Hinata Kun...
HoPE

Hmm, we just had a Maid Komaeda on the previous page. Let's continue in that spirit of flexibility with this fan art from Rachel S., who wrote in to say: "Hello there! I'm a big fan of *Danganronpa*, and I thought this picture of a yandere cross dressing Komaeda looking for Hinata-kun would be perfect for Despair Mail. I love both of the series so far, and I will definitely buy each volume of this masterpiece!! Thank you so much, and best wishes with the series!!!"

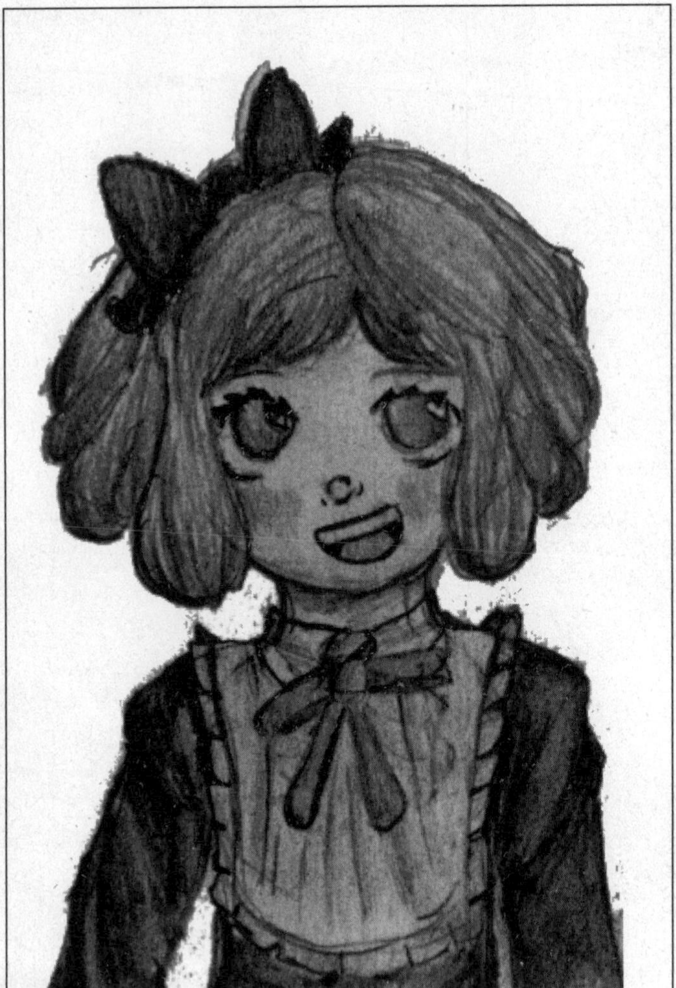

Hannah Green contributes with Monaca (aka Monaka) Towa from *Danganronpa Another Episode: Ultra Despair Girls*: "After seeing in volume two that art from the entire franchise is allowed for Despair Mail, I just had to draw my personal favorite character in the series, Monaka! I'm ecstatic that one of the manga series is getting localized, and hope that is may lead to more following. In the meantime, I'm definitely supporting this publication as much as I can, and honestly just want to thank you all for this opportunity for fans to communicate as well!" Thank you, Hannah—as you can see, your support did help lead to more *Danganronpa* manga! And there's a manga for *Ultra Despair Girls* as well—perhaps in the future we can…

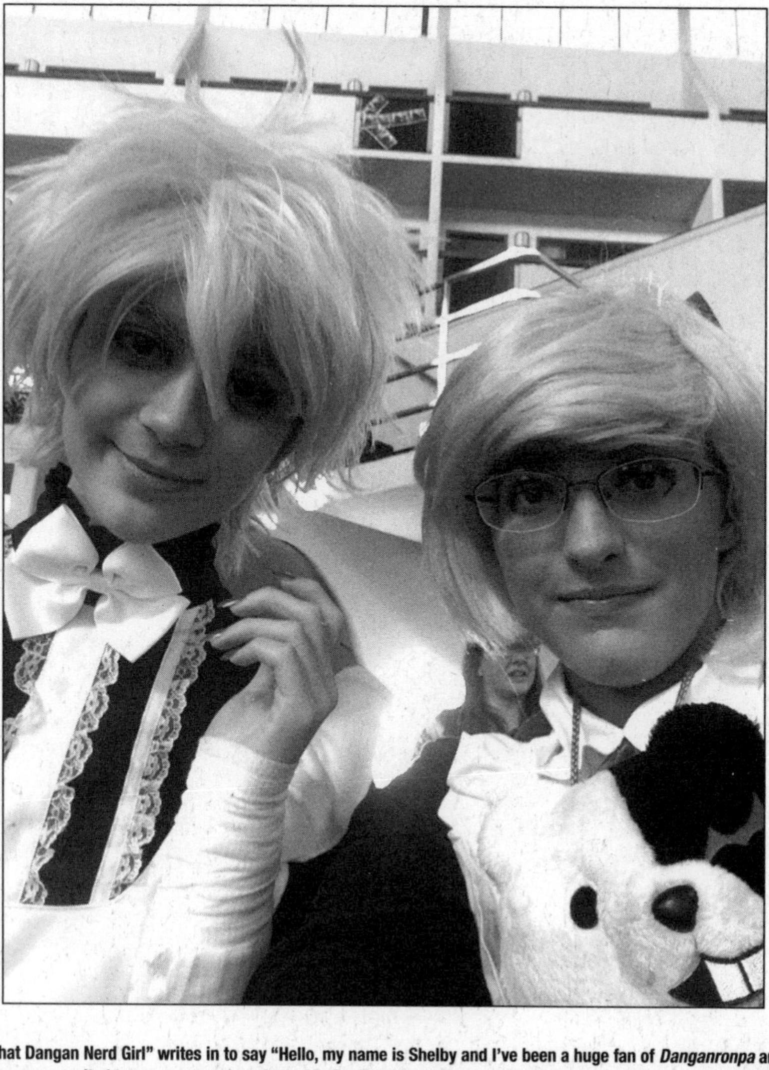

"That Dangan Nerd Girl" writes in to say "Hello, my name is Shelby and I've been a huge fan of *Danganronpa* and was super excited to see a manga be released in English. I hope I'm not too late but I wanted to send in a picture of my friend and I cosplaying. The characters we're cosplaying aren't in this part of the series but in *Danganronpa 2: Goodbye Despair* and *Ultra Despair Girls*, also known as *Danganronpa: Another Episode*. In the picture I'm cosplaying as Monaca (on the right) from Ultra Despair Girls and my friend is cosplaying as Nagito Komaeda (left) in a maid outfit from *Danganronpa 2: Goodbye Despair* and I guess I can't forget Monokuma who decided to sneak in. Thank you for the consideration and I hope this makes it into the next volume. Best of wishes, Shelby." We're seeing certain trends in character popularity . . . but why not—since Shelby sent in this letter, now we're doing *Danganronpa 2* . . . and of course, Komaeda's on the cover!

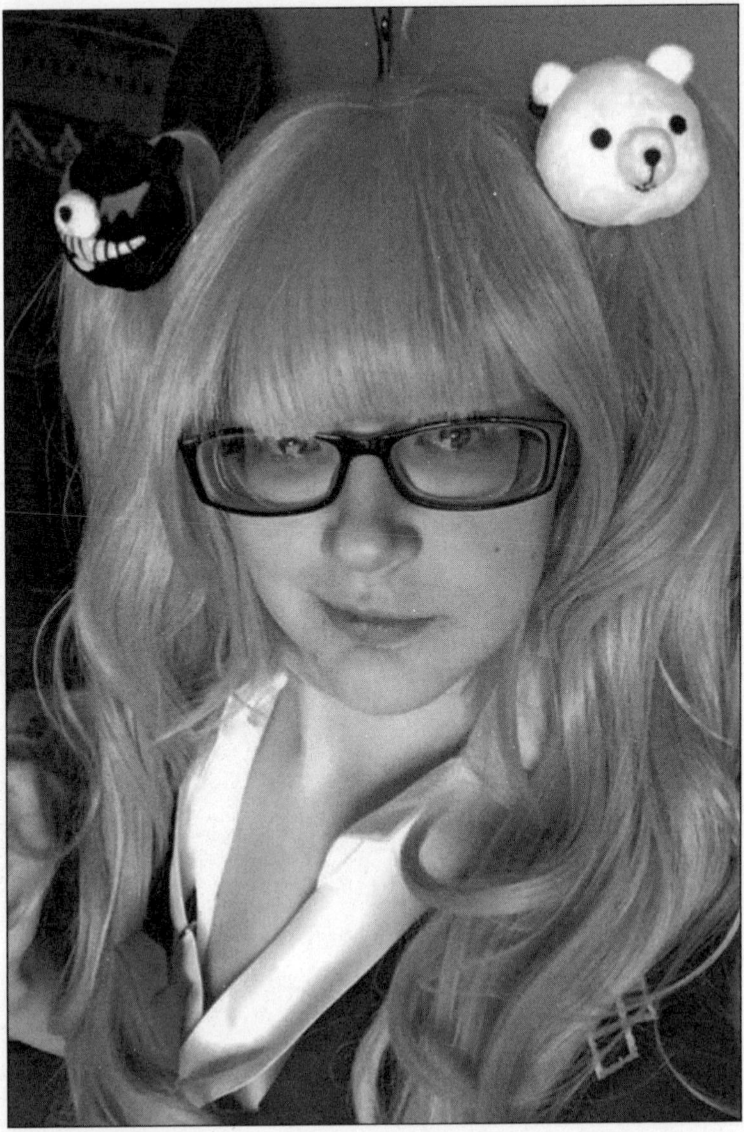

Brooke Traynor as Junko in "Ahem. Allow me to explain . . . " mode. "Time to cause some despair in this new year!" says Brooke. May it last us into 2019!

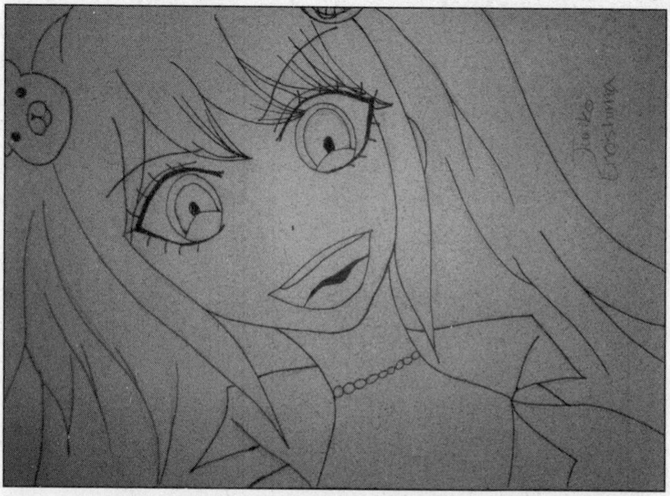

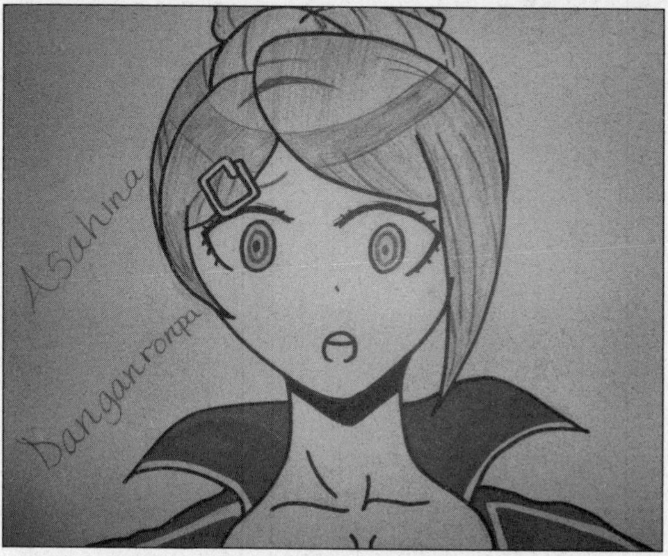
Asahina
Danganronpa

There's no escaping Junko Enoshima—she is, after all, the mastermind—but Cindy Rodriguez also gives props to aquatic champ, loyal friend, and toroidal fried dough enthusiast Aoi Asahina (Dark Horse is located in Portland, you know, home of Voodoo Donuts!). Well, we've got to take a commercial break now and leave it there until next time . . . but as I mentioned, we've still got letters from our original *Danganronpa: The Animation* manga left, so if you didn't see yours here, we'll do our best to get to it next time. And of course, we'd love to run your new letters, too. See you all in vol. 2 of *Danganronpa 2: Ultimate Luck and Hope and Despair*!

—CGH

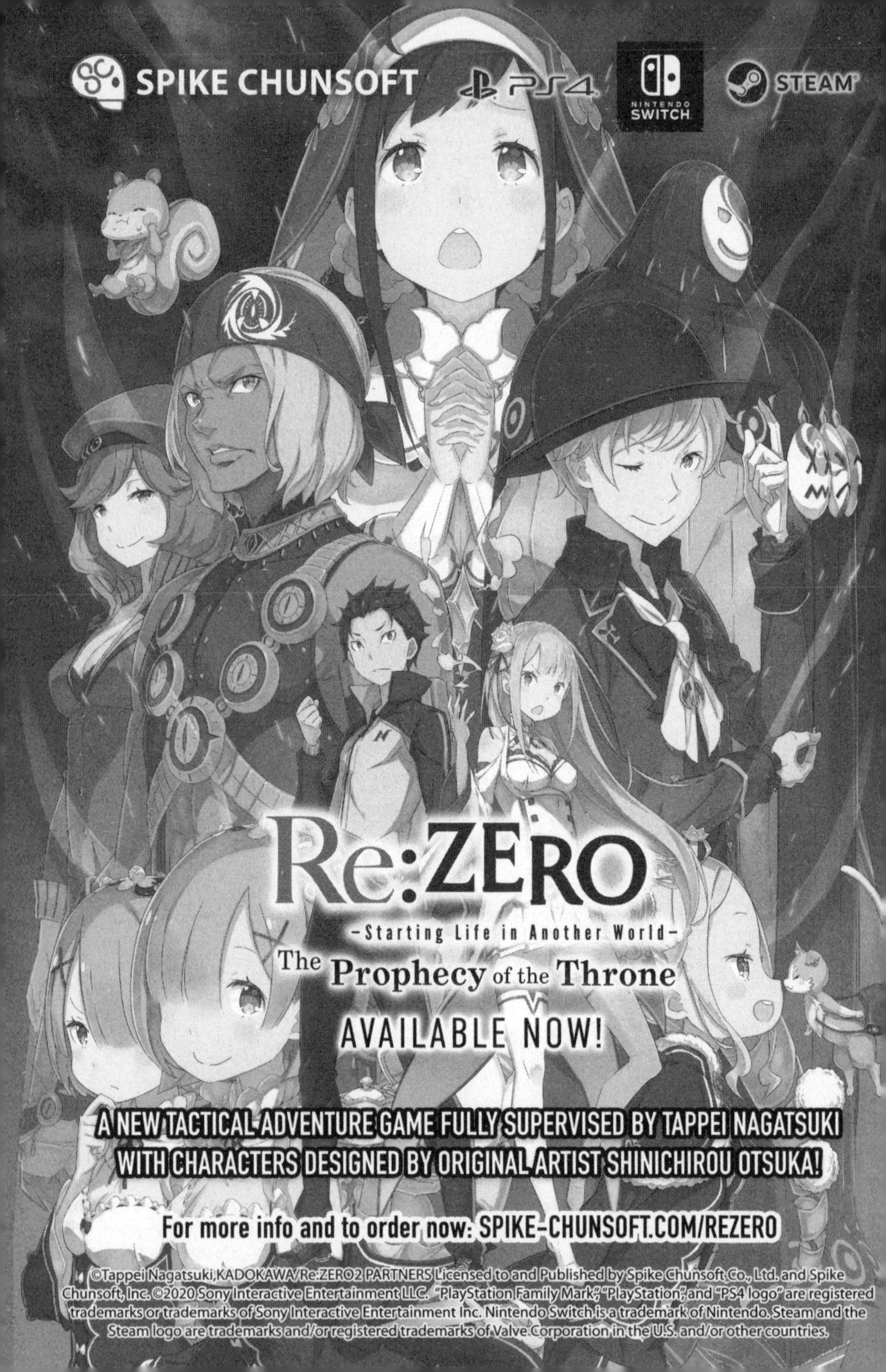
SPIKE CHUNSOFT
PS4
NINTENDO SWITCH
STEAM
Re:ZERO
-Starting Life in Another World-
The Prophecy of the Throne
AVAILABLE NOW!
A NEW TACTICAL ADVENTURE GAME FULLY SUPERVISED BY TAPPEI NAGATSUKI
WITH CHARACTERS DESIGNED BY ORIGINAL ARTIST SHINICHIROU OTSUKA!
For more info and to order now: SPIKE-CHUNSOFT.COM/REZERO
©Tappei Nagatsuki,KADOKAWA/Re:ZERO2 PARTNERS Licensed to and Published by Spike Chunsoft Co., Ltd. and Spike Chunsoft, Inc. ©2020 Sony Interactive Entertainment LLC. "PlayStation Family Mark," "PlayStation," and "PS4 logo" are registered trademarks or trademarks of Sony Interactive Entertainment Inc. Nintendo Switch is a trademark of Nintendo. Steam and the Steam logo are trademarks and/or registered trademarks of Valve Corporation in the U.S. and/or other countries.

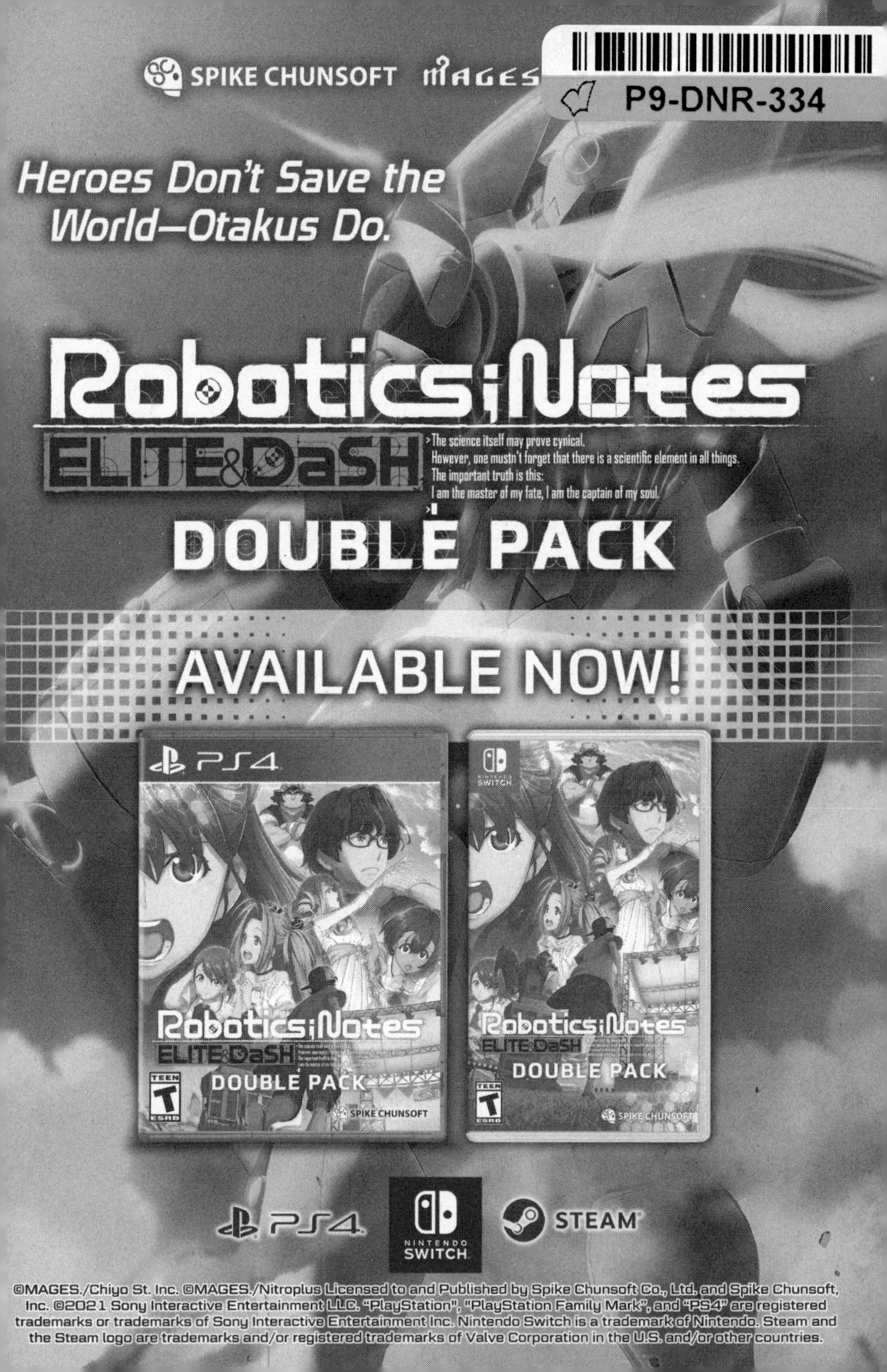
SPIKE CHUNSOFT
MAGES.
P9-DNR-334
Heroes Don't Save the World—Otakus Do.
Robotics;Notes
ELITE&DaSH
>The science itself may prove cynical.
However, one mustn't forget that there is a scientific element in all things.
The important truth is this:
I am the master of my fate, I am the captain of my soul.
DOUBLE PACK
AVAILABLE NOW!
PS4
Robotics;Notes
ELITE&DaSH
DOUBLE PACK
SPIKE CHUNSOFT
NINTENDO SWITCH
Robotics;Notes
ELITE&DaSH
DOUBLE PACK
SPIKE CHUNSOFT
PS4
NINTENDO SWITCH
STEAM
©MAGES./Chiyo St. Inc. ©MAGES./Nitroplus Licensed to and Published by Spike Chunsoft Co., Ltd. and Spike Chunsoft, Inc. ©2021 Sony Interactive Entertainment LLC. "PlayStation", "PlayStation Family Mark", and "PS4" are registered trademarks or trademarks of Sony Interactive Entertainment Inc. Nintendo Switch is a trademark of Nintendo. Steam and the Steam logo are trademarks and/or registered trademarks of Valve Corporation in the U.S. and/or other countries.